BOLSHEVIKS AND BRITISH JEWS

BOLSHEVIKS AND BRITISH JEWS

The Anglo-Jewish Community, Britain and the Russian Revolution

SHARMAN KADISH
University of London

FRANK CASS

First published in 1992 in Great Britain by
FRANK CASS & CO. LTD
Gainsborough House, Gainsborough Road,
London E11 1RS, England

and in the United States of America by
FRANK CASS
c/o International Specialized Book Services, Inc.
5602 N.E. Hassalo Street, Portland, Oregon 97213

Copyright © 1992 Sharman Kadish

British Library Cataloguing in Publication Data
Kadish, Sharman
  Bolsheviks and British Jews : the Anglo-Jewish
community, Britain and the Russian revolution.
  I. Title
  305.8924041

ISBN 0-7146-3371-2

Library of Congress Cataloging-in-Publication Data

Kadish, Sharman, 1959–
    Bolsheviks and British Jews : the Anglo-Jewish community, Britain,
  and the Russian Revolution / Sharman Kadish.
      p.   cm.
    Includes bibliographical references and index.
    ISBN 0-7146-3371-2
      1. Jews—Great Britain—History—20th century. 2. Jews—Great
  Britain—Politics and government. 3. Soviet Union—History-
  –Revolution, 1917–1921—Foreign public opinion, British. 4. Public
  opinion—Jews. 5. Public opinion—Great Britain. 6. Zionism—Great
  Britain. 7. Great Britain—Ethnic relations. I. Title.
  DS135.E5K33   1992
  941'.004924—dc20   91-18896
                                                                      CIP

Printed in Great Britain by BPCC Wheatons Ltd, Exeter

Contents

v

ז״ל

In Memory

Norman Kadish (1916–1988), my father
Esmond Kadish (1923–1989), my only uncle
Isaac Shapiro (1895?–1972), my maternal grandfather

"OUR OWN"

Jews of this happy England
   Clasped to her mother-breast,
Nestling so warm and peaceful
   Within that bosom blest,
Turn to our tortured Europe,
   Hark to the myriad moan
Of pinched lips, white with hunger,
   That stiffen as they groan,
And remember in these wan creatures runs
   The blood that is your own.

Their sires and yours together
   Bore Spain's or Poland's scorn;
With quenchless faith in marshfires
   They followed after morn.
They built their house on quicksand,
   Or the red volcano's cone,
And every age beheld it
   Engulfed or overthrown,
For never in all the ages did a home remain
   their own.

By devastated dwellings,
   By desecrated fanes,
By hearth-stones, cold and crimsoned,
   And slaughter reeking lanes,
Again is the Hebrew quarter
   Through half of Europe known;
And crouching in the shambles,
   Rachel, the ancient crone,
Weeps again for her children and the fate
   that is her own.

No laughter rings in these ruins
   Save of girls to madness shamed.
Their mothers disembowelled
   Lie stark 'mid children maimed.
The Shool has a great congregation
   But never a Psalm they drone,
Shrouded in red-striped Tallisim,
   Levi huddles with Kohn;
But the blood from the red bodies oozing is the
   blood that is your own.

Shot, some six to a bullet,
   Lashed and trailed in the dust,
Mutilated with hatchets
   In superbestial lust—
No beast can even imagine
   What Christians do or condone—
Surely these bear our burden
   And for our sins atone,
And if we hide our faces, then the guilt is as
   our own.

Laden with babes and bundles,
   Footsore on every road,
Their weary remnants wander,
   With bayonets for goad,

Alas! for the wizened infants,
   sucking at stone-dry breasts,
Alas! for the babies writhing
   In the grip of plagues and pests.
They are fever-stricken and famished,
   They are rotten of skin and bone,
Yet their mothers must die and leave them
   To suffer and starve alone.
And any one of these children might be your
   very own.

Barefoot, ragged and starving
   Like walkers in their sleep.
Feeding on bark or sawdust,
   The doomed processions creep;
Crawling through marsh or snowdrift
   Or forest overgrown,
They bear on high their Torah
   Like a flag to heaven flown;
They prove how great their spirit, let us prove
   how great our own.

At last but a naked rabble,
   Clawing the dust for bread,
Jabbering, wailing, whining,
   Hordes of the living dead,
Half apes, half ghosts, they grovel,
   Nor human is their tone,
Yet they are not brutes but brethren
   These wrecks of the hunger zone,
And their death-cry rings to heaven in the
   tongue that is your own.

Jews of this happy England,
   Who gave your sons to death,
That peace be born in Europe
   And justice draw new breath,
Will ye still endure to witness
   As of yore your kindred thrown
To races whose souls are savage,
   To tribes whose hearts are stone;.
Compared with the love and mercy that for
   ages have warmed our own?

Set your lips to the Shofar,
   Waken a fiery blast,
Shrill to the heathen nations—
   This slaughter shall be the last!
And send our old Peace-greeting
   Pealing from cot to throne,
Till mankind heeds the message
   Of the Hebrew trumpet blown,
And the faith of the whole world's peoples
   is the faith that is our own.

They cry: Shema Yisroel
   In tragic monotone,
And if ye, Israel, hear not
   By whom shall ruth be shown?
For the strength whereby God saves us is the
   strength that is our own.

Israel Zangwill's poem 'Our Own' which appeared in *Jewish Relief News*, published by the Fund for the Relief of the Jewish Victims of the War, London, February 1923

Illustrations

Acknowledgements

Sir Isaiah Berlin has probably long forgotten our conversation in his study at All Souls College, Oxford, in the autumn term of 1982. Yet, it was in the course of that conversation that the subject of this book was conceived. Now past his eightieth year, Sir Isaiah still inspires research students nearly three generations his junior who are working in the field of east European studies, and far beyond.

I would like to express my thanks to a number of other people for their guidance and encouragement. First, the supervisor of my doctoral thesis, upon which this book was based, Dr Harold Shukman of St Antony's College, Oxford. Professor Chimen Abramsky bears the responsibility for having first fired my interest in modern Jewish history while I was an undergraduate at University College London. Dr Martin McCauley of the School of Slavonic and East European Studies steered me through the complexities of Russian revolutionary politics at the same formative stage of my academic career. More recently, valuable advice has been given me by Professor William Fishman, Walter Kendall and Dr Julia Bush, and I have benefited from fruitful discussions with fellow researchers Philip Benesch, David Burke, Anne Kershen, Dr Mark Levene and Elaine Smith. Thanks are due to Ken Weller and to the late Sam Bornstein for putting me in touch with some interesting individuals to interview. I am especially grateful to the following for giving up their time to talk to me: Netty Alexander, Jack Baron, Alf Glick (by letter from Bristol), Sheila Leslie, Jack Miller, Peter Sand, Louis Wallis and Kitty Weitz. Sadly, I. A. Lisky and Israel Renson are no longer here to see the book completed. Acknowledgements are due to Charles Tucker for his expert advice on archival sources, particularly in the early stages of the project, and to the London Museum of Jewish Life.

I am indebted to Christopher Thomas for reading the entire manuscript. His labours have saved me from errors, factual, interpretative and grammatical. Any residual errors are, of course, entirely my responsibility.

ACKNOWLEDGEMENTS

Thanks to Dr Dovid Katz of the Oxford Centre for Postgraduate Hebrew Studies for teaching me Yiddish and to Valya Coe for her friendship and help with Russian.

Research trips abroad have been greatly enhanced by the warmth shown to me by senior academic colleagues: Professors Adèle and George Berlin and Professor Todd Endelman in the United States; Professors Jonathan and Edith Frankel, Dr Eli Lederhendler and Professor Avraham Greenbaum in Israel. I spent a most enjoyable year at the Hebrew University in 1986–87, during which I was also privileged to come into contact with Professors Michael Cohen and Stuart Cohen, Professor Lloyd Gartner and Dr Gideon Shimoni.

Professor Geoffrey Alderman's unerring advice over the past two years has been chiefly responsible for the transformation of thesis into book. Moreover, by giving me a job at Royal Holloway and Bedford New College he has provided me with the financial wherewithal to conclude the project.

On the subject of money, it has to be said that this book would not have been possible without financial support from the following bodies: the British Academy, the Memorial Foundation for Jewish Culture, New York, the Anglo-Jewish Association and the Jewish Memorial Council, both of London. Generous funding for my research trips to Israel (summer 1984) and to New York (spring 1986) was provided by the British Academy, the Graduate Studies Committee and the Arnold, Bryce and Read Fund of Oxford University respectively. I was the grateful recipient of a Scheinbrun Post Doctoral Research Fellowship in the Department of the History of the Jewish People at the Hebrew University of Jerusalem in 1986–87.

I would like to thank the libraries and institutions listed in the bibliography for granting me access to their holdings. I am indebted to Trude Levi for allowing me to consult the Gaster papers at the Mocatta Library within University College. Now that she has retired, her intimate knowledge of this valuable collection will be missed. Special thanks to Richard Storey for letting me look at the Aaron Rollin collection at the University of Warwick; to Dr Marek Webb and Fruma Mohrer at the YIVO Institute, New York; and to Adina Eshel at the Central Zionist Archives, Jerusalem. Finally, to the Goodman family for their kind hospitality and a peep at the Paul Goodman papers.

I would like to thank the Rothschild Archive for making available previously closed material at a very late stage in the preparation of this book (July 1990). My acknowledgements to Simone Mace.

A few formal copyright acknowledgements. Two short extracts from Chapter 1 and Chapter 5 of this book have previously appeared in a slightly different form in the *Jewish Quarterly* and *Patterns of Prejudice*. The last part of Chapter 3, 'The Letter of the Ten', was published in *Studies in Contemporary Jewry Volume IV* (Oxford University Press, 1988). The British Newspaper Library, JTS, the Mocatta and Wiener Libraries gave permission for the reproductions. Michael Joseph have allowed me to quote from Emanuel Litvinof's *Journey Through a Small Planet* in my section on the Conventionists.

A few words about the dedications at the front of *Bolsheviks and British Jews*. Originally, I dedicated my doctoral dissertation to the memory of my maternal grandfather who came to the East End of London from the market town of Shaval in Lithuania before the First World War. Like so many Jews of his generation, he had the brains but not the opportunity for scholarly accomplishment. Instead, he tried to earn his living as a compositor, working for a time on Morris Myer's *Di Tsayt*. Although he died when I was only 13, the *zider* was my link with and, no doubt, the root cause of my preoccupation with both the east European Jewish past and the immigrant experience.

Back in 1986, when I completed my thesis, I reserved my biggest and deepest thanks for my parents, Renée and Norman Kadish. Dad passed away suddenly in October 1988, a few short weeks before my marriage. That he did not live to witness the wedding or to see this book come out are my only regrets. He devoted his life to creativity, artistic rather than literary, and has left us a rich legacy in his wonderful paintings.

Lastly, I have to thank my husband Syd (Dr Sydney Greenberg), who for 12 months had to live with his bride, a mourner – and her book.

London
December 1989
Kislev 5750

Abbreviations

AJ	Archives of the Anglo-Jewish Association, Mocatta Library, UCL
AJA	Anglo-Jewish Association
AST	Amalgamated Society of Tailors
B o D	Board of Deputies of British Jews
BSP	British Socialist Party
CAB	Cabinet Papers
CO	Colonial Office
CPGB	Communist Party of Great Britain
CPSU	Communist Party of the Soviet Union
CZA	Central Zionist Archives, Jerusalem
DNB	*Dictionary of National Biography*
DORA	Defence of the Realm Act
ELO	*East London Observer*
EZF	English Zionist Federation
FJPC	Foreign Jews' Protection Committee
FO	Foreign Office
FUJ	Federation of Ukrainian Jews
HIAS	Hebrew Immigrant Aid Society
HO	Home Office
ILP	Independent Labour Party
ITO	Jewish Territorialist Organisation
IWW	Industrial Workers of the World
JAB	Jabotinsky Institute, Tel Aviv
JC	*Jewish Chronicle*
JCA	Jewish Colonisation Association
JFC	Joint Foreign Committee of the Board of Deputies and the Anglo-Jewish Association
JG	*Jewish Guardian*
JHSE	Jewish Historical Society of England
JTS	Jewish Theological Seminary, New York
JW	*Jewish World*

ABBREVIATIONS

LCC   London County Council
LSF   Lithuanian Socialist Federation
MG   *Manchester Guardian*
MOW   Mowshowitch Collection, YIVO Institute for Jewish Research, New York
MP   *Morning Post*
NAFTA National Furnishing Trades Association
NCCL   National Council for Civil Liberties
NUGW   National Union of Garment Workers
ORT   Organisation for Rehabilitation and Training
PRO   Public Record Office, London
PZ   *Poale Tsion* (Labour Zionists)
RAL   Rothschild Archive, London
RSDP   Russian Social Democratic Party
SDF   Social Democratic Federation
SPGB   Socialist Party of Great Britain
TJHSE   *Transactions of the Jewish Historical Society of England*
TUC   Trades Union Congress
UCL   University College London
UGW   Union of Garment Workers
URC   United Russian Committee
WA   Weizmann Archive, Weizmann Institute, Rehovot
WIZO   Womens' International Zionist Organisation
WJC   World Jewish Congress
WO   War Office
WSF   Women's/Workers' Suffrage/Socialist Federation
ZBPs   Zionist Bound Pamphlets, Mocatta Library, UCL
ZO   Zionist Organisation
ZR   *Zionist Review*

Introduction

Perhaps two-thirds of present-day British Jewry can trace their origin to lands which now form part of the Soviet Union and which, 80 years ago, belonged to the Empire of the Tsars. On the eve of the First World War, the Anglo-Russian Jewish connection did not appear so obscure as it might today. In 1914 about half of the $c.\,300{,}000$ strong Jewish community in Britain were recent immigrants from Russia. In the period from 1881 to 1914 waves of refugees, escaping persecution and economic pressure in the Pale of Settlement, home to the largest concentration of Jews in the world, fled west. While never rivalling the Lower East Side of New York City, the East End of London provided inhospitable sanctuary for 100,000 Russian Jews. Many Jews in Britain, then, stood in a special relationship to Russia. For indigenous Anglo-Jewry, the fate of a fellow diaspora community could no longer be a distant concern. Mass immigration brought 'Russia' to their doorstep and brought about an ultimate, irrevocable transformation in the character of British Jewry. For immigrant Jews, political interest in Russia was not merely academic; it was underpinned by sentimental attachment to the *heim* and, in many cases, by close family ties.

Britain and Russia have always been historical opposites. Physically both lie on the periphery of Europe. Politically, the former represented the epitome of liberalism and economic progress in the nineteenth century, the latter of reaction and backwardness. Culturally, Russia was inaccessible to the British public, rendered so by the mysteries of the Cyrillic alphabet and the Orthodox Church.

Before the 1880s a handful of Russian political exiles, most notably Herzen and Bakunin, had visited England. Yet, for the most part, their influence upon British politics was minimal, their activities being chiefly confined to émigré circles. Later arrivals attempted to educate British society about matters Russian, most notably the liberal coterie which formed around the Society of Friends of Russian Freedom in the 1890s. The likes of Georgi Chicherin and Maxim Litvinov also played an important role in fertilising the development of Marxist socialism in

1

Britain, before coming to greater prominence after the Bolshevik Revolution in Russia. It was above all the Russian largely Jewish (although also to a much smaller extent Polish and Lithuanian Catholic) immigration which, in a curious way, brought Britain and Russia into contact, and provided a link between these two disparate societies. The Russian Jews were the largest immigrant group to come to the United Kingdom before the Second World War. Little research has been done to set the Jewish immigration into the context of Anglo-Russian relations and to assess the political and diplomatic implications of the domestic Jewish factor.[1] It is hoped that the present book will go some way to filling that gap. The work is offered as a contribution not only to Jewish history, but also to the history of Anglo-Soviet relations. Its appearance is timely, coinciding with radical changes taking place within Russia and the Soviet Union today which may well mark a turning point in their political history.

By way of introduction, a few words need to be said about the condition of Russian Jewry under the tsars, in order to appreciate why the Revolution of 1917 was such a cataclysmic event for Jews both in Russia and abroad.[2] At the turn of the century, Russian Jewry was the largest Jewish community in the world, numbering some six million. One-third of all Jews lived under tsarist rule. Yet, for the Romanovs, the Jewish 'problem' was an acquisition of fairly recent date. Jews were incorporated into Russia with the partitions of Poland and the expansion of the Russian state in the latter part of the eighteenth century. So-called 'Russian' Jewry was, in reality, not really Russian at all, but Lithuanian, Byelorussian, Ukrainian, Bessarabian, Moldavian or Polish. The Jews were constricted in a Pale of Settlement of the tsars' own making, which extended from the Baltic Sea in the north to the Black Sea in the south. What was the rationale which lay behind the contradictions of governmental anti-Jewish policies? Russian Jewry had to endure a mixture of forcible assimilation – or 'amalgamation' – into the larger society, perpetual exclusion and frequent persecution at the hands of the regime. Even in its most liberal phase, under Alexander II (1856–81), the tsar who emancipated the serfs, abolition of the Pale and Jewish emancipation were never contemplated.

In 1881 Alexander II was rewarded for his reforming efforts by a terrorist bomb. His assassination, in which several Jewish revolutionaries were implicated, unleashed a violent backlash against the _

Jews. The period from 1881 to the First World War was one of unparalleled persecution; of pogroms and the Black Hundreds, the repressive May Laws, the notorious Protocols of the Elders of Zion and the Beilis blood libel. Mass murder by the White Russian armies in 1918–20 was only later to be overshadowed by the Holocaust. Yet this same bleak period was characterised by extraordinary vitality on the part of Russian Jewry. That enormous community was the reservoir out of which American Jewry was virtually formed, thanks to the mass migrations at the end of the nineteenth century – the biggest demographic shift in modern times. Russia, if it did not actually give birth to, certainly nurtured the two great ideological movements which have dominated Jewish thinking in the past 100 years: Jewish nationalism – Zionism – and socialism in their various guises. Amid the turmoil of political change, the forces of continuity endured almost intact, at least until the dislocation of war and revolution after 1914. Despite, or perhaps because of external oppression, the Pale of Settlement was a powerhouse of traditional Jewish life and learning, the scene of the Chassidic/Misnagdic battles of the eighteenth century and the academic excellence of the Lithuanian *Yeshivos*.

The 'watershed' crisis of 1881 elicited several different responses from its Jewish victims: individuals and groups made ideological and pragmatic choices which, ultimately, were life or death decisions. Some chose to abandon Russia entirely. Over two million Russian Jews boarded the steamships to the New World (including the 100,000 who, by accident or design, finished up in Britain), while a few thousand more chose the road back to Zion. Others decided to stay and join in the political struggle for a better Jewish future within their native land. A tiny group of middle-class *maskilim*, apostles of the German-Jewish Enlightenment, did not give up the hope that Russia could still follow the western path, and achieved fleeting success with the declaration of Jewish emancipation after the February ('Kerensky') Revolution.

Frustration with the apparent impotence of liberalism none the less goaded the young radical Jewish intelligentsia to join the Revolution: Popularism and Marxism – Menshevism, Bolshevism and Bundism. The prominence of a number of Russified Jews in the upper echelons of Lenin's party provided propaganda against 'Jewish Bolshevism' for their enemies after the October Revolution. Neither the White Russian counter-revolutionary armies, Ukrainian and Polish nationalists, nor elements within the Allied Armies of Intervention (which included the British) were averse to exploiting the accusation. The ironies of the situation were manifold. The 'Jewish' Bolsheviks, Trotsky at their head, had nothing in common with and were hardly representative of the mass of Yiddish-speaking orthodox Jewry in the Pale. Marxist atheism and anti-nationalism, while eschewing antisemitism, had scant regard for any Jewish interest, *per se*. Already during the Civil War, the Jewish Sections of the Communist Party (*Evsektsia*) embarked on a vigorous campaign to suppress Judaism, Zionism and the Hebrew language, associated with both. The attempt to subsume Jewish identity in an ideology which had little sympathy for the historical predicament of world Jewry was none too successful as the fate of the Jewish Mensheviks and the Bund after October 1917 testified. The Jewish Bolshevik Old Guard was in turn liquidated in Stalin's purges in the 1930s.

The principal aim of the present work is to highlight the attitude of Jews in Great Britain towards political and social change in Russia, during the crucial 1917–21 period when the Soviet Union was established. In 1917 Russia went through three regimes. In February (Old Style)[3] the 300-year-old Romanov dynasty collapsed under the weight of world war and its own corruption. A largely spontaneous popular uprising, which began as an outsize bread riot, brought down the government and created a power vacuum in the capital. For the next eight months, pending elections, a 'Provisional' government, originally made up of former members of the state Duma (the imperfect assembly wrung out of the last tsar, Nicholas II, during the 1905 'mini' revolution), attempted to wrest order out of chaos. But, from the outset, the authority of the interim government was challenged by the Petrograd Soviet, a grassroots socialist-dominated council which commanded popular allegiance. Attempts were made to resolve this dual power at the centre by the formation of successive coalition governments between the Duma liberals and the Mensheviks and Social Revolutionaries in the Soviet. Alexander Kerensky emerged as the dominant figure in the cabinet.

Russia's first and only experiment in liberal democracy succumbed, like its autocratic predecessor, to the intractable problems of a country still at war; military failure, the vast land question and the restless strivings of subject nationalities for independence. Mounting dissatisfaction, especially in the army, led to an abortive counter-revolution in August 1917, under the direction of General Kornilov. Meanwhile the impressive freedoms granted under the new order provided ample opportunity for agitation by the radical left. The return of Lenin from exile in Switzerland in April and effective propaganda put out by his well-organised, albeit minority, Bolshevik faction bore fruit – not in the July Days, but eventually in October. Lenin's April Theses and such slogans as 'Peace, bread, land, freedom!' skilfully pinpointed mass discontents. 'All power to the Soviets!' was a clever piece of political manipulation. The Party concentrated on cultivating support in the Soviets, realising that this was the surest road to Bolshevik power. On the night of 25 October (7 November NS) 1917, the Bolsheviks staged a successful coup, timed to pre-empt the meeting of the Second Congress of Soviets the next day. Henceforth Lenin made 'Bolshevik' and 'Soviet' power synonymous.

Having grabbed power in Petrograd, the Bolsheviks, soon renamed the Communists, had to conquer the rest of Russia. By the spring of 1918, the 'Reds' were embroiled in a bloody civil war against the 'Whites' – that is, just about everyone else. The Bolsheviks' enemies ranged from supporters of the deposed tsar, through liberal adherents of the Provisional Government, to other socialist groups, both Marxist and non-Marxist, who found themselves being excluded from the Soviets. At the same time, a large part of western Russia was occupied by the Germans, and the nationalities – Poles, Ukrainians, Georgians and others – were fighting for self-determination. In July 1918, Allied forces began to intervene in Russia. In March, the Bolsheviks had fulfilled the worst fears of the Allies. They signed a separate peace with the Germans at Brest–Litovsk, so taking Russia out of the War. With the collapse of the eastern front, Britain and France faced the prospect of a renewed German offensive in the west. Accordingly, Allied troops, eventually embracing British, French, American and Japanese contingents, were sent in initially to safeguard military supplies. However, the armistice of November 1918 did not lead to their withdrawal. Instead, military exigency gave way to an ideological crusade against Communism, reinforced by a desire to recover Russian debts which had been repudiated, and Allied assets which were being nationalised by the new regime.

In Britain, the most enthusiastic advocate of intervention 'to smother

Bolshevism in its cradle' was War Minister Winston Churchill.[4] Churchill and his supporters in the wartime coalition government, and not Prime Minister Lloyd George (whose instinct was for reconciliation) carried the day. £100 million of surplus military hardware was supplied to the White Russian generals in 1918 and 1919. British forces were stationed in Murmansk and Arkhangel to protect Allied stores and secure the strategic Murmansk railway. British volunteers served with Kolchak in Siberia and Denikin in South Russia. A British force occupied Baku and another patrolled the Russo-Afghan frontier. But Churchill's policy did not carry the country. War-weary Britain was in no mood to encourage counter-revolution against the first 'workers' state'. The Labour Party campaigned for 'Hands off Russia' and as the Whites suffered more and more reverses at the hands of Trotsky's Red Army, public opinion concurred. By the autumn of 1919 most of the British troops had been withdrawn.

In Chapter 2, and later in Chapter 5 of this book, Anglo-Jewish responses towards developments in Russia – from the February Revolution, through the Bolshevik seizure of power to the end of the Civil War in March 1921 – are charted. It may be stated at once that a coherent pattern of response emerged. All but unanimous Anglo-Jewish sympathy for the liberal Provisional Government was transformed into almost universal hostility towards the Bolsheviks. This shift in attitudes corresponded with the deteriorating situation of Russian Jewry. The high hopes which accompanied the legal enactment of Jewish Emancipation in April 1917 gave way to the chaos and pogroms of the Civil War. At this juncture physical destruction by the White Armies on the one hand, and spiritual destruction by the Bolshevik 'Jewish Sections' on the other, appeared to be the grim alternatives. Anglo-Jewry looked askance at the pogroms in the Ukraine – and at the spectacle of British intervention on the side of the White generals.

Jewish opinion did not exist in a vacuum, however. What, it must be asked, was the relationship between Anglo-Jewish views on the Revolution, held both individually and collectively, and those generally prevailing in Britain at the time? How far were the former consistent or at variance with the latter? Was there an interaction between the two? If so, how far was Jewish reaction moulded by (often adverse) government and public opinion towards not only Russia and Russian Jewry, but also, by extension, towards Jews and Russian Jewish 'aliens' in this country? This, in turn, presupposes an enquiry into the growth of antisemitism in Britain in the period. There is no doubt that anti-semitism received a great fillip as a result of the Russian Revolution, owing to the prominence of a number of 'ex' Jews in the Bolshevik leadership. In Chapter 1 we will explore the connection between an-tisemitism, anti-alienism and anti-Bolshevism in British politics at the time of the Russian Revolution and Allied intervention in the Civil War. Hostile attitudes towards Jews appeared in politics, the Civil Service, the military and the press. Such hostility which, in the heated climate of 1918–20, was by no means confined to the extreme right, was not only directed against Jews in Russia; the Anglo-Jewish com-munity – native, naturalised and immigrant – was also put under considerable pressure.

With our subject thus placed in its proper context, attention is turned to how thought was translated into action. What policies did the official institutions of Anglo-Jewry adopt with regard to the Russian Revolution, and with what degree of success? In Chapter 3, four main areas of organised Jewish activity are emphasised, each of which gives rise to a whole series of complex and important issues, with far wider implications. How did British Jewry cope with the unprecedented devastation in eastern Europe, caused by war, revolution and pogrom? What methods did Jewish leaders employ to mobilise financial aid for relief work and for the reconstruction of shattered communities? How far did Anglo-Jewry cooperate with co-religionists abroad, in Europe, America and Palestine, in this work? Above all, to what extent did Anglo-Jewish preoccupations with the 'politics of emigration' reveal real concern for the ultimate fate of Russian Jewry?

From 1919, Lucien Wolf, the 'Foreign Secretary' of British Jewry, was busy behind the scenes, intervening with the British government, at the Paris peace conference and at the League of Nations on behalf of oppressed Jewry in eastern Europe. He thus dealt with such controver-sial matters as the refugee question, Allied relations with the Whites and the problem of Ukrainian independence and the Jews.

Underlying this analysis is the assumption that Anglo-Jewish com-munal reaction to the Russian Revolution was determined as much by domestic considerations as by political change within Russia itself. For much energy was expended on countering manifestations of anti-semitism – albeit in the guise of anti-Bolshevism – at home. The tsarist forgery *The Protocols of the Elders of Zion* made its first appearance in English at the height of the British intervention in the Civil War. For some, it was regarded as the blueprint for the Bolshevik Revolution. Allegations were also made of Jewish complicity in the murder of the tsar. Thus the Jewish 'Establishment' was forced onto the defensive. A policy of answering the charges was pursued in the interests of preserving Anglo-Jewish 'respectability'. Finally, we turn from 'quiet diplomacy' to the politics of protest. There were those within the community who favoured public protest against pogroms and even against the British intervention in Russia as a whole. This was not a tactic which was based on a consensus amongst the communal leadership. The fierce controversy over the 'Letter of the Ten' in 1919 exposed the bitter divisions beneath the surface of Anglo-Jewish life.

Chapter 4 enlarges the scope of this study in a controversial direction. It examines the paradoxical relationship between the growth of Zionism in Britain during the First World War and the existence of antisemitism, parading as anti-Bolshevism. I attempt to demonstrate that the Bolshevik Revolution and the Balfour Declaration were not unrelated events. Exaggerated British perceptions of the Jewish role in Bolshevism played a not insignificant part in fostering official support for Zionism. A propaganda campaign was waged to counteract the supposed communistic tendencies of world Jewry by means of an appeal to Jewish nationalism. In the words of Winston Churchill: 'Zionism versus Bolshevism: a struggle for the soul of the Jewish people'.

Finally, in Chapter 5 we focus on the Yiddish-speaking immigrants in the East End 'ghetto'. It is apparent that, when it came to the Russian Revolution, attitudes in the 'East End' diverged significantly from those in the 'West End', reflecting very real differences in social status, religious orientation and political outlook between British-born and immigrant Jewry. Not one, but two separate Jewish communities existed in Britain in this period. The internal conflict centred on the question of military service for Russian-Jewish 'friendly aliens' during the First World War. Anti-conscription agitation in the East End, in connection with the Anglo-Russian Military Convention of 1917, fuelled anti-alien sentiment. It also caused embarrassment to established Jewry and challenged their bid to maintain communal discipline. The conscription question was the biggest single domestic complication for Anglo-Jewry arising directly out of the Russian Revolution. In the end, we ask ourselves: did the charge of 'Jewish Bolshevism' have any foundation in fact? Was Whitechapel really a hotbed of leftist subversion as the political right alleged? And just what was the level of Jewish involvement in the infant British Communist Party, the trade unions and the labour movement in general?

In investigating all of these topics, it is hoped that this study will shed light on the position of the Jew in British society during and just after the First World War.

One further note on definitions. For the purposes of this book, I use the terms 'Jew' and 'Jewish' in the double sense accepted by social scientists. I deem as Jewish anyone who considered himself/herself to be Jewish by religion and/or nationality, ethnicity or culture, in other words by the test of self-definition. I also include individuals who were regarded as being Jewish by their contemporaries, that is by the test of external definition. My definition is therefore inclusive rather than exclusive. By the 'Jewish community' I mean to denote Jews collectively organised and the institutional structures set up to preserve and promote Jewish interests. The terms 'Anglo-Jewish' and 'British Jewish' are used interchangeably with reference to Jews resident (usually permanently) in Great Britain. English-speaking and Yiddish-speaking Jews are thus covered alike by the term 'Anglo-Jewish'. We then come to the controversial labels 'East End' and 'West End' Jewry, as a shorthand method of differentiation between the two groups. I have made great use of this model in the structure of the book and make no apologies for it. The conflicts which went on between the two communities is sufficient justification for the East/West categorisation – provided it is looked upon as a social rather than as a geographical designation. I also make no apology for the fact that this study is so London-based. The bias reflects the emphasis in the available sources. As today, in 1918 two-thirds of Anglo-Jewry lived in the capital; the major communal institutions have their headquarters there. So it is natural that London should be the centre of Jewish communal political life.

1 'Boche, Bolshie and the Jewish Bogey': The Russian Revolution and the Growth of Antisemitism in Britain

[The Bolsheviks] are adventurers of German-Jewish blood and in German pay.
The Times, 23 November 1917

And please take note that the Red Shield (of Rothschild) and the Red Flag (of Communism) are not only of the same colour, but are one in essence, and the colour is the colour of blood. 'Judaism' says Professor Sombart, 'is identical with Capitalism.' But it is equally true to say that Judaism is identical with Communism.

The question is often asked; how can it profit the Jewish Capitalists to have revolutions? Whatever answer may be given to the question of the 'How', the fact remains that it does.

J.H. Clarke, *White Labour versus Red*. An address delivered before the British and Constitutional Labour Movement, 4 September 1920, and published by The Britons

'The crucial event which gave rise to post-War antisemitism was the Russian Revolution.'[1] From 1917 America and western Europe were swept by a 'Red Scare', which supplemented and ultimately superseded the 'German Menace' which originated before the First World War. In Britain, anti-Bolshevism spread to various quarters – politics, military and diplomatic circles and the press – and was by no means confined to the extreme right. This wave of antisemitism was attended by a preoccupation with the undeniable over-representation of Jews on the more extreme fringes of European socialism. Comment was passed on the 'Jewishness' of Trotsky, Béla Kun, Rosa Luxemburg and, of course, of their inspiration, Karl Marx. Fear of the 'Boche' gave way to fear of the 'Bolshies' and the 'Jewish Bogey', common to both, became, for some,

10

synonymous with the latter. The result was a reworking of the hoary Jewish conspiracy myth. The Jew, once identified with the German Capitalist, was now metamorphosed into the Russian Communist who was no less intent upon wreaking havoc in the countries of the Entente in order to dominate the world. This theme, not unnaturally, was given still greater emphasis by the appearance of the *Protocols of the Elders of Zion* for the first time in English translation, at the peak of British intervention in the Russian Civil War.

It was hardly accidental that the agitation linking Jews and Bolshevism peaked in 1919–20 at the very time when the British government was pursuing a policy of military aid to reactionary White Guard generals – the same generals who were alleging 'Jewish' Bolshevism as a pretext for their massive pogroms in the Pale of Settlement.

In the pages which follow, various aspects of the 'Jewish Bolshevik' agitation will be examined within the British context. An analysis of official government policy on the Russian Jewish question in the period of intervention provides the setting for a survey of press and other 'literary' manifestations of antisemitism in the wake of the Russian Revolution. The 'Jewish Bolshevik' campaign in the press was promoted chiefly by the arch-conservative *Morning Post* and that most highly respected of British institutions, *The Times*. In this chapter I shall attempt to assess the extent, depth and significance of what seemed to be an outbreak of antisemitism in the British press in the period 1918–20. Was it an uncharacteristic lapse, or did it have more serious implications for the future? The remainder of the chapter will consider how the 'Jewish Bolshevik' agitation coalesced with an older strand of anti-alienism in British society. This meant that, on the domestic front, the Anglo-Jewish community, native, naturalised and immigrant, was put under substantial pressure.

THE BRITISH GOVERNMENT, INTERVENTION AND THE JEWS IN RUSSIA

In March 1918 the first contingents of the British Expeditionary Force arrived in north Russia. Their purpose was plain, 'ostensibly to revive an eastern front against the Germans, but with a hope that the Bolsheviks would somehow be accidentally overthrown in the process'.[2] Once the Armistice had been signed in November 1918, this strategic objective gave way to a purely ideological struggle against Bolshevism. This meant support for the 'Whites', effectively military aid to the ex-tsarist commanders, Kolchak in Siberia and Denikin in south Russia, in order to overthrow the Soviet government by force. As a logical extension of this policy, the Allies wooed the new nation-states which were emerging in eastern Europe – especially Poland – to act as a bulwark against both the spread of Bolshevism and German revival. Neither the tsarist generals nor the Polish and Ukrainian Ultras were noted for their love of the Jews. And, owing to the prominent place held by a number of Jews in the Bolshevik leadership, counter-revolutionary propaganda could all too easily condemn Bolshevism as a Jewish conspiracy. The equation made between Jews and Bolshevism served as the perfect pretext for pogroms. Indeed, during 1919 these occurred on an unprecedented scale – even by local standards – in both Poland and the Ukraine. Conducive to this was the fact that the Civil War was being waged largely in the lands of the former Jewish Pale of Settlement. Indeed, the Pale was transformed into a battlefield between numerous warring factions – the 'Reds' and the 'Whites', Ukrainian nationalists and Polish forces, Germans, Romanians, and even assorted bands of anarchists such as the Makhnovites. In short, a situation of complete chaos prevailed.

In the period from 1917–21, it has been estimated that some 2,000 pogroms took place in the Ukraine alone; the loss of Jewish lives has been put at 100,000 or more and perhaps half a million were left homeless. The statistics show that, although all participants in the conflict were guilty of murdering Jews, including the Bolshevik Red Army, it was the White Volunteer Army which accounted for the highest number of victims – as many as all the other forces put together.[3]

By the early summer of 1919 circumstantial reports of atrocities were percolating through to the west via Constantinople. Naturally, they were exploited by opponents of intervention in Britain. Demands were made by Labour spokesmen in Parliament and in the Liberal and Labour press, that supplies to the Volunteer army be cut off and that British troops be withdrawn. Clearly, rumours of White excesses were embarrassing to the government. Notwithstanding the premiership of David Lloyd George, a nominal Liberal, the wartime coalition, which survived until 1922, boasted a growing Tory majority. At the same time, the split in the Liberal Party, which dated back to December 1916 when Lloyd George became Prime Minister, much reduced its political influence. 'Right-wing' coalition Liberals, who remained in the government, tended to acquiesce before prevailing Conservative opinion. The Conservative Party tended to support intervention in Russia to a greater or lesser degree. A policy of political, financial and ultimately military support for the Whites was adopted. True, only War Minister Winston Churchill called for a full-blooded military campaign involving the large-scale deployment of British troops in Russia, but his was an isolated voice in the Cabinet. Thus 'atrocity stories' which cast Britain's allies in Russia in a poor light created difficulties for the government, in a party political if not in a moral sense. The standard response to counter such allegations was to point an accusing finger at the Bolsheviks. Particularly after the sacking of the British Embassy in Petrograd and the shooting of Captain Cromie, the naval attaché at the end of August 1918, it was not difficult for the government – backed by the Tory press – to convince the public that the Bolsheviks were infinitely more guilty than the Whites of murder, torture and rape. When it came to White excesses against the Jews, official spokesmen professed ignorance or were curiously noncommittal. For example, when the now-famous Zionist leader Chaim Weizmann requested permission for a small Jewish delegation to call upon Denikin to urge restraint, the Foreign Office responded: 'I do not at all like the proposal. I am most reluctant to take up the question of Jews in Russia.'[4] The Anglo-Jewish diplomat, Lucien Wolf, who was widely regarded as having access to the Foreign Office, enjoyed no greater success when he raised the question of the pogroms. He was told that the British government was 'not in a position to take any useful action' as they were 'not represented in the Ukraine'.[5]

It was clear that the commitment of substantial military resources to intervention in Russia did not extend to the protection of some two million defenceless Jews in south Russia. Wolf was also assured that no real need for such protection existed, since: 'General Denikin is doing all in his power to restrain his troops, [... and ...] any excesses that have been committed are not only disapproved of by General Denikin, but are expressly against his orders'.[6] There was, in any event, a lingering doubt in the mind of Lord Curzon, the Foreign Secretary, as to whether the pogroms lacked all justification. He observed that preventive measures on the part of the British were liable to be ineffective given the 'well known' antisemitic prejudices of the peasantry which made up the bulk of the White armies:

> These prejudices have been strengthened by the belief – widely held in South Russia – that the Bolshevist movement has been led and exploited by Jews for their own ends, a supposition which they believe to be confirmed by the fact that several Jews are to be found among the Bolshevist leaders.[7]

The deputy Foreign Secretary, Robert Cecil, provided a much more detailed diagnosis:

> Tragic events such as are now taking place in Russia are the terrible results of earlier misdoings. The Tsarist Government oppressed the Jews, and drove certain of their co-religionists into an attitude of fierce antagonism to all order and government. As is well known, a large proportion of the Bolshevist administration was composed of Jews, including such men as Trotsky, Kamenev, Radek, Stekloff etc. They in turn ... have committed ... great atrocities, and have consequently aroused bitter hostility against their co-religionists, amongst many sections of the Russian population.
>
> Nor is the action of Jewish revolutionaries confined to Russia ... there is scarcely a dangerous revolutionary movement in any part of Europe which has not at the back of it a Jew, driven into enmity of the whole existing order of things by the injustice and outrage which he or his relatives have suffered from the hands of the old Governments of Russia and other states in Central Europe[8]

Representations made to those at least in nominal control of the White armies met with the frequent response that the Jews were all Bolsheviks and that the pogroms were, therefore, a natural result of the campaign to overthrow the hated regime. Apparently, the British Foreign Office was apparently willing to lend credence to such statements.

Dissatisfaction with the Foreign Office's handling of the Russian Jewish question emerged from an unexpected quarter. It was ironic that Winston Churchill, the War Minister and the biggest proponent of the intervention, should take a stand on the issue of pogroms. He sent a succession of telegrams to the British Military Mission in Russia and to General Denikin personally urging that every measure be taken to prevent the outbreak of further excesses. On 18 September 1919 he instructed General Holman to ask Denikin: 'to do everything in his power to prevent a massacre of the Jews in the liberated districts ... [and to] ... issue a proclamation against antisemitism'[9]

Commendable though these communications were, several observations need to be made by way of qualification. In the first place, it is clear that Churchill was not entirely free of the prejudices prevailing in some Foreign Office quarters. Whilst recommending that the 'special danger of Jew pogroms' be 'combatted strongly', he at the same time attributed this 'special danger' to the fact that the Jews played a 'prominent part ... in [the] Red Terror and regime'.[10] In a further letter, of 10 October, to the Prime Minister, Churchill argued that as long as Britain continued supplying arms to Denikin she would be 'constantly in a position to exercise a modifying influence' on him. But, he added:

(1) There is a very bitter feeling throughout Russia against the Jews, who are regarded as being the main instigators of the ruin of the empire, and who, certainly have played a leading part in Bolshevik atrocities.

(2) This feeling is shared by the Volunteer Army and Army of the Don under General Denikin ... [11]

Churchill was to write at length about the 'power' of the international Jewish revolutionaries in his article 'Zionism versus Bolshevism' published in February 1920, which is discussed in full in Chapter 4 below. It is, in the second place, obvious that Churchill's urgent messages were prompted as much by political considerations as by humanitarian ones. He brought to General Yudenitch's attention the fact that: 'Anything in the nature of a Jewish pogrom would do immense harm to the Russian cause',[12] and warned that 'Excesses by anti-Bolsheviks ... will alienate sympathies [of the] British nation and render continuance of support most difficult'.[13] Lloyd George was, without doubt, alive to this possibility. He wrote to Churchill:

I wish you would make some enquiries about this treatment of the Jews by your friends. Now that we are subsidising the Volunteer Army and providing them with weapons we certainly have a right to protest against outrages of this character being perpetrated.

You may depend upon it that sooner or later a discussion will be raised on the subject and I do not wish to see the British Government placed in the same position as the Kaiser when he kissed the cheek of Abdul Hamid shortly after he had massacred the Armenians. Apart from the iniquity of the proceedings and one's natural repugnance to be associated with it, it provides material for a most disagreeable debate in the House of Commons.[14]

This letter, in turn, prompted Churchill to wire Denikin another warning, pointing out to him the damage being done to the White cause in England by 'well-authenticated' reports of pogroms.[15] Moreover, a written intervention by Sir Alfred Mond (later Lord Melchett), the Anglo-Jewish industrialist and a member of the Cabinet, led Churchill to the conclusion that: 'The Jews are very powerful in England, and if it could be shown that Denikin was protecting them as his army advanced it will make my task easier'.[16]

Whatever Churchill's motives might have been, it remains true that his attempts to restrain the Whites were 'totally ineffectual' in practice. In his memoirs Churchill claimed that he 'had no responsibility either for the original intervention or for the commitments and obligations which it entailed'.[17] And even in 1920 he felt obliged to explain away the manifest failure of his policy of restraint in the following terms:

> Wherever General Denikin's authority could reach, protection was always accorded to the Jewish population, and strenuous efforts were made by his officers to prevent reprisals and punish those guilty of them. So much was this the case that the Petlurist propaganda against General Denikin denounced him as the protector of the Jews. ... [18]

Finally, it must be pointed out that all of Churchill's admonitions to the Whites were made through official channels and *not* via a public protest. Oskar Rabinowicz, in his book *Churchill on Jewish Problems* (1956), passes final judgement:

> The one drastic measure that would have stopped [the outrages] at once – the withholding of support to Denikin and his armies, Churchill could not bring himself to take. The war against the Bolsheviks was to him of much greater importance, and it was not to be abandoned or weakened by raising the question of trying to

16

prevent barbaric murders. At this time, as also later in World War II, Churchill's dominating thought was first to defeat the enemy and only afterwards to reorganise the world.[19]

In the light of the above evidence, there seems to be no reason to revise this opinion.

In July 1919, the chief of the British Military Mission to General Denikin, General Briggs, declared in the course of an interview with Reuter's:

> On my return to England my attention was drawn to certain statements as to 'atrocities' and various forms of outrage resulting from General Denikin's administration, and I am glad to take the earliest opportunity on my arrival in England to say that from beginning to end they are utterly false and are prompted by German and Bolshevist propaganda.[20]

Briggs stood by this denial at a meeting of MPs a fortnight later. Winston Churchill was present. The Whites could obviously rely on their apologists among the British military in Russia.

In April 1919 appeared the 'Bolshevik atrocity bluebook' otherwise known as the Emmott Report, entitled *Russia No. 1. A collection of reports on Bolshevism in Russia*. This was a Command Paper published by decision of the War Cabinet. It demonstrated the determination of the government to stage a propaganda counter-offensive. Whatever gross misdeeds Britain's Allies, the Whites, might be engaged in, it was argued, the Reds were immeasurably worse. The White Paper purported to contain eye-witness accounts by British residents who had been imprisoned by the Bolsheviks, and by British military and consular personnel in Russia. In reality, most of the stories were second-hand, having been supplied by anti-Bolshevik Russians to British officials in the White-controlled areas. The British Ambassador in Copenhagen, Lord Kilmarnock, and the chaplain to the British Interventionary Forces in Russia, the Rev. B. S. Lombard, made printed statements claiming that the Bolsheviks were, in fact, Jews working in the pay of the Germans. Moreover, for the first time, official credence was given to the supposed link between Bolsheviks and Jews as a justification for the pogroms. Also included was General Knox's allegation implicating Jews in the assassination of the tsar, which will be discussed presently.

Richard Ullman, in his classic study of Britain and the Russian Civil War, dismisses *Russia No. 1* as 'a wildly hysterical piece of propaganda'. It originated with Basil Thomson, the head of the Special Branch, who shared the 'widespread attitude' that 'It was desirable that atrocity stories be verified – but not necessary'.[21]

In August 1919, the Hartzfeld Affair broke. Jacob Hartzfeld was assistant military attaché to the United States Army in Arkhangel. He was an American citizen – and also a Jew. He claimed that the British interventionary forces were actively engaged in propagandising the Bolshevik–Jewish connection. He alleged that antisemitic leaflets were being produced for distribution among American and British servicemen to boost morale and to subvert the Red Army. No fewer than four separate proclamations to this effect were publicised by the intelligence departments in Arkhangel and Murmansk – with which a number of White Russian officers were associated. Hartzfeld specifically named Colonels Thornhill and Lindsay, the heads of the intelligence sections under General Ironside in Arkhangel and General Maynard in Murmansk respectively, as being behind this campaign. Some specimens were brought to the notice of the Anglo-Jewish Joint Foreign Affairs Committee, after a meeting between its chairman Lucien Wolf and Hartzfeld in Paris. The following extract comes from a document circulated among Ironside's troops in Arkhangel: 'We are ... against Bolshevism which means anarchy pure and simple ... the power is in the hands of a few men, mostly Jews, who have succeeded in bringing the country to such a state that order is non-existent.' Under the auspices of Maynard in Murmansk, this address was put out:

> To the soldiers of the Red Army
>   It is to you Russian men who have still preserved the love of country that we address ourselves, we the soldiers of Free Russia of the North, and once more call to you to throw off the Jewish yoke by uniting to us. It is now two years since the Jews have been running our country and have been trying in the person of Russia to avenge themselves on the entire world for the persecutions of which they have been the object ...
>   ... Russian men begin to understand whither the Jew-provocators are leading them for in the centre of Russia revolts

18

against their oppression are breaking out more and more frequently ... your Jewish provocators are making a supreme effort
in their struggle with us, but do not believe them, and while it is
yet not too late come over to our side.[22]

Part and parcel of the interventionist policy in Russia was, as has
already been indicated in passing, support for the new nation-states in
eastern Europe as a *cordon sanitaire* against both Bolshevik expansion
and German revival. Chief amongst these states was Poland. Although
not on the same scale as in the Ukraine, pogroms were perpetrated
against Polish Jewry – a community of some three million – in this
period, especially during the Soviet–Polish war of 1920. Protests to the
Polish nationalists merely elicited the now predictable retort that the
Jews were pro-German, pro-Russian and above all pro-Bolshevik.
Even if they were none of these things, then they were at least out for
commercial gain at the expense of the Poles. What was more disturbing
was that these excuses, like those made by the White generals, gained a
certain credence within those governing circles in Britain which
favoured intervention. The Samuel Report on Poland, commissioned
by the Foreign Office, and published in June 1920, did not entirely
sympathise with the Jewish case. This was somewhat ironic, given that
doubts had been cast in advance on the impartiality of the investigation
because the chairman of the mission was Stuart Samuel, the President
of the Jewish Board of Deputies. A third of the report was written by
Captain Peter Wright, a Foreign Office official appointed by John
Gregory, a Foreign Office diplomat who was himself a friend of the
Polish Ultras Dmovsky and Horodyski. Lucien Wolf described Wright
in his diary as being 'full of the old prejudices'.[23] In his testimony,
Wright certainly admitted that antisemitism was rife in all sections of
Polish society, but he went on innocently: 'Antisemitism is covertly and
assiduously encouraged as a protection against Bolshevism.' The
natural inference was that there was some logic in the Polish policy of
pogroms. Bolshevism, Wright maintained, was popular with Polish
Jews. On this point he contradicted Samuel, who estimated that at the
most 10 per cent of Polish Jewry was pro-Bolshevik. Wright declared
that Polish Jewry, which constituted one-sixth of the total population
of the country, had twice that representation within the Bolshevik
movement.

He explained:

> The attractions of Bolshevism are little theoretical. Bolshevism spells business for poor Jews; innumerable posts in a huge administration; endless regulations, therefore endless jobbery; big risks, for the Bolsheviks punish heavily, every offence being treated as a form of treason; but big profits. The rich bourgeois Jew also manages to get on with it in his own way, '*Judischer Weise*' as the Jews call bribery. Many Jews who are by no means poor, try at the present time to escape into Russia, so fine are the business prospects.[24]

Communism, then, did not so much appeal to the Jew's finer socialist feelings, as to his base capitalist instincts. This was a theme which was taken up by the Conservative press, which will be discussed shortly.

In Parliament, there was a group of backbench Tory 'Diehard' MPs who could be relied upon to give expression to views more extreme than those to be found among Conservative ministers within the government itself. These 'Ultra' Tories regarded Soviet Russia as the devil incarnate and called for intervention to be stepped up on ideological grounds. Without the restraints imposed by office, they were free to speak their minds much more than was Churchill. Even after the failure of intervention was obvious to all, they persisted in blocking Lloyd George's attempts to come to an accommodation with the Soviets. By 1922, their opposition had been reinforced by an increasing desire to overthrow the Prime Minister and end the coalition with the Liberals. These Tory backbenchers tended to make a mental connection between their aversion to Bolshevism abroad and their prejudice against Labour at home. The Labour Party in Parliament, socialist pacifists during the war, and trade union strikers during the wave of industrial unrest following the end of the war, were all dismissed as 'British Bolsheviks'.[25] As we shall see presently, the Tory right received significant support from sections of the press. Names such as Arnold White, Admiral Domville and Lord Sydenham of Combe cropped up frequently not only in the mainstream *Morning Post* but also in Leo Maxse's *National Review* and the Duke of Northumberland's *The Patriot*.

Backbench anti-Bolshevism reached its peak in the summer of 1919. This coincided with the White advances in the spring and with rumours of impending Allied recognition for Kolchak and Denikin. *Ad hoc* Tory pressure groups mushroomed in this period. Much activity centred on the Coalition Foreign Affairs Committee whose secretary was Walter Guinness. This body had links with White representatives in Paris and supported the Churchill line. Members made contributions to the pro-White journal *Russian Outlook*. There was also the British–Russian Society whose president was the ex-ambassador in Petrograd, Sir George Buchanan. Other right-wing groups which indulged in anti-Bolshevik propaganda and which enjoyed the support of backbench Tories included the Parliamentary Primrose League, the British Empire Union, the Anti-Socialist and Anti-Communist Union and the Liberty League. There were also the breakaway National Democratic Party, which had started life as the British Workers' League under Victor Fisher, and Brigadier-General Page-Croft's National Party. These latter two groupings stood on an ultra-patriotic ticket at the 1918 general election and were returned with nine MPs (representing 200,000 votes) and two MPs (94,000) respectively. The radical right was not unwilling to utilise the 'Bolshevik–Jewish' connection to bolster their campaign in favour of the Whites. The subject was even raised during Parliamentary Question Time. Hansard records that one such exchange went as follows:

> In the House of Commons [on 7 August] MR RAPER (Islington East C[oalition] U[nionist]), asked the Under-Secretary of State for Foreign Affairs whether he has any information as to how many Greek Orthodox priests have been done to death by the Soviet Government in Central Russia; and whether a single instance is known of the said Government having dealt in the same way with any Jewish rabbi?
> MR HARMSWORTH, Under-Secretary of State for Foreign Affairs, (Luton, C[oalition] L[iberal]); The answer to both parts of the question is in the negative.
> MR RAPER asked ... what steps are being taken by the British Government or by the League of Nations to put a stop to the pogrom of the Christian population in Central Russia, which has now been going on for the last eighteen months under the auspices of the Russian Soviet Government? ...
> ... [and further] whether the following are the leading repre-

sentatives of the Russian Soviet Government: Messrs. Trotsky, whose real name is Bronstein, Zinovieff, real name Apfelbaum, Kamenev, real name Rosenfeldt, Radek, real name Sobelson, Yoffe, Steklov, real name Nakhamkes, Sokolnikov, real name Brillant, ... and Litvinov, real name Finkelstein? ...

COL. WEDGWOOD (Newcastle-under-Lyme, Lab.): Before my Hon. friend answers, may I ask whether this and the two previous questions are intended to stir up anti-Jewish feeling and provoke pogroms in Russia?

MR HARMSWORTH: The Hon. gentleman who asked them is better able to answer that question than I am ...

MR RAPER: Is it a fact that the majority of these men are of Jewish origin, and further that these Jewish criminals, whom every decent Jew disowns, constitute the National Government in Central Russia?

LIEUT-COL. W. GUINNESS (Bury St. Edmunds C[oalition] U[nionist]): May I ask whether many of these men have not got strong German connections, and that the efforts they have made to conceal their German origins are very strong evidence of their underground connection with our former enemies?

MR HARMSWORTH: I think the facts as to the Soviet Government in Russia are very generally understood.

BRIGADIER-GENERAL CROFT: Is not Peter the Painter a trusted councillor?

No reply was given to this question.[26]

We shall now move on to a survey of antisemitism in the British press in the aftermath of the Russian Revolution. We shall also bring in here other printed sources, 'up-market' periodicals and 'literary' books and journals, and finally, some of the more scurrilous pamphlets put out on the extreme right-wing political fringe.

THE 'GUTTERCLIFFE PRESS'

'[The Bolsheviks] are adventurers of German–Jewish blood and in German pay' editorialised *The Times* on 23 November 1917. Between them the proprietor of *The Times*, Lord Northcliffe, and its editor, Henry Wickham Steed, ensured that the paper continued to fulfil its traditional role as a buttress of the Tory establishment. Throughout the period under review *The Times* consistently sided with and mirrored official Conservative policy on Russia. It thundered against Bolshevism, backed British intervention in the Civil War and urged assistance for the nascent Polish state. It waged a constant campaign against Lloyd George's attempt to reach an understanding with the Soviet government. *The Times* did not shrink from making use of the 'German-Jewish-Bolshevik' connection in order to add piquancy to its uncompromisingly anti-Communist position. On one level this strategy can be explained away if seen in the context of the bitter party in-fighting of the time. Lloyd George may have been a Liberal but the wartime coalition, which lasted until 1922, boasted a growing Tory majority. Furthermore, the Liberal Party had been divided since December 1916, when Lloyd George was appointed Prime Minister, and this effectively neutralised its political influence. 'Right-wing' Liberals who remained in the government tended to bow to Conservative opinion. Given these circumstances, no effort was spared in the Conservative attack on Lloyd George's Russian policy.

Indeed, the issue was perceived as one of a number of convenient levers with which to topple the Prime Minister and bring the coalition government to an end. Yet the fact remains that in taking up the 'Jewish-Bolshevik conspiracy' *The Times*, and the Tory press in general, succeeded in making antisemitism respectable – for a while at least.

The Times's two main contributors on Russian affairs were hardly sympathetic towards Russian Jewry. One of them, Stephen Graham, a founder member of the British–Russian Society, had attracted Jewish attention with an article he had written on Russia and the Jews for the *English Review* of 1915. The article amounted to a virtual *apologia* for the tsarist policy of persecution. In his book *Russia in Division*, written ten years later, Graham demonstrated that his attitude had only been confirmed by the intervening revolution. The book contained the following conclusion:

> The Jews interpreted certain prophecies in the Talmud as referring to the fate of Russia. And while one cannot but believe that God loves the Gentiles of today at least as much as he loves the Children of Israel, one cannot be surprised that fervent Jews see in the destruction of Russia a biblical visitation of the vengeance of

23

God upon those who have persecuted His people. With all respect, it is an incredibly exaggerated vengeance. Pharaoh and the Egyptians got off very lightly by comparison.[27]

'Jewish vengeance' in the form of Bolshevism, combined with a barely disguised religious antisemitism, is a recurrent theme throughout the revolutionary period.

Robert Wilton, *The Times* correspondent in St Petersburg from 1903, was far more influential than Graham. The son of an expatriate English mining engineer, he spent much of his youth in Russia and as an adult most of his sympathies and contacts lay with the Russian monarchist party. From the very beginning of the war Wilton identified the Jews and the Germans as conspiring together to overthrow the Romanov dynasty. When the Revolution became fact Wilton continued to blame Germans and Jews for Russia's ills, adding Bolsheviks to his list as October approached. As early as 28 March 1917 he sent a report to *The Times* from Riga which described 'hot headed and hysterical Jewish youths' forming a militia which they had refused to subordinate to local representatives of the Provisional Government. In a later report Wilton wrote: 'it is high time for the Russian Jews publicly to disassociate themselves from the demagogues', and with this advice came an unambiguous warning: 'If anarchy prevails in Russia there is bound to be a reaction in which the Jews would be the first sufferers.'[28]

The tone of Wilton's bulletins not only attracted criticism from Jews and Russian liberals, it also caused concern in the Foreign Office. *The Times* archives still contain a letter from the novelist John Buchan, who was serving in the Intelligence Department during the First World War. It reads: 'The situation in Russia is very delicate and I cannot think that Wilton's cables and articles have always been very discreet. Would it be possible for you to keep an eye on him and perhaps give him a hint?'[29]

In 1918 Wilton published *Russia's Agony*, the first of two contemporary accounts of the Russian Revolution, written while he was on leave in England between 1917 and 1918. In it Wilton gave great weight to the Jewish question. He claimed that the secret of Lenin's success lay in his reliance on 'non-Russian' support, namely 'German gold' and 'the pseudo-Jew class – the hate-laden produce of the Pale'. Wilton also ascribed the laying of the groundwork of the revolution to the Jews whom he saw as bringing both German influence and extreme socialist ideas into Russia. The Pale of Settlement is described as a fertile breeding ground for both of these elements:

> Amongst this suffering multitude [in the Pale] the devil of class hatred raised a fearsome harvest. The teachings of Karl Marx, a German Jew, were here decocted in their quintessence and spread by migrants from the Pale into more favoured lands – into the heart of Russia, into England and [as far as] America. Like many a noisome malady that has come to afflict mankind from the Near and Farther East, the worst political poisons exuded from the Pale.[30]

With the benefit of hindsight, however, Wilton recognised, albeit reluctantly, that the tsarist policy towards the Jews, beset as it was by internal contradictions, was responsible for this state of affairs:

> It becomes clear that the purpose for which the Pale and all the other anti-Jewish restrictions had been devised was mistaken and mischievous. It defeated itself. It led to the penetration of Russia by Hebrew elements of the most aggressive kind [i.e. businessmen and students] which had severed themselves from Jewry – had become pseudo-Jews – while it left the Jewish masses in congestion and misery. The purpose was one of self-preservation, yet it was misrepresented in the eyes of the world by Jews themselves plausibly enough, for motives that are easily comprehensible.

Moreover, the Jewish refugees who returned to Russia from the west in the wake of the revolution were also responsible for the spreading of Bolshevism:

> Another lamentable feature of the revolutionary period was the constant passage of Russian and pseudo-Jew revolutionaries from Allied countries. Every shipload that came from America, England or France gave trouble. The exiles would go straight from the train to the Field of Mars and 'stir up' the revolutionary pot. Whether 'martyrs of Tsarism' or merely German spies, they all considered themselves to be entitled to a share in the spoils, and had to be provided with 'fat places' in the Food, Agrarian, and other Commissariats. To these shipments we owe the advent of Bronstein-Trotsky and other Bolsheviki.[31]

Wilton's most substantial contribution to the stockpile of British press antisemitism in the aftermath of the revolution was, none the less, the publicity that he gave to the accusation that it was the Jews who had murdered the tsar. In dispatches sent from Russia between the end of 1918 and the end of 1920 for *The Times* series 'The Murder of the Tsar', and in his 1920 book *The Last Days of the Romanovs*, he repeated and elaborated on the accusations contained in the government White Paper *Russia No. 1*.[32]

> The Germans knew what they were doing when they sent Lenin's pack of Jews into Russia. They chose them as agents of destruction. Why? Because the Jews were not Russians and to them the destruction of Russia was all in the way of business, revolutionary or financial. The whole record of Bolshevism in Russia is indelibly impressed with the stamp of alien invasion. The murder of the Tsar, deliberately planned by the Jew Sverdlov (who came to Russia as a paid agent of Germany) and carried out by the Jews Goloshchokin, Syromolotov, Safarov, Voikov and Yurovsky, is the act not of the Russian people, but of this hostile invader.[33]

Wilton also announced that a monument to Judas Iscariot had been erected by the Bolsheviks in Moscow.

Wilton's activities during the Civil War are scrutinised in Anthony Summers's and Tom Mangold's book *The File on theTsar*, an investigation into the murder of the Imperial family in Ekaterinburg in July 1918. Apparently, when Wilton returned to Russia in the autumn of 1918 it was with the White Army in Siberia. He became *de facto* assistant to General Deterikhs, with whom he had much in common: 'the two men shared a mutual hatred of Bolshevism and Germany and above all of Jews.'[34] According to Phillip Knightly in *The First Casualty*, Wilton 'had compromised any claim to objective reporting by joining the staff of one of the White Russian generals ... it is clear that his part in the intervention on behalf of various White elements made his value as a war correspondent virtually nil.'[35] As Summers and Mangold observe, however, 'In 1920 Wilton's articles on the Romanov massacre had the full authority of Printing House Square, and carried considerable weight. The articles, and the later book based on them, were major factors in establishing the orthodox assassination version in Britain.'[36]

In November 1919 *The Times* printed a long letter entitled 'The Horrors of Bolshevism' which was supposedly written by an – unnamed – British officer in south Russia. It contained the stock accusations against the 'Jewish commissars' while at the same time seeking to exonerate Denikin from blame for any pogroms. This was only one of a number of Bolshevik atrocity stories published by the Northcliffe press during the intervention, but in this particular case *The Times* undertook to publish the 'evidence' in pamphlet form. According to the paper, 'thousands of copies' were sold to raise money for the White cause. The story also generated a spate of correspondence in the columns of *The Times* on the subject of Jews and Bolshevism. Israel Cohen, writing on behalf of the Zionist Organisation, was hard pressed to answer the allegations hurled at Jewry by the principal contributors, all of whom apparently preferred to remain anonymous, using pseudonyms such as 'Verax', 'Janus', 'Philojudaeus', 'Testis' and 'Pro-Denikin'. The tone of the correspondence was such that the Chief Rabbi, Dr Hertz, was moved to plead with 'the responsible editor of the world's most influential newspaper' to stop publishing material likely to incite racial hatred. It can be no accident that the fulminations of *The Times* against 'Jewish Bolshevism' occurred at the same time as Lloyd George's announcement (the famous 8 November 1919 Guildhall speech) that he was prepared to raise the blockade and establish trade relations with the Soviet government.[37]

On 8 February 1919 *The Times* carried a report on pogroms in Poland written by Israel Cohen, who was then in Warsaw for the Zionist Organisation. On 22 May further space was given to a major article by Cohen on the same subject. On both occasions the editorial passed comment by endorsing the essential veracity of Cohen's testimony and blamed the newly created League of Nations for failing to discipline the Poles. The paper argued that the League had the right to demand internal justice in the Polish state in return for international protection against its external foes. However, at the same time the leader writer took issue with Cohen's proposal for National Cultural Autonomy as a solution to the Jewish question on the grounds that 'there is no being in and out of a country at one and the same time'. What was implied was that the Poles had grounds for suspecting the Jews of dual loyalties.

On 28 June, in the light of the 'Day of Mourning' called by the

Anglo-Jewish community on behalf of Polish Jewry,[38] *The Times* approached this theme even more directly: 'that the Polish Jews are
suspected of sympathy sometimes with the Bolshevists, sometimes with
Germany, and of that excuse [for pogroms] too, they have it in their
power to deprive their opponents'. The onus was thus on the Jews to
prove that they were Polish patriots.

In his years as *The Times* correspondent in Vienna, Henry Wickham
Steed had been exposed to every dimension of the 'Jewish Question',
and by the time he was promoted to editor he had long been a confirmed believer in the 'German-Jewish' connection. Steed insisted that
this connection was consummated through the medium of 'international finance and of its clandestine associates': the operation of
Jewish financiers bolstered the strength of 'Pan-German militarism'.
Such views pervaded the paper's editorial policy. In July 1914 Lord
Rothschild made a last-ditch attempt to secure the neutrality of *The
Times* in the forthcoming conflict. In his memoirs Steed recorded the
following conversation between Lord Northcliffe and himself: ' "It is a
dirty German-Jewish international financial attempt to bully us into
advocating neutrality" I said "and the proper answer would be a still
stiffer leading article tomorrow." "I agree with you" said Lord Northcliffe, "let us go ahead".'[39]

This alliance, according to Steed, was not only financial in nature; it
was also supported by shared dislike of tsarist Russia. Steed noted that
'Jewish idealism'

> strengthened for a time the pro-German and pan-German ten-
> dencies of Jewish finance by bringing Jewish hatred of Imperial
> Russia into line with Jewish attachment to Germanism ... The
> gulf that severed Western Europe from Russia during the latter
> half of the nineteenth century was dug and kept open chiefly by
> Jewish resentment of the persecution of the Jews.[40]

More fundamentally, Jewish hatred of Russia

> sprang ... from Jewish detestation of the Russian Holy Synod and
> of the Russian Orthodox Church as survivors of Medieval Chris-
> tianity and as promoters of a crusade for the possession of 'Tsari-
> grad' (Constantinople) and of the Holy Places. Against Russian
> Christian fanaticism was ranged an intense Jewish fanaticism
> hardly to be paralleled save among the more militant sects of

28

Islam. This Jewish fanaticism allied itself with the anti-Russian forces before and during the early years of the War.[41]

All Jewish interests were thus supposed to be on the side of Germany and against the Anglo-Russian alliance. For Steed the arrival of Bolshevism, which was 'largely Jewish in doctrine and in personnel', represented the victory of Germans and Jews over the Russian Empire.

At the Paris peace conference of January 1919, Lloyd George and US President Woodrow Wilson announced their intention to call a truce with the Bolsheviks, with a view to eventual recognition. They proposed holding a preliminary conference on Prinkipo Island, to which both Red and White Russians would be invited. The conference never took place, however, since the White Russians refused to have anything to do with it. Undeterred, the British and American leaders launched a new initiative in March: William Bullitt, a junior US delegate in Paris, was sent to Petrograd on an unofficial mission to sound out the Soviet government's views on peace terms. As with the Prinkipo plan, the Soviets showed themselves surprisingly well-disposed to cooperate. In Britain, however, these negotiations were regarded with the utmost suspicion by Tory opinion and in the Tory press. A warning in *The Times* argued as follows: 'The origin of the Prinkipo policy is shrouded in mystery. There are indications that it was conceived by prominent Jewish financiers in New York, whose interest in Trotsky and his associates is of old standing.'[42]

Wickham Steed later claimed that the initial suggestion for the Bolsheviks to be invited to Paris had come from 'a Jewish writer' in the *Manchester Guardian*, ten days before Lloyd George made his announcement. In his memoirs Steed was even more specific in identifying exactly who was behind the Prinkipo and Bullitt 'plots': 'Potent international financial interests were at work in favour of the immediate recognition of the Bolshevists ... the well-known American Jewish banker, Mr. Jacob Schiff, was known to be anxious to secure recognition for the Bolshevists, among whom Jewish influence was prominent.'[43]

Jacob Schiff was, of course, one of the Jewish financiers accused of pro-German sympathies before the Americans entered the war in April 1917.

In his memoirs, Steed recounts how he succeeded in sabotaging the peace initiatives not only by using violently anti-Bolshevik rhetoric in *The Times*, approved of by Lord Northcliffe, but also, apparently, by his powers of persuasion in a frank conversation with President Wilson's right-hand man, Colonel House: 'I insisted that, unknown to him, the prime movers were Jacob Schiff, Warburg and other international financiers, who wished above all to bolster up the Jewish Bolshevists in order to secure a field for German and Jewish exploitation of Russia.'[44] Tory opposition – and no doubt the part Steed played in it – was a significant factor in Lloyd George's abandonment of the Bullitt project in April 1919.

The Times *and* The Protocols

In February 1920 the notorious tsarist forgery, *The Protocols of the Elders of Zion*, was published in English for the first time. The 'message' of this excruciatingly turgid text was that a Jewish conspiracy was plotting to take over the world. The secret conclave of the 'Elders of Zion' was variously identified with the French freemasons, the Alliance Israélite Universelle (a Jewish philanthropic organisation based in Paris) and the First Zionist Congress held in 1897 in Basle – a meeting remarkable for the openness of its proceedings. Subsequent research into the origins of *The Protocols* has revealed, somewhat ironically, that they were probably inspired by an obscure political satire in defence of liberalism written in France during the Second Empire. Maurice Joly's 1864 satire, *Dialogue aux enfers entre Montesquieu et Machiavel*, was later rewritten as an attack on the reformist Russian minister, Witte, by a Russian émigré in Paris who had connections with the tsarist secret police. Heavily antisemitic in tone, *The Protocols* were inevitably exploited by extreme right-wing propagandists and politicians in Russia: the Okhrana (the tsarist secret police) provided subsidies for the dissemination of a Russian translation in the period following 1903. As the tsar himself patronised the violently antisemitic organisation, The Union of the Russian People, there is little doubt that *The Protocols* helped to foment the bloody attacks against the Jews in both the Kishinev pogrom of 1903 and the 1905 reaction. It was, nonetheless, after the Russian Revolution that *The Protocols* had their most powerful impact with the birth of the Judaeo-Communist conspiracy myth.

In *Warrant for Genocide*, his classic study of *The Protocols*, Norman Cohn explains: 'What launched The Protocols on their career across the world was above all the murder of the Imperial family at Ekaterinburg.'[45] There were some strange circumstances surrounding the family's murder. At the scene of the assassination a mysterious poem and some symbols with Hebraic associations were found; a version of *The Protocols* written by Serge Nilus, entitled *The Great in the Small*, was found in the tsaritsa's possessions and the empress had also apparently drawn a swastika on a window. The White Russians interpreted these events as a sign from the dead empress that the Jews were responsible for regicide and that the Bolshevik Revolution represented the victory of the 'anti-Christ' in Russia. The White Russians thus used antisemitism – and in particular the world Jewish conspiracy theory of *The Protocols* – as propaganda in the Civil War. When in May 1918 the 'Zunder' forgery was 'discovered' on the person of a Jewish Bolshevik commander in the Red Army this 'confirmed' that the October Revolution had been a 'Jewish plot'.

It is clear from the foregoing that the full significance of the English translation of *The Protocols* can only be grasped against the background of British intervention on the side of the White Russians in the Civil War. The first edition of *The Protocols* appeared under the imprint of His Majesty's Printers Eyre & Spottiswoode, publishers of the Authorised Version of the Bible and the Anglican Prayer Book. Recent research has established that *The Protocols* reached the west via White Russian officers; the first English translation was made by George Shanks, the 'son of a well-known and highly respected English merchant till recently established in Moscow ... ' who 'of course' along with the rest of his family was 'now ruined and a refugee in London'.[46] In fact the appearance of the English edition did not arouse 'the slightest reaction in the British press'[47] at the time. It was only several months later, when *The Times* saw fit to take up the matter that it was brought to public attention. On 8 May 1920 the now famous article 'The Jewish Peril' appeared. Here the possible authenticity of *The Protocols* was speculated upon:

> What are these *Protocols*? Are they authentic? If so, what malevolent assembly concocted these plans, and gloated over their exposition? Are they a forgery? If so, whence came the

31

uncanny note of prophecy, prophecy in parts fulfilled, in parts far gone in the way of fulfilment? Have we been struggling these tragic years to blow up and extirpate the secret organisation of German world domination only to find beneath it another, more dangerous because more secret? Have we by straining every fibre of our national body, escaped a 'Pax Germanica' only to fall into a 'Pax Judaeica'?

The anonymous writer – now believed to have been Wickham Steed himself – continued to draw a parallel between the programme for world domination formulated by 'The Elders of Zion' and the policies of the Russian Bolshevik government. The timing of these revelations was not without significance: they were designed to pre-empt the long-awaited opening of Anglo-Soviet trade talks in London to which *The Times* had consistently been opposed. In the paper's view the British government had no business in dealing with the current representatives of the 'Jewish world government' in Moscow. Yet *The Times*'s strategy on the matter failed abysmally – Lloyd George met Krassin on 31 May 1920. *The Times*, none the less, was not above exploiting antisemitism to score political points, although within certain constraints. The paper never committed itself to claiming that *The Protocols* were genuine. On the contrary, it opened its correspondence column to letters – not all of them from Jews – arguing that the document was spurious. It was, furthermore, one of their own correspondents, Philip Graves, who eventually 'blew' the forgery in August 1921. But it was the notorious article of 8 May that propelled *The Protocols* into the public eye and single-handedly renewed and intensified press agitation on the subject of the 'Jewish-Bolshevik' conspiracy.

The *Morning Post*

On 8 October 1918, the *Morning Post* editorialised:

'Bolshevik' is the best-known word for the International Anarchist, though that international Anarchist is not by any manner of means always a Russian Jew. He is generally a Jew of some kind. The stubborn intellectual Hebraic race produces genius in all forms – literature, music, art, philosophy as well as finance: and it chiefly produces also the destructive genius, the man who has got into a big brain the mad idea that the only way to cure the world of its ills is to lay everything flat ... the intellectual Jew of the destructive type is the inspiring genius of the class war against civilisation.

It was the high Tory paper the *Morning Post*, edited by Howell Arthur Keir Gwynne, a confirmed apostle of the Jewish conspiracy theory, that led the anti-Jewish press campaign. In common with *The Times*, the chief source of information on Russian affairs for the *Morning Post* was an expatriate Englishman, Victor E. Marsden, who had taken up the cause of the Russian far right. Marsden's dispatches at the time of the Russian Revolution put the blame squarely on the shoulders of 'Russian Jews of German extraction' who were working for a separate peace. Marsden declared that their policy of disruption had succeeded in bringing about the treaty of Brest–Litovsk and that Russia was 'under the Government of Jewry' which was in turn at the mercy of the patron of the Jews, namely Germany. The extent of Marsden's prejudice, which perhaps even surpassed that of Robert Wilton, is illustrated in the testimony ascribed to him in this *Morning Post* editorial: 'When we plied Mr. Marsden with questions as to his persecutors and the destroyers of Russia, he replied in two words: "The Jews." When we asked him for proof of his statement he replied that the Jews were his gaolers, and the Inquisition and the whole machinery of the terror under which he had suffered.'[48] Of course Marsden had 'proof' in writing; none other than a copy of *The Protocols*. He had in fact been responsible for a new translation of the book undertaken by the ultra-right 'Britons Publishing Society' late in 1920.

In July 1920 the *Morning Post* published a series of 18 articles, with appropriate editorial comment, on the subject of 'the Jewish peril'. The articles appeared anonymously, but recent research attributes a large part of the authorship to the journalist Ian Colvin (who wrote for the right-wing *National Review*), with other contributions from Nesta Webster (the foremost 'serious historian' of the conspiratorial school) and Gwynne. All three had connections with the extreme right. The articles were subsequently collected together in a book entitled *The Cause of World Unrest* with a signed introduction by the *Morning Post*'s editor. In his introduction Gwynne claimed that this piece of learned research proved that 'there has been for centuries a hidden conspiracy, chiefly Jewish, whose objects have been and are to produce Revolution, Communism and Anarchy, by means of which they hope to arrive at the hegemony of the world by establishing some sort of despotic rule.'[49]

With the intention of making constant reference to his basic text, *The Protocols*, Gwynne also made the following statement by way of a disclaimer at the very outset:

> *The Protocols of the Elders of Zion* which have been published in England, have aroused tremendous interest and a storm of protest. It will be noticed by the reader that the authors of this book [*World Unrest*] have taken particular care not to assume their authenticity. They may or may not be genuine. Their chief interest lies in the fact that, while the book which contains them was published in 1905, the Jewish Bolsheviks are today carrying out almost to the letter the programme outlined in *The Protocols*.[50]

In other words, Gwynne was not prepared to enter into the debate on the authenticity of *The Protocols*. Their origin was to him irrelevant. He was more interested in their 'message'. The Russian Revolution – to say nothing of other abortive revolutions in central Europe – were *ex post facto* proof of the validity of *The Protocols*. Did not the revolution conform in all its essentials to the blueprint set out in that document? And lest anyone doubt the extent of Jewish involvement in Bolshevism, Gwynne also provided a list of Bolshevik leaders with their 'true' identities. The list, with all its inaccuracies, is printed below.[51]

By arguing that *The Protocols* were an uncanny prediction of events which had actually come to pass, confirmed believers in the tract rendered attempts to discredit it – by means of investigative journalism or historical research – somewhat futile. Philip Graves and Lucien Wolf were to learn this lesson. This fact also accounts for the enduring potency of the myth.

H. A. Gwynne gave generous space on the letters page of the *Morning Post* to Nesta Webster (1876–1960).[52] The thesis of her book *The Origins and Progress of the World Revolution* was that the roots of present-day Bolshevism were to be found in German socialism, which was in turn a product of Jewish thought from Marx and Lassalle. In the 1848 Revolution, German progressive thought had been 'hijacked' by 'the German-Jewish band of Social Democrats'. The Prussian authori-

'BOCHE, BOLSHIE AND THE JEWISH BOGEY'

	Pseudonym	Real Name	Race
1	Lenin	Oulianov	Russian
2	Trotsky	Bronstein	Jew
3	Steklov	Nachamkess	Jew
4	Martov	Tsederbaum	Jew
5	Zinoviev	Apfelbaum	Jew
6	Goussiev	Drapkin	Jew
7	Kamenev	Rosenfeld	Jew
8	Souhanov	Ghimmer	German
9	Sagersky	Krachmann	Jew
10	Bogdanov	Silberstein	Jew
11	Gorev	Goldman	Jew
12	Ouritzky	Radomislsky	Jew
13	Volodarsky	Kohen	Jew
14	Sverdlov	Sverdlov	Jew (?)
15	Kamkov	Katz	Jew
16	Ganetzky	Furstenberg	Jew
17	Dann	Gourevitch	Jew
18	Meshkovsky	Goldberg	Jew
19	Parvus	Helphandt	Jew
20	Riazonov	Goldenbach	Jew
21	Martinov	Zimbar	Jew
22	Tchernomorsky	Tchernomordik	Jew
23	Piatnitzky	Levin	Jew
24	Abramovitch	Rein	Jew
25	Solntzev	Bleichman	Jew
26	Zverzditch	Fonstein	Jew
27	Radek	Sobelson	Jew
28	Litvinov, alias		
	Finkenstein	Wallack	Jew
29	Lounatcharsky	Lounatcharsky	Russian
30	Kolontai	Kolontai	Russian
31	Peters	Peters	Lett
32	Maklakovsky	Rosenbloom	Jew
33	Lapinsky	Levenson	Jew
34	Vobrov	Natansson	Jew
35	Ortodoks	Akselrode	Jew
36	Garin	Gerfeldt	Jew
37	Glazounov	Schulze	Jew
38	Lebedieva	Simson	Jewess
39	Joffe	Joffe	Jew
40	Kamensky	Hoffman	Jew
41	Naout	Ginzburg	Jew
42	Zagorsky	Krachmalink	Jew
43	Izgoev	Goldman	Jew
44	Vladimirov	Feldman	Jew
45	Bounskov	Foundamentzky	Jew
46	Manouilsky	Manouilsky	Jew
47	Larin	Lourie	Jew
48	Krassin	Krassin	Russian
49	Tchicherin	Tchicherin	Russian
50	Goukovsky	Goukovsky	Russian

ties used this 'band' as a weapon to subvert their enemies, especially France and Russia. Marxism, according to Webster, was a foreign import into Russia, where it overcame indigenous forms of radicalism, such as Popularism (*narodnichestvo*) and Anarchism.

> Bolshevism in Russia is therefore German and Jewish. This is bringing no accusation against the Jewish race; it is merely stating a fact, for just as Anarchy is Russian, just as Syndicalism is French in its origin, so Bolshevism is German-Jewish in its origin. The Marxian faction was described by Bakunin in his day as 'the German-Jew company', or 'the Red Bureaucracy' and nothing could better describe the faction which is now ruling Russia. Bolshevism, therefore, is largely Jewish, and we cannot wonder that to many people the whole world revolution seems to be a Jewish conspiracy.[53]

So the October Revolution was the outcome of a 'German-Jewish plot' in which Lenin and his 'Jewish' lieutenants were smuggled back to Petrograd through Germany in the notorious 'sealed train'. This was arranged through the intermedium of 'Parvus' (Alexander Helphand), Radek (Karl Sobelson), Ganetsky (Furstenberg) and others. The aim of the revolution – its paying lip-service to communism notwithstanding – was to promote the capitalistic interests of the German and Jewish alliance. On this point Webster was in complete agreement with Robert Wilton, Wickham Steed and H.A. Gwynne. All three claimed that Russia had been dependent economically on German-Jewish finance before the war and that this had been the country's undoing. The Bolshevik Revolution gave free reign to 'the industrial exploitation of Russia by the German and Jewish company of super capitalists, whose real schemes were camouflaged under the guise of Communism'.[54] In 1922 Webster wrote in the *Post* that the introduction of 'state capitalism' into Russia, the Anglo-Soviet Trade Agreement, the treaties of Brest-Litovsk and Rapallo, all proved beyond doubt that what lay behind the Russian Revolution was the profit motive. As was to be expected it was a Jew, Radek, and Krassin – admittedly a non-Jew but with a Jewish wife – who had played prominent roles in the negotiations both in Berlin and London. The Bolshevik 'set-up' in the latter city was a tawdry affair:

That Krassin, living in luxury at his £19,000 house in Belsize Park
... has ever been a sincere Bolshevik no one can seriously believe
... in a word, the gorgeous office known as Soviet House is not
that of a 'Workers' Republic' but of the international capitalist
concern; 'Bolshevism Limited' limited, that is to say, to German
and Jewish financiers and their allies.[55]

Webster concluded by warning that the Germans, by deliberately
exploiting Jewish ingenuity were 'playing with fire'. The Spartacist
Rising in Germany – instigated by two Jews, Rosa Luxemburg and
Karl Liebknecht – highlighted the dangers of the subordinate partner
getting out of hand.

Nesta Webster's bracketing together of Germans and Jews makes for
ironic reading in the post-Second World War world. In fact, as early as
1922 she had incurred the wrath of Kurt Kerlen, a Bavarian member of
the Thule Society and a future admirer of Adolf Hitler, for daring to
make such a connection. The pair fought out their respective positions
on the relative responsibility of the Germans and Jews for the Russian
Revolution on the pages of the *Morning Post*. (The entire debate was
afterwards reprinted by a fringe right-wing publisher in New York
under the title *Boche and Bolshevik*.) Taking especial exception to
Webster's statement in *World Revolution* that 'I do not think that we
can call it entirely a Jewish conspiracy, for it is also largely German',[56]
Kerlen retorted that, on the contrary, the revolution was entirely the
working of 'sinister influences' – Social Democrats, Jews and, of
course, freemasons. These forces combined had subverted the blameless policies of the 'real' Germans – dependable fellows like General
Ludendorff. Webster, whose articles appeared in publications of the
far right like the journals of the 'Britons' and the Duke of Northumberland's *The Patriot*, joined the British Fascists in 1924. But it was not
until after 1933 that she was finally forced to make a choice between
blaming Germans or Jews. Predictably, she opted for the latter.

In fact, the 'Jews and Bolshevism' theme was not confined to the
national daily press. It spilled over into outwardly serious periodicals
such as the *Spectator* and *Nineteenth Century and After*.[57] There were
also a number of 'literary' magazines which made a speciality of
peddling an ultra-patriotic and antisemitic line during the First World
War period, such as Leo Maxse's *National Review* and *New Witness*,

with which the 'Chesterbelloc' group was closely associated. Hilaire Belloc's contribution to the debate, his 'admirable Yidbook' *The Jews*, was published in 1922.[58] Finally, the Russian Revolution stimulated an outpouring of first-hand accounts, contemporary histories and travelogues by British diplomats, soldiers and journalists. A good many of these observers commented on the Jewish role in the revolution – more often than not negatively.[59]

BOLSHEVIKS AND PROTO-FASCISTS

Far out on the extreme right, beyond the bounds of political respectability, were the pedlars of antisemitism in its most undiluted form. In the early 1920s a number of fringe patriotic journals and attendant publications were in circulation in Britain, all of which made full use of the 'Jewish/Bolshevik' conspiracy. There was *Plain English* founded in July 1920 by Lord Alfred Douglas, poet and consort of Oscar Wilde. Its strongly anti-Bolshevik and anti-Jewish stance was largely inspired by its Russian émigré contributor, one Major-General Count Cherep-Spiridovitch. He later wrote a book on the subject of *The Secret World Government* which was published in New York. In 1921 Ian Alan Percy, the Duke of Northumberland, founded the Boswell Publishing Company and in 1922 its associated journal *The Patriot* (circulation 3000) made its first appearance. This boasted contributions by Northumberland's fellow peer, the ex-colonial governor Lord Sydenham of Combe, Nesta Webster (whose book *The Origins and Progress of the World Revolution* and others were published by Boswell), and Ian Colvin of the *Morning Post*.[60]

But the most extreme group disseminating antisemitic propaganda in the early 1920s – indeed the very first organisation set up in Britain for this express purpose – was The Britons.[61] This 'patriotic' society was founded in July 1919 by Henry H. Beamish, an ex-serviceman from the Colonies and whose brother was Conservative MP for Lewes. From 1922 to 1925 The Britons published a monthly journal under various titles: *Jewry Uber Alles*, *The Hidden Hand* and *The British Guardian*. The Britons' brand of antisemitism was all-embracing, including religious, economic, political and racial elements. Like *Plain English* and *The Patriot*, it was heavily influenced by *The Protocols*.

Indeed, it was The Britons Publishing Company (founded in 1919 as the Judaic Publishing Company) which took over the publication of *The Jewish Peril* from Eyre & Spottiswoode in 1920. And it subsequently brought out the Marsden translation in defiance of the exposé in *The Times*. In an anonymous article entitled 'The Jew-made War', printed in *The Hidden Hand* of March 1921, was written the following:

> the Jews controlled Czars and their ministers from the beginning, and were as much responsible for the 'horrors of Czarism' as they are for the horrors of Bolshevism. The finance minister of Russia came to England to negotiate a loan. But no loan could be raised until he had obtained the authority – not of the Czar, that was nothing, but of *the Jews of Russia*. And England was not allowed to lend her ally money until England had the consent of the *Jews of England*.
>
> Oh yes: it was a Jew-made war. And the Jews of England and the Jews of Russia well know who would ultimately come to possess the money lent by England, by permission of the Jew nation ... The learned Elders were all ready with their Kerenskys, Lenins and Trotskys, to seize it when their plans were ripe for the blessed 'Revolution' they had long determined to set up, ready to murder the Czar in whose name they had been acting, and to wage war on the Czar's allies who had furnished them with the money.[62]

The Britons viewed war and revolution, capitalism and Communism, as mere functions of the Jew-inspired plot to take over the world. They similarly claimed that Jews were found to be behind the failure of the British intervention in the Russian Civil War – for did they not play a decisive role in the anti-intervention movement in the first place? Jews were also responsible for the 'anti-Polish' policy of the Paris peace conference – or rather the 'Kosher Conference' as The Britons dubbed it on account of the presence of various Jewish statesmen and delegations. The British Prime Minister, Lloyd George, was regarded as simply the head of a 'Jewalition' government.

A recurring motif in The Britons' propaganda was that of Bolshevism as the Devil Incarnate. The struggle against it was presented as a fight to the finish between the Forces of Darkness and the Forces of

Light, the latter being defined as Western civilisation and the Christian tradition. Inserted into this model was the equation between Bolshevism and Judaism (as opposed to merely the Jews), held to justify a religious war between Judaism (as represented by Bolshevism) and Christianity for the ideological domination of the world. This type of cosmological antisemitism, which like other brands operates on a dualistic mechanism, has been studied in depth by Norman Cohn. In *Warrant for Genocide* he traces such antisemitism back to demonological superstitions inherited from the Middle Ages:

> At its heart lies the belief that Jews – all Jews everywhere – form a conspiratorial body set on ruining and then dominating the rest of mankind. And this belief is simply a modernised, secularized version of the popular medieval view of Jews as a league of sorcerers employed by Satan for the spiritual and physical ruina-tion of Christendom.

This is indeed 'the deadliest kind of antisemitism, the kind that results in massacre and attempted genocide'.[63] The Britons' variation on this theme had not yet reached the more 'advanced' stage of secularisation. For example,

> when the Jew Bolshevists, Lenin and Trotsky, seized the Govern-ment of Russia the first thing they did was to abolish all Christian rites and all Christian priests, but they did not abolish rabbis. Bolshevism is the first overt attack of Judaism on Christianity.[64]

It is, on the contrary, common knowledge among specialists in Soviet religious affairs that Judaism, being numerically weaker than either Orthodox Christianity or Islam in Russia, suffered worst in the Bolsheviks' secularisation drive. The imagery used by The Britons to convey the horrors of Jewish Bolshevik atrocities also harks back to the medieval Blood Libel:

> If Bolshevism comes to Great Britain, we know perfectly well that the most respectable citizens will be killed or mutilated, and that the Empire will be brought to a speedy, inglorious end. The ritual

> never varies. If we be not hanged or flung down wells, or starved to death, our nails will be pulled out and our hands will be skinned, while a mob of idle Jews look on, grinning and smoking large cigars.[65]

The outstanding feature of The Britons' antisemitism was its racialist flavour. When discussing the 'evils of Jewish Bolshevism' once again, the leader-writer in *Jewry Uber Alles* (June 1920) commented: 'We are up against a foe of Eastern origin, with all the Oriental cruelty and disregard of human life inborn in his blood.'[66] Colin Holmes has written that 'the emergence and acceptance of a conspiratorial expression of hostility based on race contributed a significant new dynamic' to post-war antisemitism. For the existence of racial – and racialist – theories implied that 'no symbiosis was possible between Jew and non-Jew'.[67] The Britons, indeed, asserted that no Jew, whether assimilated or otherwise, could in the final analysis be a loyal citizen of Russia or of Britain or of any other country. He bore allegiance only to the World Jewish Conspiracy as it manifested itself in pro-Germanism and Bolshevism. Beyond this, the Jew was innately inferior, both physically and morally, to the 'Nordic', 'Teutonic' and even the 'Slavic' peoples. So far as Britain was concerned, The Britons argued that the Jew posed a distinct threat to the national unity and racial integrity of the Motherland and undermined the Empire. In practice, they advocated 'the eradication of alien [read Jewish] influences from political and economic life'. The recommended means to this end included strict immigration and naturalisation laws, protectionism in trade, the outlawing of intermarriage and, above all, the withdrawal of citizenship rights from all those born of non-British parentage 'by a re-enactment of the law of Edward I'. 'The Jewish problem' could be solved simply enough by the complete segregation of the Jews from the indigenous population, and their eventual deportation. The most desirable destination, at least initially, was Palestine. Zionism was, in short, to be made compulsory, and the Jewish National Home established in order to act as the 'Ghetto of the World'.

Despite the attention lavished on them by some researchers, the influence of The Britons must certainly not be exaggerated. They had very limited resources, both in terms of personnel (12 in 1919) and finance and were plagued by internal wrangling.[68] In the early 1920s they inhabited the lunatic fringe of British political life. Yet, the fact remains that The Britons anticipated things to come. In 1922 they published a tract entitled *Jewish Bolshevism* which featured caricature portraits of prominent Bolsheviks with reference to their Jewish origins. The preface was written by the future Nazi ideologue Alfred Rosenberg. The whole had originally appeared in German under the imprint of the *Volkisch Deutscher Volksverlag*. Here is a choice extract from Rosenberg's introduction:

> the Hebrew assassins in Russia will not escape ... that nemesis, lying in wait for all who pursue none but egotistical ends. These men are doomed ... the judgement of the Russian people will surely overtake them – and there will not be left in Russia one Jew to remember those glorious days, when his race, besmirched with blood and tears, danced over what it thought was the corpse of a great nation.[69]

The threat of violence as the final solution of the Jewish question was quite explicit. It is clear that the racist component of The Britons' antisemitism – the logical conclusion of which was the forcible removal of the Jews through expulsion and ultimately extermination – had more in common with Nazism than with the conventional 'drawing-room' antisemitism of the pre-First World War period. The difference was one of quality and not of degree.

The Jewish-Bolshevik agitation in the British press was, nevertheless, like British antisemitism in general, limited. First, it was limited in scope. *The Times*, for example, despite the controversy it aroused, observed certain unwritten ground rules concerning antisemitism. Moreover, what appeared in *The Times* must be seen in the broader context of the Conservative press campaign against Bolshevism in general and against Lloyd George's Russian policy in particular. Neither of these qualifications detract from the undoubtedly influential role which *The Times* played in publicising antisemitism in the political arena. However, it must be remembered that a significant section of the Tory press, including the *Daily Telegraph* and the *Daily Express*, remained free from the taint of antisemitism despite being equally hostile to Communism and equally in favour of British intervention in Russia.[70]

Second, the Jewish-Bolshevik agitation was limited over time. Even the Northcliffe press dropped the subject after *The Times*'s exposure of *The Protocols* in August 1921. Only the *Morning Post* (circulation 119,000 in 1920) and its less respectable associates *Plain English, The Patriot* and especially The Britons, persisted in propagating the Jewish conspiracy theory in its purest form. Thus, after 1921 such notions were consigned to the extreme fringe of British political life. This in itself testifies to the strength of the liberal tradition in Britain. Leading Liberal newspapers, the *Manchester Guardian* and the *Daily News*, were immune from this nasty outbreak of anti-Bolshevik-inspired antisemitism.[71] The same held largely true for the Labour press, despite a certain ambiguity towards Jews evident in the socialist movement as a whole.[72]. Editorial silence on the subject of Jews and Bolshevism in the journals of the progressive left may be attributed to various factors, both pragmatic and ideological. One good cause for reticence was the realisation that the issue was being exploited for political reasons by the right in order to drum up support for British intervention – a policy which Liberals regarded with mixed feelings and to which Labourites were adamantly opposed. There was also the awkward but inescapable fact that there *were* significant numbers of Jews involved in radical politics, not only in Russia, but also in Britain at the time. The exact figure is impossible to gauge, as this was a sensitive issue for Jewish and Gentile socialists alike.[73] The 'Jewish-Bolshevik' threat was used as much as propaganda against socialism at home as to promote the government's foreign policy. Moreover, as elsewhere in Europe and America, Bolshevism was regarded as a foreign import largely purveyed by Russian Jewish immigrants.

In the final analysis, antisemitism and the progressive conscience simply did not mix. Liberals and socialists had traditionally played a prominent role in the protests against tsarist pogroms and in upholding the right of asylum for refugees from religious and political persecution: Liberals in Parliament, after all, pressed for Jewish Emancipation in 1858. This heritage was sufficient to deter most liberals and socialists from using antisemitism for political ends. Indeed, in the battle against antisemitism the Jews' most influential allies were to be found almost entirely on the left.

How serious was this post-First World War wave of antisemitism in the long-term perspective of British political development? This is not the place to go into the wider academic controversy over 'continuity' in the modern development of antisemitism. I do not want to be drawn into the debate as to whether twentieth-century antisemitism, especially in its most lethal Nazi form, has been qualitatively different from that which preceded it. What is certain, however, is that the so-called 'Jewish Bolshevik' threat (which replaced the somewhat ironic one of Jewish pro-Germanism) fuelled antisemitism in the years after the First World War. This fear, along with the development of racial antisemitism, provided nourishment for the Fascist ideology of the following decade. Although marginalised in the 1920s, Jewish conspiracy theories persisted only to surface with greater impact in the literature of the far right in the 1930s. The significance of anti-Jewish hostility in Britain in the years 1917–20 must not be exaggerated, but it did sow the seeds for the future.

'THE DISLIKE OF THE UNLIKE': THE ALIENS QUESTION AND THE 'BOLSHEVIK BOGEY'

Our examination of the growth of antisemitism in Britain in connection with the Bolshevik Revolution in Russia is incomplete without any attempt to identify the targets of this prejudice. Such hostility was first directed at the Jewish commissars in Russia. But for the British public, these were largely an abstract concept. Antisemitism in Britain in this period was not to any great extent a reflection of preoccupations in the field of foreign affairs. It drew its strength principally from domestic conditions. On the political right the Russian Revolution was identified with the rise of Labour at home. British Bolsheviks were blamed for the development of the Parliamentary Labour Party, the emergence of anti-war factions on the left, the Irish troubles, trade union militancy – especially on 'Red' Clydeside and in Belfast in 1919, and the army mutiny at Calais. Just as certain Conservatives regarded Bolshevism in Russia as a foreign import, so they looked upon socialism at home in the same light. They blamed unrest on the 'alien', Irish Sinn Feiners, but mainly on Russian Jews. Immigrants and subversion were linked. In 1917, after the Russian Revolution, the East End of London was reputed to be a hotbed of pro-Bolshevik and anti-war feeling. Xenophobia was not confined to newcomers; it inevitably spilt over into antipathy towards the Anglo-Jewish community as a whole. Anti-alienists found it difficult to distinguish between native, naturalised and immigrant Jews. Indeed, the distinction came to be regarded as academic.

On the eve of the First World War, there were some 100,000–150,000 Jewish immigrants – refugees from persecution and economic hardship in Russia and other parts of eastern Europe – crowded into the more depressed areas of Britain's largest cities. The biggest colony was, of course, in the East End of London. By 1914 London was only exceeded by New York and Chicago as the greatest centre for immigration from eastern Europe. This influx doubled the size of the Anglo-Jewish community. It also produced an internal shift in its character. In 1914, about one-third of the community lived in the East End ghetto. The obvious 'foreignness' of the immigrants, with their Yiddish speech and distinct religious and cultural customs, meant that they constituted the most 'high-profile' section of 'British' Jewry. Since the 1880s, when large-scale Jewish immigration began, their presence had become a focus for anti-alien hostility. The Aliens Act of 1905, which effectively marked the end of Britain's open door immigration policy, was in large measure a response to the unwelcome arrival of Russian Jews.[74] The First World War brought fresh tensions and provided the opportunity for the British government to adopt a 'comprehensive aliens policy' for the first time. Unnaturalised foreigners were divided artificially into three categories. The first of these was 'enemy aliens' – those who hailed from countries then at war with Britain, mainly Germany and Austria. With anti-German feeling running high in 1914–15, many of these 'enemy aliens' were interned. By 1917, even the loyalty of the second category, the so-called 'friendly aliens', was being called into question. This category embraced citizens of countries belonging to the Entente, including France, Russia and Romania. The label 'neutral aliens' was applied to Belgian and other subjects of non-aligned states. These all-embracing categories belied the complexity of wartime politics, especially in eastern Europe. The fact was that 'Aliens could not simply be classified as "friendly" or "unfriendly" according to their citizenship.'[75] Polish Jews, in particular, suffered from their 'indeterminate national allegiance'. A Jew from Warsaw, then part of the Russian Empire, was deemed 'friendly' by the Home Office, whilst his co-religionist from Austrian-controlled Galicia was on the enemy side.[76]

The vast majority of all those designated under the general rubric of 'alien' were, in fact, Jews. Jews occupied a unique place during that period as the only sizeable immigrant group. Like all previous immigrants, such as the Huguenots and the Irish, they were entering a host society which was ethnically fairly homogeneous and with a strong cultural tradition. Thus, despite the fact that the Jewish immigration accounted for only one-third of one per cent of the total population of Britain in 1914, significance was attached to the new arrivals out of all proportion to their numbers. It was no accident that the term 'alien' was widely regarded as synonymous with the word 'Jew'.

During the war anti-alienism was fuelled by the controversy over conscription for military service. Indeed, this issue probably caused more antisemitism in the years 1914–18 than any other. The Conscription Act was finally passed in April 1916. It was applied not only to British male citizens between the ages of 18–41, and to naturalised foreigners, but also to certain categories of 'friendly' and 'neutral' aliens such as French and Belgian subjects. However the Home Secretary, Herbert Samuel, made a special exception for Russians. Himself Jewish, Samuel was aware of the fact that the majority of so-called 'Russians' resident in Britain were actually Jews. In many cases they had come as refugees from persecution and often to avoid enlistment in the brutal Russian army. Samuel appreciated their objection to serving in the British army on the same side as the Tsar. The principle of voluntarism therefore remained in operation in relation to Russian Jews alone – and it proved to be a dismal failure. Very few Russian Jews were persuaded to join up, in spite of the setting up of a special Jewish War Services Committee. There matters stood until 1917.[77]

The February Revolution saw the removal of the tsarist regime, and with it, it was assumed, the removal of the last objection on the part of Russian Jews in England to fighting on the Allied side. They were now presented with a stark choice: either to join the British Army and serve here or return home to Russia to serve there. A public campaign was launched for the conscription or deportation of 'friendly aliens'. It was spearheaded by local politicians and the press in East London. In February 1917 a joint delegation of the Bethnal Green Military Tribunal (whose function was to hear cases for exemption) and the five East London London County Council (LCC) members and borough council leaders lobbied East End MPs at Westminster. Bethnal Green council simultaneously organised an East London Aliens Conference. These activities, which 'marked a climax of anti-alien hysteria',[78] were given extensive coverage in the local papers. The *East London Observer* had made its name as a champion of the anti-alien cause as far back as 1915 and the extent of this newspaper's local support is clear from its correspondence columns. It was not an isolated voice. In July 1917 it reported with satisfaction on a meeting of the British Workers' National League at the Great Assembly Hall. This anti-alien society, the spiritual heir of William Evans-Gordon's British Brothers' League at the time of the Aliens Act, enjoyed the patronage of the mayor of Stepney. Its leading lights can only be described, for the most part, as representatives of the 'reactionary left'. The president was John Hodge, a Labour MP, and the executive included J. Havelock Wilson, the president of the Sailors' and Firemen's Union (who earned national fame for instigating the blacking of the socialist delegation to the Stockholm Conference), Victor Fisher, of the British Socialist Party (BSP) pro-war faction, and A. Seddon, an ex-president of the TUC. They all shared the platform with Admiral Lord Beresford, a Tory peer and ideological bedfellow of Lord Sydenham of Combe.[79]

Outside the East End, the campaign was taken up by the London press, the *Evening Standard* and *Evening News*, and nationally, principally by the *Morning Post* and Northcliffe's *Daily Mail*. As a result, a Home Office Conference on Aliens was held and a bill introduced in Parliament in May 1917. These developments were accompanied by a well-publicised police raid designed to round up eligible aliens in the East End. Sir Basil Thomson, head of the Special Branch, had a particular interest in surveillance of alien activities during the war; his police reports provide a wealth of information about anti-conscription and radical groups in Whitechapel and Stepney.[80] Between 600–4000 aliens were temporarily detained in May, of which a mere four were actually, on further investigation, found to be liable for military service. Julia Bush condemns this action as 'a blatant sop to the antisemites'.[81] She possibly exaggerates, however, in stating that it bore some resemblance to an official pogrom. Meanwhile, behind the scenes, the first of a planned series of military conventions with Allied governments was concluded between Britain and the Provisional Government of Russia, 'as to the mutual liability of His Majesty's subjects and subjects of Allied and other states to military service'. Once agreement was reached, the 1916 Conscription Act was extended to embrace out-standing friendly aliens by means of an order in council. The measure came into force in July 1917. Those men affected were given barely three weeks to apply for return to Russia. Those who decided to stay in Britain had a further month in which to apply to a military (or colliery) tribunal for exemption. Thereafter they would automatically be en-listed into the British Army.

Only a single East London MP, James Kiley (Liberal, Whitechapel), voted against the Convention when it was debated in the House of Commons. Party policy aside, even Liberals considered that pro-alien sympathies were too much of a vote-loser in the East End. Besides, unlike in 1905, at the time of the Aliens Act, there were no Jewish MPs representing East End constituencies in 1917. Stuart Samuel, the lone voice opposed to restrictionism in 1905, had resigned his seat for Tower Hamlets in 1916. Indeed, in 1917, no Jewish MP, whether sit-ting for the East End or not, was prominent in the debate on alien conscription at all. The silence spoke louder than words. There was a respectable contingent of Jews in Parliament, 16 in 1910, but in the main they were not so much Jewish MPs as MPs who merely happened to be Jews.[82] The possible exception was Herbert Samuel. But, as Home Secretary in 1917, he was hardly at liberty to challenge the govern-ment's policy. He was none the less instrumental in pressing for and securing a number of amendments to the Bill, such as the establishment of tribunals to hear appeals for exemption from call-up, designed to take account of alien sensitivities. Yet, as shall become clear, this was not enough to endear Samuel to East End Jewry. The Home Secretary was regarded as no friend of the Ghetto. Thus, in the Commons, the task of defending the aliens was left to the indefatigable Liberal radical Joseph King (N. Somerset) and Colonel Wedgwood (Labour, Newcastle-under-Lyme). In the Lords was the Liberal peer Lord Shef-field (the former Mr Lyulph Stanley). Sheffield's almost embarrass-ingly pro-Jewish sympathies could hardly be put down to the fact that one of his daughters, Venetia Stanley, was married to Herbert Samuel's cousin Edwin Montagu, the Secretary of State for India. Montagu was not exactly known for his own pro-Jewish sympathies. Still, the *East London Observer* could not resist making the most of the connection. As for Joseph King, he earned himself the ironic nickname of 'King of the Jews' for his spirited defence of the immigrants in Parliament.[83]

Outside Parliament, the pro-alien lobby found some sympathy on the left. Before the First World War, socialists and the trade unions had generally opposed the restriction of immigration. Ideologically, the socialist faith in internationalism and the Brotherhood of Labour transcended national and religious differences. In any case, restrictionism, like the wider issue of protectionism in trade, was regarded merely as a panacea dreamt up by the capitalist ruling class to divert the workers from their real grievances such as unemployment and the 'sweating system' – which in reality were not caused by immigration at all. Nevertheless, the existence of anti-alienism (and indeed antisemitism) on the left cannot be ignored, even if its importance should not be exaggerated.

The Trades Union Congress (TUC) passed resolutions in favour of immigration controls between 1892 and 1895. The impetus for this lay in the desire to protect the living standards of their members, which appeared to be threatened by the 'alien invasion' at a time of economic depression. Unions representing immigrant trades, such as tailoring, were most prone to this type of anti-alienism. There was discernible resentment against the poor Jewish worker's individualism and ability to get on – in short, his uncomfortable tendency to transform himself into a 'rich Jew' boss.

Liberal admiration for the Jew as the ideal 'economic man' – a symbol of Smilesian values – found little sympathy on the left. In 1917 the TUC did not come out with an unambiguous condemnation of the government's threat to deport 'friendly aliens' who refused to comply with the terms of the Anglo-Russian Military Convention; (although, at the local level, the Bethnal Green, Stepney and London trades councils, which were developing closer links with the Jewish unions during the war years, did speak out against anti-alienism).[84]

However, the TUC's failure to take a stand in 1917 was due in the main to the divisions plaguing the labour movement as a whole during the First World War. In 1914 British socialism had been torn down the middle. It had split into pro-war and anti-war factions. Hence the socialist position on alien conscription 'was largely governed by attitudes to the War itself'. The mainstream of the labour movement, as represented by the Parliamentary Labour Party, the TUC and the *Daily Herald*, was less than willing to take up the alien conscription question, doubtless on account of its official pro-war policy. The Independent

Labour Party, although strongly opposed to the war, did not take a strong stand on the issue either, despite the presence of a prominent Jewish radical, Joseph Leftwich, in the party's ranks. The conflict was most acute, however, within the Marxist-orientated British Socialist Party (BSP), the forerunner of the Communist Party. In 1914, a bitter struggle broke out between the pro-war faction led by H. M. Hyndman and Victor Fisher and the anti-war faction led by Maclean, Fairchild and Joe Fineberg. The part Fineberg played bore witness to a strong Jewish element in the party. The new BSP anti-war newspaper, *The Call*, under Fairchild's editorship, took up a very pro-alien position, in contrast to the established *Justice*, which was strongly influenced by Hyndman. The pro-war grouping in the BSP had no scruples about exploiting antisemitism in order to slur Fineberg and his associates, in spite of the fact that the majority of Jews in the party did not support the pacifist line.

Despite these divisions, the 1917 BSP conference passed a resolution in defence of the right of asylum and denounced 'the desperate attempt ... in the East End of London to foment ill-feeling against aliens'. According to the conference report, since June 1916 BSP branches up and down the country had been lodging protests with the Home Office against the conscription of aliens. BSP efforts also led to the inclusion of a clause concerning the right of asylum in the civil liberties resolution passed at the last Labour Party conference.

Two other anti-war parties active in the East End, the Stepney Herald League and Sylvia Pankhurst's Workers' Suffrage Federation, both took up the aliens' cause. Sylvia herself spoke at several rallies organised by the Foreign Jews' Protection Committee against Conscription and Deportation.

Anti-alien arguments in 1917

The passage of the Aliens Conscription Bill through Parliament was accompanied by a vociferous debate in the press as to the desirability of the legislation. This debate provided the best opportunity, since 1905, for the expression of anti-alien hostility. All the major symptoms of the anti-alien syndrome were revived – and given an extra edge in the light of the First World War and the Russian Revolution.

Pro-conscriptionists claimed that their position was founded upon a moral base. Russian Jews were indebted to England for showing them hospitality; the least they could do in return was to come to the defence of freedom and democracy in her hour of need. Yet behind this most reasonable of arguments lurked the suspicion that thousands of Russian Jews were evading the call-up. Indeed, they had often left Russia for this precise reason. There were reputed to be between 20,000–30,000 eligible friendly aliens in London in 1917, and 14,000 in the rest of the country, the vast majority of these being Russian and Polish Jews;[85] but in the absence of any accurate statistics, there was a marked tendency to exaggerate the figures. As in 1905, at the height of the campaign for immigration restriction, the 'mythical horde' was a very potent image. Against it, attempts by the Jewish press and pro-alien sympathisers in Parliament to set the record straight could cut no ice. They repeatedly pointed out that some 600,000 Jews were serving in the Russian Army on the eve of the revolution, and that there were 41,500 British and Empire-born – and naturalised – Jews fighting in the British Army. The latter statistic represented nearly 14 per cent of Anglo-Jewry. The percentage of British Jews doing their duty was thus higher than the national average, which stood at 11.5 per cent. As for the objection that this high figure had only been achieved on account of the draft, the Jews were no different in this respect from other Englishmen. The majority of 'eligibles' had, in the last resort, only joined up under duress. In any case, a number of Russian Jews had volunteered in 1914, only to be turned away when it was discovered that they did not hold British citizenship. The War Office deliberately discouraged aliens in the British Army.

Yet, in spite of the facts, and even after conscription had been imposed on 'friendly aliens', the charge of evasion stuck. For example, in October 1917, the *Morning Post* published a graphic account of how the 'swarms of aliens, Jew and Gentile, but mainly Jew' were crowding onto trains to Brighton, or failing that, down Underground stations, during air-raid scares in the East End. (It is often forgotten that there were some serious Zeppelin attacks on East London during the First World War; they have long since been overshadowed by the Blitz.) The implication of the report was not only that the Russian Jews were 'shirkers' but that they were also cowards.[86] Underlying both these assumptions was a feeling that, somehow, the alien was deficient in patriotism. 'Enemy aliens' had suffered the wrath of East Enders during the *Lusitania* riots in 1915. By 1917 even the patriotism of the 'friendly alien' was in doubt. Indeed, there was a growing suspicion that such people were actively engaged in subversion. The identification of immigrants with subversion was nothing new in British history. In the 1880s and 1890s, at the time of Fenian outrages and of anarchist 'propaganda by the deed', the East End was regarded as a haven for foreign revolutionaries. Like all myths, this contained an element of truth. Immigration control was invoked as a means of keeping out revolution. Now, in 1917, after the Russian Revolution, the East End was reputed to be awash with pro-Bolshevik and anti-war sentiment. The apparent desire of many Russian Jews to go back to their birth-place was held up in the immediate aftermath of the February Revolution as an example of true patriotism; by the summer it was interpreted as a sure sign that they were all Reds. Moreover, the prominence of the Foreign Jews' Protection Committee against Compulsion and Deportation confirmed that the aliens were pacifist to a man.[87]

'Aliens eating us out!' shrilled a *Daily Mail* leader in May 1917.[88] The Russian Jewish 'shirkers' were pinching the food, jobs and businesses of the loyal 'Brits' who had gone into the army. This was a new variation on the old economic argument against immigration, which argument accounted for a great deal of the restrictionist sentiment which existed in the trade unions and the socialist movement in general. The twin themes of unfair competition and displacement were rehashed in the context of the war. By 1914–18 it was claimed that the majority of so-called refugees, and their sons, had become prosperous and well-established businessmen. Their rise, especially in the tailoring trade, had had the opposite effect on the indigenous workforce. It produced unemployment and the depression of wages and living standards. These evils were abetted by the obstinate individualism of the alien and his or her reluctance to become unionised. Likewise, the presence of aliens in areas of high population density was responsible for overcrowding and the inflation of rents and rates. Bearing little relation to reality, these economic rationalisations for anti-alienism proved irresistible at the time, reflecting the insecurity and seasonal nature of East End industries. As if in fulfilment of the dire prophecies of the anti-alien lobby, social unrest – if not actual revolution – did materialise. Resentment against alien 'evasion' led to riots in 1917, in Leeds in the summer and in Bethnal Green in September.[89]

Thus, after the Russian Revolution, anti-Bolshevism was superimposed upon an older strain of anti-alienism in Britain. These two phenomena became inextricably mixed and antisemitism was common to both. As John Garrard has pointed out, the question of how far anti-alienism was actually motivated by antisemitism remains unanswerable. His acute observation regarding 1905, that 'what was crucial was not whether or not the agitation was in fact antisemitic, but that people thought or feared it might be', applies with equal force to the situation in 1917. Antisemitism was not, after all, socially respectable. Pro-conscriptionists were faced with a dilemma. It was very difficult to prevent an agitation against aliens from becoming an agitation against Jews, who were the only aliens to speak of. Pro-conscriptionists were all too aware that the accusation of racial prejudice was a potentially lethal weapon in the hands of their political opponents. It could be used to great effect to demolish their position. They therefore made every effort to divorce the issue from antisemitism as completely as possible. The embarrassment and reticence of the anti-alien lobby was held up to ridicule by Hilaire Belloc. The 'problem of Jewish immigration' he wrote in *The Jews*, was aggravated by the Liberal failure 'to call a spade a spade': 'We mask it under false names, calling it "the alien question", "Russian immigration", "the influx of undesirables from Eastern and Central Europe", and any number of other timorous equivalents.'[90] What was required was honesty, not Liberal double-talk. During the second reading of the Aliens Conscription Bill, Joseph King bluntly stated that the legislation was a reaction to 'a growing feeling of antisemitic intolerance in this land', and especially in the East End, which had been whipped up by an unscrupulous press. The recent riots in Leeds were fresh in everyone's mind. This antisemitism, King persisted, was directed not only against alien Jews but against the entire Jewish community. To which the Speaker hastily interjected '[it] is not relevant', and repeatedly urged the MP to stick to the matter in hand.[91] When pressed on the point, government spokesmen vehemently denied that their support for the bill had anything to do with antisemitism. As Garrard has demonstrated, however, the most eloquent testimony to government sensitivity to the charge of antisemitism was the fact that their spokesmen 'managed to get through debate after debate without ever mentioning the word Jew'.

Another tactic adopted by the pro-conscription lobby, to prove that

2 From Bondage unto Freedom? 'West End' Jewry and the Russian Revolution – Attitudes

> the chains have been removed ... the 'Jewish problem' in Russia has been solved, as so many of us longed and prayed that it would be solved, *in* Russia itself and by the Russians themselves. Five millions of our co-religionists are emancipated at a stroke.
>
> Claude G. Montefiore, *Liberal Judaism and Jewish Nationalism, Papers for the Jewish People*, No. 16 (1917)

Jewish political life in England had traditionally been based upon the 'Jewish liberal compromise'.[1] This concept dated back to the 'Era of Emancipation' in the mid-nineteenth century. In 1860 full political rights were effectively bestowed upon the Anglo-Jewish community by Parliament. This was the culmination of a gradual process of civil emancipation. The Jewish presence in England may be traced back to the Cromwellian Resettlement of 1658. The oldest families were of Dutch Sephardi or Marrano origin, but their numbers were continually augmented by a steady influx of Ashkenazim from central and eastern Europe throughout the eighteenth and nineteenth centuries. It was not until the 1880s that large-scale immigration of east European Jews began. This immigration was to double the size (300,000 in 1914) and change the face of 'Anglo'-Jewry.[2] Even in 1914, however, on the eve of the First World War, the official institutions of the community, headed by the Board of Deputies of British Jews (founded in 1760), were still dominated by the wealthy Sephardi and Ashkenazi elite – the 'West End Cousinhood' of leading families; the Rothschilds, Goldsmids, Montefiores, Mocattas, Sassoons, Cohens, Samuels and Henriques.[3] They had made their fortunes in the heyday of Victorian commerce.

Thus the 'Jewish liberal compromise' reflected the increasing security of a prosperous and influential native Jewish 'establishment'. It was a political outlook characterised by three fundamental beliefs. In the first place, it relied on a purely religious definition of Judaism, according to the Reform formula of 'Englishmen of the Mosaic faith'. This implied a rejection of the politics of cultural pluralism in favour of an absolute identification with the values and aspirations of the host nation.

Secondly, the compromise rested upon an implicit faith in western liberalism and in England as its ultimate expression. Jewish emancipation could be achieved and endure under such conditions. Finally, linked to the above, it was assumed that Jewish and British interests were inherently compatible. This had been demonstrated on various occasions in the nineteenth century by direct British intervention on behalf of oppressed Jewry abroad – intervention undertaken at the request of Anglo-Jewish leaders such as Moses Montefiore.

With the outbreak of the First World War such complacency was shaken. There were two reasons for this. First, British foreign policy, under the influence of fears about the German menace, had gradually shifted towards a *rapprochement* with tsarist Russia. The Anglo-Russian entente of 1907 bore witness to this trend and it culminated in military alliance in 1914. British policy thus directly cut across Anglo-Jewry's sensitivity about the persecution of their co-religionists in Russia. It was clear that British interests and Jewish interests no longer coincided. Second, the war fanned the flames of nationalism in England and throughout Europe. Anti-alienism, anti-Germanism and, finally, anti-Bolshevism all gave succour to antisemitism. The Jewish community was forced onto the defensive. These external pressures effected a veritable volte-face in Anglo-Jewish politics during the war years.

This about-face may be illustrated by reference to the editorial policy of the London *Jewish Chronicle*. The *Jewish Chronicle* had been founded in 1841, which made it the longest-running Jewish newspaper in the world. By 1914, it was recognised as the unrivalled mouthpiece of the English-speaking Anglo-Jewish establishment; it was the self-proclaimed 'Organ of British Jewry'.[4] In 1907, the *Chronicle* acquired a new editor, a professional journalist, Leopold J. Greenberg (1862–1931). As a provincial Jew (he was born in Birmingham) and a Zionist (he was a founder member of the English Zionist Federation),

Greenberg was representative of a younger generation of Anglo-Jews with innovative ideas. He became identified with the more liberal wing of the establishment which favoured a generous open-door policy on immigration. He was responsible for recasting the *Chronicle*'s editorial stance in a liberal-nationalist mould. Right up until the very last moment in July 1914, Greenberg advocated British neutrality in the coming conflict.[5] Yet, when war was declared, he was forced to reassess his position. The *Jewish Chronicle* now threw its editorial weight behind the war effort. The 'German menace' outweighed any scruples about alliance with Russian reaction. Russian antisemitism, it was argued, was the product of Prussian 'militarism'. The Anglo-Russian Alliance was justified in the interests of rooting out the latter. In due course, if Germany was defeated, given Russia's exposure to democratic values via the entente, tsarism would be reformed and Russian Jewry would be granted emancipation as a reward for loyal service to the state. Certainly, it would be an exaggeration to say that the *Jewish Chronicle* adopted an entirely uncritical line. Although Lucien Wolf's supplement on 'Darkest Russia' was suspended, the general policy of acting as watchdog on Russia's behaviour towards her Jews was continued, albeit in a more muted form. For example, Greenberg ran a series of articles condemning the mass evacuation of Jews from the war zone in 1915. This aroused the ire of the British Government Press Bureau for contravening DORA – the Defence of the Realm Act.

Greenberg's policy, when taken together with behind-the-scenes protestations to the Foreign Office, was not without effect. The British and French governments made joint representations to the Russians over the embarrassment that this antisemitic policy was creating for the Allied cause. The fact none the less remains that the *Jewish Chronicle* was largely obliged to toe the government line. This is evidenced above all by the paper's encouragement of voluntary enlistment for both British-born Jews and aliens. The campaign was conducted under the slogan: 'England has been all she could be to the Jews, Jews will be all they can to England.'

Thus a complete switch in Jewish communal policy occurred during the First World War. It may be explained by a 'deep-seated feeling of insecurity' – by the fear that Jewish emancipation might yet be 'on trial'.[6] As will presently become clear, a similar turnabout took place with regard to the Russian Revolution in the period from 1917 to

1921. This was, it is true, partly influenced by the general deterioration of the political situation in Russia, particularly as it affected the Jews. The unwelcome attention focused upon the Jewish community at home had at least as much influence, however. The current interest in German-Jewish-Bolshevik conspiracy theories, not to mention the related question of alien conscription, combined to force Anglo-Jewry in upon itself. Caution and circumspection – a hallmark of emancipatory politics – once again became the order of the day. At the same time, new methods of political activity were being evolved to deal with changing circumstances. These will be explored in the next chapter. What follows is a survey of the opinions expressed by 'West End' Jews as events in Russia unfolded.

THE FEBRUARY REVOLUTION

'RUSSIA FREE!' ran the *Jewish Chronicle* headline on 23 March 1917. The Jewish community experienced a brief but exultant honeymoon with the new Russia. For once the entire community, 'East End' and 'West End', English-born and Russian-born, orthodox and secular, conservative and radical, Zionist and anti-Zionist, all greeted the revolution with enthusiasm. It was most appropriate that the revolution almost coincided with the Festival of Freedom – Passover. The latter-day Children of Israel, the six million Jews of Russia, like the 600,000 Israelite slaves before them, appeared to have escaped 'from bondage unto freedom', from the darkness of tsarist persecution, pogrom and the Pale, into the light of instant civil and political emancipation in a benign democracy.

The Chief Rabbi, the Hungarian-born Dr J.H. Hertz, wrote a letter to the *Daily Chronicle*:

> The Jews of the British Empire ... are thrilled by the glorious tidings ... for 150 million human beings the sun of Freedom and Righteousness has risen with healing in its wings, and a government of the people, by the people and for the people is now and for all time breaking the political, racial and religious fetters of the old despotism ... In such a free and regenerated Russia, the martyrdom of my Jewish brethren, who were for a thousand years accounted as stepchildren of Russia, is at an end.[7]

The *Jewish World* (the *Jewish Chronicle*'s sister paper) predicted that:

'The prospects for the Jews in Russia have never been brighter for at least two centuries than they are today.'[8] Greenberg was vindicated. The February Revolution confirmed his faith in the progressive nature of the alliance between the western democracies and tsarism. Their good influences had indeed rubbed off. The *Jewish Chronicle* put its editorial weight squarely behind the Provisional Government. In doing so, the paper not only accurately reflected the unanimous feeling of Anglo-Jewry, but also correctly gauged the mood of the Jews of Russia. Both communities appreciated the enormous gains the Jews stood to make in the Liberal Revolution. Jews everywhere welcomed the evolution of a parliamentary democracy in Russia, founded upon the western principles of individual freedom and equality under the rule of law. For these principles implied the abolition of specific disabilities based on differences of religion, nationality, race and class. On 22 March/2 April 1917 the Decree on Emancipation was proclaimed. The Jewish Pale of Settlement, in a state of creeping disintegration since 1915, was finally swept away. Greenberg warned: 'Prejudices die hard and are not always killed at once by legislative action.'[9] The answer lay in education. Working on the assumptions fundamental to Russian liberalism, that a distinction existed between ruler and ruled, and that antisemitism was government-inspired and not endemic in the masses, it would now disappear with the demise of the Old Regime.

The continuing threat from 'German militarism' had, nevertheless, to be eliminated if the future of the revolution and of Jewish emancipation in Russia was to be secured. Given that there was 'an intimate connection between Russian and German reaction on the one hand and German influence and Russian antisemitism on the other',[10] it was of the utmost importance that Revolutionary Russia should contribute fully to the Allied war effort. Indeed, Greenberg argued, a Russia regenerated by progressive change would strengthen the Allied cause. Such a Russia could even sow the seeds of revolution in the enemy camp. The *Jewish Chronicle*'s belated commitment to the war was further illustrated by its editorial welcome for American involvement in April 1917 – and particularly for the decision of the American Jewish banker, Jacob Schiff, to lift his boycott on financial aid to the Allies. This boycott had originally been imposed as a protest against Allied association with tsarist antisemitism. Western Jewish financiers, including the Rothschilds, who had participated in the ban, now contributed to the Russian 'Liberty Loan'. Schiff's extravagant idea of sending a replica of the Statue of Liberty to Russia as 'a tribute of one great sister republic to the other' had a particular appeal for Greenberg.

Indeed, material confirmation of Greenberg's optimism was provided at New Court, City headquarters of N.M. Rothschild & Sons. Leopold de Rothschild, a vice-president of both the Board of Deputies and the Anglo-Jewish Association, was gratified to receive a telegram from the newly appointed Finance Minister to the Provisional Government, Tereschenko, 'asking us to continue our business relations in accordance with our existing contracts and also to extend our business relations'.[11] 'It proves', de Rothschild commented, that 'he is a thoroughly honest businessman [and] friend of the Jews.' All of which stood in stark contrast to the new government's tsarist predecessor. 'What a terrible hypocrite Protopopoff was and how he humbugged Baron Edmund [de Rothschild]. I think he fully deserves any fate.'[12]

The 'Conjoint' Committee of the Board of Deputies and the Anglo-Jewish Association had been set up in 1878. It acted as the 'Foreign Office' of the Anglo-Jewish community. A clearing house for information which reached the community about the situation of Jews abroad, it compiled reports and memoranda and cultivated channels of communication with the real Foreign Office, in the hope that the latter could be prevailed upon to intercede on behalf of Jews overseas should the need arise (the policy of *shtadlanut*). In short, the 'Conjoint' was a symbol of the 'Jewish liberal compromise'.

In 1903 Lucien Wolf (1857–1930) was coopted onto the Conjoint Committee.[13] Wolf's reign as the 'Foreign Secretary' of Anglo-Jewry lasted for around 20 years. He was the son of a wealthy German Jew who had found political asylum in England after the 1848 Revolutions. By the First World War Wolf had acquired a reputation as an accomplished journalist and historian – and as a rather anti-establishment figure. His relationship with the Foreign Office was not always cordial. Indeed, he was regarded as 'Public enemy number one of the Tsarist Government' in England.[14]

Nevertheless, Wolf's opinions on Russian politics were undoubtedly well-informed and influential. Throughout 1917 he produced a series of reports on the 'Situation in Russia', which are essential reading for anyone wishing to acquaint himself with Jewish attitudes to the Russian Revolution, especially since Wolf was being fed with up-to-date –

if not always neutral – information by Russian friends and associates, such as his loyal secretary David Mowshowitch and his 'Stockholm agent', Dr Reuben Blank. Both of these men were in direct contact and in political sympathy with liberal circles in Petrograd.

In common with Leopold Greenberg at the *Jewish Chronicle*, Lucien Wolf was ecstatic at the news of the February Revolution. The revolution, he declared, meant 'the end of the Jewish question'[15] in Russia. He described in great detail the tremendous response of Russian Jewry to the new order: the reactivation of communal life, the reorganisation and election of *kehillos* and the establishment of a plethora of political parties. There were plans to convene an All-Russian Jewish Congress which would seek representation in the future National Assembly. Individual members of the Provisional Government, his sources assured Wolf, were well disposed towards the Jews. Nekrasov, Konovalov, Shingarev and Kerensky himself were singled out. Meanwhile, prominent Jewish liberals, such as Maxim Vinaver, Baron de Gunsburg and Leon Bramson, were being promoted to high office. All in all, Wolf was confident that Russian Jewry at last had the chance to settle its own fate without assistance from abroad. Indeed, that community would now have the opportunity to play the part in international Jewish affairs commensurate with its size and importance.

The most outspoken exponent of the Russian Revolution to emerge from the ranks of English-speaking Anglo-Jewry, was the author and playwright Israel Zangwill (1864–1926)[16] – not that he was in any way typical. Zangwill had lately achieved considerable literary success and with it an entrée into British society. For all this, he had been born in Whitechapel, the son of immigrants from Latvia and Poland who had arrived in England in the mid-nineteenth century. He was closely in touch with East End Jewish life and his writings reflected this. Before the First World War, Zangwill published his *Children of the Ghetto* series and a play entitled *The Melting Pot*, set at the time of the Kishinev pogrom in 1903. In 1914, the play was banned by the Foreign Office at the request of the Russian government. In 1916, Zangwill crossed swords with Stephen Graham of *The Times* regarding the latter's attempt to defend tsarist maltreatment of the Jews in the eastern war zone. In 1919, Zangwill composed a poem entitled *Our Own* which was dedicated to the victims of the pogroms in the Ukraine. It was an emotional outburst which, like much of Zangwill's work, teetered on the brink of melodrama. On his own admission a liberal and a pacifist, Zangwill enjoyed wide personal contacts with English socialists, for instance with Sylvia Pankhurst (he was a staunch supporter of Votes for Women), and amongst Russian progressives such as Peter Kropotkin. He was on the executive of the Union of Democratic Control. Thus it could be said that Zangwill stood astride the 'East End' and the 'West End'. He was something of a maverick. His views, often original and usually unrepresentative, were always controversial. His utterances on the issues of the day never failed to stir up lively debate, both inside and outside the Jewish community.

On 31 March 1917, Zangwill addressed a packed meeting at the Royal Albert Hall in London. It had been organised by the British Labour Movement in honour of the Russian Revolution. The *Manchester Guardian* reported that Zangwill 'spoke chiefly for the Jews' and that he delivered 'the longest and naturally the wittiest speech of the evening'.[17] Certainly, Zangwill introduced himself to his audience 'as a representative of the race which has suffered more than any other from the Old Russia'. He declared his satisfaction with the final triumph of the 'real Holy Russia' that is 'not the Russia of church candles and ikons, but the Holy Russia of the struggle for liberty'. He was proud of the important role played by Jews in this achievement. The Jews were entitled to regard themselves as in every way equal with their Russian neighbours. Zangwill continued:

> For the great gesture with which the new Russia has freed my people at a stroke I do not thank her: I congratulate her. (Cheers) I rejoice with her that Russia is at last able to look civilisation in the face, for the persecution and massacre of her Jews weighed upon all her noblest sons. Gorki, Andreiev, Sologoub, Mereshkovsky – all confessed that it was staining their own history, humiliating them before the world. I rejoice that this burden has been lifted from the Russian soul as from the Jewish body. Hand-in-hand with their Russian brothers will the Jews, drawing over their agonies and oppressions the veil of forgiveness, go forward with them to build the great Russia of the future ...

However, the greater part of Zangwill's speech was given over to a scathing attack on the hypocritical treatment of Russian affairs exhibited by the British press. The Conservative papers which had so recently engaged in 'a literary and political conspiracy to beslaver and bolster up despotism, superstition and reaction', and in the manufacture of that romantic image of Holy Russia in the name of the Anglo-Russian Alliance, were now insolent enough to cheer the revolution. *The Times* indeed had the *chutzpa* to point a guilty finger at the opponents of the pact with tsardom:

> And now that Russia has been proved the friend of liberty, not its enemy, now that the objection to our Alliance with her is seen to have been unjust, 'will the Labour pacifists and pro-Germans,' asks *The Times*, 'have the manliness to recant?' Such an appeal from such a champion of liberty, the only begetter of the Russian Supplements and of Mr Stephen Graham, would, I thought, be irresistible. (Loud laughter.) I expected to see all of you Labour leaders – all of you, at any rate, with any spark of manliness – standing here at the penitent's table, draped in white sheets. Nay, editors like Mr Lansbury wrapped in their own journals. But you seem to think that this demand of Lord Northcliffe's is only the brazen crowing of the weathercock. (Cheers and laughter.) You seem to imply that it is rather Lord Northcliffe who should be standing here doing penance, wrapped in *The Times*. I should agree with you but for one small consideration – *The Times* is not a white sheet.

As far as Zangwill was concerned, no such confession was necessary: 'We democrats never denounced Russia: we denounced only the Russian government.' On the contrary, it was the right-wing journalists, who painted such a 'rosy' picture of the former Russian Empire, who ought to be worried now:

> What in the name of the Prince of Lies are they rejoicing over? How could the Paradise they depicted be changed, except for the worst? Do they not see that their jubilations over the new Russia are a judgement upon themselves, that every cheer they raise is their own condemnation? (Loud applause.) They confess now, these Judases of journalism, these Parliamentary parasites of success, that Russia was always a dead weight in the Alliance, a political incubus; that, in fact, England was ashamed of her. And this was the real truth, and the best Russians knew it, and it distressed them.

That was not all Zangwill had to say. The remainder of his speech consisted of an attack on the record of Lloyd George's government in office. Zangwill spoke as a liberal disillusioned by the illiberalism of a nominally Liberal administration in wartime. He concluded that 'If Russia has turned into England, England has turned into Russia.'[18]

'HOCUS-POCUS ANARCHISM': FROM FEBRUARY TO OCTOBER

As the political situation in Russia deteriorated during the summer of 1917, so the initial euphoria felt by Jews in England dissolved. Communal unanimity disintegrated. The inability of the Provisional Government to resolve the urgent problems facing the country – the war, land and nationalities question – became apparent to all observers. The government's difficulties were compounded by the fact of sharing 'dual power' with the Petrograd Soviet and by the latter body's contradictory pronouncements. Governmental authority was further undermined by an almost obsessive attachment to the rule of law. The exigencies of legitimacy, legality and accountability all militated against the rapid convening of the long-awaited Constituent Assembly. An 'intoxication with liberty'[19] extolled voluntary cooperation and unrestrained freedom of expression without a counterbalancing stress on discipline and responsibility. In sum, the political situation in Russia came to be characterised by the lack of any coordination from above, combined with degeneration into anarchy from below.

Even as far back as March/April 1917, it was one thing for individual West End Jews to express their delight at the Russian Revolution. It was quite another matter to organise a coordinated community-wide response. Lucien Wolf, forever the diplomat, did all he could to discourage the Board of Deputies from making a precipitate official statement about the revolution on behalf of the Anglo-Jewish community. Wolf advocated delay. It was not the Board's function to preempt the British government, he argued, and it would be presumptuous for the Jewish community to make a statement independently of the government. The Board should confine itself to an appropriate endorsement of the emancipation decree when – and only when – it was made public, since that was the only aspect of the revolution which directly concerned the Jews. Wolf's recommendations were meticulously carried out, even though this involved having to rein in de

Rothschild, who was engaged in an ecstatic telegraphic correspondence with Baron Alexander de Gunsburg in Petrograd. 'Mr Leo' apologised to Wolf: 'I was so excited about the Revolution that I was inclined to be impetuous ...'[20] In the event, it was not until 10 April that a carefully worded private message, written on behalf of the Conjoint Committee, was dispatched to Prince L'vov. Any allusion to the revolution as such was conspicuous by its absence. Letters expressing solidarity were also sent to leading Russian Jews. No special meeting of the Board was called and when the regular meeting did take place, a full two weeks after the revolution, deputies had to be content with a prepared statement read out on behalf of the president, David Lindo Alexander, who could not attend, apparently due to ill-health. Some were not impressed. An unedifying row broke out as to the manner in which the so-called representative organisation of British Jewry had welcomed the Russian Revolution. Wolf stood firm and defended Alexander in his absence. He was supported by Sir Philip Magnus, the Tory MP for London University, who asserted that it was none of the Board's business to greet revolution 'which was purely a political matter'.[21] Dr Israel Gollancz, the scholar and uncle of Victor Gollancz who founded the Left Book Club in the 1930s, walked out in protest. In contrast, Rabbi Samuel Daiches, a lecturer at Jews' College and also a member of the Conjoint, spoke up in favour of a proper resolution worthy of the Board. It was fitting, he argued, that Jews in Britain should make public their satisfaction not only with the granting of emancipation to their brethren in Russia, but with the triumph of the cause of freedom in general. He was strongly supported by S. Gilbert.

Inevitably, the controversy spilt over into the Jewish press. Both the *Chronicle* and the *World* sided with the Daiches camp. Indeed, Greenberg had already sent a congratulatory telegram to the Russian Jewish deputy to the Duma, N.M. Friedman. Now the *Jewish Chronicle*'s mysterious weekly contributor 'Mentor' – who was none other than the editor himself – inveighed against what he regarded as an ineffectual communal leadership – 'A race of Brer Rabbits, lying low and saying nuffin'.[22] He lashed out at their ghetto mentality, their failure to appreciate the full significance of the momentous events in Russia, other than from a narrow Jewish perspective. Greenberg took particular delight in sending up the pomposity and irrelevance of Alexander's statement, which seemed to imply that the *shtadlan* diplomacy of the Board of Deputies had had a 'considerable' impact on 'the general movement for national liberation in Russia'. The idea that a conservative body like the Board of Deputies of British Jews could have been 'one of the palpable causes of the [Russian] Revolution' struck Greenberg as ridiculous. A 'communal revolution' against an inept leadership might be more appropriate. As for Lucien Wolf's contribution to all this, the editor summed it up in the following terms: 'The Conjoint will not say "Revolution", but carefully deletes the "R".'[23] Greenberg was determined that the press would strike the middle way between over-enthusiasm and the excessive caution demonstrated by the official institutions. The latter could all too easily be construed as either indifference to or distrust of the revolution.

Dr Moses Gaster (1856–1939), the *Haham* or Chief Rabbi of the Sephardi community in Britain (although he was, in fact, of Romanian Ashkenazi descent), must have been in sympathy with the Wolf/Alexander line. In April and May 1917, he turned down several invitations to address public meetings in the provinces, called to demonstrate Jewish solidarity with the revolution. He too doubted the wisdom of members of the Jewish community pre-empting the British government on matters political – especially since the revolution was 'not an exclusively Jewish problem but one of a larger political character'. Therefore 'To reduce it [the proposed meeting] only to a Jewish demonstration would be out of place and I think out of the question ... Let it be a demonstration of British citizens.' The Jewish community would be ill-advised to commit itself in advance as there was the danger that it might find itself out of step with prevailing public opinion later. The situation in Russia was still in a state of flux – 'very obscure and complicated'. And moreover 'The solution of the Jewish problem in Russia is far from being definite. Many difficulties will have to be overcome and much trouble is still ahead before we shall be able to breathe freely and see light.' Gaster went on:

> One cannot say from today what the next day will bring and whether the change that may supervene will be in strict harmony and accord with the wishes of the British Government, especially in connection with the issue of the war ... I have my own doubts as to whether the British Government sees eye to eye with the

development that has taken place, especially in view of the two governments that are fighting one another for political supremacy in Russia.

He ended his letter with a piece of advice and a warning:

> I think that we Jews in this country ought to cultivate a little more caution, and the exposed position which I occupy renders that caution still more desirable, not because it might affect me, for I fear no consequences from what I think right, but it might have an adverse effect on the general situation ... Mind, I am not afraid of the future, but whether the future which I contemplate will be the same which others would like to see accomplished is to me still an open question, and to ventilate it from a public platform might perhaps bring us within the compass of the Defence of the Realm Act.[24]

As matters turned out, those communal leaders who had erred on the side of caution in matters Russian were shown to have been the better judges. Leopold Greenberg admitted as much when he asked rhetorically 'Were we wrong?' in a *Jewish World* editorial of 18 April 1917. He proffered to his readers the pessimistic analysis of a leading expert on Russian affairs concerning the anomaly of 'dual power':

> The difficulties of the situation are ... enormous, mainly because there are two distinct powers holding the reins of government, neither having them entirely in its hands and each dependent upon the other. For the time being suspicion and mutual distrust prevent their coalescing. Until they do there must be trouble ...[25]

Yet Greenberg still overestimated Kerensky's ability to overcome the problem: 'that brilliant young statesman... has taken the helm... he seems to be morally, mentally and spiritually a very giant, and so probably will be able to bear it unfalteringly.'[26] By the autumn, however, when the Moscow Conference and the Pre-Parliament had manifestly failed to salvage the coalition, he could only lament that the resulting chaos was the product of 'Generations of repression under Tsarism'.[27]

Lucien Wolf was more concerned about the effect of the revolution on the eastern front. Initially, he subscribed to an interpretation of the February Revolution which had found favour in Russian liberal circles:

the revolution was basically a patriotic revolt against the failure of the tsarist war effort – which, it was alleged, was all along being subverted by the pro-German 'Black Bloc' at Court.[28] By May 1917, Wolf could see that the new regime was enjoying no more military success than its predecessor. 'I see no prospect of a wholehearted Russian cooperation in the War', he wrote.[29] Government inaction regarding fundamental economic problems was fuelling the growth of extreme socialist and anti-war feeling. Thus revolutionary zeal, instead of bolstering the Allied cause, could seriously undermine it. To paraphrase General Brusilov's famous dictum: it was not beyond possibility that the revolution could kill the war. Alternatively, the war could kill the revolution. The continuation of a war which was going badly, and the increasing reluctance of the domestic population to take part, could lead to total collapse. The political consequences for Russia herself were alarming. Wolf wrote: 'I am afraid I do not regard the danger of a counter revolution as negligible.' He keenly appreciated the decisive role of the army in making or breaking the revolution:

> The overwhelming mass of the army is still outside the authority of the Provisional Government and is in the hands of the old Army Administration. It is true that the Chief-Commanders, including the Grand Duke Nicholas, have given their adhesion to the Revolution, but this adhesion will certainly not be continued if the Provisional Government interfere with the discipline of the Army, or otherwise pursue an extreme democratic course. In that case, the pendulum will swing back to an autocratic restoration.[30]

Thus Wolf accurately predicted the effect of Order No. I on the Kornilovs of the Russian High Command.

In short, an alarming polarisation was taking place in Russian political life, the outcome of which could be civil war and a German victory in the east. Such a situation was fraught with danger for the Jews. The bitter lesson of experience was that the Jews were the first to suffer in times of political instability. The prospect of counter-revolution in Russia was not a happy one. The tsarist history of persecution was all too familiar even in the west. With awful regularity, right-wing reaction tended to be accompanied by antisemitic outbreaks.

As early as March 1917, Wolf saw the necessity of down-playing Jewish interest and Jewish involvement in the revolution. In a letter to his colleague on the Conjoint Committee, Claude Montefiore, Wolf set out the reasons why he was opposed to a demonstrative show of support for the revolution on the part of British Jews:

> I said at once I thought it would be exceedingly dangerous. Apart from the fact that the situation is still a little obscure, there can be no doubt that anything that might savour of foreign interference in the crisis would be strongly resented by all sections of Russians, and not least by the revolutionists themselves. Moreover it must be remembered that the new Government consists entirely of well-known friends of the Jews, and we must take care not to compromise them. Anything that would accentuate their friendship for the Jews would render it difficult for them to act on our behalf, and at the same time would enable the antisemitic reactionaries to clamour that the whole revolution was a Jewish conspiracy.[31]

In his Conjoint report, Wolf concluded:

> It would not take much … to raise a cry that the Revolution was the work of the Jews, that the leaders of the Revolution were the instruments of International Jewry and that the object was to play into the hands of the Germans.[32]

Clearly, observers of the Russian scene had been conditioned to fear counter-revolution most of all. For Jews especially, the example of 1905 was uppermost, when 'a revolution was drowned in Jewish blood'.[33] Yet the events of October 1917 proved that history is never an entirely reliable guide to future political developments. If the threat of right-wing reaction remained – and indeed grew – then the more or less universal liberal belief in *pas d'ennemi à gauche* was to be equally severely tested. The Bolshevik Revolution created more complex problems for Anglo-Jewry.

THE BOLSHEVIK REVOLUTION

The 'Maximalist' *coup d'état* which took place in Petrograd on 25 October/7 November 1917 was greeted with dismay by Anglo-Jewry. The community – like its counterpart in Russia – now faced an unappetising choice. In effect, they were being asked to choose between the devil of 'autocracy' and the deep blue sea of 'demagogy',[34] between monarchist restoration and Communist revolution. The first possibility still could not be countenanced. In the words of the *Jewish Chronicle*:

> So far as our co-religionists are concerned, anything in the nature of the reversion of a great people, like the Russian, from the ideals of liberty and freedom – however faultily expressed – to those of reincarnated Tsarism, must prove a disaster to the world of the greatest seriousness.[35]

Greenberg shed no tears over the murder of the Imperial family in July 1918. On the other hand, the Bolsheviks were by no means an attractive alternative. In the estimation of the *Chronicle*'s Russian correspondent, the Bolsheviks had 'not done a single thing to win the Jews. They have, however, done much to estrange the Jews from them.'[36] This was an exceptionally perceptive remark. Some explanation of Lenin's theoretical position on the Jewish question, as well as of Bolshevik policy in practice, will be necessary, in order to arrive at some understanding of the reasons for Anglo-Jewish hostility towards the new regime.

Lenin, unlike Marx, wrote no separate treatise on the Jewish question. His views on the subject can therefore only be examined in the context of his nationalities policy in general. Lenin could not nevertheless afford to ignore the Jews entirely, owing to the 'on-going' conflict with the Bund – arguably the most advanced wing of Russian Social Democracy at the beginning of the twentieth century. The conflict culminated in an open split in the movement at the 1903 party congress.

Lenin was adamantly opposed to the subjugation of national minorities: 'No nation is free if it oppresses other nations.'[37] It followed that he condemned antisemitism. Recognising that Jews were the most oppressed of all peoples in tsarist Russia, he, like Marx, favoured Jewish political emancipation in the era of 'bourgeois democracy'. Lenin's views represented an advance on Marx, however. He was aware not only of the existence of a Jewish capitalist class, but of a Jewish proletariat as well. Antisemitism, like all forms of nationalism, was a diversion used by the ruling class to divide the workers and thus preserve its ascendancy.

Lenin came out in favour of 'national self-determination', i.e. that each nationality has the right to form a separate self-governing state. He none the less failed to extend this principle to Jews, for two reasons.

In common with Marx, Lenin denied that Jews qualified as a nationality in the first place, since they were in a minority everywhere, they had lost their national culture and political independence and lacked both a homogenous economic base and common language. The distinctions which existed between Jews and the rest were merely artificial; they had been created by discriminatory government legislation. In the second place, Lenin did not believe that nationalism could be expressed in anything other than territorial terms. This was the basis for Lenin's argument with the Bund (the General Jewish Workers' Union, founded in Vilna in 1897). By 1903, the latter had made up their mind that the Jews did constitute a nationality like other non-Russian nationalities in the Empire, and aspired to equal economic, civil and political rights. Moreover, they demanded 'national cultural' rather than territorial autonomy for the Jewish minority.[38]

In general, Lenin saw the nationalities question in class terms. As a Marxist, he put the class above the national struggle. Nationalism was simply a red herring, a reactionary ideology employed by the bourgeoisie to hoodwink the workers into submission. Founded upon this assumption, Lenin's stand on 'national self-determination' proved to be qualified and highly ambivalent. It was temporary and conditional. He realised that nationalist aspirations (like peasant grievances) could be exploited as a means of overthrowing both tsarism and the Provisional Government. They were merely a tactical weapon in the achievement of the ultimate goal – the victory of the proletariat. Once the 'bourgeois' stage had given way to the Social Revolution, it was axiomatic that the national proletariats, the only element that counted – 'We, for our part concern ourselves with the self-determination of the proletariat in each nationality, rather than with the self-determination of peoples or nations'[39] – would voluntarily agree 'to accede to a fraternal union of all peoples based on socialist principles'.[40] By this point, the national proletariats would have turned against their own national bourgeoisies and joined the Great Russian proletariat in a union of socialist states. Moreover, on the subject of 'national culture', Lenin stated that, on the contrary, within each nation there existed two cultures: the dominant 'national culture' of the aristocracy, capitalists

71

and clergy and the 'democratic and socialist culture' of the proletariat. Lenin believed that, after the Revolution, the separate cultures of the national proletariats would amalgamate to form a new and superior international culture. Not the 'bogey' of assimilation, but 'fusion' was the question at issue. As for the Jews, Lenin extolled their internationalism rather than their conflicting tendency to 'ghettoisation'. It was the 'great world-progressive features of Jewish culture ... its identification with the advanced movements of the epoch' that Lenin approved of most of all; Jewish universalism rather than Jewish particularism.[41]

If national aspirations were subordinate to the 'dictatorship of the proletariat', they were also subject to the power of the Party, the 'vanguard of the proletariat'. Lenin demanded unity and centralisation in the party which transcended national distinctions. In 1903, therefore, he opposed the Bund's quest for federative status within the party. He also objected to the Bund's bid to become the sole representative of the Jewish masses to the RSDP. To Lenin, these demands smacked of separatism – if acceded to, they would undermine the supranational character of the Party. Lenin rightly foresaw that other national groups, who, unlike the Jews, did have territorial claims inside the Russian Empire, would demand similar rights. This could lead to the disintegration of the socialist movement as a whole.

It may thus be concluded that Lenin was not anti-Jewish; but he was no philosemite either. He had little sympathy for the historical predicament of the Jewish people, nor interest in Jewish culture. Jewish commentators in the west sensed this early on, and their suspicions were borne out by subsequent events in Russia. With the onset of civil war, Bolshevik policy developed in ways hardly calculated to win the approval of liberal Jewish opinion. Indeed, in the words of the *Jewish Chronicle*'s Russian correspondent, they did 'much to estrange the Jews from them'. This was despite, or perhaps because of, the fact that a number of high-ranking Bolsheviks were of Jewish descent. In January 1918, Lenin took the decision to create 'Jewish organisational forms' in both the Party and the government apparatus. In the government (SOVNARKOM), a commissariat for Jewish Affairs (EVKOM) was set up within the Commissariat for Nationalities (SOVNATCOM). Semyon Dimanshtain, the only prominent Bolshevik familiar with Yiddish life and language, was put in charge. (He was an ex-rabbinical student from Vitebsk). This department was designed primarily as an administrative organ – merely as a 'transmission belt'. In contrast, the Jewish Sections of the Communist Party (EVSEKTSIA) were intended to be 'the supreme political force in Russian Jewry'. The EVSEKTSIA's function was twofold: to aid the economic rehabilitation and social welfare of the Jewish masses, and above all, 'TO CARRY OUT THE DICTATORSHIP OF THE PROLETARIAT ON THE JEWISH STREET'. This process was to be achieved in three stages: (1) The destruction of the Old Order; (2) The 'Bolshevisation' of the Jews; (3) The construction of Socialism. Stages 1 and 2 were largely accomplished during the Civil War. They involved a frontal assault on all manifestations of 'bourgeois ideology'. This included religion (and not merely clericalism), nationalism – that is, Zionism – and the Hebrew language, associated with both. This likewise entailed the destruction of the traditional communal organisation – the *kehilla* and charitable bodies – and Jewish political parties, a large variety of which had emerged in 1917. When such pseudo-democratic means failed, the EVSEKTSIA was not averse to the use of force to impose its will upon the Jewish community. These Jewish Sections duly made their contribution to the 'Red Terror' which got under way from the end of 1917. This campaign was remarkable for the fact that it was carried on almost exclusively by Jewish Communists against other Jews. The personnel of the EVSEKTSIA was drawn from new Party members who had joined since the October Revolution – most notably from the Bund which was in a state of disarray – and not from the Jewish Bolshevik Old Guard. The phenomenon of left-wing Jews denouncing other left-wing Jews dated back, at least, to the 1903 battle between Trotsky, Martov and the Bund. In any event, non-Jewish participation, especially in the attack on religion, would have conjured up uncomfortable parallels with tsarist persecution. As the ex-Bundist M. Rafes commented: 'The ban on Zionist activity ... was put into effect on the initiative of *Jewish* Communists. This means that we are dealing with a manifestation of Jewish Civil War ... this concretizes the dictatorship of the Jewish proletariat on the Jewish Street.'[42]

It is thus not surprising that the *Jewish Chronicle*, an organ dedicated to the promotion of Jewish culture in both the religious and the national sense, found Bolshevism unpalatable. Greenberg accused the new regime of perpetrating pogroms (or, at the very least, of being powerless to stop them), harbouring Black Hundred[43] elements and of conniving with the Germans. It was an exaggeration. There was nothing in Leninist ideology which could be construed as antisemitic. Indeed, the Red Army was often the only defender of the Jews during the Civil War, and Lenin made several statements expressly condemning antisemitism. Yet, can Greenberg be blamed if he failed to appreciate the subtleties, when confronted with the doings of the EVSEKTSIA? Perhaps, ironically, the *Jewish Chronicle* was as much a victim of current anti-German and anti-Bolshevik sentiments as was the British press at large. Greenberg perhaps felt obliged to overstate the antisemitic nature of Bolshevism in order to repudiate allegations that the revolution had been the work of the Jews, which were common in certain British newspapers. No doubt, with this end in view, the *Chronicle* gave prominence to an interview with ex-premier Alexander Kerensky, who was in England to attend the Labour Party conference in July 1918. Kerensky is quoted as making the following allegation: 'Bolsheviks and renegade Jews have fostered ... the antisemitic movement especially in the Ukraine and South Russia where it is acquiring a tremendous force.'

The majority of Russian Jews – as was to become one of the *Chronicle*'s constant refrains – were by contrast in fundamental sympathy with liberal democracy and with the war effort:

> 99 per cent of Russian Jews opposed the Bolsheviks [claimed Kerensky] ... The Jewish intellectuals and the Jewish masses ... were the most faithful supporters of the Revolution ... The Jews everywhere worked together with the parties coalesced to organise and support the Provisional Government. The Jewish bankers, firms, the workers' unions, the Bund – they all were for national defence, and for cooperation with the moderate bourgeois elements in the upbuilding of the new state.[44]

The Kerensky interview was, in all likelihood, printed with an eye to external consumption. Englishmen who wished to know what was going on in the Jewish world automatically turned to the *Jewish Chronicle*. Consciousness of this fact sometimes created a problem for editorial policy as to what should and what should not be published. The role played by the *Chronicle* in communal defence will be examined in the next chapter.

Let us concentrate for the moment on some of the internal discussion the Bolshevik Revolution generated within the Jewish community. Much of this debate took place on the pages of the Jewish press. There was, for instance, general agreement amongst British Jews that the 'Bolshevik-Jewish' connection was unreal, but several commentators were not content to leave matters there. They rather unwisely embarked on a deeper examination of the nature of Bolshevik theory. This was in large measure a response to the tendency of antisemites to equate Bolshevism with a 'Jewish' assault on 'Christian' civilisation. Did some link between Communism as a political ideology and Judaism as a religion exist after all? If Bolshevism could not in fact be described as 'Jewish', then just what was it? Israel Zangwill tried to lay the blame at the door of the daughter religion. On more than one occasion, he described Bolshevism as 'merely an applied form of Christianity'. The editor of the *Jewish Chronicle* himself was equally guilty of treading on sensitive ground in this area. In the course of his 'Mentor' column during April 1919 (in the very same issue which provoked the infamous 'Letter of the Ten'), Greenberg made the following, highly controversial remark: 'The ideals of Bolshevism at many points are consonant with the finest ideals of Judaism, some of which went to form the basis of the best teachings of the founder of Christianity.'[45] Reverend Morris Joseph of the West London Reform Synagogue immediately took issue with this statement, on behalf of the Anglo-Jewish ecclesiastical establishment. The editor was obliged to cross swords with the clergyman in the columns of his own newspaper, at the same time as he was attempting to fend off the very public challenge posed to him in connection with The Letter. 'Mentor' was forced to explain the offending sentence. He meant merely that Judaism and Christianity shared with Communism a common vision of social justice and a better world. After all, 'It has often been said that the Hebrew Prophets were the first socialists', he wrote. In pursuit of this line of argument, Greenberg claimed that he was divorcing theory from practice. If it was possible for him, as a believing Jew, to sympathise with the ultimate aims of Communism, this did not mean that he approved of the 'means' and 'methods' used by Bolsheviks to achieve their goals. Greenberg did, nevertheless, imply that, under certain circumstances, the end could justify the means. In support of this contention, he referred to the numerous bloodthirsty exploits of the

Children of Israel recorded in the Hebrew Bible, which were sanctioned in the interest of the Divine Plan. Could not a case also be made for revolutionary violence in furtherance of some noble principle – such as the Principle of Liberty held to have inspired the French Revolution? It was not inconceivable, that, despite its 'temporary aberrations', the Communist Revolution in Russia might one day be regarded in a favourable light.

Morris Joseph profoundly disagreed. In 'Sermon of the Week', he posed the obvious question: Since Bolshevism preaches atheism in theory and has 'abolished religion and slain its prophets' in practice, then how can 'this godless policy [have] any affinity whatsoever with Jewish ideas?' On the contrary, 'Is it not the very negation of them?' On a deeper level, Joseph argued that Judaism as a system is founded upon the Rule of Law; the Law is intended to promote morality and a higher, more spiritual type of freedom whereas communism seeks to destroy law and overthrow morality. Judaism stands for 'the brotherhood of humanity, and looks towards universal peace and love as essential characteristics of the Golden Age'. Bolshevism – whilst it may claim to do the same – in fact calls for class war and social division in order to achieve the domination of one sectional interest over the rest. In other words, the means had become the end. Joseph took particular exception to 'Mentor's' reference to the Levitical law of the Jubilee as evidence of the socialism inherent in Judaism. Bolshevism, he wrote:

> instead of ordering the return of the land to its owners ... sanctions their expropriation in favour of the proletariat. Instead of establishing justice it legalises robbery ... [The *Torah*] declares that the land belongs to God, the other declares that it belongs to the man who can grab and keep it ... Mosaism affirms the sacredness of Property; to the Communist it is anathema.

Such a theological debate was necessarily inconclusive. Greenberg was probably ill-advised to broach the subject at all. Joseph certainly thought so, and pleaded in the *Jewish Chronicle* that its editor show a little more responsibility in view of the fact that careless utterances on this subject would only provide ammunition for the antisemites. On that score, Rev. Joseph was indeed proven correct.

Another favourite subject with the Jewish press was Trotsky. After all, Trotsky was the ultimate 'Jewish' revolutionary. In both Russia and the west, the Jewish response to his prominence was ambivalent; in the words of Robert Wistrich, 'compounded of mixed feelings of pride and fear'.[46] The *Jewish Chronicle* fell neatly into this pattern. Greenberg was in no doubt that Kerensky had Trotsky chiefly in mind when he had spoken of 'renegade Jews'. For Trotsky's approach to the Jewish question was to avoid it completely by assuming a militant cosmopolitanism. Trotsky's attitude is admirably illustrated by his oft-quoted exchange with the Bundist leader Vladimir Medem:

> Medem: 'You consider yourself, I suppose, either a Russian or a Jew.' 'No,' Trotsky responded, 'you are wrong. I am a Social Democrat and only that.'

On 30 November 1917, the *Jewish Chronicle* carried a report that Trotsky had turned away a Jewish delegation which sought his protection against pogroms. He apparently did this with the 'insolent' reply that, as an internationalist, he saw no reason to defend the Jews in particular. Greenberg could nevertheless not quite resist evoking the image of Trotsky as 'a new type of Jew ... the avenger of Jewish sufferings and humiliation under the Tsarist regime'.[47] On the one hand, he roundly condemned the 'Red Peace' of Brest–Litovsk as indisputable evidence of the weakness and moral bankruptcy of Bolshevism. On the other hand, he delighted in the ability of Trotsky to outwit the Germans with his non-policy of 'neither war nor peace': 'the spectacle of the envoy of German militarism ... dancing attendance on an extreme socialist, impotent to do anything but his bidding'.[48]

Greenberg recognised that Trotsky's extremism had been incubated under conditions of tsarist repression. His rise to power was, at least in part, attributable to the failure of the Western Allies to press for meaningful reform in Russia before the revolution. Trotsky's outspoken demand for peace with 'no annexations, no indemnities' contrasted favourably with the Allies' consistent refusal to revise their war aims. If dangerous, Trotsky's idealism was unmistakably genuine. The allegation by the British that Trotsky was a German spy (it dated back to his internment at Halifax whilst en route from New York to Petrograd in 1917) was dismissed as totally out of character by the *Jewish Chronicle*. Greenberg wrote: 'He [Trotsky] would appear to be no traitor, nor an international double dealer. He is just consistent and true to a principle for which he has been content to suffer a life of martyrdom.'[49] The editor could not help himself. He ended up by claiming the anti-religious and anti-Zionist leader for the Jewish people:

> His career exhibits not a little of the persistence of the Jew amid the most disheartening circumstances together with that curious aloofness to prevailing conditions in pursuit of his ideals which is a sure mark of Jewish origin ... Trotsky possesses certain typically Jewish qualities ... great facility and fertility of brain power and indomitable perseverance ...[50]

As in Russia itself, Jewish pride in Trotsky's achievements was tempered by the fear that, were the Bolsheviks to fall, the Jews would be made to suffer for the deeds of the 'Jew Government'. Indeed, the religious leaders of Russian Jewry had long warned that the sins of the tiny Jewish revolutionary movement would be visited upon the community as a whole. Greenberg certainly shared the sentiments of the Chief Rabbi of Moscow, who was once overheard to observe that 'The Trotskys make the revolutions and the Bronsteins pay the bills'.[51] Trotsky notwithstanding, the Anglo-Jewish establishment was undoubtedly hostile to Bolshevism. It was also in no doubt that Bolshevism was hostile to Jews. The Red Terror finally gave the lie to the Jewish-Bolshevik conspiracy theory. The *Jewish Chronicle* concluded:

> Bolshevism for all its alleged Jewish origin, has been a nightmare and a curse to the Jewish population of Russia. Under its wings anarchy has flourished again and the Jews of Russia are living today under a terror rarely matched in all the dark days of Tsarism.[52]

The series of assassination plots masterminded by Jewish terrorists in 1918 – the murder of Uritsky (himself a Jew) by Leonid Kanegiesser, the murder of the German Ambassador, Count Mirbach, by L. Blumkin and the attempt on Lenin himself by Fanny (Anna) Kaplan-Roid – all bore symbolic testimony to Jewish hatred of the revolutionary regime.

Even Israel Zangwill, who had been so outspoken in support of the new Russia, began to have second thoughts about Bolshevism. Compare the following speech which Zangwill made at the Kingsway Hall,

East London, with that delivered to the Labour rally at the Albert Hall in March 1917, quoted above:

> I should be no honest advocate of liberty if I endorsed the Russian method of imposing socialism by brute force; and even socialism proper – divorced from violence ... holds grave danger for the human spirit, however welcome be the tardy justice it does to the human body. It is moving towards us so swiftly in these latter days that the question of the due boundaries between the State and the individual may be upon us sooner than any of us can foresee ... socialism encroaches too far upon individual liberty. 'The strongest man', said Ibsen, 'is he who stands most alone.' And similarly, I say the strongest state is that which lets him stand alone. Not to make the world safe for democracy, but to make it safe for minorities, is the true human ideal[53]

A purer statement of classical liberal principles, echoing De Toqueville and John Stuart Mill, could not be wished for. From such a perspective, Zangwill could not but look upon the Socialist Experiment in Russia with severe misgivings. In a new play entitled *The Forcing House*, published in 1922, Zangwill explored the phenomenon of 'Socialism while you can't wait'. The action was set in an imaginary country, Valdania, which had undergone a revolution. It was clearly inspired by Revolutionary Russia and the revolutionary hero was modelled on Trotsky. Zangwill put the following lines into the mouth of one of his characters:

> [Valdania was] not a Paradise of blossoming brotherhood, not a natural growth under God's heaven, but a socialism ripened prematurely under the heat of compulsion and watered with blood, a socialism that can be perpetuated only by ever-renewed compulsion.

In his anthology *The Voice of Jerusalem* (1920), Zangwill declared that 'The Red Road is not the path to Zion'. As for the Bolshevik brand of socialism, he regarded it thus:

> Mr Grimstone, the schoolmaster in *Vice Versa*, remarked that he could establish a spirit of unmurmuring happiness and unreasoning contentment in his school if he had to flog every schoolboy to

achieve it, and Bolshevism in its Russian caricature is only Grimstonianism writ large.

BRITISH INTERVENTION AND THE RUSSIAN CIVIL WAR

The Anglo-Jewish establishment was anti-Bolshevik. This did not mean, however, that it was prepared to give its blessing to the British intervention. The *Jewish Chronicle* would have preferred to see a peaceful end to the 'blood-stained tyranny' either through voluntary Bolshevik cooperation with 'moderate elements' or through the natural emergence of a 'strong democratic leader'. Such possibilities were becoming increasingly remote by the middle of 1918. The editor was thus moved guardedly to sanction Allied intervention to over- throw the Bolsheviks by force and to restore the eastern front – provided that it was carried out in a 'prudent manner'.[54] For the Conjoint, Lucien Wolf hinted that he was in agreement with the new policy. At the beginning of December 1918 – significantly, after the Armistice – he wrote the following in a note to Lord Curzon:

> Russia, plunged into chaos by the Revolution [amended to read 'Bolsheviks'] awaits order and reorganisation at the hands of the Allied powers. Great Britain itself is dependent upon their advice and help and will require their formal recognition when a stable Government is established.[55]

By 1919, Jewish attitudes to intervention had undergone a dramatic change. This was a result of the White campaign in South Russia, accompanied by an unprecedented wave of pogroms in which more than 100,000 Jews lost their lives. The Civil War turned the former Pale of Settlement into a bloody battlefield for competing armies, Russian, Ukrainian and Polish. Nationalist forces effectively made war on the Jews for their alleged collusion with the Bolsheviks. This turn of events shocked Anglo-Jewry. Greenberg lamented: 'The Jewish con- dition in Eastern Europe is ... one long pogrom.'[56] Later still, in 1923, the Chief Rabbi, Dr Hertz, summed up his feelings of indignation at the blood-letting in the Ukraine:

> Three million Jews of the Ukraine were handed over, helpless and hopeless, to murder and dishonour ... Historians have for cen-

turies dwelt on the tragedy and inhumanity of the expulsion of the 150,000 Jews of Spain. But throughout 1919 and 1920 we have had in the Ukraine not merely the expulsion of a similar number of human beings, but their extermination by the wild hordes of Denikin, Petlura, Grigoriev, Makhno, and other bandits, raging like wild beasts amid the defenceless Jewries of South Russia. The massacres of the Jews in the Ukraine can find, for thoroughness and extent, no parallel except in the massacres of the Armenians ... Wholesale slaughter and violation, drownings and burnings and burials alive, became not merely commonplaces, but the order of the day. There were pogroms that lasted a week; and in several towns the diabolic torture and outrage and carnage were continued for a month. In many populous Jewish communities there were no Jewish survivors left to bury the dead, and thousands of Jewish wounded and killed were eaten by dogs; in others, the synagogues were turned into charnel houses by the pitiless butchery of those who sought refuge in them. If we add ... the number of the indirect victims who, in consequence of the robbery and destruction that accompanied these massacres, were swept away by famine, disease, exposure, and all manner of privations – the dread total will be very near half-a-million human beings.

Yet all this persecution, torture, slaughter, continued for nearly two years without any protest by the civilised Powers, with hardly any notice in the English Press of this systematic extermination. And if you even consult the latest volumes of the *Encyclopaedia Britannica*, and turn to the article 'Ukraine', you will find not the slightest reference, not by a single word, to this black page in all the dark and blood-stained annals of Europe. This conspiracy of silence has been but too successful.

The Chief Rabbi further reflected on a unique aspect of Jewish pogroms. In contrast to other forms of atrocity, they were liable to be repeated at regular intervals:

Jewish massacres alone – remain unchanged by the lapse of time, nay, they increase in volume and in murderous fury. The single pogrom of Kishinev in 1903 with its scores of victims, was succeeded by a wave of pogroms in 1905, with thousands of victims; and this in its turn was followed by the whole cycle of mass massacres of 1919 and 1920 and 1921. Would to Heaven that these remained the last. May God in His mercy have pity on this sorely afflicted people.[57]

The mass murder of Ukrainian Jewry during the Russian Civil War was, in actual fact, only to be surpassed by the Nazi Holocaust in the 1940s.

Anglo-Jewry felt quite impotent in face of the hopeless plight of Russian Jewry. When persecution had occurred under the Tsars, the communal *shtadlanim* had at least had recourse to diplomatic protest. Urgent notes were dispatched to the Foreign Office — sometimes backed up by public meetings — to impress upon the government the extent of communal concern. It was hoped that such action would, in turn, induce a British complaint to the Russians. This, it seemed, in the years 1918–20, was no longer a realistic option. The *Jewish World* observed: 'Unfortunately we can here do nothing – absolutely nothing – in present circumstances – to help them [Russian Jewry].'[58] On the one hand, the paper recognised the following, self-evident truth: 'No protest [by the west] can avail where there is no Government to which to carry the protest: – and it is precisely because there is no Government in Russia worthy of the name that our people are made victims of mob violence.'[59] On the other hand, there appeared to be little use in appealing to the British authorities. They were, after all, supporting the Whites, the chief perpetrators of the pogroms. Intervention had had just that consequence which the Jewish leaders had feared — alliance with counter-revolution.

Thus 'the Jews of England were outraged by the antisemitism of those to whom Britain was giving military support.'[60] The old dilemma, which the February Revolution had briefly banished, now returned to plague Anglo-Jewry with renewed force. When it came to Russia, Jewish interests and British interests patently did not coincide. The difference was that now, with the war over, the community felt somewhat freer to say so. The Anglo-Jewish press, for the first time since 1914, indulged in some outspoken criticism of government policy. In June 1919, the *Jewish World* (which was always more forthright than its sister the *Chronicle*) allied itself with the opponents of intervention. It questioned the wisdom of sending war-weary British troops to Russia with no certain end in view. What amounted to an invasion of Russia by foreign armies would only give a 'fillip' to the Bolshevik cause. The Communists would be able to portray themselves as the nationalists, fighting to defend the independence of the Mother-land – a situation seemingly reminiscent of that during the French Revolution. Allied intervention might also precipitate the fall of the Bolsheviks and a consequent monarchist restoration or military dic-tatorship. In either event, the Allies were likely to become embroiled in a prolonged civil war. Leopold Greenberg showed clear distrust of the Allies' motives. He accused them of hypocrisy. Before the revolution, they had been loath to put pressure on the Tsar to liberalise his rule, invoking as an excuse the principle of non-interference in the internal affairs of a sovereign state. Now that hallowed principle had been superseded by another, more urgent, one: namely the necessity of overthrowing Bolshevism. Besides, the editor hinted, there was a more material motive at work. General Kolchak had promised to repay Allied debts which the Bolsheviks had repudiated. Financial con-siderations notwithstanding, support for the Volunteer Army was also unlikely to bring the Allied Powers much long-term benefit: 'The White terror, which is associated with Kolchak and his friends ... does not seem a very attractive alternative to the Red Terror of Bolshevism.'[61] As far as the Jews were concerned, Greenberg totally rejected the White generals' protestations that they were not antisemites. The most that could be said in their favour was that they were powerless to prevent excesses on the part of their troops.[62] When obliged to choose between the grim alternatives, the *Jewish World* made the following – qualified – judgement:

> There is no question that the Bolshevik regime is terrible from many points of view for Jews – if half the stories told of it be true – but even if the worst imputed to it be the fact, it is not so utterly hopeless, so entirely a set-back to every Jewish aspiration as is evidently Kolchakism.[63]

As has already been observed, the experience of tsarism had condi-tioned Jews, both in Russia and the west, to fear the extreme right more than the extreme left. The latter was still largely an unknown quantity. By the end of 1919, it was apparent that Russian Jewry was being driven into the arms of the Bolsheviks by the cruelty of the White

Guard. Lucien Wolf grudgingly acknowledged this truth. He confessed to his diary:

> I was convinced that doctrinally the overwhelming mass of Jews of all classes were opposed to Bolshevism; but what could these poor people do when all the anti-Bolshevik forces – the Poles, the Ukrainians, the Roumanians, the armies of Kolchak and Denikin, the Siberian armies and now even the British Expeditionary Forces – were insisting that they were all Bolshevists; and were making war on them as such?
> They were, in fact, being driven into Bolshevism whether they liked it or not.[64]

To the *Daily Telegraph* he wrote in the following terms:

> If Jews have reluctantly turned to Bolshevism, it is because they have been forced to it by the anti-Bolsheviks. They cannot but be alarmed by the persistency and passion with which the charge of Bolshevism is levelled at them, and the threat which comes from all sides to avenge in their persons the sins of Lenin and Trotsky. They have had a bloody instalment of the St. Bartholomew in the pogroms of the Polish borderlands and the Ukrainian plains. What wonder, then, if some of them – and they can only be relatively few – turn for protection to the Soviets, especially in the lands where the Soviets rule?

He added that, in any case, Jewish Law exhorts obedience to the civil authorities.[65]

The *Jewish Guardian* of 7 November 1919 – the second anniversary of the October Revolution – estimated that about half the Jews in Russia were now pro-Bolshevik. In the end, Leopold Greenberg pleaded with the Allies to let the Russians sort out their own affairs:

> Bolshevism, however crazy as a form of government, however ... undemocratic – and Lenin himself has had to make vast concessions of his communistic theories – is not necessarily a creed of bloodshed and slaughter ... such as it has been represented doubtless with some substratum of truth, but equally doubtlessly, with immense exaggeration. The stand that Bolshevism has made rather goes to show that it has a great hold upon the Russian

people and ... it is surely for the Russian people only to determine the form of Government they themselves wish.[66]

By early 1920, direct British intervention in Russia was all but at an end. Lloyd George, encouraged by the French and Winston Churchill, none the less decided to send military aid to the Poles in their struggle against the Bolsheviks. On 10 May, London dockers 'blacked' a consignment of ammunition bound for Danzig. The government acquiesced in the ban for as long as the Poles were winning. In July they were routed and the Red Army began its march on Warsaw: the situation came to a head. The labour movement, taking a cue from the dockers, organised Councils of Action and threatened to call a general strike in a bid to stop the intervention. The tactic had some effect. Lloyd George declared that Labour was 'knocking at an open door'.

The *Jewish World* did not hesitate in bestowing its blessing on the policy of the left.[67] Direct action might not be strictly constitutional, the journal argued, but it was justified given that 'circumstances are exceptional and need exceptional measures'. The necessity of averting the greater evil – a renewal of war – overrode any other considerations. Greenberg himself went on to assert that Labour was entitled to withdraw itself in order to put pressure on the government. After all, by so doing, was not it simply imitating the tactics of capital? It was not unknown for bankers to withdraw loans in order to get their own way. The only sensible solution to the current dispute was a ceasefire, the mutual recognition of Poland and Soviet Russia and, above all, the recognition of the latter by the British government. This was not an unreasonable demand, the *Jewish World* insisted. Instances could be multiplied where diplomatic relations existed between Great Britain and regimes whose political systems she did not approve of. Tsarist Russia was the precedent which came to mind. Thus the Anglo-Jewish press welcomed the Anglo-Soviet Trade Agreement with relief, when it was finally signed in April 1921. It held out promise of a new era of cooperation between the two countries. At the same time, the introduction of the New Economic Policy (in reality the Old Economic Policy, since it restored a limited free market) in Russia raised hopes that the economic conditions of Russian Jewry, at least, would be improved. It was clear that the Trade Agreement had also released Anglo-Jewry from a painful dilemma.

3 'Our Own': 'West End' Jewry and the Russian Revolution – Policy

The preceding chapter dealt with Jewish political opinion in Britain concerning the revolution in Russia, and the situation of the Jews therein. It is now time to focus on official communal policy. How did Anglo-Jewry, as a collective, act in response to the Russian Revolution? Four main areas of organised Jewish activity may be highlighted, this activity being most intense during 1919 and 1920. It was initially limited to the traditional spheres of relief-work and *Shtadlanut* – that is, to philanthropy and diplomacy. Relief funds were collected for the victims of the pogroms. Appeals had been launched at the time of the mass evacuation of Jews from the war zone by the tsarist authorities in 1915; now they were renewed in greater earnest. Lucien Wolf, the *de facto* 'Foreign Secretary' of Anglo-Jewry, simultaneously engaged in diplomatic intercession behind the scenes, not only with the British government but also at the Paris peace conference and at the League of Nations. On behalf of oppressed Jewry in eastern Europe, Wolf raised such issues as the refugee question, Allied relations with the Whites and the problem of the Ukraine. Thus 'quiet diplomacy' was revived, after its almost total suspension during the war, owing to the delicate circumstances of the Anglo-Russian Alliance.

Such tactics were soon found to be insufficient, however. The Jewish establishment now began to engage in a policy of communal self-defence, designed to counter manifestations of antisemitism – albeit in the guise of anti-Bolshevism – which appeared with increasing regularity in the press. External pressure upon Anglo-Jewry was mounting, and the leadership was forced onto the defensive. Finally, the tactics of public protest were invoked – although as will become clear, this development was not unanimously endorsed by all of the communal powers-that-be. In studying Anglo-Jewish communal reaction to the revolution, it is contended that it was determined as much by domestic considerations as by political change within Russia itself.

RELIEF, REFUGEES, RECONSTRUCTION

The relief effort was an object lesson in Jewish self-help. In August 1918, the Joint Foreign Committee received an urgent request for aid from the Central Jewish Relief Committee in Moscow. It claimed that: 'The better half of the Jewish population in Russia must now rely on public assistance',[1] – and that half of the necessary funds would have to come from abroad. A sombre picture was painted of the uprooting of the Jewish population: famine, epidemics, the dislocation of trade and industry, transport and communications and rampant inflation under conditions of war and revolution. Food, clothing, shelter and medicines were all needed for the refugees. (It is worth noting that such a miserable economic situation prevailed in the lands of the former Pale before the advent of widespread pogroms during the course of 1919.) Accordingly, a plethora of home-grown relief committees were created or reactivated within Anglo-Jewry. These included the Fund for the Relief of Jewish Victims of the War in eastern Europe, chaired initially by Leopold de Rothschild (who died in 1917), , the London Committee for the Relief of Polish Jews and the Federation of Ukrainian Jews (FUJ) – these latter two East End based. There were also various *landsman-schaft* societies in the ghetto which took a direct interest in this work. In 1920 an east European 'Forwarding and Distribution Committee' was set up as a supplement to the official Fund. All of these bodies cooperated with major western Jewish relief agencies such as the Alliance Israélite Universelle (France), the Hilfsverein (Germany) and the American Joint Distribution Committee and Hebrew Immigrant Aid Society (HIAS).

Similarly they cooperated with the international Jewish relief organisations[2]: the Jewish Colonisation Association (JCA), the Organisation for Rehabilitation and Training (ORT) and the World Zionist Organisation. Of all these it was ORT, originally an indigenous Russian society, the JCA and the 'Joint' which played the most important role in post-revolutionary Russian relief work.

However, in 1918–19 relief work was very haphazard and hazardous. In March 1918 the *Jewish World* reported that the Fund had suspended its operations temporarily because the political and economic chaos in Russia made their efforts 'impracticable'.[3] Communications with the Moscow-based Russian Central Jewish Relief Committee and the Jewish Medical Society were unreliable. Contact with Baron Gunsburg himself, chairman of the former, was interrupted by his three-week arrest in September 1918. Leon Bramson, *trudovik*, former member of the Duma and the Soviet and friend of Kerensky, had to flee from Russia for his life when he was declared an 'enemy of the Revolution' by the Bolsheviks. He managed to re-establish ORT in exile – the ORT Union centred on Berlin. Henceforth this emigré organisation tried to come to an understanding with 'Soviet' ORT which was being brought more and more under Bolshevik control. But during the Civil War, it was impossible to get relief through. It was not even a case of lack of cooperation on the part of the Russian authorities; there was simply no authority in Russia to cooperate with. This situation was compounded by the disintegration of the former Russian Empire into its constituent national units. This meant the break-up of the Jewish Pale of Settlement. Moreover, in 1918, some of the most seriously stricken areas were under German occupation. Permission to send supplies to these sensitive areas was refused by the British Ministry of Blockade. So the Jewish relief agencies had to contend with the obstructionism of the British government as well as with the existence of no government at all in Russia. Throughout the period of intervention, the Foreign Office treated Jewish requests for official assistance in emergency relief with suspicion. In 1918, at least, the communal representatives were still in a position to put some pressure on the government. Lord Swaythling warned Sir Adam Block of the Ministry of Blockade – himself Jewish – that

> The danger to this country is, if the English Jewish community refused to help the Jewish victims of the war in Russia, they will be forced to turn for assistance to our enemies and German propagandists will say that England left them to starve and it was eventually German funds that saved the remnant left over.[4]

If it had little effect in this particular instance, this was the kind of language the Foreign Office understood. Labouring under an exaggerated belief in the political and financial influence of world Jewry, the government had, throughout the war, attached some importance to wooing both American and Russian Jewry to the Allied side. A propaganda war was being waged in competition with the Central Powers for the heart of Jewry, as the increasing importance attached to

Zionism testified. The above quotation illustrates Anglo-Jewish (anti-Zionist as much as Zionist) willingness to play upon Foreign Office prejudice in order to promote their own interests, even at the risk of perpetuating the myth of world Jewish power.[5]

It was not until July 1920 that relief was put on a sounder footing. IDGEZKOM – the Jewish Social Committee – was set up under the auspices of the Bolshevik EVKOM, the commissariat for Jewish affairs. Desirous of acquiring foreign capital and expertise for the rebuilding of Russia, IDGEZKOM negotiated the first of a series of agreements between the Soviets and the Jewish relief agencies abroad. The American Joint was willing to cooperate on the condition that other non-Communist Jewish organisations, both in Russia and overseas, be allowed to participate. The Soviets acceded to this demand and ORT, EKOPO (the Jewish Help Committee), OZE (the Society for the Health of the Jewish Population) and the religious-socialist SETMAS (the Union of the Jewish Working Masses) were enlisted internally, the JCA and ORT Union externally. The scheme worked fairly efficiently until January 1921. The Jewish Communists (mostly ex-Bundists) of the EVSEKTSIA (the Jewish Sections of the Communist Party) , jealous all along of their monopoly in Jewish work and resentful of foreign interference, made an attack on SETMAS and the other welfare bodies pulled out of IDGEZKOM in protest. This crisis brought the 'on-going' political debate on the *Russkii Vopros* (Russian Question) within the western organisations to a head. ORT Union, which had been cut off from its roots in Russia, was particularly torn over the advisability of conducting operations under conditions and within bounds imposed by the Soviet government. A 'pro-Soviet' and an 'anti-Soviet' faction emerged in ORT in exile. The enthusiasm for the Soviet Experiment shown by a number on the 'left' – including the Yiddish writer David Bergelson, who subsequently returned home – was counterbalanced by those on the 'right' who adopted a blanket opposition to any relief work in Russia at all, as it would only serve to bolster the Soviet regime. Many Zionists in particular took this view, preferring to see scarce resources expended on the development of Palestine rather than sunk in bottomless Russia. This political conflict over priorities also dogged the emigration programme, as will be seen presently. The official line adopted by the ORT leadership was something of a pragmatic compromise between these two extremes. They were determined to take maximum advantage of any opportunity afforded by the Soviet government to get aid through to beleaguered Soviet Jewry, while at the same time they had no intention of subscribing to Soviet ideology. Agricultural settlement programmes would be funded because they conformed to ORT's own policies and not because they were acceptable to the Soviet authorities – although that was an undoubted bonus.[6]

Meanwhile, on the Soviet side, the EVSEKTSIA regarded relief work with distaste and the IDGEZKOM was finally dissolved in 1924. This forced the western organisations to reassess their relationship with the Bolsheviks all over again.

By 1921, the whole problem of relief had broadened out into the areas of reconstruction and the renewed emigration of refugees. ORT and the JCA turned their attention to what was termed 'reconstructive relief', that is, helping devastated communities to rebuild their social and economic fabric on the spot in eastern Europe. The preferred methods were agricultural settlement, vocational training and bank loans, with a view to the encouragement of self-help and 'productivisation'. However it soon became apparent that such efforts were indeed but a drop in the ocean, and they received a serious setback with the famine of 1921. An estimated 200,000 Jewish refugees were 'clogging' the exit points along the Soviet frontier with Poland and Romania in the summer of that year.[7] Was the pre-war exodus about to be resumed? Certainly, the high hopes of 1917 that the liberalisation of Russia would check this human stream once and for all had been sadly misplaced.[8] Not that the new refugee problem was confined to Jews. It is estimated that about one million people fled the former Russian Empire in the revolutionary period. White Russians and Ukrainians formed the majority of those escaping the effects of political upheaval and famine. The principal outlets for the emigration were:

(1) In the south: by sea via the Odessa–Constantinople shipping lanes. Some 190,000 were evacuated by this route alone.
(2) In the north: via the Baltic states.
(3) In the west: overland via the Polish and Romanian borders.
(4) In the far east: via the Trans-Siberian Railway to Manchuria and the Pacific coast. (Harbin and Shanghai developed thriving emigré communities.)

The most popular destinations included other parts of eastern Europe (especially Poland and the Baltic), the Balkans (Bulgaria, Romania) and western Europe (mainly France and Germany). Indeed, Paris and Berlin became the centres of the Russian Emigration. As for England, she received a mere 4000 Russian refugees. The Hope-Simpson report on the refugee problem, published on the eve of the Second World War, makes the following observation regarding this low figure: 'Very few other than well-to-do educated people were able to remain in England, except those Jews who were absorbed in the existing Jewish Community in the East End of London.'[9] He quotes no statistics on the proportion of Jews amongst the immigrants, however. Smaller numbers of 'Russians' made their way overseas, to the USA, Argentina and, of course, in the case of Jews, to Palestine, in the first half of the 1920s.

The scale of the emigration was such that it received international attention. The League of Nations set up a High Commission for Refugees (the Nansen Commission) in 1921 and a conference on Russian refugees was held in Geneva the same year. Voluntary relief organisations, including the Jewish ones, were invited to form a standing Advisory or Consultative Committee to the High Commission and to participate in the conference. League agencies like the International Labour Office (ILO) and the Health Section also took an interest in this work.

As far as Jews were concerned the new emigration revived the old question: *Wohin?* – Where could they find refuge? In 1919 Britain extended the provisions of the 1905 Aliens Act; more importantly, Republican legislation in the United States (1921 and 1924) all but slammed the door on immigration from Europe. Access to *Di Goldene Medina* (the Golden Land) – the traditional destination for Jewish emigrants – was virtually at an end. The Zionists, naturally, looked to Palestine. But Arab unrest forced the British periodically to restrict Jewish immigration under the Mandate. In any case, even the Zionists were obliged to admit that the Palestinian economy was not sufficiently developed to absorb more than a fraction of the potential influx at once.[10] Others advocated an internal migration within eastern Europe itself. Israel Zangwill suggested resettlement in Siberia, in the context of his 'Territorialist' schemes, whilst Lucien Wolf had another novel idea. In 1919 he speculated:

There would be no peace in Poland whilst the Jewish population remained at its present abnormal density. Further emigration westwards was out of the question, and was, besides, unnecessary. Russia could take the whole Jewish population of Poland without feeling it, and as soon as stable conditions were reached in that country emigration thither should be encouraged ... Not only could Russia easily take the Polish Jews, but she wanted them, more especially in so far as they were artisans.[11]

He talked in terms of a liberalised Russia as a 'New America' which would act as a powerful – and more accessible – magnet for east European Jewry. Wolf's optimism proved short-lived.

On a practical level, Wolf worked closely with the Paris-based Jewish Colonisation Association and its newly created Jewish Central Emigration Council. This latter body held its first conference in Brussels in June 1921, to coordinate the international programme for Jewish relief and refugees. Wolf cooperated with the Central Council to put pressure on both the League of Nations and individual governments to ease immigration restrictions in western and overseas countries and for the issue of visas and provision of transport; and campaigned for the reunification of divided families. The men who had returned to Russia under the Convention in 1917, and now sought to rejoin their wives and children in England, were a case in point.[12] Successful representations were also made to the Polish and Romanian governments to forestall their threatened expulsion of Jewish refugees back to Soviet Russia in 1923. Wolf welcomed the efforts made by the High Commission for Refugees, and appreciated the importance of the fact that the League recognised that the Jewish emigration problem was part and parcel of the general question of displaced populations in post-war Europe. The legal and political protection of a non-sectarian organisation like the League could be of great value to the Jewish relief workers.[13]

Even so, Jewish hopes vested in the League were disappointed. Despite the sympathy shown by Fridtjof Nansen himself and by the British Chairman of the International Emigration Commission of the ILO, Viscount Ullswater, the bureaucracy in Geneva moved tantalisingly slowly. The prevailing post-war economic situation also made west European, American and Dominion governments all reluctant to countenance renewed immigration. The South Africans, Australians and Canadians operated strict quotas which favoured agriculturalists of British stock to the detriment of all 'Russians' except those 'of good character'. In July 1921, Wolf reported to the JCA that even the trade union representatives, who accounted for one-third of the membership of the International Emigration Commission, were hostile to any further influx of labour.[14] Neither was the Commission eager to get mixed up in 'the politics of emigration',[15] nor to make any substantial financial commitment for the benefit of Jewish relief. Although the private Jewish organisations had undertaken sole responsibility for 'sheltering, transporting, receiving and settling the emigrants' no public funds were made available from either League or government sources for this purpose.[16] The Jewish organisations were thus wise to insist on the retention of their financial autonomy and independent initiative.

Squabbles amongst the Jewish bodies themselves did not help matters either. Rivalry existed between the JCA's Central Emigration Council and the Carlsbad Committee set up under the auspices of the Jewish World Relief conference held in Carlsbad in July 1920. Behind the latter was the Zionist Comité des Délégations Juives which, like the JCA, was also based in Paris. Both organisations sought representation on the High Commission's Advisory Committee. In December 1921 Wolf declared that it was 'impossible' for the JCA and allied organisations (i.e. the Anglo-Jewish Association (AJA), Hilfsverein and Alliance) to share representation with that 'irresponsible' committee: 'we could not contemplate without the greatest aversion the appearance at the Consultive Committee of two Jewish organisations which were not in agreement with each other.' Unless 'a single delegation or at least a unified delegation' could be agreed upon, 'I was afraid we should have no choice but to retire from the Consultative Committee.' At length, Wolf rescinded his threat.[17] Nevertheless the dichotomy between Zionist and non-Zionist policy was real. Wolf accused the Carlsbad Committee of 'set[ting] itself deliberately to stimulate further emigration from Russia'[18] – with the intention, he could have added, of redirecting the stream towards Palestine rather than towards the west (a conflict of interests that is still with us today, in the tension which exists between the Israeli government and diaspora Jewish organisations, most notably HIAS, over the question of the Soviet Jewish emigration movement).

In the light of these problems, by mid-1923 Jewish emigration policy was back to where it started, despite the fact that Lucien Wolf had adamantly declared on behalf of the western agencies as a whole: 'We are dead against repatriation.' Anti-Zionists and pro-Zionists alike were agreed that

> the famine, the epidemics, the general economic misery, the persecutions of religious minorities and the obscure prospects of the present regime with the certainty that a reactionary revolution would have as its first result a colossal massacre of Jews, all this forbids us to countenance any schemes of repatriation. Even if ... there are Jews who wish to go back we should be disposed to advise them to abandon the idea.[19]

Several weeks later, however, Wolf had acquiesced. He reluctantly gave his backing to the High Commission's negotiations with the Soviet government for the repatriation of refugees. This turnabout in policy was on pragmatic rather than on ideological grounds: 'In principle, of course, no one was enamoured of repatriation, but it was clear that, to some extent, it might become inevitable, and hence it would only be prudent to make it the subject of a detailed agreement with the Soviet Government.'[20]

Such a task, indeed, was not an easy one. The Soviets were apt to treat League 'interference' with the refugee question with suspicion. They maintained that the extension of League of Nations protection to Russian émigrés, deliberately deprived of Soviet citizenship in the years 1921–4, encouraged the perpetuation of the White Russian 'émigré plot' against the new regime. In the end, the Soviet government did re-admit some 181,000 ex-Russian citizens, but only on their individual merits – with a strong preference for 'useful' elements such as farmers as opposed to 'petit bourgeois' traders and artisans. At the same time, by the mid-1920s further legal emigration from the USSR had become all but impossible.

The repatriation negotiations exacerbated both conflicts: those between the Jewish organisations and the High Commission, and those among the Jewish organisations themselves. Regarding the Zionists, Wolf reported to the JCA that the proposal to negotiate a repatriation agreement with the Soviet Government for the benefit of our refugees was made by my Association alone, [i.e. the JCA], and it was received with very scant cordiality, if not with actual hostility, by the representative of the only other Jewish Society [i.e. the Carlsbad Committee] in the Consultative Committee.[21]

Repatriation was in fundamental opposition to the thrust of Zionist policy. Many Zionists were also, as is already clear, opposed to any form of negotiation with the Soviets. As for the Nansen Commission, its discussions with the Soviets made slow progress. They dragged on from April to November 1923. Wolf became impatient. In October he complained that 'We ask nothing from the High Commission except assistance in the political domain and if we cannot get that we have no reason whatever to remain in the Consultative Committee.'[22] Given that the JCA had initiated talks in the first place, he proposed direct JCA-Soviet negotiations which would bypass the machinery of the League altogether. While willing to 'make use' of the High Commission's 'moral clout', Wolf concluded that 'it [was] not indispensable'.[23]

Thus by the beginning of 1924, Jewish relief work in eastern Europe had come full circle. The Jewish voluntary organisations had been forced back into traditional self-help methods, and the emphasis had shifted from emigration back to reconstruction within Soviet Russia. The JCA, ORT, the American Joint and HIAS all concluded agreements with the Soviet government to provide financial support and technical know-how for Jewish agricultural colonies inside the USSR.

WOLF'S 'QUIET DIPLOMACY' – THE PARIS PEACE CONFERENCE, 1919

In one respect, the Russian Revolution made Wolf's battle on behalf of Jewish rights in eastern Europe a vastly more complicated one. The Conjoint Committee had long fought for the civil and political emancipation of Russian Jewry. In 1914, they urged that this be written into the declared war aims of the Allied Powers. The exigencies of the British alliance with the tsar none the less necessitated that Wolf's demands be muted. When the monarchy was swept away and the Provisional Government made the April Decree, it appeared that the Jewish question in Russia had been solved. It soon became apparent, however, that the Declaration only applied to the *c*. 1.5 million Jews in Great Russia. The revolution had precipitated the disintegration of the Empire into its constituent national units. The emergence of new nation-states – Poland, the Ukraine, Lithuania, Latvia, Estonia and Finland – brought the *de facto* dismemberment of the former Jewish Pale of Settlement. Four-fifths of 'Russian' Jewry was now separated from Russia proper. In future, instead of having to deal with just the one government – however intransigent the tsarist regime – western Jewish diplomats would be obliged to negotiate with an assortment of different powers. This prospect led Wolf into a preoccupation with minority rights at the Versailles peace conference, to which he had been invited to lead a delegation on behalf of the Anglo-Jewish community.

In April 1917, in an article entitled 'The Jewish National Movement', published in the *Edinburgh Review*, Wolf came out in favour of the principle of 'national cultural autonomy' for the Jews in eastern Europe. He claimed that this concept was supported by the vast majority of Russian Jews, as organised in a variety of political parties such as the liberal *Folkspartai* of Simon Dubnov, the socialist *Farainigte* and especially the Bund. Initially, Wolf assumed that this solution would be worked out within a democratic, federated and decentralised Russian Empire. Even when that possibility faded, he still hoped that reunification could eventually be achieved. In the meantime, he set about securing guarantees for Jewish minority rights from the rulers of the new east European states in return for Great Power recognition of their independence. He also wished to ensure a Jewish right of appeal to the League of Nations against infractions of the Minorities Treaties.

Wolf's work at Paris with regard to the Minorities Treaties is largely outside the scope of this study. It has been dealt with in detail elsewhere.[24] Some attention must, however, be paid to the Anglo-Jewish delegation's negotiations with the Ukrainians at the peace conference. By 1921 the Ukraine had reverted to Russian – Soviet – rule.

The Ukraine

By the 'First Universal' of 10 June 1917, the Ukrainian Central Rada declared equal civil and political rights for all minorities living within the borders of their new state. They went on to enact 'national cultural autonomy' for the benefit of Ukrainian Jewry – some 1.6 million, the third largest ethnic grouping in the Ukraine, and constituting the largest component part of the former 'Russian' Jewish community. No fewer than 50 Jewish deputies were elected to the Rada, and the post of Minister for Jewish Affairs was created in the central government. It was occupied by Mr M. Zilberfarb of the *Farainigte*. This was the first case in history of a Jewish ministry.[25]

These developments were, naturally, welcomed by Jewry abroad. David Mowshowitch reported from Stockholm that 'The principle of the sovereignty of all the nationalities inhabiting the Ukraine is carried out so thoroughly that even the banknotes of the Republic ... have inscriptions in several languages – Ukrainian, Russian, Yiddish and Polish.'[26]

The Ukrainian delegation at the peace conference included two Jews, Mark Vishnitzer and Arnold Margolin, as proof of the new regime's good faith. Both men subsequently found themselves in London, Vishnitzer serving as secretary of the Ukrainian Mission in England.

However, when complete Ukrainian independence was declared by the Fourth Universal in January 1918, Jews in the west began to have misgivings. Lucien Wolf doubted whether an independent and liberal Ukraine could survive. Its very existence was an implied affront to Russia. It was threatened on every side, not only by the Bolsheviks and the Whites, but by the Germans, Poles and Romanians. Moreover, the Ukrainian government was internally unstable. The Skoropadsky régime came to an accommodation with the Germans and Petlura with the Poles – but neither could exactly be relied upon to guarantee Jewish rights. Yet Ukrainian representatives abroad continued to court the Jews. As late as December 1920, Wolf received a letter sent on behalf of the Directory assuring him of Ukrainian toleration towards the Jews. 'The Jews', it said,

> can consider the Ukraine as *sui generis* their second home (after Palestine) for they inhabited the country from times immemorial (Khazars). In helping actively to restore order in the Ukraine they (1) will show themselves good patriots of their second fatherland ... (2) they will help to create a marvellous country ... (3) they will give a smashing *dementi* to the ludicrous accusations of

which they are today an object – accusations as to their *soi-disant* destructive scheme against the civilised world.[27]

That final sentence reveals the extent to which Ukrainian toleration could be stretched. The advent of the Directory under the militantly nationalist, and militantly antisemitic Petlura indeed put paid to any hopes Wolf had vested in an independent Ukraine.

The Ukraine now became a major battleground in the Russian Civil War – and the setting for the bloodiest pogroms in the history of eastern Europe to that date. At the peace conference, Wolf repeatedly sought assurances from the Ukrainian delegation that their government was doing all in its power to put a stop to the excesses. He never received a satisfactory reply, only excuses. It was true that the Ukrainians never actually denied that pogroms were taking place, but they pleaded extenuating circumstances: they blamed the presence of a hooligan element in the Ukrainian army over which the government had no control, or the general instability created by the Civil War. Antisemitism was a regrettable legacy of tsarist days which the Ukrainians were desperately trying to shake off. There was also the inevitable claim that the atrocity stories were being made up or grossly exaggerated by the enemies of the struggling little Ukrainian state. The favourite excuse put forward by the Ukrainians, however, like their arch-enemies the White Russians and the Poles, was that the Jews were involved in Bolshevism. Mr Zarchi, a member of the Ukrainian delegation in Paris, informed Wolf that the pogroms 'were not, however, so much anti-Jewish as they were a consequence of the struggle between the Ukrainians and the Bolshevists. In the intensity of this struggle the allegations of Jewish complicity in Bolshevism had found very ready acceptance.'[28]

Everyone and everything, except the Ukrainians themselves, were thus held up for blame. Even the Ukrainian Jewish delegates, Vishnitzer and Margolin, found themselves cast in the role of apologists for the activities of the Directory. They lost credibility in the eyes of Jews abroad as a result and were branded as *Yiddishe meshorsim* (Jewish lackeys).[29] Wolf thus treated the Ukrainian-inspired proposal of sending a Jewish commission of inquiry to the Ukraine, like the one sent to Poland, with appropriate scepticism: 'There seems to be a mania for these missions ... I suppose the Ukraine wants one because it thinks that the result would be to whitewash its own Government.' Given this, and the suggested make-up of the commission - 'pretentious medio-cracies [*sic*] ... and blatant nationalists' – 'such a Commission would carry no weight in the Jewish community, and no one would pay any attention to it outside.'[30]

There was also the attitude of the Jews living in the vicinity to be considered. Ukrainian Jewry had, in large part, long been opposed to the creation of an independent state. The Bund voted against the Fourth Universal; the other Jewish parties – liberal, socialist and Zionist – all abstained. They too suspected that the country might fall into the wrong hands. Like Wolf, they were perturbed at the break-up of the Russian Jewish community which the creation of a separate Ukrainian republic implied. They put their faith in a reconstituted democratic Russian Empire instead. The Jewish liberals on the Russian side agreed, as did the mainstream Zionists. Indeed, the Russian Zionists Rosov and Goldberg, in spite of supplying Wolf with infor-mation on the pogroms, went so far as to deny Denikin's antisemitism, in the interest of promoting Russian reunification under the Whites. In the process, they incurred the wrath of Mark Vishnitzer. In a memo to Wolf, he pointed out that the attitude of the Zionist Organisation, if publicised, could 'cause the Jews great prejudice in Russia'. They thus ran the risk of becoming associated with counter-revolution.[31] They were equally liable to be accused of lack of patriotism by the Uk-rainians. Jewish opposition to Ukrainian national aspirations was a fine way of showing gratitude to the only government in eastern Europe proposing to agree to Zionist demands at Versailles. Last, but not least, it was crass hypocrisy: 'While they were asking the Peace Conference to restore the Jewish nationality in Palestine they were opposing other non-Jewish nationalities in Russia.'

In Wolf's eyes, the Zionists were mere opportunists. He surmised that: 'In view of an early decision on the Palestine question ... [the Zionists were] anxious to place themselves in fullest accord with what they imagined to be the settled policy of the Powers in Southern Russia.' Wolf at this stage (January 1920) reckoned that the Zionists had got it wrong. He thought

> they were making a mistake as it was quite on the cards that the
> cause of Ukrainian independence would still triumph either

through a direct understanding between Petlura and the Bolshevists or through the recognition of the Ukraine by the Powers
which had been rendered very probable through recent developments in South Russia.[32]

Wolf did, nevertheless, find himself in sympathy with a declared
Zionist aim for once, if only with regard to the future character of
Russia. All the same, he feared that the liberal elements who supported
the federal solution would be outmanoeuvred by the pro-tsarist right.
This fear was justified. Wolf thus came to be faced with an unappetising choice: to support either antisemitic Ukrainian nationalists, or
equally antisemitic White Guard generals. Both were contributing
heavily to the physical destruction of the Pale. Wolf's hands were in any
event tied by the fact that the British government had come down in
favour of the White demand for 'Russia – one and indivisible'. Wolf, in
his capacity as the head of the Anglo-Jewish delegation to the peace
conference, was not in a position to go against the declared policy of his
own government. So he took the advice of his Foreign Office contact,
Rex Leeper, who wrote: 'Personally, if I were you, I should hesitate to
express an opinion on Ukrainian affairs at the present moment until it
becomes possible to see a little more light than we can at present.'[33]

So Wolf abandoned the Ukrainian morass as utterly hopeless; the
Ukrainians themselves did not know whether they were 'running with
the hare' or 'hunting with the hounds'.[34] By the beginning of 1921 he
was sitting on the fence. He politely informed the Ukrainian Mission in
the UK that:

> I am afraid I have not been able to render any material services to
> the Ukrainian cause but you are right in assuming that I sympath-
> ise with the assertion by your country of the principle of self-
> determination and with the efforts it has made to stem the flood
> of Bolshevism in Russia. My personal attitude must however not
> be confounded with that of my committee which is necessarily
> neutral in questions of this kind.[35]

Wolf realised that a liberal solution, either by way of an independent
Ukraine or of a federation with Great Russia, was now impossible. It
was the fate of Ukrainian Jewry to be caught up between warring ultra-
nationalist factions:

For us to give any advice to the Jews of the Ukraine is impossible. We cannot advise them to be good Ukrainians without risking the imputation that we are setting them against the Entente and asking them to be traitors to Russia. We cannot ask them to support the cause of an undivided Russia without pillorying them as enemies of their country's national cause. We cannot advise them to be neutral without recognising a Jewish nationality and setting both Russians and Ukrainians, and probably also Bolshevists, Poles and Rumanians against them.[36]

Thus Wolf understood the dilemma. The only solution he could devise was a warning against the dangers inherent in the 'expedient of Jewish neutrality'. Far better, he argued, that the Jews should support the dominant nationality in any given country; the Russians in Great Russia, the Ukrainians in the Ukraine and so on. On this point, Anglo-Jewish opinion was divided. Israel Zangwill took a diametrically opposite view:

A Jew of Kieff, which has been taken and retaken seventeen times, would have had to be ringing the changes on Russian, Ukrainian, Pole, (not to mention Bolshevist and anti-Bolshevist) about once a month. Only a quick-change patriot could have kept pace with the permutations. The Jew in any city wrangled over by rival elements was thus justified by prudence as well as by humour in remaining neutral and just a Jew.[37]

The question, at least as far as the Ukraine was concerned, soon became an academic one. The refusal of the Powers to recognise the Ukrainian delegation and the triumph of the Bolsheviks put paid to Ukrainian aspirations.

The Whites

If Wolf could do nothing to influence the situation of the Jews in the Ukraine from Paris, he certainly could not ameliorate the plight of Jews in Russia proper either. The fact was that Great Russia – including 1.5 million Jews – stood outside the scope of the settlement. It is worth adding that since Germany and Austria were also excluded, three of the major east European communities had no representation at the peace conference. Wolf's satisfaction at the signing of the Armistice – especially in so far as it nullified the Treaty of Brest–Litovsk – was somewhat diminished by the realisation that a 'just' and enduring peace could not be attained until the situation in Russia had been stabilised. This feeling was shared by Leopold Greenberg at the *Jewish Chronicle*. In 1918, he wrote an editorial welcoming President Woodrow Wilson's pledge to 'stand by Russia', even at the cost of prolonging the war. And in January 1919, he gave his blessing to Wilson's peace note to the Bolsheviks.[38] For Greenberg, like Wolf, understood that an accommodation with the Reds would simplify matters regarding representations on behalf of the Jews. As things turned out, Wolf had to deal with the Whites.

Throughout 1919, both the London Conjoint Committee and the British Jewish delegation in Paris received a steady stream of pleas for help from Russian and Ukrainian Jewry. All these communications solicited Wolf's intercession with the British government to provide facilities for relief measures and to restrain the Whites. The Russian Zionists were particularly insistent. They furnished the anti-Zionist Wolf with much useful factual material on the pogroms which he was able to forward to the British, Russian and Ukrainian delegations in Paris. In July, the Zionists submitted a special report on the pogroms carried out by Denikin's troops. It was recommended reading matter for the Foreign Office and its Russian allies. The compiler warned the Whites that they would 'be held responsible for all pogroms against Jews in occupied territory'. The Zionists demanded that a Jewish officer and a representative of the local Jewish community be appointed to Denikin's staff.[39] For his part, Chaim Weizmann urged British approval for an official commission of inquiry, composed of leading Jews from Britain, France and the USA, to be sent to the Ukraine. In October, as noted earlier, the Ukrainians came up with their own proposal for an investigation, which never came to anything. Both Denikin's office in Paris and the British government vetoed the whole idea, the former asserting that since Denikin was not in the least bit antisemitic, it would be superfluous. The Foreign Office merely assured Wolf that the newly appointed High Commissioner in South Russia, H.J. Mackinder MP, would exhort Denikin to 'exercise a moderating influence' on his men. He was also being asked to prepare a report on the pogroms.[40] This did not materialise. Wolf then unsuccessfully requested that the Foreign Office order its officials in Constantinople and Palestine to conduct a fact-finding survey among refugees from the Ukraine. Norman Bentwich was meanwhile appointed to conduct such a survey on behalf of Anglo-Jewry. Rabbi Samuel Daiches was also given the task of interviewing Ukrainian refugees who found their way to England. A further demand, made by the Aliens Committee of the Board of Deputies, for British government sanction of relief supplies to their relatives back in the Ukraine, was likewise ignored. The Foreign Office's evident lack of cooperation forced Claude Montefiore to the conclusion that:

> It is in my opinion hopeless to expect any firm pressure to be applied by the English military or civil representatives on the *de facto* Government in Siberia [he was referring to Kolchak, but the observation could apply with equal force to Denikin]. They are too deeply infected with the antisemitic virus. Of the two, the civil branch, i.e. the High Commissioner and the Foreign Office are more liberal than the military.[41]

Wolf, however, felt himself hindered not only by the attitude of the Foreign Office, but also by conflicting accounts about the pogroms he received from the spokesmen for Russian Jewry. As noted, Zionist policy was contradictory. Certain elements sought to play down the pogroms in the hope of promoting Russian reunification under – it was hoped – liberal White control. The Zionist Organisation was also, simultaneously, insisting upon the gravity of the situation and was most active in lobbying abroad on behalf of their co-religionists. In so doing, the Zionists were criticised by the Russian Jewish liberals, Gunsburg and Vinaver, for allegedly exaggerating the extent of the pogroms. The latter too, were inclined to play down the whole issue. For example, speaking of the armies of Kolchak and Denikin, Vinaver stated: 'all their civilian advisors were Kadets, and they, of course, knew better than to make the Jews responsible for Bolshevism.'[42]

Captain Wright, a member of the Samuel Mission to Poland, although not to be counted upon as an impartial witness, had a point when he claimed – somewhat uncharitably – that the Russian and Polish conservatives, had a common 'interest' with the Zionists 'in perpetuating antisemitism', that in reality 'Dmowsky and [Nahum] Sokolow were acting in tacit alliance'. Vinaver was so concerned about what he considered to be the sensationalist and at times unsubstantiated information put out by the Copenhagen Zionist Bureau and by Sokolov's Comité des Délégations Juives in Paris, that he felt that some counter-propaganda was desirable. This was one of the motives behind the establishment of a new journal, *La Tribune Juive* in Paris. The editor was Wolf's old anti-Zionist contact, Dr Reuben Blank.[43]

Wolf agreed that the testimony of the Zionists could not be relied upon. But he also had misgivings about the partiality of his liberal informants. He wrote in his diary:

> I confess I did not feel very satisfied with Vinaver's optimism [*re* the improbability of pogroms]. He is quite in the inner circle of the anti-Bolshevist organisation, and is consequently apt to see things as they want the world at the moment to see them. That is to say that quite unconsciously he is disposed to cover up the dark reactionary elements which exist in the anti-Bolshevist camp and to belittle the dangers with which they are fraught.

and he predicted:

> I am afraid that when the triumph comes these elements and the army officers will make short work of the Liberals and Jews, including Vinaver himself.[44]

Although his efforts on behalf of Russian Jewry were frustrated, Wolf was not prepared to take his campaign into the public forum. He had two good reasons. In the first place, he felt that his prime objective at the peace conference was to secure Jewish minority rights in the rest of eastern Europe. This was a realisable aim in so far as Poland, Romania and the Baltic Provinces fell within the purview of the discussions at Versailles. He could not afford to run the risk of alienating the Powers by stressing the situation of the Jews in Russia, which issue was, in any case, beyond the scope of the agenda. Attainable goals should not be sacrificed to unattainable ones. In the second place, Wolf was aware that public protest could be counter-productive. British intervention on the side of the Whites had placed Anglo-Jewry in a very delicate position politically. The supposed existence of an identity of interest between Great Britain and the Jews, touted by Jewish liberal emancipationists and Zionists alike, appeared to have broken down.

There was an understandable temptation to protest loudly and publicly against the pogroms being perpetrated by Britain's allies in Russia. Such a policy, it had also to be acknowledged, could very well boomerang. It could all too easily invite allegations, especially in the Conservative press, that British Jewry was anti-interventionist. It was but a short step from this premise to the conclusion that British Jewry was actively pro-Bolshevik. Given the tendency on the part of right-wing newspapers to equate Jews and Bolshevism at the slightest excuse, Jewish leaders sought to avoid any action which might generate public controversy on the subject of Jewish involvement in Bolshevism. Because the charge could never be entirely refuted, Anglo-Jewry was clearly vulnerable to accusations of mass disloyalty to the state. Wolf's assessment of the dangers inherent in the situation proved to be remarkably perceptive.

COMMUNAL SELF-DEFENCE

All Israel should set up a statue to Lenin for *not* being a Jew.

Israel Zangwill, *The Voice of Jerusalem* (1920)

British Jewish opinion was generally, if not universally, hostile to the Bolshevik Revolution. It is therefore ironic that the Jewish community should have been the target for an agitation which sought to prove a confluence of interest between Jews (and Judaism) and Bolshevism. Anglo-Jewry was put under considerable pressure, especially by sections of the right-wing press, on account of the fashion for German-Jewish-Bolshevik conspiracy theories. They were forced onto the defensive. Feeling vulnerable, the established Jewish leadership felt the need to restrain internal debate on the subject of the Russian Revolution – a difficult task, given that interest was so intense. At the same time, they felt obliged to adopt a policy of communal self-defence; namely, one of answering the charges of Jewish complicity in Bolshevism, and exposing the scarcely concealed antisemitism which lay behind them. This strategy was carried out on an *ad hoc*, essentially reactive basis until October 1920, when the Board of Deputies finally set up a Press Agency. Behind the policy of communal self-defence lay a desire to preserve Anglo-Jewish respectability. It was above all essential to disassociate Jews, British as well as Russian, from any form of revolutionary extremism. It could thus be said that the predominant reaction of the Anglo-Jewish community to the Russian Revolution was dictated as much by domestic considerations as by political developments within Russia itself.

The Board of Deputies was in no hurry to issue a statement of greeting on the occasion of the first Russian Revolution in March 1917. This was partly, as noted above, out of fear that such official endorsement by a Jewish organisation abroad could have an adverse effect on the position of the Jews in Russia, in the event of a conservative backlash. Leopold Greenberg, however, writing in the *Jewish World*, put his finger on a more likely reason for establishment caution, which was to be found much closer to home: 'when ... an opportunity arose [to greet the revolution], it was "turned down" by the Alexanders and the Magnuses who are led by *The Times* Petrograd correspondent and the reactionary press in this country.'[45]

For his part, the *Haham*, Dr Moses Gaster, advised Joseph Super of the East End based (but West End controlled) National Union for Jewish Rights against sending a message of support to the revolutionary government:

> It would be a very dangerous step to take on the part of the National Union. If the English Jews like to do it, they are perfectly entitled to do so like the American Jews have done, but you will notice that even in America the telegram to Milyukov was not signed by the Russian Jews in the U.S.[46]

He doubtless suspected that the immigrants in the Whitechapel ghetto were an even 'softer' target for the attentions of the 'reactionary press' than the established community. In March and April 1917, then, the extent to which Jewish responses to events in Russia were to be determined by conditions at home was apparent.

It was also in March 1917 that *The Times* correspondent in Riga, Robert Wilton, despatched his report claiming that 'hot-headed and hysterical Jewish youths' in Yuryiev (Dorpat) had formed a private militia which they refused to subordinate to the local representatives of the Provisional Government. He suggested that Russian Jews who engaged in extremist activities ran the risk of retribution. It was, he subsequently added: 'high time for the Russian Jews publicly to disassociate themselves from the demagogues'. Wilton recommended that 'their co-religionists in Great Britain' ought somehow to keep them in check.[47] At the Board the implied threat was taken seriously. Considerable effort was exerted behind the scenes to amass evidence to prove that *The Times* report was without foundation. A correspondence took place between London and Petrograd, between Lucien Wolf and Leopold de Rothschild on the one hand, and Senator Vinaver and Baron Gunsburg on the other. The latter admitted in private: '[I] am much grieved [by] tactless behaviour of some [of] our young co-religionist revolutionists. They are very few but troublesome and we try our best to persuade them that every conspicuous Jewish action would be disastrous to us.'[48] He did none the less warn that *The Times* was given to exaggerate in order to promote its own, notoriously antisemitic, ends. Armed with a detailed brief from the Russian *Maskilim* proving that '*The Times* message [was] untrue from beginning to end', Wolf, encouraged by Leopold de Rothschild, entreated Geoffrey Robinson to retract. His letters remained unanswered in private, nor were they printed in public. Instead, *The Times* stood by the version of events related by its Russian correspondent and merely remarked that the facts were contested 'in various Jewish quarters'. It was not until January 1918 that the paper, somewhat belatedly, conceded that:

> As regards the Jew factor in the Revolution, we know that the great majority of the Russian Jews have openly condemned their extremist co-nationalists [*sic*]. The fact that Trotsky and others of his political class belong to the persecuted race is notorious. But the pseudo-Jew Bolshevists have been denounced and disavowed by Jewry both in Russia and in the Allied countries.[49]

In the course of the correspondence over the Dorpat incident, Baron de Gunsburg let it be known that he was in favour of a proposal put forward by the French Alliance to send a western Jewish delegation to Petrograd. The intention here was to promote the Allied cause among Russian Jews who, it was feared, were gravitating towards socialism and pacifism. Gunsburg requested Anglo-Jewish participation in this venture because 'British influence would greatly help regulating our general evolution – developing rather fast!'[50] But he did not meet with a ready response. De Rothschild replied: 'Intervention by us would, we think, be improper.'[51] Wolf agreed: 'I do not see what we, as Jews, can do. He [Gunsburg] is clearly referring more to the general than to the Jewish situation.'[52] In any case,

> It is obviously impossible for us to interfere in what is not only an internal Russian question, but a question of party politics. The Jewish socialists of Russia are just as much opposed to Jewish non-socialists as they are to Gentile non-socialists, and this opposition would be increased ten-fold were interference to come from foreign non-socialists.[53]

Wolf clearly viewed the proposed delegation as potentially counterproductive. It would, at the very least, suggest to *The Times* that the British Jewish community took seriously reports of Russian Jewish extremism. On the other hand, a public refusal to send representatives to Petrograd could lead to further accusations that Anglo-Jewry was not prepared to do its bit for the Allies. Wolf wisely let the matter drop.

A similar request for direct Anglo-Jewish intervention in the affairs of its sister community was made in February 1918, that is, after the Bolshevik Revolution. Only this time it was the Foreign Office which proposed that Jews in Britain should issue a public appeal to Jews in Russia, urging them to remain loyal to the entente.[54] At the instigation of Lord Robert [Cecil], a confidential letter was sent to Leopold Greenberg asking him to draft a suitably worded statement and secure the signatures of 'a number of representative Jews in England'. Greenberg, although reluctant to comply ('I was not very much in favour of the idea and did it only because the Foreign Office asked me'), nevertheless came up with what can only be described as a gushing declaration. He made much of the fact that in 1914: '... the Jews of Great Britain and the Jews of Russia found themselves in this war fighting side by side' for the 'Jewish ideals' of liberty, justice and the rule of law, in opposition to the barbarism and antisemitism perpetuated by Prussian militarism etc., etc. ... The one inconvenient fact which marred this cosy picture of solidarity in the face of the common enemy was lightly dismissed by Greenberg in the following terms:

> This [solidarity] mitigated the natural regret which it was inevitable we should feel that the conditions and circumstances of world politics brought into the Alliance, struggling for the free-

dom of the world, the wickedness and cruelty of Tsardom. But that was, after all, an incident.[55]

Nothing came of Greenberg's appeal owing to the reluctance of other leading British Jews to affix their signatures to it. Israel Zangwill, for one, doubted the wisdom of the plan. He wrote directly to Lord Robert, regretting that he could not bring himself to sign the letter as: 'there is no political unity in Russian Jewry to which an appeal could be addressed, and to assume that there is, might be to endanger the general Jewish position there.' Thus, Zangwill raised the same objection as Wolf had done in response to Gunsburg's original request for Anglo-Jewish intervention back in April 1917. Like Wolf, Zangwill had another misgiving:

> Moreover, I do not know the exact footing on which England and Russia now stand; but in today's *Evening Standard* I see a violent article treating the Russian Jew in our midst almost as an alien enemy. A message from English Jews to Russian in the present dubious situation, might well be misunderstood in both countries.[56]

Once more, domestic circumstances – this time press agitation which linked anti-Bolshevism with anti-alienism – contributed to the modification of Anglo-Jewish responses to the Russian Revolution.

It was natural that, after the October Revolution, the community desired to put as great a distance as possible between Jews and Bolshevism. Beginning with a letter from Leopold Greenberg to *The Times* in November 1917, numerous statements were put out by leading British Jews repudiating the connection between Jews and Bolshevism – and, more fundamentally, between Judaism and Communism. Given that 'Bolshevism has lately been represented as a Semitic movement to undermine the foundations of Christian civilisation', the Zionist leader Israel Cohen found it necessary to point out that:

> Those who engage in such a demonstration must be utterly oblivious both of the sources of the Christian faith and also of the character of Jewish doctrine. For Jesus drew his spiritual ideas from Jewish teachers, and the fundamental principle of Judaism in practice is social righteousness.[57]

109

The standard argument against the political involvement of Jews in Bolshevism ran as follows: Whilst it could not be denied that a handful of leading Bolsheviks were 'of Jewish extraction' – that, indeed, was the whole problem – they were entirely unrepresentative. Even within the context of the Bolshevik Party itself, these Jews did not accurately reflect the make-up of the rank and file membership, which was predominantly Gentile. As the Russian Jewish liberal Reuben Blank pointed out in a report to the Conjoint Committee:

> The first generator of Bolshevism was the fleet at Kronstadt, into which not a single Jew was admitted; the second was the proletariat of Petrograd, a town into which only a rare Jew could find entry. From these two centres it spread to Great Russia, where the Jews constitute less than one per cent of the population.[58]

In the broader context of Marxist socialism, a far greater number of Jews were to be found among the Mensheviks than amongst the Bolsheviks – leaving aside the Bund. Above all, the Jewish Bolsheviks, 'long estranged from their co-religionists',[59] could in no way be considered representative of the Jewish community in Russia. Socially, the Jewish Bolsheviks were assimilated, Russified intellectuals, who had often spent many long years in the Emigration. They thus had little in common with the traditional Yiddish-speaking inhabitants of the Pale. Ideologically, they were renegades. As Israel Cohen put it:

> There is not a single active Jewish Bolshevist, I make bold to say, who is a conforming member of the Jewish community. Jews who have become Bolshevists, and especially Bolshevist leaders, have long ago severed their connection with the communion in which they were born. Neither Trotzky nor Radek nor any other Bolshevik leader of Jewish blood is a member of a synagogue or of any other Jewish institution.

Moreover,

> Their whole outlook, policy, and system of thought are anti-Jewish. They are not Jews by religion but free thinkers, nor are they Jews by nationality since they are anti-nationalists. The true Jew is a believer and a nationalist. The Bolshevik scoffs at all creeds and would efface all nationalities.

Marxist atheism and anti-nationalism ran directly counter to the attitudes of an overwhelmingly traditional Jewish community – and one, moreover, increasingly affected by Zionism. Cohen concluded that 'Jews who have adopted Bolshevism have left the Jewish community, which is no longer responsible for them.'

Bolshevism in practice meant not only an attack on all things Jewish, but also an attack on the basic structures of organised Jewish life: the synagogue, religious education – especially the teaching of Hebrew – social welfare institutions and Zionist clubs. This endangered the physical existence of the *kehilla*. Added to this, the fact that the majority of Russian Jews were occupied as artisans and traders made them likely victims, to a disproportionate degree, of Bolshevik economic experiments. For Bolshevik economics had no time for 'petty bourgeois' elements.

Having disposed of political and economic explanations for Jewish involvement in Bolshevism, Anglo-Jewish apologists were nevertheless willing to accept the 'education theory' as containing some validity. Israel Zangwill was fond of quoting the Samuel Report on Poland:

> Bolshevism requires a vast administration and propaganda, which in turn requires that men shall at least be able to read and write. But in the proletariat of Eastern Europe only the Jews possess these accomplishments, and therefore the administrators and propagandists of Bolshevism must necessarily be Jews.[60]

In all of the above arguments, Jewish polemicists were on sure ground. Unfortunately, however, at least one, Israel Cohen, was guilty of 'spoiling his own case' by exaggeration. This Zionist accused the Communists of being old-fashioned antisemites. In his contribution to *The Times* debate on 'Jews and Bolshevism' (December 1919), Cohen claimed that 'The Red Army carried out regular pogroms in the summer of 1918 ... the antisemitism of the Red Army is notorious.' Whilst it is true that, in some instances, atrocities were committed by Soviet troops, antisemitic violence or discrimination against Jews was nowhere sanctioned by Bolshevik theory. Thus Cohen erred when he wrote that Lenin was 'an apostle of Jewish pogroms, by which he thought, through the massacre of the Jewish bourgeoisie he could hasten his communist paradise.'[61] The fact that Bolshevik formulations on the Jewish question were far too sophisticated to be equated with antisemitism in the recognised sense, had not yet been grasped by the Zionist publicist.

The publication of the *Protocols of the Elders of Zion* and the allegation of Jewish complicity in the assassination of the tsar, contained in the government white paper *Russia No. I*, marked the high point of antisemitic agitation in Britain in the immediate aftermath of the Russian Revolution. When taken together, these two *bilbulim* (calumnies) posed a challenge to the Anglo-Jewish community which could not be ignored. Certainly the *Jewish Chronicle* would have liked 'to treat [this] rubbish with the silent contempt which Jewish self-respect demands. If *The Times* and other equally well-disposed journals wish to rummage in such literary garbage, they can find it at almost every street corner in Russia.'[62] But a policy of 'no comment' would make no difference in the propaganda war. Lucien Wolf made up his mind not to let the case go by default, above all as he did not doubt that the campaign was being waged for sinister political ends. Right-wing elements in Britain were working hand in hand with White Russian emigrés to promote the war of intervention against the Bolsheviks. They deliberately manipulated the 'Jewish Bogey' in order to give their propaganda greater impact. There was no alternative but to go onto the counter-offensive. Wolf took the responsibility upon himself. He spent a good deal of time researching into the background of the *Protocols* and the murder of the Tsar. His findings on the former subject appeared in a series of letters to the press during 1920. Regarding the Imperial family, Wolf amassed a dossier of evidence to disprove the indictment against the Jews.[63] His file contained three important documents:

(1) The conclusions of the investigation carried out by Professor Nikander Mirolyubov, the Procurator of the High Court of Kazan (which administered the Ekaterinburg region) at the behest of Kolchak's Ministry of Justice, dated December 1918.

(2) The testimony of the Minister of Justice himself, Starynkevitch, made in an interview with Wolf's self-appointed Russian adviser, Reuben Blank.

(3) A report of the inquiry conducted by the Soviet authorities in Perm

in September 1919 and published in a Russian emigré paper in Paris.

Not a single Jew was incriminated in any of these statements. Wolf duly sent all of this material to the Foreign Office, together with a covering note demanding to know just where General Knox had got *his* information from. The original source, it transpired, had been General Deterikhs, friend of *The Times* correspondent Robert Wilton and notorious antisemite, who was responsible for the circulation of a nasty little pamphlet entitled *The Jews have Murdered the Tsar* amongst the White forces in Siberia. This fact raised several awkward questions which the Foreign Office was loath to answer. Since it was established that the British High Commissioner in Siberia, Charles Eliot, had been presented with a copy of the Kolchak report on the murder, why had he not handed it over to Whitehall? Assuming that he had, why had the official report been excluded from the government white paper, while it had been seen fit to include Knox's unsubstantiated allegations? The Foreign Office's reluctance to answer these questions, plus their apparent desire to keep their correspondence with Wolf as confidential as possible, goaded the latter into print. He sent all the evidence, including the Kolchak report, to the press, where it appeared in full on 18 August 1920.[64] As in the case of the *Protocols*, Wolf arranged for the publication of a special edition under the aegis of the Board of Deputies. However, he did not go as far as the *Jewish Guardian* which demanded that the whole affair be raised in Parliament.

By October 1920, the Board of Deputies had decided that a more coordinated response to newspaper – and indeed officially sanctioned – antisemitism was called for. Since the existing Press Committee (established in April 1918) was not capable of meeting the present need, it was expanded into a fully fledged Press Agency, modelled upon the B'nai Brith Anti-Defamation League in the United States. Its functions were divided up between two sections: a publicity department, whose job it was to monitor and deal with specific cases of antisemitism, and the Press Agency proper designed to disseminate information on Jewish affairs to the media in general on a regular basis.[65] The *Jewish Guardian* welcomed the development; the *Chronicle* was not so sure. Greenberg felt that the existence of the agency might only serve to create still more unsolicited publicity for the community, with further distortion of the facts a likely result. Above all, he was sceptical about the agency's effectiveness at fending off attacks. After all, the editor ruefully observed, the *Jewish Chronicle* itself had been 'fighting antisemitism for the last three-quarters of a century without much to show for it'.[66] It was a thankless and somewhat futile task.

The charge of 'Jewish Bolshevism' was strenuously denied by established Anglo-Jewry. Unfortunately, in the political climate following the First World War and the Russian Revolution, the case for the defence, coloured by over-sensitivity anyway, failed to convince. Indeed, it was in many respects inadequate. It was simply not sufficient to argue that Trotsky was not 'Jewish' because he did not practise the Jewish religion or because he did not identify with the Jewish community. It was also useless to protest that Bolshevik ideology, unsympathetic to Jewish concerns in theory, persecuted Jews in practice – if not physically, by pogrom (although this was claimed too), then spiritually, by a campaign against religion, Zionism and the Hebrew language; for this line of argument did not 'wash' in the face of the primarily racial type of antisemitism which emerged after the war. Trotsky could indeed be identified as a Jew on a 'racial' criterion, however far removed he was from Jewish life in Russia.

The inadequacy of the community's response is most evident *vis-à-vis* the *Protocols* and the allegation that the Jews had murdered the tsar. Here, Lucien Wolf abandoned his own rule of never becoming embroiled in public controversy on the question of Jews and Bolshevism.[67] He was fond of quoting Disraeli's maxim: 'Never complain and never explain'. He now set out to 'expose' the allegations, but given the dearth of hard evidence, any debate was bound to be inconclusive. All he succeeded in doing was to give some credence to the charges. The *Protocols* anyway did not lend themselves to rational scrutiny. This particular myth was made of the most durable stuff.

Finally, it is hard to say what Anglo-Jewry could have done in the situation. They were trapped in a dilemma, as Wolf's uncharacteristic change of tactics testified. Not to reply, effectively meant that the case would go uncontested. The alternative course of action ran the risk of being interpreted as apologetics. The Jewish community had lost the initiative to the antisemites at the very outset. They were therefore placed in an unenviable position.

PUBLIC PROTEST

> We Jews have to be more careful than other people.
>
> > Hermann Gollancz in the *Jewish Chronicle*,
> > 11 May 1917

> 2000 years of tact are enough for any nation: in face of the pogroms going on everywhere despite it, it is high time to try another policy.
>
> > Letter of Israel Zangwill, 29 March 1919
> > (Central Zionist Archives, A36)

> He quite saw that the Zionists could not remain silent on the subject, but he would prefer them to wait a little longer before starting a public agitation. And he saw a difficulty in the fact that a Zionist protest against anti-Jewish excesses may be met by the counter charge that the Jews were responsible for excesses in Russia. ... I told Sir George that I fully appreciated his point of view but could not regard it as absolutely satisfactory. We were already told that Jews were responsible for Bolshevik misdoings and it did not need a protest against anti-Jewish excesses to stimulate that accusation.
>
> > Chaim Weizmann: interview with Sir George Clarke at the Foreign Office, 28 November 1918 (Weizmann Archive)

'Quiet diplomacy' did not suit the disposition of all members of the Anglo-Jewish elite. On the contrary, Israel Zangwill and others favoured the greatest possible publicity for the desperate plight of the Jews in eastern Europe. They wanted a campaign consisting of broadsheets, relief appeals, letters, petitions and mass meetings to draw attention to the issue. In current terminology these leaders wanted an organised Jewish lobby to make a foray into 'pressure-group politics'. Even in 1919, indeed, such a concept was by no means new. Precedents had been set with the Mansion House meetings of 1840, 1881 and 1892. Protests had also been organised in 1903, in both Britain and America, following the Kishinev pogrom. So 26 June 1919 was declared a 'Day of Mourning' for Polish Jewry and an estimated 100,000 people marched through central London. The event was given considerable coverage in the press. A *Times* leader commented that it had 'made a deep impression on public opinion'.[68] Yet a concensus among the communal *makhers* (bosses) on the question of tactics was totally lacking. The sharp division between those who emphasised discreet diplomacy and those who advocated public protest was profound. It was natural that the conflict over tactics should reflect deeper differences within the community regarding essential issues: the political course of the Russian Revolution, British intervention, the nature of Bolshevism itself and the Jewish role in the Bolshevik regime.

The Polish demonstration provides a good illustration of this disunity. 'In view of the delicate nature ... of the political situation',[69] the Board of Deputies opted for a purely religious format: a memorial service addressed by the Chief Rabbi and Reverend Morris Joseph at the Queen's Hall in the West End. In his sermon, Dr Hertz rounded upon the Polish antisemites' 'tooth-and-nail' policy of exterminating the three million Jews in Poland, on the mere pretext that they were all Bolsheviks.[70] He also attacked the Allied governments who, despite high-sounding phrases about liberty and equality, had done nothing to put an end to the massacre and he publicly announced that he was placing a proposal for an Allied commission of inquiry before the Foreign Office. Dr Hertz's criticisms, however, and those of the Day of Protest as a whole, were confined exclusively to the situation in Poland. It is significant that only a passing reference was made to the Ukraine, where, after all, pogroms were taking place on a far larger scale. That fleeting reference was to absolve Great Britain from any 'responsibility' for the anarchy in south Russia in spite of her part in the intervention.

It was clear that the majority of Anglo-Jewish leaders were not prepared to overstep certain limits when making a public protest. They were reluctant to indulge in overt political activity, especially with regard to the pogroms in the Ukraine. This, they feared, could all too easily be misinterpreted – or misrepresented – as anti-interventionism or even pro-Bolshevism by right-wing opinion at home. Sir Philip Magnus was indeed so concerned about the possible damage which the Day of Mourning could do to the Jewish community's public image that he informed the Foreign Office of his opposition to it in advance. He felt that the demonstration could scupper all of Lucien Wolf's 'back door diplomacy'. In the event Magnus's private approach to the powers-that-be simply earned him the condemnation of both the Board and the *Jewish Chronicle* for his 'little exercise in communal Bolshevism'.[71]

The East End, in contrast, suffered from no such compunctions. Schools, shops and businesses closed down for the day out of solidarity with Polish Jewry. The Yiddish newspapers were printed with thick black borders. Two large public meetings were organised, one at the Peoples' Palace at which the Sephardi *Haham* Dr Gaster was the principal speaker, the other at the Pavilion Theatre, presided over by Israel Zangwill. Later a procession of an estimated 30,000–40,000 people marched to a rally in Hyde Park. In short, the ghetto had seized the initiative. The *Poale Tsion* (Labour Zionist) newspaper *Unzer Veg* commented that perhaps for the first time, the East End had shown its strength in terms both of numbers and organisation. The unity and discipline displayed in Whitechapel stood out in stark contrast to the wavering of the 'plutocrats' and '*golukhim*' (literally 'priests', i.e. 'non-Jewish' Jews) of the West End, who had merely been 'ready to liquidate the protest movement with a prayer'.[72] Meetings also took place in the provinces – most notably in Manchester.

Lucien Wolf's position *vis-à-vis* the Foreign Office predisposed him towards 'quiet diplomacy' rather than 'public protest'. Wolf's attitude is well illustrated by the stance he adopted during the Hartzfeld affair in August 1919.[73] Hartzfeld had already submitted his report on antisemitism in the British Army of Intervention to the United States government. It was, according to Wolf, 'couched in very strong terms'. He was now seeking an interview with Felix Warburg, Louis Marshall and with President Wilson himself, with the intention of putting pressure on them to make representations to the British. Wolf strongly disapproved of this attempt to make 'international mischief'. His reason was that it was likely to be counterproductive.

> The British Government would not listen to a foreign Government in such a matter, and British public opinion, whether Jew or Gentile, would resent any attack by foreigners on British officers, who are fighting the battles of their country, however badly they have acted.

Such a move would also focus further unfavourable attention on the Anglo-Jewish community:

> All sorts of bad blood would be made, all the unhappy facts about

Jewish participation in Bolshevism would be raked over afresh and exaggerated, and in short the Jews would end by making fresh enemies and getting no redress at all.

Wolf regretted that Hartzfeld had sent his findings not only to the US government, but also to the *Jewish Chronicle*, although this had been on the understanding that they were confidential and were not to be published without the assent of Stuart Samuel, 'I [Wolf] said it was very unfortunate that he [Hartzfeld] had taken Greenberg into his confidence, as his discretion was not to be relied upon. He [Hartzfeld] rather discomforted me by saying that I had introduced him to Greenberg.'

Hartzfeld himself did not agree with Wolf's 'softly-softly' approach: 'He was inclined to think that some outside pressure was necessary.' Wolf discouraged him: 'I replied that it was not necessary at all.' Because, as he recorded in his diary, 'We might be trusted to "wallop our own niggers" [*sic*] and if he had confidentially communicated the facts to us we should have placed them before our Government with the absolute certainty that the mischief would be dealt with without any scandal.'

Wolf at length managed to persuade the American to wait upon the decision of the Conjoint Committee before taking any further action. Meanwhile, Claude Montefiore raised the issue with Lord Milner, and Wolf himself with E.H. Carr the historian, who was then at the Foreign Office and a member of the British delegation to the Paris peace conference. The latter, apparently, took the matter very seriously. At the interview 'he said nothing', but ten days later produced an official statement confirming the allegations and containing an apology of sorts:

> [The antisemitic materials had been published] at a moment of great pressure and were the work of Russian officers attached to the intelligence sections of the Expeditionary Forces who had not been properly controlled. The technical responsibility for them, however, rested with the British Generals.

For 'Ten thousand copies ... [had been] ... issued under their general authority and distributed by British aeroplanes.' The government 'regretted the incident' and promised it would not happen again. Thus, Wolf's brand of 'quiet diplomacy' had succeeded in extracting this, not entirely satisfactory, disclaimer from the Foreign Office. It remains questionable whether the public lobby tactics favoured by American Jewish leaders would have produced any better results in the British context. Wolf may have been right after all.

Hands off Russia!

It was not necessary to go 'down the East End' in order to find views on the Russian Revolution at variance with those held by most of the Anglo-Jewish establishment.

The 'maverick' writer Israel Zangwill was in the vanguard of public protest tactics. He was not prepared to restrict himself to mere demonstrations against pogroms, but was determined to place his protest where he believed it rightfully belonged – in the broader political context. He was most outspoken in his criticism of British policy in Russia – and against Anglo-Jewry's apparent willingness to acquiesce before it. Nor was he content to vent his feelings on the pages of the *Jewish Chronicle*; he was quite ready to take his protest into the forum of public debate. On 8 February 1919 Zangwill addressed an anti-intervention rally organised by the Marxist British Socialist Party, at the Royal Albert Hall. He shared the platform with prominent figures in the labour movement, and made a rousing speech in which he advised the Allies to keep their 'Hands off Russia ... until they are clean'.[74]

Zangwill had thus asserted his right to speak out publicly against government policy. As a British citizen he demanded and took full advantage of the right of free speech. As a thinking liberal, he insisted that this right was indivisible; it extended to all – even to the British Bolshevik. He wrote to the *Morning Post*:

> I cannot understand what you mean by regarding even the British Bolshevist as the enemy of his country. Bolshevism ... does not necessarily imply revolution or violence; and to seek to change the economic structure of one's country has never hitherto been considered disloyal.[75]

It followed therefore that British Jews – even Bolshevik ones – should also enjoy free speech in a democracy. Zangwill agreed with Leopold Greenberg, who wrote in the *Jewish World* that, since Bolshevism was 'not illegal as a principle', then why should not Jews 'merely because they are Jews' be allowed to 'join in its propagation if they believe in it?'[76] Fundamentally, both writers realised that the Jewish right to speak out was a yardstick by which the progress of Jewish emancipation in Britain could be measured. If Jews really had obtained *de facto* as well as *de jure* civil and political equality with other British citizens, then they shared, in equal proportion, the right *as Jews* to dissent.

The fact nevertheless remains, that Zangwill, *the Jew*, had appeared on a platform in compromising company. That he professed not to have seen 'The famous red flags draped in black for Rosa Luxemburg and Liebknecht' at the 'Hands Off Russia' demonstration was irrelevant. That he was the only Jewish speaker present was also no defence. Indeed it was precisely the fact that he *was* the only Jewish speaker, and a well-known Jewish writer at that, which landed Zangwill in trouble. Predictably, his lack of circumspection was pounced upon by the ultra-Conservative press. The *Morning Post* portrayed him not only as an opponent of intervention, but as a Bolshevik sympathiser, and as such somehow representative of Jewish opinion. The *Post* and its allies had no qualms about employing antisemitism as a weapon with which to discredit the anti-intervention movement.

It is arguable that Zangwill's stand was politically inept.[77] There is also some evidence that he regretted it. Yet his refusal to be bullied into silence by the likes of the *Morning Post* was courageous. Leopold Greenberg, in his capacity as the leading English-speaking journalist within Anglo-Jewry, took the same line. Barely a month after the Zangwill affair, Greenberg found himself at the centre of another, not dissimilar, controversy; only this was a vastly more serious one. It precipitated not just an assault on the community from without but led to a serious internal row.

THE 'LETTER OF THE TEN'

> Thou shalt not go up and down as a tale bearer among thy people, neither shalt thou stand against the blood of thy neighbour.
>
> Leviticus 19:16, quoted in the *Jewish World*, 30 April 1919

Under the heading 'Bolshevism and Jewry: A Repudiation', the following letter appeared in the London *Morning Post* on 23 April 1919:

The 'Letter of the Ten' as it appeared in the *Morning Post*, 23 April 1919

SIR – We have read with the deepest concern and with sincere regret certain articles which have recently appeared in two closely associated Jewish newspapers in this country on the topic of Bolshevism and its 'ideals'. In our opinion, the publication of these articles can have no other effect than to encourage the adoption of the theoretic principles of Russian Bolsheviks among foreign Jews who have sought and found a refuge in England. We welcome, accordingly, your suggestion that British Jews should 'disassociate themselves from a cause which is doing the Jewish people harm in all parts of the world'. This is profoundly true, and we, on our own behalf and on behalf of numbers of British Jews with whom we have conferred, desire to disassociate ourselves absolutely and unreservedly from the mischievous and misleading doctrine which these articles are calculated to disseminate. We repudiate them as dangerous in themselves and as false to the tenets and teachings of Judaism.

Partly in order to counteract the mistaken policy of the newspapers referred to, the League of British Jews was founded in November 1917. The proceedings and views of the League are published in a monthly bulletin, entitled *Jewish Opinion* which can be obtained at the offices of the League 708–709, Salisbury House, EC2, and which may eventually be merged in a larger journal appearing at more frequent intervals. For we thoroughly concur with your criticism that 'the British Jewish community, most of whom', as you rightly say, 'are by no means in sympathy with this [Nationalist] crusade, are being served very badly by their newspapers'. Meanwhile we take this opportunity of repudiating in public the particular statements in those newspapers to which you have felt it your duty to call attention. – Yours & c.

> Lionel de Rothschild, Swaythling, Philip Magnus, Marcus Samuel, Harry S. Samuel, Leonard L. Cohen, I. Gollancz, John Monash, Claude G. Montefiore, Isidore Spielman

The letter was signed by ten leading Jews who between them represented the cream of the Anglo-Jewish establishment. They numbered within their ranks three Conservative MPs (Rothschild, Magnus,

Harry Samuel), a privy councillor (Samuel again), a former lord mayor of London (Marcus Samuel), a couple of highly respected academics (Montefiore, Gollancz), a theatrical entrepreneur (Spielman) and two of the richest men in England (Rothschild and Marcus Samuel, later Lord Bearsted). Their communal connections were unrivalled. Rothschild was president of the United Synagogue, Swaythling of the Federation, Magnus an ex-president of the West London Reform synagogue and Montefiore a founder of the Liberal Jewish Religious Union. Cohen was president of the Jewish Board of Guardians and Montefiore of the Anglo-Jewish Association. Finally, there was Lieutenant-General Sir John Monash, the only non-Briton on the list, who was the commander of the Australian forces in France during the First World War.

At the time, this celebrated 'Letter of the Ten', as it very soon came to be called, had a dramatic effect. Externally, it focused hostile attention on Anglo-Jewry; internally, it led to a communal row of the first order. The episode remains somewhat controversial even now. According to the dominant view favoured by Zionist historians, the letter should be regarded as a function of the contemporary debate over Jewish nationalism, as a symptom of the continuing battle between English Zionists and British Jews for the domination of the community. The purpose of this section is to trace the development of the dispute about the 'Letter of the Ten' and to analyse the issues it raised. In so doing, I shall venture an alternative and really much more straightforward explanation of the letter's purpose and significance, one that challenges the traditional interpretation.

In the *Jewish Chronicle* of 28 March and 4 April 1919, there appeared a two-part special article entitled, 'Peace, War – and Bolshevism'. It was written by the regular contributor, 'Mentor', who was none other than the editor himself, Leopold J. Greenberg. In the course of the article, Greenberg declared: 'Bolshevism is at once the most serious menace to, and the best hope of Civilisation ... in Bolshevism there lies, today, the hope of Humanity'. He went on to argue that Bolshevism was a protest against the old social order that had tolerated both Russian tsarism and German militarism. Bolshevism was, therefore a terrible warning to the west to come to grips with its own social problems in the era of reconstruction. In this way, and in this way alone, was Bolshevism to be seen as a progressive force. But intrinsically 'it is a political disease, an economic infliction, a social disaster'. 'Mentor' was not content to leave his somewhat paradoxical thesis at that, however. Having drawn a distinction between the ideals of Bolshevism and its methods, he continued: '[T]he ideals of Bolshevism at many points are consonant with the finest ideals of Judaism, some of which went to form the basis of the best teachings of the founder of Christianity'. It is for this reason that Bolshevism has found 'so many' adherents among Jews, 'the Jew ... is an idealist or nothing'.

The dialectical character of Greenberg's article unfortunately proved too subtle for some. It was susceptible to misinterpretation and to misquotation.[78] But it was not *The Times* or the *Morning Post* that first drew attention to the *Jewish Chronicle*'s apparent Bolshevik sympathies, but the ten highly respectable members of the Anglo-Jewish establishment. They took it upon themselves to send their letter of protest not, as might be expected, to the editor of the *Jewish Chronicle* but to the editor of the *Morning Post*. The 'Letter of the Ten' was duly published on 23 April. 'The Ten' accused the Jewish press (i.e., the *Jewish Chronicle* and the *Jewish World*, Greenberg's papers), although not by name, of 'encourag[ing] the adoption of the theoretic principles of Russian Bolsheviks among foreign Jews who have sought and found a refuge in England'. They set on record their endorsement of the *Morning Post*'s editorial of 8 April that had called on British Jews to 'disassociate themselves from a cause that is doing the Jewish people harm in all parts of the world'. Since 'the Ten' found this statement to be 'profoundly true', they desired 'to disassociate ourselves absolutely and unreservedly from the mischievous and misleading doctrine which these articles are calculated to disseminate. We repudiate them as dangerous in themselves and false to the tenets and teachings of Judaism'.

The rationale that lay behind the letter was subsequently spelled out by a member of the League of British Jews in the *Jewish World*:

> [Its] object was to obtain from the *Morning Post* a cessation of its antisemitic writings against us Jews who belong to this country, by showing that we are truly British to the very core, and are associated heart and soul with the British people in our detestation of Bolshevism.[79]

In other words, the 'Letter of the Ten' was the latest move in the long-running campaign on behalf of Anglo-Jewry to meet the external challenge of antisemitism in the form of anti-Bolshevism. It was written with the express purpose of denying Jewish connivance with Bolshevism in the interest of upholding the good name of the community. The letter was moreover, stimulated in the first instance by the internal political debate about the Russian Revolution that, despite attempts to discourage it, now continued with even greater fervour than hitherto.

The publication of the letter led to a full-scale confrontation within the community. Greenberg, not unnaturally, was incensed. He immediately fired off a note to the *Morning Post* in which he wrote that the *Jewish Chronicle* and the *Jewish World* 'have never given the slightest encouragement or support to Bolshevism'.[80] As for 'the Ten', he accused them in the columns of his own papers of committing a grave political blunder. If, as they claimed, their object had really been 'to obtain from the *Morning Post* a cessation of its antisemitic writings', then they had somewhat ingenuously played right into the hands of that same antisemitic press. For it was clear that the letter itself could be taken as proof that Jews, to a significant degree, were indeed Bolsheviks.

H.A. Gwynne, the editor of the *Morning Post*, was certainly gratified:

> We have never alleged, nor do we believe, that the leaders of the British Jews, nor the British Jews as a community, have approved of or countenanced this [Bolshevik] propaganda. We have, however, remarked more than once that their silence may be misinterpreted. That misinterpretation is no longer possible after the letter which we publish today.

A few days later, the *Morning Post* intoned further:

> We received a very striking testimony to the honesty as well as the truth of our warning in a letter signed by ten leading British Jews. That letter is a sufficient answer to the charge that we have been influenced to make the statements [on the association of Jews with Bolshevism] by the spirit of antisemitism. If these statements are supported by Major Lionel de Rothschild, Lord Swaythling, Sir Philip Magnus, Sir Marcus Samuel, Sir Harry Samuel, Mr Leonard Cohen, Professor Israel Gollancz, General Sir John

Monash, Mr. Claude Montefiore and Sir Isidore Spielman, we are sufficiently absolved from the charges both of bearing false testimony and of antisemitism. It would be absurd to suppose that these ten representative Jews would join in a baseless charge inspired by antisemitism. These ten Jews also saw the danger to England and the Jewish community and they felt it their duty to support and emphasise our warning. If the Jewish press publishes articles which are likely to prejudice the Jewish community in the eyes of the British public, and if distinguished Jews attend Bolshevik meetings in London, it is the part of the good Jew to denounce these things.[81]

This distinction between supposed good (loyal) and bad (subversive) Jews was one of Gwynne's favourite themes. As he later wrote in his book *The Cause of World Unrest*:

[I]t would be downright wicked to ascribe to Jewry as a whole this mad and dangerous policy [of promoting 'World Unrest']. In that direction lies the danger, the hideous danger of a violent and indiscriminate antisemitism. It must be averted by the Jews themselves. The honest, patriotic Jews must come forward and denounce ... the revolutionaries of their race ... for the time has come when there can be no sitting on the fence; those who are not with us are against us.[82]

In short, the onus was on the Jews. They were assumed to be guilty until they proved they were actually innocent. The *Morning Post*'s constant reference to the 'Letter of the Ten', with the implication that the repudiation it contained needed constant reiteration, also bore witness to the failure of 'the Ten' to achieve their declared aim. A public plea of not guilty did not mean that the charge was dropped.

The week following the publication of the letter, 'Mentor' contributed another article to the *Jewish Chronicle*, this time about the role of *mosrim* in Jewish history. *Mosrim* were Jews who betrayed their community in order to curry favour with a foreign master. It was a thinly veiled attack on 'the Ten' that was not lost even on the *Morning Post*. As far as Greenberg was concerned this *minyan mosrim* (quorum of traitors) had committed the cardinal sin of 'denouncing fellow Jews in circles outside their own people', and in an antisemitic journal to boot: 'At a time when our people are surrounded by alert and active foes, these men think it wise, and prudent, and tactful – and Jewish – to mumble the stock accusations of our enemies, and to carry a domestic quarrel to them for arbitrament.' They were guilty of stupidity if not of downright treachery: 'They sought to exculpate themselves ... from the *Morning Post*'s ridiculous charge of the association of Jews with Bolshevism, by fixing that charge upon other Jews.'[83] In other words, 'the Ten' had been intimidated by the antisemitic press into breaking ranks: 'The "Letter of the Ten" associated with Bolshevism a large proportion of the Anglo-Jewish community, while the signatories dis-associated themselves from their brethren by calling them "foreign".'[84] 'The Ten' aimed at nothing less, Greenberg clearly suggested, than creating a distinction between the East End and the West End branches of British Jewry – between natives and immigrants, rich and poor, British and Russian.

Down in the East End ghetto, where perhaps some 100,000 im-migrants from eastern Europe were congregated by 1914, the 'Letter of the Ten' was certainly interpreted in this way. The Yiddish press, led by Morris Myer's influential *Di Tsayt*, condemned the ten *yehudim* for their betrayal of the great mass of *yidn*.[85] It was a divisive act by a privileged few calculated to ingratiate themselves at the expense of the many. It was also dishonest. As Greenberg put it: 'We refuse to coun-tenance a division of our community into those who came here yester-day and those who came here the day before.'[86]

The essential expediency that lay behind the policy of 'the Ten' was satirised by Israel Cohen in a letter to *The Times* in December 1919. He wrote in reply to the contribution by a self-styled 'English-born Jew' that had been published by *The Times* in its series on 'Jews and Bolshevism':

> Your correspondent ... would seem to belong to the class of Jew ... always anxious to cast overboard any fellow Jews who are pointed to as inconvenient Jonahs. Today he is bent upon disas-sociating himself as an English Jew from his Russian brethren because the latter are involved in Bolshevism. Yesterday he was anxious to disassociate himself from his German brethren be-cause they were involved in Prussian militarism. He is desirous of disclaiming a Trotsky as a fellow Jew, while doubtless willing to bask in the reflected glory of an Einstein.[87]

The 'Letter of the Ten' was the subject of a stormy meeting of the Board of Deputies on 29 April. After much argument, the following resolution was passed:

> That this Board deprecates the letter which appeared in the *Morning Post* of the 23rd [April] inst. signed by ten members of the 'League of British Jews', as it differentiates between British and foreign Jews. This Board, on behalf of the Anglo-Jewish community which it represents, repudiates any sympathy with Bolshevism.[88]

This resolution was welcomed by synagogues, trade unions, friendly societies and Zionist clubs, especially in the East End. It was also endorsed by the Yiddish press. As socialists and with strong grass-roots links, journalists like Morris Myer and his colleague Joshua Podruzhnik regarded the motion that had been passed by the Board as a victory for the forces of democracy within the Anglo-Jewish establishment over an irresponsible oligarchical elite. The battle over the 'Letter of the Ten' was part of the class struggle between the East and the West Ends for control of the institutions of Anglo-Jewry. Leopold Greenberg, who was identified with the more liberal wing of the establishment, having always taken it upon himself to speak for the East End, was also well pleased. He was satisfied that 'the Ten' had been duly rebuked for their 'fit of communal Bolshevism', their attempt to arrogate to themselves the prerogative of the Board in speaking on behalf of the community.[89]

Even so, Greenberg had some misgivings. He questioned the wisdom of an official Jewish body making a formal repudiation of Bolshevism. Although condemning the action of 'the Ten', the Board had at the same time adopted much of their logic. It, too, sought to disassociate itself formally and publicly from Bolshevism in the interests of the Jewish community's reputation. The only difference was that the Board claimed to speak in the name of all sections of that community, British and foreign-born alike. Greenberg feared that by publicly denying the legitimacy of the original letter, the Board could be seen as acknowledging – and perhaps even condoning – the existence of Bolshevik sympathies among Jews. The *Morning Post* certainly took the resolution in this way.

> We are bound to say that we are considerably disturbed by the fact that the Board of Deputies, while it repudiates any sympathy

with Bolshevism, should deprecate the Letter of the Ten. For if it is to be regarded as a crime for Jews to be Englishmen first and Jews afterwards, we are led to conclusions which will be as obvious to logical Jews as to thinking Englishmen.[90]

In sum, neither the letter itself nor its repudiation by the Board had succeeded in achieving that which their authors had intended.

Serious as this situation was, the baleful consequences of the 'Letter of the Ten' were not likely to end there. Greenberg was equally concerned about its possible repercussions on the position of the immigrants in the East End and on their relatives in Russia itself. After all, these relatives were in a far more vulnerable position. He quite rightly regarded the letter as obvious ammunition for the anti-alien lobby at home. Xenophobia directed against German spies and Russian Communists tended to go hand-in-hand with hostility to immigrants from central and eastern Europe in the years before, during and immediately after the First World War. Pressure for immigration restriction had borne fruit with the Aliens Act of 1905, the Aliens Restriction Act had been hurriedly passed on the outbreak of war.

By 1919, agitation was growing for the extension of the latter measure in both time and scope. The original legislation already provided for the compulsory wartime registration of all aliens in Britain (not only 'enemy' but also 'friendly' and 'neutral' aliens) with the police. It gave the Home Secretary wide powers of exclusion and deportation without appeal. It was now decided, for the first time, to make certificates of naturalisation purchased by immigrants liable to revocation. The Anglo-Jewish community could not but look on these developments with alarm. The status of long-time Jewish residents would now be at risk. Moreover, as the situation in Russia deteriorated, a renewed outpouring of refugees to the west became increasingly likely. Yet the door was being slammed shut – not only in Britain but, more importantly, in America – at the very time when a massive flight from the *pogromshchiki* was about to take place.

In these circumstances, 'the Ten' provided the perfect pretext for the *Morning Post* to write:

> Ten of the most prominent of the British Jews were recently forced to protest in our columns against the Bolshevism of the Jewish press; that Bolshevism ... is manifest in the great con-

gregation of Eastern Jews which has swarmed of late years into this country, and is working in accord with the Bolshevist Jews of Russia.[91]

If English Jews felt it was fitting to imply that their Russian brethren were harbouring Bolshevik sympathies, then the *Morning Post* and the entire anti-alien camp was free to make the same allegation with impunity. Indeed, Greenberg suspected that 'the Ten' were deliberately stirring up anti-alienism in order to protect their own position. A recognisable pro-restrictionist element had certainly existed on the right wing of the established Jewish community since the beginning of mass immigration in the 1880s. The League of British Jews tended toward this approach. It was a position based, ultimately, on fear that the presence of aliens might lead to hostility against the existing community and threaten its hard-won civil and political rights. Within this group, there was no doubt some sympathy with the *Morning Post*, which had 'often thought that the British Jews were injuring their own position in this country by fathering all that dubious [Russian immigrant] community'.[92]

For his part, Greenberg rejected such attitudes outright, seeing them as the product not only of cowardice but of self-delusion. Following the serious pogrom perpetrated by the Poles at Pinsk, he wondered, ironically, '[W]hether there is a League of Polish Jews and, if so, whether some of them have been accusing their brethren in the public press'.[93] He almost seemed to be implying here that the League could be exposing the Jews to possible anti-alien riots in England as well as doing damage to the Jews in Russia.

In 1919, Russian Jewry was caught in the midst of a civil war. Jews were being massacred in their thousands by White Russians, Ukrainians and Poles on the pretext that they were Bolsheviks. In this situation, the Yiddish press in the East End of London was appalled that ten leading members of Anglo-Jewry had apparently lent a measure of credence to the idea that Bolshevism was attractive to eastern European (foreign) Jews.

In February 1920, the *Jewish Chronicle* gave due prominence to an interview with Captain D.I. Sandelson, a former financial adviser to the British Military Mission in Siberia, and also a Jew. According to his testimony, the 'Letter of the Ten', on its publication in Russia, had further encouraged the vitriolic antisemitic campaign that was then being waged in the Kolchak camp. Sandelson quoted a certain official of the Omsk government as expressing his approval of the fact that 'the English Jews [had] made such an outspoken statement'. The letter, he concluded, had proved to be 'a potent weapon in the armour of the Russian antisemites'. Sandelson also graphically described how the beleaguered Jewish community in Siberia, which had looked to western Jewry for some measure of protection, was shattered by the 'Letter of the Ten'. He praised the Haham, Dr Gaster, and the *Jewish Chronicle* as well as the various communal institutions that had registered their disapproval in an effort to salvage what they could from the situation.[94]

Clearly, the 'Letter of the Ten' had inadvertently lent ammunition to those who saw the Jews as Bolshevik and could only further strain the relationship between Russian Jewry and the Whites. On the other hand, its publication could hardly benefit Soviet-Jewish relations. The letter, after all, denounced Bolshevism as mischievous, misleading, dangerous. Months later, we find Greenberg loudly criticising Rabbi Samuel Daiches of the Polish Relief Committee for his claim that 'only two per cent' of Russian Jewry supported the Bolsheviks. This was, the editor scathingly remarked, 'by way of excuse or palliation in case the Committee should be charged with the heinous offence of having sent means to prevent some fellow Jews of communistic tendencies from starving'.[95] What, asked Greenberg, about the other 98 per cent? Were they to be portrayed as disloyal to their own *de facto* government? If so, they would no doubt have to face the consequences. In short, the publication of the 'Letter of the Ten' had, in the foreign arena, been irresponsible. Against the background of the Russian Civil War, the outcome of which was by no means certain, it could be dangerous for Jews in the west to make pronouncements that could be construed as identifying Russian Jewry with one side or the other in the conflict.

In June 1919 at the Paris peace conference, the Russian Jewish liberals, Maxim Vinaver and Baron Gunsburg, approached Lucien Wolf with a proposal that leading Jews in the west should affix their signatures to a new and international document that would follow the line of the 'Letter of the Ten'. Wolf objected in the strongest terms, not merely on the classic anti-nationalist grounds that the Jews as a 'religion had nothing to do with politics', but also because:

I feared too, that if we were to publish a manifesto ... we should only provoke a counter-manifesto from Jews in favour of Bolshevism, or at any rate some form of revolutionary socialism. We should then have it on permanent record that there was a strong tendency in this direction in the Jewish community. Hitherto we have been able to some extent to hide or obscure this fact.

Wolf agreed with Stuart Samuel, the president of the Board of Deputies, who reportedly thought

[T]hat Bolshevism is very much like the French Revolution, and ... one of these days we shall be honouring it in much the same way as we now honour the Revolution. He is also afraid that it may succeed, and in that event we shall have backed the wrong horse.[96]

The significance of the 'Letter of the Ten': alternative views

Traditional Anglo-Jewish historiography sees the political development of the community in terms of a power struggle for control of its important posts and institutions. A cleavage began to occur within the communal establishment during the period of mass immigration from Eastern Europe that began in the 1880s. One school of thought maintained that two distinct factions appeared within the leadership. On the one hand, there were those who favoured a generous open-door policy on immigration and concerned themselves with the social welfare of the new arrivals. They were, broadly speaking, pro-alien and during the First World War were critical of, or downright opposed to, the conscription of 'friendly aliens' into the British Army. This group took a prominent part in advocacy and public protest on behalf of Russian Jewry. It is further suggested that a linear correlation existed between this liberal accommodation of the immigrants and the growth of Zionism in Britain. Sympathy with the immigrant predicament tended to accompany sympathy with the supposedly most popular immigrant political cause – Jewish nationalism. In any case, the essential unity of the Jewish people, a fundamental tenet of Zionist theory, logically implied the protection of all Jews, including penniless refugees, in practice. On the other hand, there existed an opposing faction within the communal leadership that took up a contrary position on all of these issues.

Stuart Cohen in his *English Zionists and British Jews*[97] refers to the above interpretation as a 'type of Whig history', one favoured by Zionist historians. According to the model, the pro-immigrant and Zionist lobby was dynamic and democratic in character. It was bound to win because it was an expression of deep social change within the community. In contrast its opponents represented the status quo. They were a privileged elite intent on defending their vested interests. The battle was between nationalists and assimilationists, liberals and conservatives, for the soul of the community.

In May 1917 the split became open. Lucien Wolf had written to *The Times* criticising the negotiations between the Foreign Office and the English Zionist Federation over Palestine. At the Board of Deputies, this provoked a vote of censure of the Conjoint Foreign Affairs Committee, which was carried by a narrow majority. This apparent victory for the Zionists only resulted in greater polarisation, however. In November of that same year, the anti-Zionists formed themselves into the League of British Jews. The theoretical position of this organisation was founded on the Reform definition of Jewishness as being a purely religious and not a national attribute. It therefore denied the validity of the Zionist thesis that the Jews formed a separate political and national entity that needed a territorial base.

The League's philosophy amounted to an optimistic defence of the 'Jewish liberal compromise'. It was motivated by reasons both of principle and of expediency. On principle, the League asserted the importance of the struggle for emancipation in the east and the west. It was part of the general battle for liberalism and was related to the concept of the universalist Mission of the Jews. More practically, the spread of Zionism could undermine emancipation in the west by provoking accusations of dual loyalty. Zionism, the League argued, could and did inspire antisemitism.

In terms of numbers the League was tiny – it boasted only 18 members in 1917. Nevertheless, it wielded surprising influence. Its membership may have been small, but it was select, made up of representatives of the 'Cousinhood', prestigious for both wealth and intellect. Indeed, as Cohen points out, the vigour of their ideological argument has not been fully acknowledged. In October 1919 the

League founded its own newspaper, the *Jewish Guardian*, in order to propagate its views. The editor, Laurie Magnus, regarded it as a bid to break the monopoly far too long enjoyed by the pro-Zionist *Jewish Chronicle* and *Jewish World* under Leopold Greenberg.[98]

Stuart Cohen accepts this 'Whig' interpretation only up to a point. He certainly sees the anti-Conjoint Committee vote as something of a watershed. It represented a partial victory for the Zionists and a 'communal revolution of sorts' for the forces of democracy; but he regards such an explanation as too simplistic by itself. He questions the underlying assumption that a necessary correlation existed between Zionism and the defence of unrestricted immigration, between immigrants and democracy.

In the context of the problem we are examining here, it is significant that Cohen sees the 'Letter of the Ten', like the anti-Conjoint vote itself, as a pivotal stage in the development of the division within the Jewish establishment. Its importance is explained in terms of the debate over Zionism. The letter is used to illustrate the thesis that the Zionists had not achieved the 'conquest of the community' by the vote of censure. The Board of Deputies was not willing to pass the following motion that expressly defended Zionism against the League:

> That this Board disapproves of the letter in the *Morning Post* of the 23rd inst. signed by members of the League of British Jews, in as much as it casts the stigma of favouring Bolshevism on the Nationalist [Zionist] section, and many others of the Jewish community not members of the League, which is untrue ...[99]

Cohen is right to perceive the 'Letter of the Ten' as symptomatic of the debate over Zionism. Nevertheless, the fact remains that this was not made explicit at the time. Neither the actual wording of the letter nor the subsequent debate in the press were posed in terms of Zionism or anti-Zionism.[100] Greenberg was angry with the Leaguers for omitting to explain to the *Morning Post* that their action had been motivated by an internal conflict within the Jewish community over the merits of Jewish nationalism. Perhaps this was precisely because more immediate, external motivations had been primary.

We have seen how Anglo-Jewry was put under considerable pressure, especially by the right-wing press after the Russian Revolution. This pressure intensified with the Bolshevik takeover and the start of the Allied Intervention. Jews in Britain – both indigenous and immigrant – were suspected of anti-interventionist and pro-Bolshevik sympathies. Public relations, the communal image and self-defence became more than ever matters of crucial concern to the Jewish leadership. On this reading, the 'Letter of the Ten' should be taken at face value. It was simply the latest shot in a continuing campaign of Jewish self-defence, designed to stop the ceaseless accusations of Jewish involvement in Bolshevism made by the *Morning Post* and its ilk. Its purpose was to preserve the good name of Anglo-Jewry.

The difference was that in this instance, those who initiated the policy of reply had not obtained the sanction of the entire communal establishment. They could not claim, therefore, to be in any way representative of the whole of Anglo-Jewry in the broadest sense of that term. For the League of Jews, 'British by birth and nationality', recognised the connection made in right-wing propaganda between anti-Bolshevism and anti-alienism, and it endeavoured to disassociate itself from the immigrant wing.

The Leaguers took this step *not* because the East End was reputedly pro-Zionist – which, paradoxically, they also believed – but because it was supposed to be pro-Bolshevik. Both doctrines were regarded as alien imports and equally capable of undermining the loyalty of the newcomers to Britain. Winston Churchill was to argue in his article 'Zionism versus Bolshevism: A Struggle for the Soul of the Jewish People', published in 1920,[101] that a battle was taking place between these two ideologies for the mind of Russian Jewry. It seems that this battle had spilt over into the Russian Jewish community in London. Conflicting claims were made. English Zionists, wishing to project a popular image, maintained that Zionism was the most widely supported political position in the East End. Anti-Zionists, including Lucien Wolf, claimed that, on the contrary, primacy belonged to socialism, especially Bundism. In 1919 the League of British Jews simply accepted the thesis, inspired by antisemitism, that Russian Jews were Bolsheviks. Their subsequent display of patriotism was inspired by the anti-Bolshevik and anti-alien climate around them.

4 Zionism versus Bolshevism: 'A Struggle for the Soul of the Jewish People'

... it may well be that this same astonishing race [the Jews] may at the present time be in the actual process of producing another system of morals and philosophy, as malevolent as Christianity was benevolent, which, if not arrested, would shatter irretrievably all that Christianity has rendered possible. It would almost seem as if the gospel of Christ and the gospel of Anti-Christ were destined to originate among the same people; and that this mystic and mysterious race had been chosen for the supreme manifestations, both of the divine and the diabolical ...

There is no need to exaggerate the part played in the creation of Bolshevism and in the actual bringing about of the Russian Revolution by ... international and for the most part atheistical Jews. It is certainly a very great one; it probably outweighs all others ...

Zionism has already become a factor in the political convulsions of Russia, as a powerful competing influence in Bolshevik circles with the international communistic system ... The struggle which is now beginning between the Zionist and Bolshevik Jews is little less than a struggle for the soul of the Jewish people.

> Winston Churchill, *Illustrated Sunday Herald*, 8 February 1920

On 2 November 1917, the Balfour Declaration was made. Written in the form of a letter to 'Dear Lord Rothschild', it pledged British support for the creation of a 'national homeland for the Jewish people in Palestine'. Whatever its obscurities, this document represented, both then and now, a diplomatic victory for the Zionist leadership in

London. On 7 November 1917, the Bolshevik Revolution took place in Petrograd, marking the end of the liberal interlude in Russia. Leon Trotsky oversaw the planning and execution of the coup. These two historic events were entirely unconnected, yet they had one thing in common – the fact that Jews, and east European Jews in particular, played a central role in both. This coincidence focused the interest of government and press in Britain upon the Jewish 'problem'. British thinking on this subject was characterised by contradiction.

The Russian Revolution produced alarm about the 'peril' of 'Jewish Bolshevism', yet significant advance in the fortunes of the Jewish national cause took place despite this unpropitious atmosphere. Zionism evoked a positive response in Britain. A greater awareness of political and social change in Russia and misconceptions about the Jewish role in this upheaval each played an important part in the debate over Zionism in England. This applied with equal force to the discussions taking place within the Anglo-Jewish community, the Zionist leadership and, above all, within the government itself. In official circles, a paradoxical relationship existed between the growth of Zionism in Britain during the First World War and the development of antisemitism parading as anti-Bolshevism.

In February 1920, an article by the Secretary of State for War, Winston Churchill, appeared in the *Illustrated Sunday Herald* entitled, 'Zionism versus Bolshevism: A Struggle for the Soul of the Jewish People'. There were, in Churchill's view, three different political types within Jewry: one 'good', one 'bad' and one 'indifferent'. First, there is what he terms the 'national' Jew, who defines himself thus: 'I am an Englishman practising the Jewish faith.' Such a person exemplifies the diaspora Jew, in both east and west, who believes in the promise of emancipation and who responds with undivided loyalty to the host nation. To Churchill this is a 'worthy conception', for the contribution of such Jews to finance and industry and in the spheres of progressive politics and military service, was considerable.

In sharp contrast to the 'national' Jew, Churchill maintained, was the 'international Jew', that is the revolutionary Jew, and the Marxist revolutionary Jew in particular. This type was destructive and dangerous, as had been clearly witnessed in the Russian Revolution. Churchill explicated the intimate connection between Jews and Bolshevism:

ZIONISM versus BOLSHEVISM.

A STRUGGLE FOR THE SOUL OF THE JEWISH PEOPLE.

By the Rt. Hon. WINSTON S. CHURCHILL.

SOME people like Jews and some do not; but no thoughtful man can doubt the fact that they are beyond all question the most formidable and the most remarkable race which has ever appeared in the world.

Disraeli, the Jew Prime Minister of England, and Leader of the Conservative Party, who was always true to his race and proud of his origin, said on a well-known occasion : "The Lord deals with the nations as the nations deal with the Jews." Certainly when we look at the miserable state of Russia, where of all countries in the world the Jews were the most cruelly treated, and contrast it with the fortunes of our own country, which seems to have been so providentially preserved amid the awful perils of these times, we must admit that nothing that has since happened in the history of the world has falsified the truth of Disraeli's confident assertion.

Good and Bad Jews.

The conflict between good and evil which proceeds unceasingly in the breast of man nowhere reaches such an intensity as in the Jewish race. The dual nature of mankind is nowhere more strongly or more terribly exemplified. We owe to the Jews in the Christian revelation a system of ethics which, even if it were entirely separated from the supernatural, would be incomparably the most precious possession of mankind, worth in fact the fruits of all other wisdom and learning put together. On that system and by that faith there has been built out of the

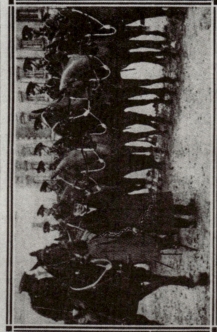

Mr. Churchill inspecting his old regiment, the 4th Hussars, at Aldershot last week.

The National Russian Jews, in spite of the disabilities under which they have suffered, have managed to play an honourable and useful part in the national life even of Russia. As bankers and industrialists they have strenuously promoted the development of Russia's economic resources, and they were foremost in the creation of those remarkable organisations, the Russian Co-operative

people, most of whom are themselves sufferers from the revolutionary régime. It becomes, therefore, specially important to foster and develop any strongly-marked Jewish movement which leads directly away from these fatal associations. And it is here that Zionism has such a deep significance for the whole world at the present time.

A Home for the Jews.

Zionism offers the third sphere to the political conceptions of the Jewish race. In violent contrast to international communism, it presents to the Jew a national idea of a commanding character. It has fallen to the British Government, as the result of the conquest of Palestine, to have the opportunity and the responsibility of securing for the Jewish race all over the world a home and a centre of national life. The statesmanship and historic sense of Mr. Balfour was prompt to seize this opportunity. Declarations have been made which have irrevocably decided the policy of Great Britain. The fiery energies of Dr. Weissmann, the leader, for practical purposes, of the Zionist project, backed by many of the most prominent British Jews, and supported by the full authority of Lord Allenby, are all directed to achieving the success of this inspiring movement.

Of course, Palestine is far too small to accommodate more than a fraction of the Jewish race, nor do the majority of national Jews wish to go there. But if, as may well happen, there should be created in our own lifetime by the banks of the Jordan a Jewish

like Bukharin or Lunacharski cannot be compared with the power of Trotsky, or of Zinovieff, the Dictator of the Red Citadel (Petrograd), or of Krassin or Radek—all Jews. In the Soviet institutions the predominance of Jews is even more astonishing. And the prominent, if not indeed the principal, part in the system of terrorism applied by the Extraordinary Com-

With the notable exception of Lenin, the majority of the leading figures are Jews. Moreover, the principal inspiration and driving power comes from the Jewish leaders. Thus Tchitcherin, a pure Russian, is eclipsed by his nominal subordinate Litvinoff, and the influence of Russians like Bukharin or Lunacharski cannot be compared with the power of Trotsky, or of Zinovieff, the Dictator of the Red Citadel (Petrograd), or of Krassin[1] or Radek – all Jews ... although ... there are many non-Jews every whit as bad as the worst of the Jewish revolutionaries, the part played by the latter in proportion to their numbers in the population is astonishing.

Finally, Churchill proposed the 'Zionist Jew' as a constructive alternative to the 'revolutionary Jew'. The creation of a Jewish homeland in Palestine, under British auspices, would serve not only as 'a refuge for the oppressed' but would embody 'a national idea of a commanding character' for the benefit of world Jewry. Not only would it 'be especially in harmony with the truest interests of the British Empire', but it would be in the interest of Europe as a whole. The heart of Churchill's message was that a Jewish centre in the Middle East would syphon Jewish energies away from radical politics in the west. In short, Zionism presented itself as an antidote to Bolshevism, a constructive ideal to neutralise destructive tendencies.

Churchill's thesis epitomised a trend of thought which had been present in the minds of British ministers, diplomats and civil servants almost since the beginning of the Russian Revolution. The first part of this chapter will examine the role of the 'Russian Jewish' factor in fostering the appeal of Zionism to the British government, leading to the formulation of the Balfour Declaration. It is here assumed that the Declaration was primarily dictated by reasons of exigency, that is, for the purposes of wartime propaganda to boost the Allied cause, rather than for long-term strategic or idealistic motives. It also served to forestall German attempts to exploit Zionism as an instrument of propaganda.

While the government initiated policy, the Zionist leaders were willing junior partners. The second part of this chapter concentrates on Chaim Weizmann (1874–1952), who, interposing himself between the government and the Anglo-Jewish community, was mainly responsible for the conduct of Zionist diplomacy in London. In contrast to the English Zionist Federation which was largely run by Jews of British birth, Weizmann and his associates such as Sokolov were born in Russia and, as it turned out, only temporary residents in Britain. They were not averse to exploiting exaggerated Foreign Office fears about the Jewish role in Bolshevism in order to secure British support for a Jewish Palestine. Finally, we shall turn to Anglo-Jewry itself and ask 'What impact did the Russian Revolution have on the debate about Zionism within the community?'

THE 'PROPAGANDA CARD': THE BRITISH GOVERNMENT, THE BALFOUR DECLARATION AND THE RUSSIAN REVOLUTION

During the months following the February Revolution, there were reports of growing anti-British sentiment within the Russian Jewish community. Although this community traditionally had been disposed to regard the 'Mother of Parliaments' with respect, since 1914 and the Anglo-Russian Alliance a certain disenchantment had set in. This feeling had been reinforced by the British government's failure to exert pressure on the tsar to stop the forcible evacuation of Jews from the war zone in 1915. Nor had Milner made any effort to contact Jewish leaders during his visit to Petrograd on the eve of the revolution. Overtly biased reporting by British journalists alienated Russian Jewry further, whilst the Anglo-Russian Convention regarding the mutual enlistment of 'friendly aliens' did nothing to restore their sensibilities.

After the revolution, however, anti-British attitudes among Russian Jews were regarded as a significant threat to the British diplomatic and military position. The revolution had thrown up the image of the revolutionary Jew, who was inspired by socialist, pacifist and anti-annexationist idealism. The part played by Jewish Mensheviks and Bundists in the Soviet served to confirm this view, even before Bolshevism became prominent. It was but a short step from such suspicions to the conclusion that Russian Jewry was actively pro-German. In April 1917, the Foreign Office considered utilising the appeal of Jewish nationalism to counteract the growing influence of Jewish socialism. Prompted by Lord Robert Cecil, the Deputy Foreign Secretary, Harold Nicolson and Sir Ronald Graham of the Political Intelligence Department wrote to the British Ambassador in Petrograd,

Sir George Buchanan, to seek his opinion on the advisability of such a course:

> We are advised that one of the best methods of counteracting Jewish pacifist and socialist propaganda in Russia would be to offer a definite encouragement to Jewish nationalist aspirations in Palestine ... The question of Zionism is full of difficulties, but I should be glad ... to learn your views as to whether a declaration by the Entente of sympathy for Jewish Nationalist aspirations would help or not in so far as concerns internal and external situation of Russia.[2]

A revision of war aims making the creation of a Jewish homeland in Palestine conditional upon Allied victory would, perhaps, strengthen Russian support for the war effort. Such a strategy was based upon two (unproven) assumptions: that the political and financial power of Russian Jewry was such as to be capable of swaying opinion in the new Russian democracy; and that Zionism was the most popular political creed within Russian Jewry itself.

The former was, without doubt, a wild overestimation; the latter is still open to debate. Opinions differ as to the relative strength of Bundism as a serious rival to Zionism. It is remarkable how Foreign Office representatives who favoured the pro-Zionist policy insisted on the validity of these two assumptions. The theme of 'Jewish power' was a recurring one. William Ormsby-Gore, for example, noted:

> The emancipated Jewish intelligentsia is an organized section of the Russian body politic which must be taken into account politically ... I really believe our Petrograd people underestimate the power of the Jews in Russia. It may be small in Petrograd but in Odessa and the South it is really something to reckon with. The Jewish provincial press is a great force and the Germans realize it and will capture the machine unless we do something to counteract their efforts.[3]

Indeed, it was the vice-consul in Nikolayev, Henry Brown, who provided some of the most colourful commentary upon this subject:

> The Jew is heart and soul for a separate peace, though with his customary caution he works warily ... it is not convenient for him

139

to show his hand yet, nor is it desirable that his views should be known, as a large section of his community is interested in the Zionist movement. Russia is hardly able to preserve her own territories, France and Italy have their hands full with their own business, and the United States is too far off [from Palestine]. Great Britain is already there and is fast smashing up the Turkish power, and therefore it is to Great Britain they must look for the realisation of their hopes. The stigma of concluding a separate peace must be on the Russian, not on the Jew, and he – the Jew – will then secure Palestine, and at the same time preserve for himself the rich Russian fields.[4]

The notion that there was a secret Jewish conspiracy manipulating the press, politics and finance in its own interests was also held in government circles. The juxtaposition of latent antisemitism and Zionist sentiment among British politicians, diplomats and journalists has been noted by other writers. Leonard Stein[5] comments upon the apparent contradiction in the pages of *The Times* between Robert Wilton's reports from Petrograd, peppered with antisemitic remarks, and foreign editor Wickham Steed's consistent support for Zionism from May 1917 onwards. If historically, antisemitism is the antithesis of Zionism, *The Times* ended up by identifying the two. It demonstrated that it was possible to be an antisemite and a Zionist at the same time. This synthesis was achieved by the conceiving of Jewish nationalism as an answer to excessive Jewish influence in the diaspora. This was, in short, a more 'civilised' version of that 'Zionism' advocated by openly antisemitic writers such as Arnold White and the 'Britons', a mere pretext for the removal of European Jewry *en masse* to a glorified ghetto in the Middle East.

Churchill's *Sunday Herald* article is probably the best example of this 'double-edged'[6] Zionism in operation. It is difficult to escape the impression that Churchill's depiction of the 'international Jew' is heavily coloured with the imagery of the *Protocols of the Elders of Zion*, as can be seen in the following passage:

This movement among the Jews is not new. From the days of Spartacus–Weishaupt to those of Karl Marx, and down to Trotsky (Russia), Béla Kun (Hungary), Rosa Luxembourg [*sic*] (Germany), and Emma Goldman (United States), this world-

Caricatures of Lenin, Radek, Martov and Emma Goldman from Aldred
Rosenberg's *The Jewish Bolshevism*, published in English by The Britons in
1922

wide conspiracy for the overthrow of civilisation and for the reconstitution of society on the basis of arrested development, of envious malevolence, and impossible equality has been steadily growing.

According to Churchill, the Russian Revolution is merely the latest manifestation of the 'schemes' of 'this sinister confederacy' of 'international Jews' who are seeking to create a 'world-wide communistic state under Jewish domination'. Churchill's thesis is based upon the underlying conviction that the ideological conflict between Zionism and Bolshevism within Jewry is of vital significance for the rest of the world. This conviction is itself founded upon the belief that the 'formidable race' enjoys an undue influence over the affairs of the rest of the world. Quoting Disraeli's maxim: 'The Lord deals with the nations as the nations deal with the Jews', he claims that the contrasting fortunes of Great Britain and Russia in the recently ended war prove the truth of these words. Above all, however, the struggle between Zionism and Bolshevism 'for the soul of the Jewish People' is presented in cosmological terms as a struggle between Christ and the Anti-Christ, between 'the divine and the diabolical'.

The assumption that Zionism was the most popular ideology among Russian Jews was no less fixed in the minds of British policy-makers in 1917. According to Ronald Graham, for example, it was critical to secure a connection with Zionism especially in Russia, 'where the only means of reaching the Jewish proletariat is through Zionism, to which the vast majority of Jews in that country adhere'.[7] In the event, Buchanan warned that as the 'Jew question here is always a delicate one ... the less said about Jews the better'.[8]

At this juncture, the whole idea was abandoned. There was, in any event, the ever present fear that open encouragement of Zionism might lead to Turkish reprisals against the Jewish settlements in Palestine. By the summer, however, owing to the setback in the Allied war effort occasioned by the Russian collapse, the scheme was being resurrected. The end of fighting in much of the Balkans freed large German forces to be sent to the western front. It also undermined the Allied economic blockade, since the Central Powers could now gain access to Russian supplies – especially to the Ukrainian 'breadbasket'.

It was simultaneously feared that the withdrawal of Russia from the

Caucasus would lead to the strengthening of German influence in Turkey, indeed to the creation of a 'Teutonised Turkey' (Lord Curzon), controlling both Syria and Palestine. This posed a direct threat to British imperial interests in Egypt and the trade route to India and the Far East. Lloyd George held the view that it was essential to intensify the campaign in Palestine. In August the 'Allenby' offensive was launched. It was, therefore, the gravity of the military situation created by the Russian collapse and the fear of her total withdrawal – even of a separate peace – which once more impelled the British government to interest itself in Zionism. If properly exploited, Zionism could provide the perfect propaganda pretext for a forward policy in Palestine. Steps were accordingly taken to depict the forthcoming offensive as a campaign to liberate Arabs, Armenians and Jews from Turkish rule. It was also tacitly implied that Jewish national self-determination in Palestine would be promoted under British protection.

The prevailing balance of military forces once again led authoritative observers to link the questions of eastern Europe and the Middle East. An appeal to Jewish nationalism focused on the restoration of Zion was thought to be a means of counteracting anti-annexationist sentiment in Revolutionary Russia, which would depict an outright British conquest of Palestine as a 'self-seeking imperialistic' move. After the February Revolution, the newly formed Soviets repudiated the tsarist war aims of the partition of the Turkish Empire and the seizure of Constantinople and the Straits. They also denounced 'secret diplomacy' and declared for 'peace without annexations and indemnities', for the 'self-determination of peoples' and for the revision of Allied war aims as the prelude to a general negotiated peace. After the April crisis, precipitated by Pavel Milyukov's 'decisive victory' note and demonstrating the extent of public support for the Soviet policy, the Provisional Government was effectively obliged to acquiesce.[9]

Moreover, Zionism also could be brought into play against American anti-annexationist sentiment. This sentiment was summed up in President Wilson's Fourteen Points (January 1918), outlining the conditions upon which the United States had forsaken its position of neutrality in favour of the Allied cause. The appeal of Zionism to Russian and American Jewry was distinctly a bonus, and belief in Jewish power was thereby revived. Indeed, with regard to American Jewry, this notion considerably predated US entry into the war in April

1917. The boycott of loans to the Allies instigated by American Jewish financiers had been attributed not so much to their anti-Russianism as to their alleged pro-Germanism. After April, Foreign Office attention simply shifted to the attitude of Russian Jewry. Any residual sympathy on the part of the latter for the Ottomans could soon be dealt with.[10]

'Pro-Germanism' was more difficult, as the Central Powers were also aware of the potential uses of Zionism. Germany and Austria had long been putting out feelers to their own resident Zionists, above all to the Berlin Executive. The British (and indeed the French) felt obliged to counter the designs of the enemy, and hoped to subvert 'enemy' and 'neutral' Zionist opinion into the bargain. In short, convinced of the propaganda value of Zionism, in 1917 the powers 'were competing for Jewish support'.[11]

Given all these considerations, Graham suggested that the Foreign Office publish a written declaration of sympathy with Zionism in time for the Petrograd Zionist Conference, scheduled to open on 6 June. Conveyed to the conference by a delegate from England (for example, Nahum Sokolov), such a note would strengthen the hand of the pro-British Zionists in Russia. It was quite deliberate that a Russian Jew was chosen to undertake this delicate mission in the light of the belief that this was 'the best medium for working upon the Russian Jewish community'.[12]

No action was taken, however, until the outcome of the Conjoint vote at the Jewish Board of Deputies was known.[13] It was only at a meeting with Weizmann and de Rothschild on 19 June that Balfour consented to an official declaration. Cecil lamented: 'I wanted to do this several weeks ago but was deterred by the advice of Sir G.[eorge] Buchanan.'[14] It was indeed too late to influence the Petrograd conference which had ended on 13 June. The resolutions passed reflected the continued adherence of Zionist activist Yehiel Tschlenov to the hallowed wartime principle of 'neutralism'. Reaction in Whitehall was mixed. While some officials felt that a more emphatically pro-British orientation would in any case have been embarrassing, Charles Webster of Military Intelligence regretted that 'the aspirations of the Russian Zionists were more international in character than those of the London Bureau.'[15]

Questions of propaganda nevertheless exerted a stronger and stronger influence on British government thinking during the final months prior to the Balfour Declaration. They played a significant role in the discussions which preceded the creation of the Jewish Legion in the summer of 1917. Since 1916, Vladimir (Ze'ev) Jabotinsky had been campaigning for the establishment of an Allied Jewish force to be posted in Palestine. Its aim would be to liberate that country from the Turks; in return for their contribution to the Allied victory, Jabotinsky envisaged that Britain would return Palestine to the Jewish people. He was not unsuccessful in winning adherents for this imaginative scheme in the Foreign Office (especially in the Intelligence Department), the War Office and in the press (C.P. Scott and Wickham Steed). All believed that an identification between Britain and Zionism, through the medium of a Jewish regiment established initially in Britain, would be a most effective way of counteracting pacifist and anti-British sentiment among both American and Russian Jews. As Lloyd George's Private Secretary, Philip Kerr (later Lord Lothian, H.M. Ambassador to Washington), put it somewhat euphemistically: 'It might produce a very beneficial effect in making the Jews of America and Russia much keener on helping to see the war through.'[16]

The creation of the regiment was delayed until August 1917, owing to problems regarding the application of the Anglo-Russian Military Convention to Russian-Jewish 'aliens' in Britain, and to the fact that the whole idea raised 'wider questions of policy'[17] for the government, that is, that their adoption of it might well be interpreted as a commitment to the 'full Zionist programme'.[18] This they were not prepared to do, not least because of the vociferous opposition to such a course mounted by the anti-nationalist wing of the Anglo-Jewish community.[19] Lucien Wolf and his associates did not hesitate to brand the regiment a fundamentally Zionist enterprise. Thus the national character of the regiment, as it finally emerged in late 1917, was somewhat diluted to meet the misgivings of these critics, and its propaganda value was seriously undermined.

Elizabeth Monroe writes that the argument about Russia was the 'crowning reason' that enabled Balfour, at last, to get the Declaration accepted at the two vital Cabinet meetings of 4 and 31 October 1917. Balfour claimed:

> The vast majority of Jews in Russia and America, as indeed, all over the world, now appeared to be favourable to Zionism. If we

144

could make a declaration favourable to such an ideal, we should be able to carry on extremely useful propaganda both in Russia and America ...

Failure to seize the opportunity could also have proved disastrous, for at this time, Balfour noted, the German government was simultaneously seeking Zionist support.[20] Ronald Graham, concerned at the delay in the publication of the Declaration, consequently warned that:

> further delay will have a deplorable result and may jeopardise the whole Jewish situation. At the present moment uncertainty as regards the attitude of His Majesty's Government on this question is growing into suspicion, and not only are we losing the very valuable cooperation of the Zionist forces in Russia and America, but we may bring them into antagonism with us and throw the Zionists into the arms of the Germans who would be only too ready to welcome this opportunity ... Information from every quarter shows the very important role which the Jews are now playing in the Russian political situation. At the present moment the Jews are certainly against the Allies and for the Germans, but almost every Jew in Russia is a Zionist and if they can be made to realise that the success of Zionist aspirations depends upon the support of the Allies and the expulsion of the Turks from Palestine we shall enlist a most powerful element in our favour.[21]

A clearer expression of Foreign Office faith in the twin assumptions of 'Jewish power' and Jewish enthusiasm for Zionism could not be wished for.

The Balfour Declaration may thus be viewed as a desperate bid to avert the almost certain withdrawal of Russia from the war. Indeed, Lloyd George, Prime Minister and a prime mover in the drafting of the Declaration, confirms this in his memoirs. In 1939 he reflected:

> the actual timing of the declaration was determined by considerations of war policy; ... the launching of it in 1917 was due ... to propagandist reasons ... In 1917 the issue of the War was still very much in doubt ... Public opinion in Russia and America played a great part, and we had every reason at that time to believe that in both countries the friendliness or hostility of the Jewish race might make a considerable difference.

It was his general opinion that Jewish sympathies were for the most part anti-Russian. This, in his view, held potential dangers for the Allies, given that the Germans were no less aware of the influence of the Zionist movement and just as eager to win its worldwide support. The editor of *The Times*, Henry Wickham Steed, agreed with the essence of Lloyd George's retrospective analysis. Setting the Declaration squarely in the context of the First World War, in 1945 he wrote that 'a British undertaking to establish a Jewish National Home in Palestine would decisively influence the Zionist organisations in Russia and the United States.'[22]

The historiography, nevertheless, is not unanimous when it comes to an analysis of the various motives behind the Declaration and their relative importance. The majority of writers, however, including authorities like Leonard Stein and Isaiah Friedman, agree that the propaganda argument, particularly in relation to Russia, cannot be ignored.

The journalist Conor Cruise O'Brien, in a review of Ronald Sanders's study of the Declaration,[23] identifies three categories of possible reasons to explain why the British government threw its weight behind Zionism in the autumn of 1917: 'Reasons connected with the conduct of the war', i.e. propaganda; 'Reasons connected with the nature of a desired postwar settlement', i.e. British imperial designs on Palestine and the desire to forestall French claims there; and 'Transcendental (or sentimental) considerations', i.e. religious and liberal nationalist idealism. The second interpretation is favoured by Hardie and Herrmann in *Britain and Zion*[24] ('Empire came first, wartime propaganda second'), while both the pro-Zionist Arthur Koestler and the anti-Zionist Elizabeth Monroe are convinced that ultimately, pure altruism, for better or for worse, was decisive. O'Brien is no less sure which motive to opt for:

> in October 1917 the British War Cabinet was thinking about the War. The Cabinet minutes record that it was discussing the utility of the declaration for Britain's war effort and there does not seem to be any good reason to believe either that they really had something quite different in mind, or that they were altogether mistaken in their view that the declaration might help them win the war.

After the Declaration

The response of Russian Jewry to news of the Balfour Declaration was, by all accounts, overwhelming. Demonstrations of support took place in all the main centres of Jewish population. An official Russian Zionist delegation called on the British Ambassador in Petrograd to express its gratitude on behalf of the community. The *Jewish Chronicle*'s correspondent summed up the atmosphere in these terms:

> The Jewish resolutions of appreciation of the Balfour Declaration on Zionism, the demonstration of joy and praise of England, the articles in the Jewish press with the heading 'Long Live England' and finally the greetings of the young Zionist working men's organisations to the British democracy ... were unmistakable signs of the warm sympathy of the Jews towards England.[25]

Questions about the precise extent of Russian Jewish support for Zionism remained – and still remain – but it is indisputable that the Declaration gave a decisive boost to Zionist fortunes. Foreign Office faith in the assumption that the majority of Russian Jews were Zionists had apparently paid off. Mark Sykes observed with some satisfaction: 'In Russia and the United States of America, the spontaneous response is even greater than I could have expected.'[26]

The fact remains, however, that the Balfour Declaration had come too late and its timing could hardly have been worse. A few days later the Bolsheviks were in power. It was now manifestly clear that the Declaration had failed to achieve its acknowledged objective, to forestall the development of extreme socialism in Russia. All the evidence suggests that the government was keenly aware that it had not acted in time and regretted the consequences. Graham, for instance, lamented: 'It is a misfortune that our Declaration was so long delayed.' To which Balfour laconically replied: 'Not my fault.'[27] Hardinge commented that if the government had issued a statement last spring, 'it might possibly have made all the difference'.[28] The War Office agreed with this assessment, claiming that it was 'even possible that, had the Declaration come sooner, the course of the Revolution might have been affected'.

Such judgements were truly an exercise in self-delusion. The Foreign Office had all along been labouring under an exaggerated notion of Jewish political power. The subsidiary argument regarding the popularity of Zionism in Russia was now irrelevant: 'Most Russian Jews may well have been pro-Zionist, but the course of Russian history was not about to be determined by counting heads, whether of Gentiles or Jews.'[29]

The failure of official policy none the less did not put an end to the illusions upon which it was based. Once the Bolshevik coup was a *fait accompli*, the spectre of separate peace arose anew to haunt Foreign Office thinking. For the purposes of forestalling such an eventuality, the Jews were still considered to be an important factor. In February 1918 the Department of Information made a request to the Anglo-Jewish community, through the offices of Leopold Greenberg, the editor of the *Jewish Chronicle*. At the instigation of Lord Robert Cecil, the Department solicited an appeal to '[your] brethren in Russia' urging them to stay loyal to the Allied cause against the greater evil of Prussian militarism. It was not difficult to divine the logic which lay behind this move: 'It seems to us that if ... this letter could be signed by a number of representative Jews in England and transmitted by us to Russia, it would have considerable good effect in the interests of England and the Allies.'[30] Owing to the reluctance of other leading British Jews to affix their signatures to it, Greenberg's appeal failed.

The notion that Russian Jewry exercised great political and financial power persisted, in revamped form. It was now reckoned that Jewish financial influence could be used to obstruct German exploitation of the grain resources of the Ukraine. The idea that the Jews of the Pale enjoyed a special commercial relationship with the Germans due to their exclusion from Russian markets dated from the early days of the war. Now it experienced a revival. In a memorandum which was later circulated among the British delegates to the Peace Conference, Charles Webster wrote:

> Even now, in the question of economic control, the support of the Jews of South Russia is of fundamental importance ... the connection between Russian and German Jews makes the Jew the natural channel for the exploitation of Russian resources by the Central Powers.

After the Declaration he added: 'This channel has now been to some extent interrupted.'[31]

Apparently, Zionism still had its uses. Once again, however, the

British Foreign Office overestimated the power of the Russian Jews. Jewish middlemen were not indispensable to the Germans in their search for supplies. The Germans did not report any hostility on the part of Jewish traders, nor is there any evidence of widespread anti-German activity on the Jewish side. Even if they had all been Zionists, it is unlikely that the Russian Jews would have risked overt opposition to the occupying power which had, after all, shown them more tolerance than their erstwhile tsarist overlord.

The twin policy of mobilising Zionism against Bolshevism was no less inappropriate, yet it continued to be pursued with the onset of the Civil War. General Barter in Petrograd had already suggested in November 1917 – after the October Revolution – that one way to frustrate Bolshevik peace overtures to the Germans would be:

> for Allies to make some sort of conditional promise that in the event of a successful termination of War, Palestine would be given to the Jews[?] Such an announcement would immediately have a powerful effect in this country where Jewish influence is great and where craving for Promised Land and distinct nationality is greater even than in England.[32]

Lloyd George concurred. He wrote in his memoirs:

> I could point out substantial and in one case decisive advantages derived from this [Zionist] propaganda amongst the Jews. In Russia the *Bolsheviks* [italics added] baffled all the efforts of the Germans to benefit by the harvests of the Ukraine and the Don, and hundreds of thousands of German and Austrian troops had to be maintained to the end of the War on Russian soil, whilst the Germans were short of men to replace casualties on the Western Front...we have good reason to believe that Jewish propaganda in Russia had a great deal to do with the difficulties created for the Germans in Southern Russia after the Peace of Brest–Litovsk.[33]

This was an unfounded claim. As Stein points out, 'the Jews among [the Bolsheviks] were the last people likely to be moved by the Balfour Declaration.'[34] Such misguided notions must be compared with more realistic views which were in circulation at the same time, such as this remark made by Cecil: 'We could hope for nothing from Trotsky, who was a Jew of the international type and was solely out to smash Russia and to revenge himself, not only on the governing classes, but upon the peasants of Russia.'[35]

There was, clearly, a good deal of confusion in Foreign Office thinking on this point. As some Russian Jews were *not* committed Bolsheviks, Cecil proposed the idea of rallying the Jews to the side of the anti-Bolshevist forces in the Ukraine. Since 'the Jews were very powerful in the Ukraine', he commented, 'it might be possible to obtain their support.' He suggested that Jews in Odessa and Kiev might be persuaded to help finance the Whites in south Russia through the representation of 'friendly Jews in western Europe, such as the Zionists'.[36]

The notion that Russian Jews, whether Zionist or not, would ever consider giving assistance to the army of Denikin which was responsible for the perpetration of large-scale pogroms in 1919, was quite divorced from reality. This was not to say that Russian Jewry, as a whole, was naturally predisposed toward Bolshevism. The distinction was a subtle one, which was wholly lost on some British leaders. Take, for instance, the following statement made to the War Cabinet Eastern Committee in December 1918 by General MacDonogh: 'if the Jewish people did not get what they were asking for in Palestine, we should have the whole of Jewry turning Bolshevik and supporting Bolshevism in all the other countries as they have done in Russia.' Upon which Cecil commented ironically: 'Yes, I can conceive the Rothschilds leading a Bolshevist mob.'[37]

'Zionist Bolsheviks'

The chosen emblem of Bolshevism is the five-pointed Zionist star.[38]

> Lord Sydenham of Combe, 'The Jewish World Problem', *Nineteenth Century and After*, November 1921

Your Britisher here is obsessed by the notion that Zionism is incipient Bolshevism, and has no less an object than in the very near future to drive off the native Moslem and Christian to the desert ..., sweep up the mess of the Holy Sepulchre, and – remarkable though it seems in a Bolshevik – pull down the Dome of the Rock, and rebuild the Temple! It is all utter nonsense, but the fact remains that the Jews, and especially the Jews here in Palestine, fail to convince the non-Jews to the contrary.

> Rev. H. Danby to Samuel Landman, written in Jerusalem, 3 May 1920[39]

While we have to fear the activities of Jewish Bolshevist leaders in many countries in Europe, ... there need be no fear of Bolshevism in Palestine. I am convinced of that. I am convinced that your [Zionist] Organisation will not endeavour or seek to create a communistic system in Palestine which is now being preached all over Europe and that your ideas and ideals of development are such as are the ideals of development which Great Britain would wish to see applied to her own Crown colonies or in Mesopotamia, or any other region under her domain.

> William Ormsby-Gore in an interview with Herbert Samuel and Chaim Weizmann, Tel Aviv, 10 May 1919[40]

If Churchill saw Zionism as a solution to Bolshevism, it is indeed ironic that by May 1921, after the Jaffa riots, he was concerned that the Arabs were opposing Zionism as simply a pretext for the infiltration of Palestine by Bolshevik Jews.[41] The Haycraft Report traced the disturbances to a May Day rally in Tel Aviv, organised by a group of Jewish Communists, in defiance of a government ban.[42] They then paraded through the town with banners in Yiddish calling for a Soviet Palestine, and clashed with a larger – and legal – procession led by the Jewish socialist *Ahdut Ha'Avodah*. The police intervened and the local Arab population rioted. According to the British High Commissioner Sir Herbert Samuel, the latter had been provoked by the news of the impending arrival of a further boatload of 'Jewish Communists' at the port. The unrest lasted a week and the gravity of the situation led Samuel to impose a temporary suspension of Jewish immigration.

At a Cabinet meeting on 22 June, Churchill, who as Colonial Secretary had overall responsibility for Palestine, endorsed Samuel's policy. He elaborated further:

> the Zionists, in order to work up enthusiasm for their cause, have to go all over the world preaching the return of hundreds of

thousands of oppressed peoples from the persecuted countries of
Europe, Russia, the Ukraine, Poland and so forth, to the
Promised Land. This terrifies the Arabs ... the idea they have in
their minds is that they are going to be swamped and over-
whelmed by hundreds of thousands of Bolsheviks from Central
Europe ...[43]

Churchill accordingly sent strict instructions to Samuel to 'purge the
Jewish colonies and newcomers of Communist elements and without
hesitation or delay have all those who are guilty of subversive agitation
expelled from the country'.[44]

In Cabinet he had gone further in advocating a policy of virtual
immigration control, explaining:

The stories of Bolshevism have been much exaggerated ... the
number of those who are infected with this horrible form of
mental and moral disease are not at all great, but I have given to
Sir Herbert Samuel, himself a keen Zionist and a Jew, directions
which he is carrying out with vigour, to search the camps for men
of Bolshevik tendencies and to send them out of the country with
the least possible delay, and this is being done. It is not a question
of making war upon opinion, but of not allowing a great experiment which deserves a fair chance, to be prejudiced by persons
who are guilty of a breach of hospitality.[45]

Churchill was, it is true, well aware that the Arabs were making use of
the 'bogey of Bolshevism' in an attempt to bring the British to abandon
their pro-Zionist policy in Palestine. He agreed with Wyndham
Deedes, who wrote that the 'whole movement' of Arab discontent was
'anti-Jewish' and it was therefore wrong to blame a handful of Jewish
Communists.[46] Churchill nonetheless bowed to this Arab pressure
when he issued his orders to Samuel.

Both the Arab population and British administrators of Palestine
were susceptible to such ideas. Bernard Wasserstein has observed:

The Judeo-Bolshevik myth gained easy credence among British
soldiers and officials in Palestine, partly because a large proportion of the Jewish population was Russian by origin, and
frequently of socialist (although generally anti-Bolshevik) sentiment ... The Jewish Bolshevik bogey was an obstinately recurrent

theme in British thinking about Palestine throughout the Mandatory period.[47]

Chaim Weizmann attested to the lack of sympathy displayed by the British administration towards the Jews of Palestine. In his memoir *Trial and Error*, he wrote:

> The scanty Jewish population, worn out by years of privation and isolation, speaking little English, seemed to them to be the sweepings of Russian and Polish ghettos. And Russia at this time was hardly in the good books of the Allies, for it was soon after the Bolshevik Revolution, which on the whole they identified with Russian Jewry: Russians, Jews, Bolsheviks were different words for the same thing in the minds of most of the British officers in Palestine in those days, and even when they were not entirely ignorant of developments, they saw little reason to put themselves out for the Jews — Declaration or no Declaration.
>
> This peculiar situation had not, however, developed of itself. In an early conversation with General (now Sir Wyndham) Deedes (he was one of the few men who *did* understand our position), I learned of at least one of the sources of our tribulations. Suddenly, and without introduction, he handed me a few sheets of typewritten script, and asked me to read them carefully. I read the first sheet and looked up in some perplexity, asking what could be the meaning of all this rubbish. General Deedes replied quietly, and rather sternly: 'You had better read all of it with care; it is going to cause you a great deal of trouble in the future.' This was my first meeting with extracts from the *Protocols of the Elders of Zion*.
>
> Completely baffled, I asked Deedes how the thing had reached him, and what it meant. He answered, slowly and sadly: 'You will find it in the haversack of a great many British officers here — and they believe it! It was brought over by the British Military Mission which has been serving in the Caucasus on the Staff of the Grand Duke Nicholas.'
>
> It would be a mistake to imagine that the views of the whole British army were tainted by the ideas expressed in the *Protocols of the Elders of Zion*; but at a time when the horrors of the Bolshevik revolution were fresh in everyone's mind the most

fantastic rumours and slanders – operating frequently on existing backgrounds of prejudice – gained credence, and the extracts from the *Protocols* which I then saw had been obviously selected to cater to the taste of a certain type of British reader.[48]

The 'Jews equal Bolsheviks' agitation among the Arabs, and as reflected in the attitude of British officials in Palestine, found a sympathetic hearing in sections of the British press and in Parliament. Between February and July 1922, while the British Mandate for Palestine was in the process of ratification at the League of Nations, the Harmsworth family spearheaded a public campaign against the 'Zionism' of the government. With heavy antisemitic overtones, its chief feature was an attack on the supposed 'Bolshevism' of the Jewish settlers. In February *The Times* published a series of reports on Lord Northcliffe's trip to Palestine and his press conference in Cairo.[49] Under the scaremongering headline 'A Second Ireland', it was stated that the press baron had called for the setting up of an independent inquiry to investigate what he had previously termed 'the recent importation of undesirable Jews, Bolshevists and others' into Palestine, and into Zionist 'extremism' in general. On 23 February the *Daily Mail* ran a headline which read: 'PALESTINE WASTE AND BOLSHEVIKS. INCESSANT ARMS SMUGGLING. LORD NORTHCLIFFE'S REMEDY: STOP THE IMMIGRATION.'

The 'Jews equal Bolsheviks' agitation in relation to Palestine found a ready parallel in the anti-Bolshevism and anti-alienism which was directed against the Jewish community in Britain during this period. This was somewhat ironic, given that not a few on the right of British politics had been attracted to Zionism's cause as a means of solving the 'problem' of Jewish immigration domestically, by diverting Russian Jewish refugees to Palestine.[50] Arab opposition, however, convinced this school of thought that the disadvantages outweighed the advantages.

WEIZMANN'S 'QUIET DIPLOMACY'

From February to October

It appeared that the Russian Revolution had superficially weakened the bargaining position of the Great Russell Street Zionists *vis-à-vis* the British government. The Emancipation Decree had apparently 'knocked the bottom out of the Zionist case in so far as it had rested on the intolerable conditions of Jewish life in Eastern Europe.'[51] Moreover, if Zionism recommended itself to the Allied Powers chiefly on account of its propaganda value, then:

> The collapse of the Tsarist régime had made Russia respectable in Jewish eyes and ... had [thus] deprived pro-German propagandists of their trump card – the partnership between the Western Allies and the Russian antisemites ... The idea of counter-propaganda by way of an appeal to Zionist sentiment among the Jews was, therefore, no longer as interesting ...

The impression that Zionism had suffered a setback on account of the revolution was, however, misleading. Chaim Weizmann was entirely convinced that the internal momentum of the movement was not fuelled solely by the existence of antisemitism. At the London Zionist Conference in May 1917 he – somewhat optimistically – declared:

> Some of us – some of our friends even, and especially some of our opponents – are very quick in drawing conclusions as to what will happen to the Zionist movement after the Russian Revolution. Now, they say, the greatest stimulus for the Zionist movement has been removed. Russian Jewry is free. They do not need any places of refuge outside Russia – somewhere in Palestine. Nothing can be more superficial, and nothing can be more wrong, than that. We have never built our Zionist Movement on the sufferings of our people in Russia or elsewhere. Those sufferings were never the cause of Zionism. The fundamental cause of Zionism was, and is, the ineradicable national striving of Jewry to have a home of its own – a national centre, a national home with a national Jewish life. And this remains now stronger than ever. A strong and free Russian Jewry will appreciate more than ever the strivings of the Zionist Organisation. And truly we see it even now. Russian Jewry is formulating its national demands in a proud, open, free way, which may well serve as an example and an encouragement to the free Western communities of Jewry. You have all read of meetings which have taken place all over

Russia – of a meeting which took place only recently in Moscow, and was attended by seven thousand Jews. Many Western Jews could learn from these meetings how a free and proud Jew ought to speak. We therefore look forward with confidence to the future of Zionism in Russia.[52]

It is arguable that the Zionists were in a stronger diplomatic position than they had been before the revolution, for two reasons. First, matters were made simpler by the removal of Tsarist Russia as a contender for the spoils of the Turkish Empire. This left the rival claims of Great Britain and France, either for a British protectorate or an Anglo-French condominium over Palestine. In such a situation, the Zionists could make themselves useful to the British government as a counterbalance to French ambitions.[53] Second, the spectre of Jewish 'pro-Germanism' was about to be superseded by the spectre of Jewish 'Bolshevism' in the minds of some Foreign Office officials. Weizmann, for one, had no scruples about exploiting the latter, as well as the former, in the interests of promoting his cause. He was quite willing to present Jewish nationalism as a counterweight to Jewish socialism.

In his speech of 20 May, Weizmann stated that it was the 'task' of the Zionist Movement worldwide 'to contribute as much as it is in their power to the stabilisation of conditions in Russia'. Weizmann was not acting merely out of expediency. There is every evidence in his own writings that he was genuinely concerned about the spread of revolutionary socialism in Russia. In promoting the antithetical connection between Zionism and socialism, he was, however, running the risk of perpetuating the misconceptions which were current in Foreign Office circles regarding the Jews. The twin beliefs in the extent of Jewish influence and Zionist strength in Russia were implicit in his argument. Weizmann's policy bore fruit only because it fitted in with existing British interests. The Foreign Office appreciated the advantages to be derived from Zionism as an instrument of wartime propaganda. Indeed, this appreciation predated Weizmann's appearance upon the diplomatic scene. Britain's longstanding imperial interests in Palestine and neighbouring regions were also significant. As Mayir Vereté has observed, Zionism served as an 'adjunct' to established British policy.[54] It is important, therefore, not to exaggerate the extent of Weizmann's influence. He was by no means the living embodiment of Jewish 'world power', manipulating the British government in the interests of Jewry. On the contrary, his diplomacy could only be conducted within predetermined limits. He took every opportunity to make himself indispensable to the British government, but the fact remains that it was they who were doing the 'using'.

While it would be unjust to suggest that this was his sole motive, it is undoubtedly true that Weizmann backed Jabotinsky's plan for a Jewish Legion in the teeth of both English and Russian Zionist opposition, partly because he saw it as another means of convincing the British government of the 'propaganda card' case for Zionism. He fully endorsed Jabotinsky's memorandum, which was presented to the War Cabinet in January 1917, and was subsequently summarised in a *Times* leader, thus:

> The great majority of Jews in the world could, in view of these two events [i.e. the Russian Revolution and the US entry into the war], be considered as entirely pro-Entente, but that, at the same time, they had no special interest in the prosecution of the War to complete victory. The suggestion was made that, by inspiring the unassimilated millions of the Jewish people in America and Russia with an ideal of which the realisation would be essentially dependent on victory, a living link would be created between the Jews and the fortunes of the War. The suggested idea was the liberation of Palestine with the help of a combatant Jewish Legion.[55]

In a private note to Harold Nicolson of the Intelligence Department, Jabotinsky spelt out his intentions with regard to Russia: 'There is in Russia plenty of inflammable material for a great pro-War movement and ... setting it ablaze is only a question of a strong concentrated will and of a good battle cry. The battle cry, so far as Jews are concerned, is Palestine.'[56] It was also true that the Regiment could counteract pacifist sentiment amongst Russian Jews in England and encourage them to enlist.[57]

Weizmann fully appreciated the utility of Zionism – from the British point of view – in the policy of depicting the Palestine campaign as a war for the liberation of oppressed nationalities from Turkish rule. This would make it more palatable, given growing anti-annexationist and pacifist opinion in both the United States and Revolutionary

Russia. He further recognised – as many Zionists, especially in the above-named countries, did not – that the movement had a shared interest with the British government in countering such tendencies. After all, they carried with them the danger of a negotiated peace with Turkey. Weizmann wrote in the following vein to C.P. Scott, the editor of the *Manchester Guardian* and an enthusiastic supporter of the Zionist cause:

> Two big democracies like Russia and America may have a very decisive voice in the future settlement of the map of the world. These two countries contain the largest number of Jews who are at present articulate and if it is to be known that Palestine has simply been mutilated in order to satisfy certain strategic policies which are not real ... a cry will ring out from one end of the world to the other: where is the principle of justice for small nationalities for which everybody is fighting? These principles are not a mere battle cry at present but they are a reality to be reckoned with.[58]

A British protectorate over a Jewish Palestine would be mutually beneficial: 'A Jewish Palestine under a British Protectorate could not be interpreted simply as an annexation of Palestine by Great Britain ... it would be easily understood that Great Britain [was] keeping the country in trust for the Jews.'[59] In *Palestine*, the journal founded by the British Palestine Committee to promote the Anglo-Zionist connection, Weizmann elaborated further:

> Between ... holding Palestine in trust for the Jewish people ... and 'annexation' in the vulgar sense there is all the difference in the world. It is the difference between adopting a child and kidnapping a child; and we take the declaration of the Russian Government to be against kidnapping, not against adoption.[60]

Accordingly, Weizmann launched a parallel campaign among American and Russian Jews to secure their support for a Jewish National Home in Palestine under British protection. On 27 April 1917 he sent the first of a stream of telegrams to Yehiel Tschlenov in Petrograd, urging the Russian Zionist Central Committee to issue an 'official declaration' of sympathy for the policy being pursued in London. The cooperation of the Provisional Government was also sought. In the course of a subsequent letter, Weizmann assured his opposite number that:

> England is not yearning to annex Palestine, and were it not for the combination with us [i.e. France], she would hardly oppose the internationalisation of the country. On the contrary, one fears here that, in view of the present feeling in Russia and in America, it is difficult to work in favour of a British Protectorate save on the condition *that the Jews themselves wish it*: in other words Great Britain is ready to take Palestine under her protection in order to give the Jews the possibility of getting on their feet and living independently ... It is, therefore, extremely important that Russian Jewry proclaim the importance of this question and bring it home to the Russian Government.[61]

Weizmann implored Sokolov, who was then in Paris, to make the trip to Russia and deliver this message in person – as a representative Russian Jew – to the forthcoming Zionist conference.[62] In the event, Sokolov was delayed in Paris, the conference could not be postponed and Boris Goldberg, who was suggested as a substitute envoy, did not leave London till July. Despite Weizmann's efforts, the Russian Zionist Conference clung obstinately to the principle of 'neutrality'. Tschlenov, following the lead of the Berlin Executive, reasserted the international nature of the Zionist movement. 'In harmony with traditional Zionist thinking, he pictured the establishment of a Jewish National Home in Palestine as part of a negotiated peace settlement to which both groups of belligerents would be parties.'[63] In pursuing this policy, Tschlenov was influenced as much by considerations of expediency as by ideology. Above all, there were nagging doubts as to the final outcome of the war. What if the Central Powers were *not* defeated? There was a real danger of Turkish reprisals against the Palestinian *Yishuv* – to say nothing of the fact that two and a half million Jews were hostage to the German and Austrian occupation of eastern Europe. In the context of domestic politics in Russia, Tschlenov, as a Kadet (a member of the Constitutional Democratic Party, the Russian 'liberal party' founded after the 1905 revolution), could ill afford to compromise his reputation with the left by committing himself to 'imperialistic' British war aims; he was mindful of Milyukov's fate. The Provisional Government had in any event shown itself not entirely unsympathetic to the fortunes of the Zionists. Why, then, should Russian Zionists count solely upon the British? Especially since no firm commitment had yet been received from the British government. Weizmann was guilty of exaggerating British assurances in his telegrams to the Russian Zionist Conference – several of which had been sent without the knowledge or approval of the Foreign Office. In June 1917, the British government was not yet in a position to give solid pledges to the Zionists. Consequently, Tschlenov was moved to write back to Weizmann:

> For the last six months you have been demanding from us a public statement in favour of your conception ... you will surely agree with us that before making such a statement we must have clear and positive promises. So far we have not got them even from England ... in Russia we have been given much more definite pledges.[64]

Tschlenov was on solid ground when arguing that it was impolitic to give the British *carte blanche* before having any written guarantee of support from them. Weizmann despairingly sent back a lengthy reply in which he complained about what he called 'the hostile neutrality' of the Russian Zionists, which would only result in their 'fall[ing] between two stools'.

> The whole Russian conference, impressive as it turned out to be as a great Zionist demonstration, paid, in my view, too much lip service to the doctrines that are now in the air in Russia and because of which poor Russia is now falling to pieces. You have all been trying far too hard to be *à la mode*, and this is a major political mistake, or, more correctly, a weakness unbecoming a great organisation ...
>
> I expected more support from your Conference, not publicly but at least privately. But Russian Zionism is far too eclectic, far too much under the banner of the Soviet of Workers' Deputies, and we, as always in Jewish history, are too impressionable to evaluate the facts coolly, dispassionately and in a mature fashion. I must admit that in recent months I have become very depressed. Was it worthwhile to devote one's whole life for three years to a task which is not even appreciated by comrades now intoxicated with other people's wine?

And he concluded:

> [Y]ou must support our work more intensively and ... you in
> Russia, where very little can be done in the larger political field,
> must consolidate the Zionist Organisation and protect it from
> too large a dose of 'Helsingforsism' and – pardon my expression
> – of 'Maximalism'.[65]

Weizmann made one final attempt to persuade Tschlenov to modify his
position at the end of July. He sent Boris Goldberg to see him in
Copenhagen where a meeting of the German dominated 'Actions
Committee' had been convened. But Tschlenov chose to defer to the
wishes of the German Zionist leaders, who declared that the cooperation of Berlin as well as of London must be secured for any Palestinian
plan. To both Weizmann and Sokolov it was 'axiomatic' that Germany could never be counted upon as a friend of Zionism. Even
Sokolov was driven to observe that the Russians were being entirely
unrealistic and were 'the victims of too much talking in too many
committees'.[66] The fact remained, however, that they had good reasons
to keep their options open. Russian Zionists in Petrograd and Russian
Zionists in London did not necessarily share the same priorities – or
even the same interests. Each group was operating under different
political conditions. When Tschlenov finally turned up in London at
the end of October, he had not changed his mind one iota. Vera
Weizmann, rather unsympathetically, noted in her diary that 'Every-
body is most enthusiastic [about the impending Declaration] except
Tschlenov, who still advocates Jewish neutrality, and [the] policy of
sitting on the fence.'[67] A different view is proffered by Dr Gaster who, it
must be said, had every sympathy with the Russian Zionists' position –
and had a long-standing and bitter personal dispute with Weizmann.
According to Gaster's version of a conversation which took place
between himself and Tschlenov in November 1917, the latter stated
that:

> the Russians as well as he personally were *not* in agreement with
> the policy of Weizmann and Sokolov which was one-sided, dan-
> gerous and ultra-British instead of being Hebrew and Jewish.
> They all favoured rather an international solution which would
> place the English/Entente Zionists in a harmonious position to

the Central Power Zionists. He and they had their grave doubts about the Declaration and feared it would lead to schism and danger.

And reportedly, Tschlenov complained further that:

> Weizmann, Sokolov, Sacher and the hangers-on were now rabid Englishmen and did not see anything else but from an ultra-patriotic point of view, which struck him rather ludicrous in the mouth of these Russian Jews, who had no long-standing connection with this country and simply played up to the Government and to a rather peculiar gallery. They had forgotten that Zionism was neither English nor does it affect many English Jews. It was the ideal of the continental masses and above all the Russian. But he added plaintively, what am I to do [?]. They will not listen to me and even try to shut me up and warn me not to hinder their work by incautious speech.[68]

Tschlenov died in Brighton in January 1918.

After the Balfour Declaration and the Bolshevik Revolution

> The effect of the November *coup d'état* was ... to weaken the [Zionist] Movement internally [in Russia], but, as against this, the Bolshevik threat to the established order of society, and exaggerated ideas as to the extent to which Jewish brains were behind it, served to strengthen the position of the Zionists in presenting their case to the Western World.[69]

The Zionist Organisation in the west was about to be deprived of its chief source of inspiration: Russian Jewry. Since the foundation of the movement, the majority of its leading personalities had been drawn from this vast reservoir in the east. As a consequence Weizmann predicted a shift in the political balance. In a note to Louis Brandeis in Washington (April 1918), he made the following prophetic remarks:

> In view of the situation in Russia, and the chaotic state of Russian Jewry, the burden will not be lifted from your shoulders, I am afraid, for a long time to come. For some years to come, until Russia has settled down, we shall all still turn to you and to your

great country for help, advice and guidance – for help in men and money.[70]

Weizmann was able to turn the fact that 'Jewish' Bolshevism had come to power in Russia to his short-term advantage. It might have been thought that this very circumstance proved the whole policy of 'Zionism versus Bolshevism' bankrupt, both as far as the British and the Zionists were concerned. On the contrary the notion became even more entrenched. Churchill's article on the subject appeared at the beginning of 1920, in the midst of the Civil War. Exactly a year earlier, Weizmann had made this statement to the Paris peace conference:

> The solution proposed by the Zionist Organisation [i.e. the crea-tion of a Jewish National Home in Palestine] was the only one which would in the long-run ... transform Jewish energy into a constructive force instead of its being dissipated in destructive tendencies.[71]

Such remarks anticipated, to a remarkable degree, the words employed by Churchill. Later, before the Twelfth Zionist Congress in 1921, Weizmann invoked a similar metaphor:

> Britain with her political farsightedness, understood sooner and better than any other nation ... that the Jewish question, which hangs like a shadow over the world, may become a gigantic force of construction or a mighty instrument of destruction.[72]

In common with the British government, he still genuinely believed that he could influence events in Russia through the Zionist movement there. Not only in Russia, indeed, but in Poland too:

> Polish Jewry if driven to despair might form a bridge between Germanism and Bolshevism which were at present separated by it and this would be a danger to the whole world: Mr Balfour seemed to see the force of this argument and expressed the opinion that the Zionist solution must be supported if only to avoid this grave danger which would otherwise threaten.

Weizmann added an NB to this memo:

> Made a point of this.[73]

Hard on the heels of the Declaration – and of the Bolshevik Revolution – he wired to Rosov in Petrograd: 'Your sacred duty now to strengthen pro-British sympathies in Russian Jewry and counteract powerfully all adverse influences. Remember providential coincidence of British and Jewish interests.'[74] He intended to follow this up with the despatch of a delegation consisting of Sokolov, Tschlenov and Jabotinsky to Russia 'to promote the joint aims of the Zionist Organisation and the Allied Powers'.[75] A similar mission, headed by Aaron Aaronsohn, was to go to the United States. This plan, with regard to Russia at least, proved impracticable, owing to the October *coup d'état*. By February 1918, Weizmann was beginning to realise the limitations of his policy – and that, perhaps, his expectations had been too great:

> The total effect of this [Zionist] propaganda in Russia has been considerable though perhaps hardly as much as had been hoped. The Revolution occupied most of the attention of the Russian Jews and the consolidation of their newly-won liberty was their main object. The general feeling among them was far from friendly to Great Britain.

He nevertheless arrived at the same conclusion as some Foreign Office officials 'that had the Declaration come sooner the course of the Revolution might have been affected'.[76]

Weizmann certainly did not share the illusory belief entertained by less well-informed elements in the Foreign Office that somehow the 'Jewish' Bolsheviks could be made more amenable to the Allied cause through the machinations of the Russian Zionists. Indeed, he had scant sympathy for Bolshevism to which '99 per cent of the Jewish people' were 'deadly enemies'.[77] Nor did he subscribe to the opposite notion that Russian Zionists were capable of mobilising the whole of Russian Jewry against the Bolsheviks in conjunction with the antisemitic White Russian generals. He did, however, share the Foreign Office's faith in the efficacy of Zionism as an antidote to the spread of German influence in the Ukraine. The German advance in the east and the concomitant possibility of a separate peace there was the primary danger to British – and therefore to Jewish – interests in the winter of 1917–18. Weizmann therefore gave Whitehall his full cooperation in their attempts to avoid such an eventuality.

He telegraphed Brandeis in Washington thus:

Information received that Germans contemplate during Armistice to establish purchasing companies South Russia ... and to obtain produce and petrol which would render our blockade ineffective ... we think that Jews of South Russia who control trade could effectively counteract German and Bolshevik manoeuvres in alliance with Ukraine. We have telegraphed to our friends Petrograd, Rostov, Kiev, Odessa, and beg you to do the same, appealing to them on behalf of Allied and Palestinian cause ... Jews have now splendid opportunity to show their gratitude England and America.[78]

Weizmann counted not merely on the cooperation of the international Zionist 'network', but on Jewish financial power ('Jews of South Russia who control trade'). Somewhat prematurely in February 1918, he gave guarded testimony to what he considered to be the success of this policy:

Even now in the question[s] of economic control the support of the Jews of South Russia is of fundamental importance and this undoubtedly appears to have been secured. The connections between Russian and German Jews makes the Jews the natural channel for the exploitation of Russian resources by the Central Powers. This channel has now been to some extent interrupted and this negative result may compensate for the small influence which has hitherto been obtained in the political sphere.[79]

It is certainly the case that Jews played a major role in Ukrainian commerce. Weizmann was none the less, like some Foreign Office officials, guilty of exaggerating the strength of Jewish financial power in Russia. The fact remains that the Jew is as susceptible to myths about the character of his own community as any Gentile. The Germans and the Bolsheviks signed the Treaty of Brest–Litovsk in March 1918, and this opened the way for German economic exploitation of the Ukraine.

'ENGLISH ZIONISTS VERSUS BRITISH JEWS': THE IMPACT OF THE RUSSIAN REVOLUTION UPON THE DEBATE WITHIN ANGLO-JEWRY

What was the future for Zionism in the new Russia? Would the cause of Jewish nationalism be strengthened in a free society which, for the time being at least, invited open political debate? Or would it, by contrast, succumb to the competing lure of assimilation? What about the other alternatives confronting Russian Jewry, such as the Bundist solution of 'National Cultural Autonomy' within the borders of the transformed state, or renewed emigration to the west? Indeed, was Zionism still relevant now that Russian Jewry had gained their emancipation? These were just some of the questions which proponents and opponents of Zionism within the Anglo-Jewish community had to address in the aftermath of the Russian Revolution. During 1917, a pamphlet war was waged within – and without – that community, in which these issues were central to the arguments of both sides. This public war mirrored the parallel – almost symbolic – struggle taking place within the government – between the Zionist Herbert Samuel and his anti-Zionist cousin Edwin Montagu.

Anti-Zionists and the Revolution

I regard with perfect equanimity whatever treatment the Jews receive in Russia.

Edwin Montagu to Sir Eric Drummond,
Earl of Perth, 3 August 1916[80]

If Russian Jews obtained freedom in November, there would be no more Zionists in December.

attributed to Lucien Wolf, c. 1916

Zionism, Wolf maintained, was founded upon antisemitism. It enjoyed no independent existence of its own; it was rather a wholly negative reaction to antisemitism, and one which held out an entirely illusory hope of escape from persecution in eastern Europe. It was, in short, merely a formula arising out of 'the political exigencies of the times'.[81] Proof of this lay in the fact that Jewish nationalism drew its leadership and popular support principally from the Pale of Settlement and not from west European and American Jewry, who had already achieved civil and political emancipation. It followed, therefore, that the case for Zionism collapsed with the dawn of emancipation in the east – that is, with the coming of the Russian Revolution. Now Russian Jewry would tread the same path towards individual freedom and legal equality in a parliamentary democracy as its counterparts in the west. As Laurie Magnus, Philip's son, put it:

> The star of freedom has risen in New Russia, and Prussian *kultur*, which reinvented antisemitism, is setting in baths of blood. The Jewish problem to Jewish eyes in 1902 was how to escape persecution. Theodore Herzl was a desperate man. Jewish conditions under Francis Joseph were intolerable, and the situation was even worse in Roumania and Russia. Today this despair is lifted ... Imperial Russia is finding her own soul. The remedies devised by the new Zionists to cure the evils they could not bear, disappear with the evils that engendered them.[82]

The Jewish anti-Zionists were irrepressibly confident that emancipation could ultimately be achieved everywhere. Basing themselves on the premiss, formulated by the German Reform School, that 'Jewish' identity was a purely religious and not a national characteristic, they rejected the Zionist argument that the Jews formed a distinct political and national entity which required a territorial centre. The struggle for equal rights was thus a cardinal principle of the anti-Zionist creed. The 'Jewish liberal compromise' was applicable to both west and east. The Jewish struggle was part of the general battle for liberty taking place in Europe and, as such, was bound up with universalist tendencies in the Jewish religion. To embrace Zionism was a denial of the Jewish Mission to Mankind in favour of a narrow nationalism. In relation to Russia it meant an abdication of political responsibility. Philip Magnus wrote:

> In the recent Revolution ... the Jews are known to have taken an active part: but they did so, not with a view to the restoration of Jewish nationality in Palestine, but in the endeavour to secure for the Russian people, as a whole ... freedom ... It has been said that the Revolution will prove to be the deathblow to the general acceptance by Russian Jews of the idea of National Zionism, and so it should be, for the Jews in Russia, as loyal subjects of the present Provisional Government, should devote their energies, their well-known organising abilities, and their intellectual efforts to the building up of a new and free Russia, occupying a foremost place among the civilising nations of the world.[83]

Laurie Magnus concurred:

> We used to hear about Little Englanders. Surely Little Jews is the
> right term for the neo-Zionists, bred in persecution ... [who]
> urged the remedy of flight ... But the ... moral purpose [has]
> always lain in the direction of an improvement of Jewish con-
> ditions from within. Russian Jews, by remaining in Russia will
> help Russia to become a modern state.[84]

Such high-mindedness apart, the anti-Zionists had another, far more
prosaic concern: the spread of Jewish nationalism could undermine the
process of emancipation in Russia at just that moment when it was
being achieved – by conjuring up the spectre of 'dual loyalties'. Lucien
Wolf summed up the dilemma:

> The Zionists say that the Jews are a nation. Most eagerly is this
> false and foolish assertion laid hold of by antisemites who are
> always eager and sympathetic Zionists. For, if the Jews are a
> nation, how can they be citizens of other nations? A man cannot
> belong to two nations. If he is a Jew by nationality, he can't be a
> true Russian or Englishman.

Zionism could thus inspire antisemitism, rather than provide a
solution to it. To Wolf the Zionist programme amounted to a uni-
lateral declaration, by a section of Jewry, that the Jewish masses were
'in a state of homelessness' throughout the world. This was without
doubt a 'deplorable' declaration which 'may be calculated to wreck
whatever chances of liberty and happiness there may be at the present
moment for the seven millions of unhappy Jews in eastern Europe'.[85]
In his sermon for *Shavuos* (Pentecost) 1917, which was appro-
priately entitled *The Mission of the Jew*, Rev. Ephraim Levene of the
New West End synagogue said:

> A few weeks ago the world was ringing with the glad tidings of
> the Revolution in Russia. Jews were devoutly thankful that the
> era of liberation had dawned for our Russian brethren. The
> nationalist aspirants almost went beyond themselves in their
> enthusiasm. They were clamouring at the Board of Deputies be-
> cause that body had not been impetuous enough to send tele-
> grams to Russia and acclaim the happy event. 'The greatest event
> in Jewish history', they proclaimed. The emancipation of millions

of Jews one week, the granting to them [of] all the rights and privileges that belong to Man – the preaching of the Jewish Nationalism the next week.

Is it consistent?

If the Revolution in Russia endures, who knows what the attitude of the millions of emancipated Russian Jews will be ... It would seem to be an inopportune moment to preach the doctrine of Jewish nationality ...

Clearly, there was a fundamental conflict of priorities here. Lucien Wolf was in no doubt where his lay:

The Russian question is vastly more important than the Palestine question

he declared, and therefore:

Nothing must be said or done as regards Palestine and the Jews which would, or could, possibly injure the cause of the Russian Jews. Far better that no more Jews ever entered Palestine than that the emancipation of the Russian Jews be put back or hindered at this crisis of their fate ...

Thus, any action in Palestine, or in relation to Palestine, whether by Jews or on behalf of Jews, which makes the Jewish claim for emancipation in Russia less cogent, less true, less urgent, does the Jews a grave injury. Any such action which lessens the possibility of pressure being exercised upon Russia, which removes public attention from the persecution and the disabilities, does the Jews a grave injury.[86]

Wolf's justification for his view was that it was a realistic one. The fact of the matter was that between six and seven million Jews lived in eastern Europe: the continued growth in population there could never, on current trends, be offset by the colonisation of Palestine. That was a very long-term objective indeed. The Zionist Dream was 'pie in the sky' compared with the pressing economic and political problems facing the Jews in the former Pale of Settlement. It would be unfair, however, to accuse Wolf of being an out and out 'assimilationist' on account of his opposition to Zionism as a solution for the Jewish question in eastern Europe. He was aware that 'nationality [was] a unit of state life' beyond the Danube in a way that had no parallel in the west. Therefore it would not be enough simply to prescribe a recipe of civil and political freedom for the individual on the western liberal model. The peculiar conditions of eastern Europe, with their plethora of competing nationalities, forced Wolf to the conclusion that the Jewish minority could only be adequately safeguarded by the insistence on Jewish *national* as well as individual rights. In his article, 'The Jewish National Movement', which was published in the *Edinburgh Review* of April 1917, Wolf came out in favour of 'National Cultural Autonomy' for the Jews in eastern Europe. He gave his approval to Simon Dubnov's concept of 'Spiritual Nationalism' whereby religion was regarded as the chief medium for the preservation of Jewish identity in the diaspora. (Indeed, one of Wolf's objections to Zionism was its predominantly secularist tone.) The Jewish 'national' identity was merely 'a state of mind' which need not conflict with the political demands of allegiance to a non-Jewish state.

Wolf also professed to being a disciple of the Springer Plan. This scheme was originally designed as a blueprint for a reformed Austro-Hungarian Empire. It provided for the representation of minority nationalities within the national diet of each of the majority nationalities, by means of proportional representation for extra-territorial 'linguistic circles'. Minority, as well as majority national groups, would also have representation in the federal parliament. This framework would guarantee that scattered minorities, such as the Jews, would have a voice in the affairs of the multi-national state. They would, in so doing, act as a break against chauvinistic excesses on the part of the larger nationalities. Obviously, the Springer Plan could equally be applied to a decentralised and democratised Russian Empire. The advantage of 'National Cultural Autonomy' in Wolf's eyes was that 'it was entirely in harmony with its Russian environment'. This confirmed the existing political aspirations of the revolution:

> Today, national autonomy, more or less on the Springer Plan, is an accepted principle of all shades of Russian liberal politics. The principle of self-government and equal rights for all nationalities has taken its place as a necessary corollary of the principle of individual freedom and equal rights for all the many varieties of Russian citizens.[87]

The real importance of 'National Cultural Autonomy', for Wolf, lay in the fact that it offered a solution to the Jewish predicament in Russia – *within Russia itself*. This was something Zionism – or indeed mere emigration to wherever it was directed – could never claim to do. These 'solutions' simply turned their back on the problem altogether.

In pressing his case, Wolf insisted that the vast majority of politically aware Russian Jews were in favour of 'National Cultural Autonomy'. The Jewish liberal *Folkspartai*, the Jewish socialist *Farainigte* and the Bund had all adopted it as party policy. Indeed, the Bund had virtually made the slogan of 'National Cultural Autonomy' their own. Wolf consistently maintained that it was the Bund, rather than the Zionists, who commanded the most support among Russian Jews in 1917. When, in an interview at the Foreign Office (May 1917) Rex Leeper posed the following question: 'Suppose the British Government were to authorise an official statement expressing their readiness to establish a Jewish state in Palestine, do you think this would make the Jews [in Russia] more friendly to England?', this was part of Wolf's reply:

> I said I believed the Jews knew all about the intentions of the British Government in regard to Palestine, indeed much more than the British Government itself knew, and I was sure that they were already very grateful. I did not think that anything that might be said would alter the practical political aspects of the situation. The Zionists would no doubt be very enthusiastic, but their political influence *qua* Zionists was inconsiderable. They were a minority among the Russian Jews, and the great bulk of Russian Jews at this moment were more concerned in establishing their National Autonomy in Russia itself than in founding a state in Palestine. Moreover, the extreme left among the Jewish politicians were irreconcilably opposed to the Zionists, and ... the question was the subject of a lively controversy. Hence, an official statement by the British Government might have an effect quite contrary to what was intended, in as much as the Jewish socialists who have far more political influence at this moment than the Zionists, would regard it as an interference against themselves and would resent it accordingly.[88]

Thus when the British government solicited the views of leading British Jews on the issue of Zionism during 1917, Lucien Wolf was at the forefront of the anti-nationalist lobby. He poured scorn on the 'propaganda card' case for Zionism. On the contrary, 'The Revolution', he declared, '... has relieved the Allied Governments of any absolute necessity to deal with the Zionist question at all.'[89] On this point, Claude Montefiore, Anglo-Jewry's most intellectual exponent of Liberal Judaism and anti-nationalism, was Wolf's staunchest ally. In an interview with Lord Milner, also during May 1917, he stated quite categorically that 'It has obviously been represented to His Majesty's Government that the Russian Jews are all enthusiastic Zionists. I said that I did not believe that this was by any means the case.'[90]

Montefiore recorded that Milner agreed with him that the Russian Jews were 'very revolutionary, anti-monarchical, anti-annexationist and anti-British', and that any message from the British government 'even about Palestine' was unlikely to have any effect on them.

So the anti-Zionists vigorously challenged the dominant view held in the Foreign Office (and cultivated by Weizmann) regarding the utility of Zionism as an instrument of wartime propaganda. Conflicting opinions about the political situation in Russia lay at the heart of the controversy. Wolf and Montefiore cast doubt on the extent of support for the nationalist cause within the Russian Jewish community. With this assumption removed, the whole strategy of 'Zionism versus Bolshevism' was liable to collapse. Yet, as it turned out, the anti-Zionist case failed to convince. This was, at least partly, due to the fact that they were guilty of putting forward contradictory arguments. On the one hand, Lucien Wolf was insisting in public that Russian Jewry was a moderate and level-headed body. On the other hand, he claimed in private that the influence of the Jewish socialists was very strong. The former pronouncements were obviously designed for home consumption, to allay the stock accusation of Jewish involvement in Bolshevism. The latter, made behind closed doors at the Foreign Office, were intended to forestall British entanglement with Zionism. Since Wolf's arguments did not add up, the British government went on believing in the destructive potential of Jewish extremism – and this belief, as already shown, played no small part in the final publication of the Balfour Declaration.

Israel Zangwill devised his own personal solution to the problems faced by Russian – and indeed world – Jewry: Territorialism. This concept owed something both to Zionism (it started life as a breakaway from mainstream Zionism in 1905) and to Bundism's

'National Cultural Autonomy'. The aim of the Jewish Territorial Organisation (ITO), as stated in its Constitution, was 'to procure a territory upon an autonomous basis for those Jews who cannot, or will not, remain in the lands in which they at present live'. To clarify, 'The territory shall be one in which autonomy shall be attainable, and in which the predominant majority of the population shall be Jewish.'[91] Providing it fitted these criteria, the 'Itoland' could therefore be anywhere in the world. East Africa, Texas (the Galveston Project), Tripolitania, Mexico, Australia and Canada were all toyed with, at one time or another, as possible destinations for Jewish immigration. In 1917 Zangwill came up with another idea. How about an 'Itoland' inside the borders of the new Russia? He wrote to Stephen Wise in America: 'The happy Revolution in Russia needs to ... be digested before the Jewish future is finally shaped. I am of [the] opinion that a Jewish state in Russia itself is now possible, and would be far superior to the Weizmann concept of a Palestinian State.'[92] In his article 'Siberia as a Jewish State',[93] written for *New York American* and reprinted in the London *Jewish World*, Zangwill advocated the creation of a 'United States of Russia', that is, of a decentralised federation on the American model, but divided up along national lines. Before the revolution, the Pale of Settlement had acted as an – admittedly involuntary – guarantor of Jewish 'national culture' in the diaspora. Now that the Pale had been broken up, it was essential to maintain this 'national culture' artificially on a territorial basis. This could be achieved by setting aside some 'virgin region' – such as Siberia – for Jewish settlement. In other words, there should be an internal migration of Russian Jews to an 'Itoland' within Russia itself. Later, in 1923, Zangwill enlarged upon the merits of Siberia for the purpose:

> In Siberia only ten millions of people eke out a livelihood and a Continent half as large again as the United States has been left almost in primaeval forest. Is there any reason why the Jews, instead of being cooped up in the stinking towns of the Pale, should not be invited to carve out a province with the plough-share from these vast neglected territories?[94]

Here, Zangwill was, remarkably, anticipating Soviet experiments with 'alternative Zionism' by means of Jewish agricultural colonisation in the Crimea and Birobidzhan during the 1920s.

Zionists and the Revolution

The English Zionist Federation (EZF), following the lead of Weizmann and Sokolov ('the EZF made virtually no independent contribution to Zionist theory'),[95] rejected out of hand the hypothesis that their ideology had been made redundant by the Russian Revolution. They welcomed the February Revolution because it granted emancipation to Jews as individuals. But, they argued, it gave nothing to the Jews collectively, as a nation. Not for the Zionists the half-way houses of 'National Cultural Autonomy' or 'Territorialism' – concepts, it was true, that the revolution did not oppose. As Leon Simon pointed out: 'the claim for Jewish national rights in Russia is a local matter, whereas the demand for a national centre in Palestine touches the whole of Jewry.'[96] The Zionists aimed at nothing less than the creation of an autonomous Jewish National Homeland in the territory of the ancient Jewish Commonwealth, recognised by the Great Powers, in just the same way as the 'self-determination' of all other small nations was to be recognised after the war.

In an interview[97] with Leopold Greenberg of the *Jewish Chronicle*, Nahum Sokolov maintained that the Zionist movement would derive benefit from the establishment of a democratic Russia – which he referred to as 'a sort of USA' – in three main ways. In the first place, now that the Zionist parties had been legalised, there was tremendous opportunity for open Zionist propaganda. Weizmann, too, was alive to this, as his speech of 20 May to the Zionist Conference testified. The movement, freed from the fetters of 'obsession with the Russian Jewish problem' would henceforth be able to concentrate, without distraction, upon its real aim – the upbuilding of Palestine. In the second place, the improved economic position of Russian Jewry, liberated from the strait-jacket of the Pale, meant a new source of finance for the *Yishuv* to supplement the contribution made by American Jewry. Finally, there now existed another sizeable free Jewry as a pool of potential *olim* (immigrants) for *Erets Yisrael* (the Land of Israel). Far from fearing that immigration thither would now dry up, the Zionists argued that, on the contrary, it would be stimulated. It would also be more selective. Only the cream of Russian Jewry would be attracted by settlement in Palestine. On this subject, Weizmann wrote:

[Emancipation] should serve to check that stream of Jewish emigration which is primarily economic in origin. But it should create no problem for a Jewish Palestine. The appeal of Palestine to the Jews is not simply or racially economic. The Jew who seeks a fortune rather than the opportunity to achieve inner freedom and to cooperate in the revival of the national life of his people will do well to seek another home than Palestine during the first genera- tion of the new society. There was hitherto the possibility that the close of the war might send into Palestine a flood of such im- migrants greater than the country in its early years could easily absorb. The Revolution should correct that possibility into an improbability, and select for Palestine ... precisely that kind of Jewish settler who is most needed to build up the new Jewish State.[98]

Thus the Zionists concluded that the advent of liberalism in Russia was a necessary precondition for the achievement of the Jewish national dream in Palestine. The former, insufficient in itself, would help to promote the latter. Liberalism in Russia, however, was a mixed blessing. Certainly it brought with it freedom of choice. But the Rus- sian Jew could just as easily choose assimilation as opposed to nationalism. This danger made the realisation of Zionism more urgent than ever. The break-up of the Pale of Settlement, as a result of emigration and war, had already loosened the bonds of Jewish obser- vance and cultural values in Russia. Dr Jochelman (in making the case for ITO) made some very startling, and, as it turned out, very accurate, predictions about the future character of the Russian Jewish com- munity: 'A migration of Jews within Russia there will be after the War, such as has never happened before ... In one or two generations the necessity for instructing children in Yiddish will disappear.'[99] The founder of the Women's International Zionist Organisation (WIZO), Rebecca Sieff, noted in an article in the *Zionist Review* that

> It is quite within the realms of possibility that Yiddish will disap- pear more quickly in Russia than in America, for in New York there exists a much greater aggregation of Jews than in any town in Russia; and, in consequence of the Revolution, it is likely that this aggregation will have a longer lease of life than any similar one in Russia.[100]

Many Zionists shared the view held by traditionalist religious leaders that the passing of the Pale was, in some respects, a matter for regret. Weizmann took up this theme:

> It is already obvious that [the war] will deal a shattering blow at what has been for centuries the great reservoir of Jewish strength. Thus the war brings the Jewish problem into tragic relief. It is not merely that hundreds of thousands of Jews have been turned into homeless wanderers, exposed to the ravages of famine and disease with but the slightest prospect of ever recovering such economic stability as they had before ... of even more awful significance for the Jewish people, is the destruction of the home of Jewish life and learning, the breakup of the social organism which, despite its lack of freedom and of material and political strength, has embodied most fully in the modern world what is vital and enduring in the character and ideals of the Jewish people. The havoc brought by the war to the Jews of Poland has been compared to the destruction of Jerusalem by the Romans, and the comparison is by no means fanciful. For the fearful blow strikes beyond the individuals at the very heart of the nation.

Zionism offered a third alternative to the two extremes of the ghetto and assimilation. The prospect of the dispersal of the Jews all over Russia, after the revolution, invested the Zionist goal – the creation of a central spiritual reference-point in Palestine – with increased urgency. Only such a homeland could be a truly 'national centre' for the Jews – a status which the Pale as a compulsory ghetto could in any case never have attained. Weizmann warned:

> It is ... no exaggeration to say that East European Jewry has been for some centuries the real centre of Jewish life, and that its disruption, not accompanied by the establishment of another centre, would threaten the very existence of the Jews as a people.[101]

Implicit in the Zionist case was the belief that: 'The great mass of the 6,000,000 Jews in Russia [were] more or less in sympathy with the Zionist cause.'[102] And it was in the Zionists' interest to foster this assumption in the mind of the British Foreign Office. As seen earlier, they were successful on this front, despite the fact that the government was being fed at the same time with directly contradictory information by Lucien Wolf and his associates. Weizmann cited voting patterns at the various assemblies called by Russian Jewry during 1917 to prove that the Zionists were the strongest party (for example, the Jewish conference held in Kiev in May, which recorded a 300 plus majority for the Zionists over the Bund). In reality, all the figures quoted by both sides were open to dispute, given that, under conditions of war, revolution and German occupation, no truly representative Jewish assembly met that year. The most reliable statistics – which were constantly referred to by the Zionist Organisation in the west – were the results of the elections held for the All-Russian Jewish Conference in the autumn of 1917. But, since these elections took place in the aftermath of the Balfour Declaration, which undoubtedly gave Zionism a terrific boost in Russia, they shed no light at all on the precise fortunes of the 'nationalists' (Zionist and cultural) *vis-à-vis* the 'assimilationists' (the socialists), in the interim between the February and October Revolutions. Yet the EZF, following Weizmann's lead, insisted on the popularity of Zionism in Russia to the extent that it gave further credence to the 'propaganda card' thesis – the idea that a British declaration on Palestine could have a significant effect on Russian Jewish opinion, and through it, ultimately, on the general political situation in Russia. Thus, the EZF, like Weizmann, bore some responsibility for perpetuating the myth of 'Jewish power'.

Behind the Zionist promotion of the 'propaganda card' lay one further assumption: the identity of interest between the Jews and the British Empire. Indeed, this was a fundamental plank of Weizmann's policy, and led directly to the setting up of the British Palestine Committee. When, in February 1918, the Foreign Office approached Leopold Greenberg, the editor of the *Jewish Chronicle*, to draft a manifesto from British Jewry to their Russian brethren, this is what he wrote:

> The fact that England which throughout its history has stood for the freedom and liberty of mankind and which has never left an opportunity unembraced for help to the Jewish people, has, we can well believe, impressed you. So we doubt not has the fact that England has declared that Peace shall see the last shreds of civil and political disability to the Jew existing anywhere wiped away

and the first beginning made of the recognition of Jews as a national entity in the world. Whatever may be our views upon the Jewish National Movement, there can be no question about England's attitude towards our people and her unflinching championship of human rights.[103]

More extravagant claims on behalf of the supposed existence of a British/Jewish alliance could not be wished for. An essential ingredient of the 'Jewish liberal compromise' in England had been lifted out of context to serve a very different and, the anti-nationalists would argue, contradictory purpose.

The whole problem as to whether Jewish nationalism flourishes or not in a free society, as to the influence of the Zionists *vis-à-vis* the Bund, soon became academic, at least as far as Russia was concerned: '[t]he aftermath of Jewish emancipation in Russia in the Spring of 1917...confounded the theory of Wolf and his friends. It took only a few months for their cloudless optimism to give way to mounting concern about the recurrence of antisemitism.'[104] At the same time, the Bolshevik Revolution put paid to any hopes the Zionists entertained about the advantages to be gained for their cause from the existence of a liberated Jewry in the east. Some Zionists, however, had never suffered from the illusion that the revolution heralded the complete disappearance of antisemitism in Russia. The thesis that antisemitism is endemic, whatever the system of government, goes back a long way in Zionist thought. Lev Pinsker claimed that an invisible vicious circle operated in Europe. Emancipation of the Jew from the ghetto led to assimilation into the host society; this process, in turn, only stimulated antisemitism and renewed exclusion. As neither native nor foreigner in the land of his birth, the Jew was a perpetual outsider.

As early as April 1917, Lord Rothschild wrote to Weizmann:

> Apart from the first and foremost great national aims and sentiments of our people ... there is to my mind a very much greater need for establishing the real Jewish nation again in Palestine. We must think of the future; the bulk, quite 90 per cent of the Russian nation is illiterate and uneducated and have been urged on for centuries against the Jews. Our people are the educated class in Russia, therefore now that they have equal rights they will forge ahead and outstrip the rest of the Russian peoples in all walks of

178

life and thus raise up a new form of hatred and envy. Therefore, we ought by urging on our Government here to adopt the Zionist cause as their own to enable us to reduce the number of Jews remaining in Russia as much as possible and so lessen the chances of future trouble. The national aspirations must, of course, take first place but I feel sure we shall do wrong if we do not keep the possibility of *future Russian trouble* well to the front of the Zionist programme.[105]

By 1920, with civil war raging, every Zionist regarded the outlook for Russian Jewry with profound pessimism. The *Zionist Review* (August) captured the prevailing mood: 'Those who believed that with the accomplishment of the Soviet Revolution in Russia the Jewish question in that country would vanish must by now be sadly disillusioned. Never has the Jewish problem in Russia been so acute.'

Finally, the Zionists rejected the fear expressed by their opponents that pursuit of the Jewish nationalist goal threatened the position of the Jews in Russia. The issues of Russia and Palestine were entirely unrelated. Harry Sacher denied that there was any conflict inherent in the striving after national as well as after individual rights:

> The inspiration of the Russian Revolution is the political equality of all citizens coupled with the rights of nationality. These two great principles are proclaimed by the Russian Revolution each as the natural complement of the other, and the conflict between them upon which the emancipation 'contract myth' has rested is repudiated in a most decisive fashion.[106]

The Russian Revolution, unlike the French Revolution, did not insist that Jewish emancipation was conditional upon the renunciation of allegiance to world Jewry or to the Land of Israel. Citizenship was not synonymous with nationality. And it did not matter whether the territorial centre of the nationality in question lay *outside* the Russian state. Perhaps, in arguing thus, the Zionists were guilty of displaying a faith in the generosity and endurance of western liberal values – not to mention their application to Russian conditions – which would have been more becoming in Lucien Wolf and his friends. As for the assertion that Zionism would only lead to still more antisemitism, Leon Simon had this to say:

179

But there is a simple answer to that argument. If the nations which have granted equal rights to the Jews are capable of retrogressing so far as to substitute a policy of persecution for one of toleration, it would be absurd on the part of the Jews to expect to find in their own homelessness a shield against the evil which threatens them. Experience in Russia (under the Old Regime) and elsewhere proves that a country which for one reason or another is predisposed towards an antisemitic policy is not deterred from carrying it out by the consideration that the Jews have no country of their own. If, then, it be assumed that other states will in future model their treatment of the Jews on Czarist Russia, what ground is there for supposing that it will make any difference whether there is or is not a Jewish National Home? The fact is that the Jews, as a scattered people, must always depend on the liberality and enlightenment of the states in which they live ... and if the civilised world is going to relapse into chauvinistic intolerance, the outlook for the Jews is so bad that they would be well advised to secure at least a corner of the earth where they can hope to be beyond the reach of antisemitism.

But, he added,

There is no reason so to despair of human progress, at any rate within a year of the Russian Revolution.[107]

CONCLUSION

In 1917 and 1918, the ideology of Jewish nationalism was pitted against Jewish socialism as a 'propaganda card' in British government policy with regard to the Jewish 'problem'. The irony was that, on the part of policy-makers, enthusiasm for the former was based to some extent on the assumption of certain antisemitic stereotypes. It has been pointed out elsewhere that antisemitism *per se* is not an adequate explanation for any given state policy in relation to Jews. Antisemitic notions can be entertained as much by supporters as by detractors of the Jewish cause. As Brian Cheyette has shown in his study of Jewish stereotypes in literature, all images of the Jew tend to be dualistic in character, that is, 'bifurcated' into 'good' and 'bad', 'positive' and 'negative' by supporters and opponents alike.

Churchill's article of 1920, which provided the linchpin for this chapter, is a prime illustration of Cheyette's thesis. For the very policy he advocates of 'Zionism versus Bolshevism' operated on the antithesis between the 'constructive' Jewish type – the nationalist – and his 'destructive' counterpart (one is tempted to say *alter ego*), the internationalist. In Churchill's defence, it must also be set on record that the Zionist leadership in London encouraged this over-simplification.

Chaim Weizmann was exploiting exaggerated Foreign Office fears about the Jewish role in Bolshevism in order to engender British support for a Jewish Palestine. Nor were Zionists acting merely out of expediency. There is ample evidence in Weizmann's own writings that he shared the anxiety of the British government to contain whatever 'Jewish' part there was in Russian revolutionary extremism through an appeal to Jewish nationalist sentiment. In promoting the antithetical connection between Zionism and socialism, however, Weizmann was running the risk of perpetuating the misconceptions which were current in governing circles regarding the Jews.

The question must also be posed: Can allowance be made for the fact that Churchill's obsession with revolutionary Jews was incidental to his wider campaign for an ideological struggle against the threat of Bolshevism, conducted in the context of the British intervention in the Russian Civil War? As Norman Cohn has pointed out, it was the First World War and the Russian Revolution which were, in a sense, responsible for bestowing legitimacy upon the Jewish conspiracy theory. Israel Zangwill judged that Churchill's policy was a 'perversity of vision' created 'in a brain that is seeing red, and seeing falsely'.[108] That did not constitute an excuse.

Finally, from the vantage point of the British government, the policy of 'Zionism versus Bolshevism' was an abject failure. The October Revolution rendered it obsolete, although this fact was lost on Churchill himself, who persisted with the notion with even greater insistence during the Civil War. On the other hand, for the Zionists it yielded an immediate benefit: 'Zionism versus Bolshevism' played no small part in the publication of the Balfour Declaration. Yet Zionist success in the short-term notwithstanding, this policy was fraught with danger even for the Zionists themselves. Not only were they responsible for encouraging the myth of 'Jewish power'; with the advent of the British Mandate, the charge was levelled against them that 'Zionist Bolsheviks' were invading Palestine.

Meanwhile, a debate of far profounder import was taking place between 'English Zionists and British Jews' regarding the destiny of Russian Jewry in the light of the revolution. What was to be the overall relationship between the issues of eastern Europe and the Middle East, as far as the Jews were concerned? For anti-Zionists, the February Revolution vindicated their optimistic view of the world. It confirmed their faith in emancipation and in the Jewish Mission. They could now sit back and observe the development of a free and vibrant Jewry in the east. At the same time these 'Englishmen of the Mosaic faith' were anxious that the notion of an extra-European Jewish nationalism could endanger the rights won by Jews in Russia, in England and elsewhere, by raising the sensitive question of 'dual loyalties'. Insisting then, that the fortunes of Russia and Palestine were intimately bound up with each other, they asserted that it was simply a matter of priorities – in which the remoter Zionist dream must take second place.

The Zionists took a diametrically opposite view. To them, the Russian Revolution was only a stepping stone on the road back to Zion. It did not in itself address the underlying problem of antisemitism which was with the Jew in perpetuity, given his anomalous situation of homelessness in Europe. Indeed, the destruction of the ghettos of the Pale invested the search for a solution to this problem with renewed urgency. The opening up of the Russian interior to the Jew meant accelerated assimilation into, and along with it, the increased risk of rejection by, the host society. In the internal debate, the Zionists maintained, then, that Russia and Palestine were for all practical purposes separate issues. It was ironic that at the same time, Weizmann was stressing to the British government the connection between Zionism and Bolshevism.

In the end, it must be acknowledged that serious critics of Zionism, like Wolf, Montefiore and also Zangwill, were motivated quite as much as their opponents by genuine concern for the fate of Jewry in eastern Europe. Furthermore, they were deeply committed to the preservation of the rich cultural and religious life of that Jewry. Not all anti-Zionists were thorough-going 'assimilationists', as much Zionist historiography would have us believe. They based their position on what they considered to be a realistic analysis of conditions as they then were. Take, for example, Wolf's views expressed in 1917 on the competing claims of Hebrew and Yiddish for the loyalties of east European Jewry (a much politicised subject):

> The Yiddishists, of course, won; for Hebrew, whatever its historic associations and the zeal with which its study was promoted, was an exotic, while Yiddish was a living language; the natural outcome of Russian Jewish life, the language of the people and the home.[109]

That the anti-Zionist position was made redundant by the course of events – the enormity of which even the Zionists could not have predicted – was no fault of their own. The fact remains that the radical Zionist viewpoint, founded upon a fundamentally pessimistic reading of the Jewish situation in Europe, proved, in retrospect, to be the only answer in the face of extremity.

5 Jewish Bolsheviks? East End Jewry and the Russian Revolution

The February Revolution

There is no doubt, that the nightmarish *tsorres* [trouble] of our brothers have now disappeared together with Tsarism.

Der Yiddisher Ekspress, 21 March 1917

If the Russian Revolution has been practically ignored in 'official' quarters, apart from the Chief Rabbi ... this has not been the case in that large section of the Community whose connections with their Russian brethren are closer. Throughout the London Ghetto, and in all other parts of the country where Russian Jews or their English-born children are to be found in any numbers, the rejoicings have been thorough and sincere. A spirit of optimism has spread throughout the poorer Jewish centres ... In other quarters doubts may still linger: but the Russian Jew in England believes without any reservation that his kinsman in Russia is at length free.

The Zionist Review, May 1917

The sentiments towards England entertained by the Russian Jew in England are not as deeply-rooted as are his sentiments towards his fellow-Jews in Russia; nor can they be expected to be ...

I. Wassilevsky, *Jewish Refugees and Military Service*, Manchester, 1916

For 'East End' Jews, the majority of whom originated in eastern Europe, news of the Russian Revolution had an immediacy which was inevitably lacking in the response of their counterparts in the 'West

184

End'. Political developments in the 'Old Country', to which ties of kinship were in many cases still strong, were of direct consequence to the immigrant community. At first, the collapse of the tsarist government was greeted with disbelief. The sad precedent of 1905, when expectations had been raised, only to be cruelly dashed, was uppermost in everyone's mind. But, as more certain information arrived, caution went to the winds. The Ghetto was jubilant.

The East End boasted its own home-grown and very lively Yiddish press. The leading Yiddish daily, '*Di Tsayt*' had no regrets about the passing of the Romanovs. Under the heading 'The red Tsar with the black heart', its editor Morris Myer wrote: 'For us, Nicholas II was a red Tsar, up to his eyes in Jewish blood. Under his rule occurred one of the most tragic pages in the history of the Jews in Russia ... The Tsar Nicholas was ... an enemy of the Jews.'[1]

Myer was a professional journalist who had been born in Romania and emigrated to England in 1902. In 1913 he founded *Di Tsayt* – the Yiddish answer to the London *Times* – and in 1914 its sister evening paper *Ovend Nayes*. Politically, Myer was a socialist and a Zionist. He had strong connections with the Jewish trade union movement, was a member of the Workers' Circle and of the *Poale Tsion* London Executive. In 1919 he was elected to represent the East End on the Board of Deputies and thus gained a foothold in the communal establishment. By 1922 he was a vice-chairman of the English Zionist Federation and a member of the Conjoint Committee. 'Up West' Myer was regarded as the unofficial representative of immigrant Jewry. Yet his position as a bridge between the two communities earned him the distrust of elements further to his left. Myer had 'sold out' to the 'bourgeoisie' – his migration to an address in Golders Green being the outward symbol of his defection.

'*A moyra tsu friiyen*' (A fear of freedom), commented Aron-Tsvi Romanovsky, on the month-long failure of the Board of Deputies to greet the revolution.[2] Romanovsky was a colleague of Myer's who had come to London in 1906 and was president of *Poale Tsion* in England. In the East End, on the other hand, a series of public meetings was called in honour of the momentous events in Russia. These were organised by the socialist movement and by various Russian émigré groups. At the end of March 1917 the *Manchester Guardian* reported that about two thousand people were packed into the Kingsway Hall and that 'There was a strong Jewish element, for there are many Jews who call Russia home.'³ *A Wanderer* (Jacob Capitanshchik) recorded his impressions of a similar 'gigantic' mass meeting at the Great Assembly Hall. 'In ten minutes' he wrote, the hall which was 'decked in red flags' was packed to overflowing and 'hundreds' outside had to be turned away. Speaker after speaker was accompanied by the throwing of caps, cheering and singing. Jewish enthusiasm was not dampened by the fact that the majority of the speeches were made in Russian, a language with which the average immigrant from the Pale was not very familiar. Nevertheless, the Jews applauded and stamped their feet at the mention of the word *revolutsia*, as if, the writer commented, they were blotting out the 'Hamans' at the traditional reading of *Megillas Esther* (the Book of Esther) on the festival of *Purim*. This scene must have inspired a piece of fantasy entitled 'The Future Russia: The Month of March 2017', which appeared in *Ovend Nayes* a couple of weeks later. Written by Sh. Zumd, this was a rather far-fetched science-fiction account of the hundredth anniversary of the revolution as he imagined it would be celebrated in the capital 'Freeburg' (that is the renamed Petersburg) of the 'United States of Russia'. The story owed something to both the French Revolution and H.G. Wells.⁴

Yiddisher Ekspress (the *Jewish Express*), the main rival of Myer's papers and one of the oldest Yiddish newspapers in England (founded in 1896 in Leeds and edited by Jacob Hodes), predicted that not only would the revolution mean that immigration to England would dry up, but that 'thousands' of Jews from the East End would want to return to Russia after the war. The population of Whitechapel would decline. Meanwhile Leo Kenig, *Di Tsayt's* literary critic, who had come to England from Odessa in 1914, observed that the relationship between east European and west European Jewry was about to change: 'We [the Russians] were against them indeed scroungers [*taka schnorrers*] and they, against us men of substance [*nogidim*] ... Now, we will be just as rich and equal as they.'⁵ One gets the impression that Kenig was referring as much to the relationship between 'East' and 'West End' Jewry, as to that between the Jews of east and west.

From February to October

They talk day and night ... they will talk, talk and talk. From generation to generation the jaws of the Russian citizens were locked. They were not permitted to speak but one word, and now, when the locks have been torn away, the jaws have suddenly opened and will speak out for the whole time that they were silent ... Passionately they talk, all together and one does not listen to the other and one wants to shout the other down ... [Meanwhile] ... anarchy in the country is growing from day to day ...

Yiddisher Ekspress, 10 October 1917

The mainstream Anglo-Yiddish press was dominated by Labour Zionists. We have already encountered the names of Morris Myer, Jacob Hodes, Aron-Tsvi Romanovsky and Leo Kenig. Other contributors of similar ilk were Joshua Podruzhnik and Dr Joseph Kruk, both of whom had originated in Poland. Podruzhnik was a professional journalist who settled in England in 1914 and served in the Jewish Legion in Palestine. Kruk was a Doctor of Law who lived and studied all over Europe; in 1926 he returned to Poland to engage in socialist politics and in 1939 escaped to Palestine. In terms of British politics, all of these Yiddish writers identified with the Labour Party. In 1917 they shared the 'majority' socialist viewpoint that the war against German 'militarism' was paramount. In the context of Russian revolutionary politics, their sympathies lay with the Petrograd Soviet, and its declared policy of 'revolutionary defence', with an eye to a future general negotiated peace. Thus the Yiddish press welcomed both the June Offensive and the calling of the Stockholm Conference.

Morris Myer's great hero was Alexander Kerensky. Kerensky was 'destined' (*beshert*) to be the ruler of Russia, safeguarder of democracy, moderation and national unity, 'The wonderful truly revolutionary figure of Kerensky, the man of constructive action, and not of provocative words and wild disruptive deeds'. For *Yiddisher Ekspress* too, Kerensky was 'The embodied soul of freed Russia: [the] embodiment of a ruler of a land which is poised to realise the noble ideals of socialism: a land which has begun to breathe freely, to live freely'.[6]

Kerensky's task was not an easy one. As early as March, Myer voiced his concern about 'Sinister forces which might be looking to turn the clock back ... and groups of extremists who would like to wind the clock on so quickly, that the whole machinery of the revolution might give'.[7] In the successive crises which plagued the short life of the Provisional Government, extremists and reactionaries were regarded as the root cause of the trouble, while Kerensky himself was held to be blameless. Myer welcomed the formation of a coalition government in the aftermath of the Milyukov 'Decisive Victory' note crisis in May. On balance, this was a 'wise' move which would enhance the prestige of the Soviet. Nevertheless, a natural distrust of alliance with the 'bourgeoisie' in the government remained. During the July Days, Myer not only condemned the far left, 'who thought that mere wild and stormy outbursts were revolutionary deeds', but also the Kadets – the landowners and industrialists – who were attempting to undermine Kerensky and Soviet power. These vested interests set their face against the economic reform of land and labour urged by the socialists. As for General Kornilov, Myer dismissed him as an 'adventurer' and 'intriguer', who was in collusion with the 'Black Hundreds' and egged on by the Tory press in Britain. Kornilov seized upon the unrest caused by the Bolsheviks in July, as an opportunity to make counter-revolution. More importantly, the Kadets were seriously implicated in the plot. In hindsight, Myer wrote: '[The Kadets] instigated the Kornilov uprising, which had the aim of completely suppressing the Soviet and of bringing back a regime which would exclusively suit the bourgeoisie.'

Kerensky himself was cast in the role of 'Saviour' of the revolution. He was forced to take over as the effective dictator of Russia, but a dictator dedicated to the revolution and to democracy. Indeed, Myer claimed that if Kerensky had been installed as the ruler of Russia at the very beginning, the present chaos might have been avoided. And, clearly afraid of the consequences of anarchy, Myer concluded: 'if freedom succumbs, it will succumb together with Kerensky.'[8]

The Bolshevik Revolution

Di Tsayt was no more in favour of October than was the *Jewish Chronicle*. Morris Myer had no illusions about Lenin. He boasted that he was well qualified to pronounce on this subject, as he had met both Lenin and Trotsky at the 1907 RSDP Conference in London. Lenin, Myer wrote, may look like a cossack, but was a first-class thinker and a ruthless, natural leader.

If Lenin were a king, I am sure that he would be more autocratic than Nicholas II and even than William II. If he were a general, he would be more brutal than Hindenburg or Nero. He cannot tolerate any other opinion. He cannot make any compromise with a differing world-view. Since he was not a king, he has always striven to be the dictator of the proletariat, and the proletariat is not permitted to have any other aim but his, any other aspiration [*einshoyaungen*] than that which Lenin has. For Lenin, the proletariat is his own property, and he wishes that, as far as the world is concerned, Lenin is the proletariat.

Myer did not believe that such a man could ever have been a German spy: 'This is an absurdity. There is no power in the world which could buy him off to serve them. But it may be, that he has used German resources to attain his goal.'[9]

In short, Lenin was a 'formidable' personality who should not be underestimated. Neither should Trotsky. Myer, like Leopold Greenberg, had kinder words for the 'Jewish' revolutionary. He was 'honest' and 'courageous', 'wilful' and with a 'touch of genius'; he possessed 'such a delectable brain'. The Treaty of Brest-Litovsk was a shameful sell-out, but it revealed more about the 'imperialist psychology' of the Germans than the sinister motives of the Russians. The Bolsheviks were perceived as the victims, driven to make terms out of sheer desperation. For the Russians had been betrayed by the Allies who consistently ignored the Soviet's call for a revision of war aims. So Trotsky was making a last-ditch attempt to salvage the honour of Russia through his defiant non-policy of 'neither war nor peace'. But in the end 'Prometheus' was overruled by 'Mephistopheles', 'the evil spirit' of the revolution – Lenin. Trotsky was little more than a 'slave' to the domineering and undemocratic will of his master. Yet, somehow, he had achieved a 'moral victory' over the Germans.[10]

The London Yiddish journalists, for the most part, agreed with the Menshevik analysis, which regarded the attempted social revolution as 'premature'. The Bolsheviks had 'used military methods to seize power' and the inevitable result was violence. Myer again:

> [Lenin] organised the counter-revolution against the first revolution and incited brother revolutionaries to shoot brother revolutionaries. He drowned the first bloodless revolution in a sea of blood and as soon as he had the power in his hands, he began to rule by force and through terror.[11]

For six whole months, Myer clung to the belief that an escape route from Bolshevism still existed, via Allied recognition of the *Soviet* government. By that term he meant the Soviets in their original form, as opposed to the Bolsheviks. Myer had invested a great deal of faith in these workers' councils, with their broad representation of socialist parties and social classes, as the foundation of Russian democracy. Foreign recognition, he argued, would enhance the prestige of the Soviets and revive the moderate elements therein. If, in the event, the Bolsheviks remained the dominant party in the Soviet then so be it. For 'We must let the Soviets choose whichever leaders and rulers they like.'[12]

Myer wrote this line in May 1918; the Bolsheviks had shut down the Constituent Assembly, where they had not achieved a majority, the previous January. At the very least, Myer hoped that the Bolsheviks themselves would see the error of their ways. However, by the summer the editor was forced to relinquish such notions as unrealistic, the occasion being the Labour Party conference, at which his erstwhile hero, Kerensky, was guest speaker. Myer was thoroughly disillusioned, and dismissed the ex-leader of the Provisional Government as being a 'gasbag'. His speech consisted of a catalogue of complaints (*taynes*) against Bolshevism. In marked contrast to his 'constructive deeds' of a year ago, Kerensky's words were now a godsend to the reactionaries:

> For us, Kerensky appeared at the conference not as a statesman, and not as the architect of a great free land, but as a symbol of an unhappy people, who wanted so much and achieved so little ... who reached for the sun and sank into the depths. ... who destroyed with so much passion and are so reluctant to build. ... who are so sharp in their criticism and so weak in positive reconstructive plan[s] ... who have such grandiose dreams and such a horrible reality ... A very poignant symbol of Russia's unhappiness is Kerensky. But can symbols save Russia from unhappiness?

Romanovsky, in *Ovend Nayes*, agreed that Kerensky was the very symbol of '*golos*' (exile) today.[13]

Where did all this leave the Jews? Like their opposite numbers in the 'West End', the Yiddish papers had few regrets about the passing of the tsar. They were only concerned that the assassination might have created a martyr in the style of Charles I and Louis XVI, a focus around which reactionary forces could regroup. For the Jews, there was no doubt that counter-revolution was a 'terrible' (*shreklikh*) prospect. On the other hand, in the estimation of Aron Romanovsky, 'For us Jews, the new Russia is as bad as the old.'[14]

For his part, Myer could not bring himself to believe the personal assurances given him by Maxim Litvinov – the Bolshevik emissary with '*a yiddishe ponim*' (a Jewish face) – that the new government of Russia would respect the 'national, cultural and political rights' of the Jews 'completely', and moreover that 'The Jews who want to be a nation can do so' (although this statement, apparently, did not mean that Litvinov was prepared to give his blessing to the Zionist enterprise in Palestine). It did not take long for Myer to discover that the Bolshevik's secularism, anti-nationalism and anti-individualism were in direct conflict with every Jewish aspiration. Russian Jewry was mainly orthodox in religion; liberal, moderate socialist or Zionist in politics; and in economic terms 'a nation of shopkeepers'. As early as February 1918, *Di Tsayt* accused the Bolsheviks of carrying out pogroms 'under cover of the Red Flag':

> In four months of the Russian Revolution the Russian Jews have had more pogroms than in the time of Nicholas I, Alexander II, Alexander III and Nicholas the Last ... This is the sum total of Bolshevism: defeat, shame, collapse, disgrace, robbery, murder, theft and slaughter.

Not, as Leo Kenig conceded, that this meant that pogroms had a place in Bolshevik ideology. It was simply that they were all for utilising the 'revolutionary instincts' of the masses, and pogroms were, from that angle, considered to be 'revolutionary deeds in every respect'. The revolutionaries recognised the thirst for revenge on the part of the 'sans culottes' and so tolerated excesses. Jewish life was cheap in revolutionary epochs.[15]

British intervention and the Russian Civil War

עַד־מָתַי, עַד־אָנָה, עַד־מָתַי?[16]

The Yiddish press was uncompromisingly opposed to intervention against the Bolsheviks. But not until after the Armistice did *Di Tsayt* make public its disapproval. Bolshevism, Morris Myer consistently argued, was a by-product of war, and of German 'militarism' in particular; therefore it would but thrive on a war of intervention. The commitment of Allied forces in Russia would give credence to Communist propaganda against 'capitalist counter-revolution' and would encourage the build-up of a national Red Army. The Bolsheviks would benefit from the ill-deserved sympathy of western socialists and workers. In short, Myer, like Greenberg at the *Chronicle*, did not much like Lenin, but he had severe misgivings about intervention as a means of overthrowing him.

There was also the ever-present fear that if the Bolsheviks fell, Russia might get something even worse. The Ghetto had no illusions about the White Guard generals: after all, a great many of its inhabitants had fled to England in order to escape the attentions of similar elements. A situation of civil war boded no good for the Jews. In April 1919, Myer predicted that 'The Jews will be between two terrible fires. For sure, the Bolsheviks will shout that the Jews are on the side of the Entente and the reactionaries will shout that the Jews are Bolsheviks.'[17] It needed no special power of prophecy to realise that the result would be a *khurban* – a massive destruction of Jewry. *Yiddisher Ekspress* sadly observed:

> Great was the hope that the word 'pogrom' would disappear together with Tsarism; we could not but believe that Jewish salvation had come through the fall of Tsarism ... It is already over a year since we have been freed from Tsarism and still this word 'pogrom' is not yet forgotten, indeed we come across it now perhaps more often than before.[18]

During 1919 and 1920, for weeks on end the Yiddish press carried graphic reports of widespread pogroms and lists of towns and individual victims in the Pale of Settlement. These lists, in particular, bring home the fact that the East End was directly involved in events *in der heim* (the old country). The report of pogroms in Poland and in the Ukraine did not have that quality of detachment that one finds in the English language Jewish press – for it was dealing with the fate of friends and relatives.

The utter helplessness of the Jews, trapped in 'a hellish gehenna' comes across vividly in these reports. *Yiddisher Ekspress* likened the victims to '[S]heep in the slaughterhouse ... quite ready for the knife of the wild destroyers. They do not protest. Because it is not worth protesting: to whom can they protest and for what can they protest?'[19] Their brethren in the west were equally powerless to help: for 'our hand is too short'. Protests would be 'like a voice in the wilderness' (*a kol bmidbar*). Indeed, the slaughter in the Ukraine surpassed in scale even that which had occurred in Poland – and the world seemed even less concerned. Joshua Podruzhnik commented that since Poland was 'a creature of the Allies' – and of the League of Nations – they were forced to accept some responsibility for her. Whereas, in the case of the Ukraine, which had never been on the Allied side, they could afford to maintain 'a sort of unhappy neutrality'.

Nevertheless, the East End took the lead in organising the national Day of Mourning for Polish Jewry in June 1919, and had no doubts about the efficacy of that particular public protest in stopping the pogroms in Poland. Accordingly, regarding the Ukraine, Myer demanded: 'Why are we silent? Why are we doing nothing?'[20] whilst *Yiddisher Ekspress* called for an 'on-going' 'people's protest' against pogroms. In March 1920 the Federation of Ukrainian Jews held a memorial meeting in Mile End for the victims of the pogroms in south Russia.

As far as the Yiddish press was concerned, the Russo-Polish war of 1920 represented just one more tragedy for the Jewish people. Myer wrote: 'After the lightning comes the thunder and after an offensive comes a pogrom ... It appears that these wars have no other aim[s] than to make pogroms.[21]

Allied involvement with the Poles – among whom rather than among the Bolsheviks, bitter experience had taught, the majority of the *pogromshchiki* were to be found – was to be condemned. The Yiddish press approved of Labour's 'Direct Action' to prevent the shipment of supplies to the Poles. Nevertheless, the Jews would be wise to remain strictly neutral regarding the rights and wrongs of the conflict. Once again, 'We find ourselves between two fires, and however dear the Jews of Russia are to us – so too are the Jews of Poland, and we cannot let either one of them be sacrificed.' Myer welcomed the Treaty of Riga with relief as 'the best thing that Soviet Russia has done up till now'.[22]

British intervention in Russia itself, not surprisingly, did not enjoy a good press in the East End; Winston Churchill was less than popular. *Yiddisher Ekspress* dubbed the intervention 'Churchill's War'. It wrote with venom:

> And now that he has fulfilled his ambition [for high office] he wants to show what he can do as War Minister. He wants to show that he can conduct a war; ... he desires to conduct war against the Bolsheviks ... He wants a war.

Had not Churchill disgraced himself enough with the disastrous Gallipoli campaign in 1915?, the paper enquired.[23]

Non-interference, not intervention, would be the best turn the Allies could do for Russia. Give her a chance to sort out her own destiny, urged Morris Myer. The only way to deal with Bolshevism was by relaxing the external pressure, and establishing some sort of dialogue with the Soviet regime. This would encourage the most effective type of reform: that which comes from within. Thus the Yiddish papers welcomed the abortive Prinkipo peace proposal in January 1919 and Lloyd George's attempts to revive it the following November. They praised the Prime Minister's role in this initiative, although doubting his moral stamina to carry it through, and avidly followed the tortuous progress of the negotiations leading up to the Anglo-Soviet Trade Agreement of March 1921. Myer argued all along that the economic blockade of Russia was having as dolorous an effect as direct military intervention. On the other hand, the restoration of trade relations could be a means of exerting a beneficial influence on the Soviet government. As Leo Kenig put it: 'There will not be shooting with bullets, but with goods and products and men will not be killed, but hearts will be bought.'[24]

Perhaps as a result, the Russian people would be encouraged to demand reform and the government itself to adopt more moderate policies. In February 1920 Myer, somewhat optimistically, speculated that the Bolsheviks might even be induced to convene a democratic parliament. In any case, the onset of famine provided an irresistible humanitarian imperative for the restoration of trade relations. Against this, Myer dismissed the so-called 'moral' arguments against treating with the Reds as '*tsu frum*' (too pious).[25] After all, the British had been allies of the tsar, pogroms notwithstanding, and talked with the sultan of Turkey despite the Armenian massacres. England, he declared, would have negotiated with cannibals if to do so was in her national interest. Myer clearly regarded trade relations as a prelude to diplomatic recognition. For this reason, he grew impatient and frustrated at the high-handedness of Bolshevik conduct at critical stages of the negotiations – which behaviour threatened to break them up altogether. *Di Tsayt* described the Bolshevik rejection of Prinkipo as '*a chutzpa*' (cheek) and disapproved of Bolshevik propaganda abroad, feeling that it was quite reasonable for the British to demand that it be stopped, as one condition for the continuation of talks. Lenin's *Letter to the British Workers* in June 1920 and the *Daily Herald* 'Bolshevik Gold' scandal of September 1920 irked Myer greatly. Lenin's letter was a 'death blow' to the endeavours of the British Labour Party to convince public opinion that the Bolsheviks were not so bad after all. It was an insult:

> In reality, Lenin's letter is not so much an attack on Capitalism as an attack on the English Labour leaders, on the whole English Labour Party, which will not declare itself in love with Soviet Communism and with the Dictatorship of the Proletariat, which, in reality, has absolutely nothing to do with socialism.

It was a gift to the reactionaries who were opposed to the trade agreement – a gift which the Soviets could ill afford, given their desperate need for western relief supplies. In short, the *Letter* was 'senseless' and 'an utter sin'.[26]

When the trade agreement was finally signed, *Di Tsayt* hailed it as the most significant peace treaty since the end of the war. The paper predicted that it would be followed up by British recognition of the Soviet government. (This did not, in fact, come about until the first Labour government took office in 1924.) Myer's analysis of internal reform in Russia seemed to be borne out by the introduction of the New Economic Policy (NEP) early in 1921, which was accompanied by an announcement that foreign investment would, once more, be tolerated. NEP was 'the greatest counter-revolution' in Russia since the October Revolution – and one carried out by the Bolsheviks themselves. *Yiddisher Ekspress* hailed it as 'the beginning of the end' of the Communist Experiment. Even so, the west now had no choice but to resign itself to the existence of Bolshevism. A few months previously Myer had written:

> Every sensible person, who is familiar with the situation in Russia, knows that it is impossible to have another type of government there ... and all of the disturbances [oysbrukhen] which will take place, and which must take place are absolutely inevitable.

Accordingly, he treated the Kronstadt Revolt with trepidation; no good would come of it, only further bloodshed. Russia was no longer at the stage where she could tolerate another change of regime. The events of 1917 had shown that it was impossible to make the transition from autocracy to democracy in one giant leap. In the meantime, Russia was obliged to settle for dictatorship. It could only be hoped that democracy would one day develop, even out of Bolshevism itself.[27]

A working conclusion from our survey of the East End Jewish press can now be arrived at: the Yiddish press was no more 'Bolshevik' than the English-language Anglo-Jewish press. To be sure, it was more outspoken and less self-conscious in its opinions. But this in itself is not surprising, given that the Yiddish press was not subject to the same external scrutiny as was the *Jewish Chronicle*. While it was concerned with the internal welfare of the Ghetto, it was not so much preoccupied with the business of 'communal defence' and relations with the larger society. Nevertheless, the same pattern held true for the 'East End' as well as the 'West End', if the marginal elements on the far left are discounted (see below). Universal support for the Provisional Government turned into antipathy towards the Bolsheviks. Whatever residual sympathy for the Russian Communists still existed in Whitechapel by 1919 tended to be of the 'lesser evil' variety. The Ghetto treated British intervention on the side of the White generals with severe reservations. The sympathies of Morris Myer and his associates lay with the British Labour Party and with democratic socialism. The Yiddish papers adopted Labour policy on Bolshevism and, especially, on intervention to a remarkable degree. The problem was that, during and after the First World War, there was a tendency for Conservatives to label all opponents to their left as 'Bolsheviks'. And, as will become evident, it was the presence of a small, unrepresentative, but vociferous radical

Posters in English and (overleaf) Yiddish advertising the mass meeting called by the Foreign Jews' Protection Committee in Aldgate on 25 March 1917

דער פערטהיידיגונגס קאמיטעט
פון די אויסלענדישע אידען געגען צוריקשיקונג קיין רומ־
לאנד און געצוואונגענע מיליטער־דיענסט.

א מאסען פערזאמלונג
צו פערטהיידיגען דאס אזילרעכט

און פייערען די רוסישע רעוואלוציאן
וועט אבגעהאלטען ווערען

זונטאג דעם 25 מערץ
אין
קעמפערדאון הויז.
האף מן פעסערדזש, אלדגיט.

דער זעהר געעהרטער
לארד שעפיעלד
וועט זיין דער פארזיצענדער.

מר. דזשאזעף קינג, מ.פ.,
קאונסילער דיטמאן, דר. וואלטער וואלש, ד.ד.,
דר. י. מ. וואלמינד, דר. א. מארגאלין, מרס. יוער,
מיסס סילוי פאנקהערסט און אנדערע וועלען ריידען.

איינטרים פריי. טהירען אפען 1.30.

אין אויפטראג פון פערטהיידיגונגס קאמיטעם
געגען צוריקשיקונג און צוואנג־דיענסם,
אברהם בצלאל, סעקרעטאר.

געדרוקט ביי י. נאראדיצקי, (טרייד יוניאן), 48 מייל ענד דוד, א.

element in the East End, which was mainly responsible for making the label stick.

'FRIENDLY ALIENS' AND THE CONSCRIPTION QUESTION

Nowhere did foreign affairs and domestic Jewish concerns coalesce more strongly than in the controversy surrounding the conscription of Russian Jewish 'friendly aliens' during the First World War. The Russian Revolution brought the problem to a head. It stimulated an outbreak of anti-alienism on a scale not seen since 1905. Inevitably an attack on aliens in the East End meant, in practice, an attack on Jews, which even the 'West End', that is native and naturalised Jews, could not entirely escape. And the position of the latter was made even more uncomfortable by the militant hostility of the Russian Jews to the Anglo-Russian Military Convention.

The Foreign Jews' Protection Committee

In June 1916 the Foreign Jews' Protection Committee against Deportation to Russia and Compulsion (FJPC) had been set up in the East End of London. Its primary aim was to resist veiled government threats to deport back to tsarist Russia 'friendly aliens' who did not volunteer for service in the British army. During the first half of 1917, the committee organised several large demonstrations in the East End 'to protect the right of asylum and cheer the Russian Revolution'. The best publicised of these was the Camperdown Hall meeting of 25 March. Handbills in English and Yiddish were posted around the East End and advertisements placed in the Yiddish and local press. The second public meeting was scheduled for 2 June at the Great Assembly Hall – except that the proprietor was issued with a police order to withdraw permission for the use of his premises. The FJPC meeting was hastily shifted to the Old King's Hall in Commercial Road, while the anti-alien British Workers' League was given free run of the original venue. According to a police report, the final open meeting of the FJPC at 'Wonderland' in Whitechapel Road attracted some 6,000 people, despite the fact that it had not been advertised. In itself this figure reveals that the committee's cause enjoyed considerable sympathy amongst the Jews of East London.[28]

What was the nature of the FJPC's demands? Who were its active members during its year-long existence? And above all, the question must be asked, whether the organisation was politically inspired or not.

The FJPC insisted that in the light of the Russian Revolution 'friendly aliens' should be given a real choice between volunteering for the British Army or the right to return to Russia, all expenses paid. In fact, the British government accepted this demand and the option of voluntary repatriation for males eligible for the call-up was granted. Although, as at least one civil servant in the War Office remarked: 'While there was an option in form, there was little or none in fact.'[29] The shortage of shipping and prevailing wartime conditions made the undertaking a perilous one, quite apart from the cost involved. No government department was enthusiastic about encouraging returnees, preferring enlistment in the British Army as the simplest solution. Nevertheless, the FJPC further demanded that facilities be provided to enable the families of the 'alien eligibles' to accompany them home. Failing this, they wanted 'separation allowances' for the dependents left behind in England, to be paid for out of central or local government funds. Lastly, the committee asked for a guarantee that the men would eventually be readmitted in order to rejoin their families in England. At the very least, the British government must be prepared to reunite divided families in Russia at the end of the war.

If the requests were turned down, the FJPC declared that they would emulate the 'glorious' example of the Conscientious Objectors and refuse to comply with the terms of the Convention. This latter document, it did not escape notice, had been signed by the Russian Provisional Government in flat contradiction to Soviet policy, which called for an end to the fighting. Indeed, the chairman of the committee, Abraham Bezalel, attempted to send a telegram to the Petrograd Soviet to enlist its support for the plight of the Russians in Britain. Prompted by the anti-alien disturbances in Leeds in June 1917, he drew a parallel between the treatment of Jews in Britain and in the former Tsarist Empire, and called for Soviet condemnation of the Convention. Bezalel sent a similar message to the Stockholm socialist peace conference. Both cables were intercepted by the censor and referred to the Foreign Office. They led directly to a police raid on the FJPC's headquarters on 27 July 1917 and to the deportation of Bezalel in August.[30]

Most of the information we have about the FJPC comes from police reports in the Home Office files at the Public Record Office. Basil Thomson, the head of the Special Branch at Scotland Yard, made surveillance of 'revolutionary movements' in Britain his speciality, almost to the point of obsession. He even recruited Yiddish-speaking Jews to attend meetings of organisations he deemed 'subversive' and to inform on the proceedings.[31] Many of the reports, filed at Leman Street police station, are simply translations of speeches made by 'trouble-makers' like 'Beelzebub' (alias Bezalel). If these sources are to be believed, the FJPC was no more than a cover for anti-war and pro-Bolshevik activity. How much truth was there in these allegations? An analysis of the makeup of the central committee and its leading personalities may help us arrive at some conclusion.

Bezalel's real name was Solly Abrahams. He was born in 1885 of Russian Jewish parentage in the Dobrecjia province of Romania. He apparently arrived in Britain via France, either in August 1914 or January 1915, and settled initially in Glasgow. In 1916, he migrated with his family to Whitechapel. Unfortunately, beyond these scanty biographical details, nothing has come to light regarding Bezalel's political affiliations.[32] The same cannot be said of the committee's other leading personality, Joseph Meir Salkind (1875–1937).[33] Salkind is generally described as an anarchist; but this would be to dismiss him too simply. His was a contradictory and very colourful personality. Salkind came to England from Russia in 1904. One of his earliest appointments was as rabbi to a congregation in Cardiff, for Salkind, descended on both sides from rabbis – his mother could reputedly trace her line back to Rashi – had taken *semicha* (ordination) at Volozhin *Yeshiva*. But he combined traditional Jewish learning with a wide secular education at the *Gymnasia* and afterwards at German and Swiss universities. He gained his PhD in Linguistics at Berne. In short, Salkind was a *maskil*, a product of the Jewish Enlightenment, a deeply religious and observant Jew familiar with Western thought – and, more unusually, active in radical politics. Salkind's original affiliation was with Zionism; after the Kishinev pogrom he organised a self-defence group in Berne and between 1913 and 1915 was in Palestine, where he was a founder member of *Moshav* Karkur. However, back in England in 1916, Salkind fell out with organised Zionism – although his sympathies with the Zionist ideal remained – over Jabotinsky's scheme for a Jewish Legion. Salkind denounced Jabotinsky as a 'Jewish Garibaldi'. He made known his opposition to militarism in general and to the First World War in particular. In collaboration with A. Vevyorka and Dr Arnold Margolin (the Ukrainian Jewish nationalist who attended the Versailles peace conference in 1919), Salkind produced an anti-war newspaper *Di Yiddishe Shtimme* in the East End between November and December 1916. He was arrested and spent a short spell in prison. Nevertheless, in 1917 Salkind spoke out against the Convention, hence his association with the FJPC.

Salkind's association with anarchism also dates from this period. Jewish anarchism in England had its origins in the 1890s, but enjoyed its 'Golden Years' from 1905–14. During these years the German Gentile and Yiddish-speaking, Rudolph Rocker was active amongst the Jewish workers of East London.[34] Famous names like Kropotkin, Malatesta and Emma Goldman all spoke at the Jubilee Street Anarchist Club. The anarchist paper *Arbayter Fraynt* enjoyed its longest uninterrupted run from 1903–14. But, on the outbreak of the First World War, Rocker was interned in Alexandra Palace as an 'enemy alien', his ideological opposition to the war notwithstanding. Both the club and the paper were closed down. The rump of the Yiddish Anarchist Federation moved to Gore Street, Hackney. However, the existence of the FJPC, and the substantial anarchist involvement with it, showed that anarchism in the East End had not simply died in 1915. Indeed, in 1920, the remnants of the anarchists approached Salkind to become editor of the revived *Arbayter Fraynt*. He accepted, and was associated with the paper until he finally left England for the United States and thence Palestine in 1932.

A list of committee members of the FJPC which was 'acquired' by the Special Branch in 1916 provides a useful insight into the political constituency of the organisation.[35] For example, the name of Jacob Capitanshchik appears. His presence indicates not only the anarchist interest in the FJPC, but also the role played by the Jewish trade unions; he was secretary of the Jewish Bakers' Union. Capitanshchik wrote under the pseudonym of 'A Wanderer' for Morris Myer's *Di Tsayt*,[36] the most widely read of the Yiddish dailies, with a vaguely socialist-

Zionist bias. Of similar ilk was the anarchist Sam Dreen, a close associate of Rudolph Rocker's, who was active in the mainstream Amalgamated Society of Tailors. Two of the three East End branches of this union gave their support to the FJPC, as did its West End Jewish branch and the two East End branches of the rival United Garment Workers (UGW).[37] Salve Josephs, the secretary of the London Ladies Tailors, took over as secretary of the FJPC after Bezalel's arrest. The Jewish furnishing unions, the United Furnishing and the Hebrew Carvers, supported the FJPC as well. Together, these unions represented a considerable body of organised Jewish support behind the committee. Indeed, as early as July 1916 a delegation of leading Jewish unionists had met with Herbert Samuel to protest against the threat of deportation of 'friendly aliens'.[38] This demonstrated the strength of Jewish union opposition to the government's policy.

The FJPC could also count on the support of the above-party Workers' Circle. Founded in 1903, this was essentially a secular friendly society, set up to rival the multiplicity of religious friendly societies among East End Jewry. Its headquarters in Great Alie Street became a focus for workers' education. Although the secretary was Nathan Weiner, an anarchist, the Circle was an umbrella organisation for all Jewish radicals and sought, through its classes, concerts and other events, to promote a Yiddish secular culture.[39]

Even more overtly political elements played a part in the FJPC. Representatives of the British counterparts to both the major left-wing Jewish parties in eastern Europe – the Marxist Jewish Social Democratic Party, the Bund, and its arch ideological rivals the Labour Zionists – *Poale Tsion* – also figured on the membership list. The Bund connection is not surprising, for, shortly after the Russian Revolution, the Bund in Britain became officially affiliated to the larger British Socialist Party (BSP), and was closely identified with its anti-war faction. Bundist delegates, such as P. Himmelfarb (the editor of the short-lived Bundist newspaper *Dos Arbayter Vort* from 1915–17) and Solomon Schwartz attended the BSP annual conferences in this period. In 1920 the majority of British Bundists entered the Communist Party.

J. Pomerantz, the secretary of *Poale Tsion* (PZ), joined the FJPC's central committee, as did the respected Labour Zionist Yiddish journalist Dr Joseph Kruk. PZ was in a period of rapid expansion at this time, from a mere 100 members in 1915 to some 1,000 by 1918.[40]

The Jewish Territorial Organisation, which had split from main-stream Zionism over the Uganda offer in 1905, also had links with the FJPC. Dr David Jochelman and the Anglo-Jewish novelist Israel Zangwill, both of whom had influential contacts in the 'West End', showed a sympathetic interest in the plight of the Russian Jews in London, although neither actually joined the committee. Zangwill became perceptibly lukewarm after the Convention became law in July 1917, whilst Jochelman limited himself to looking after the welfare of the dependents of the returnees.[41]

Thus the central committee of the FJPC clearly boasted the leading names of radical politics in the Jewish East End. But it also drew support from political organisations beyond the psychological, if not the physical borders, of the Ghetto. In September 1916 the Metro-politan Police reported to the Home Office that, in their opinion, the FJPC was not acting alone.[42] Indeed, two other left-wing, anti-war organisations with 'larger financial resources' and operating on 'a larger scale' were, in reality, running the show. In character, both were Russian émigré groupings rather than exclusively Jewish, but with a sizeable Jewish membership. The first of these was the Marxist Russian Anti-Conscription League. Inspired by the national No-Conscription Fellowship, this had been founded in March 1916 with its head-quarters at 12a Colchester Street – the same address as the local branch of the AST. The secretary was P. Himmelfarb of the Bund. The rank and file included Bundists and some anarchists. The second and more important body mentioned in the police report was the Committee of Delegations of Russian Socialist Groups, which was set up in March 1916. Its leading lights were Georgi Chicherin, who afterwards became Soviet Foreign Minister, and Mary Jane Bridges-Adams (1855–1939), an English socialist, suffragette and educationalist.[43] In 1915 they had organised the Russian Political Prisoners and Exiles Committee which had its offices in Mrs Adams' home in Kensington (96 Lexham Gar-dens). Mere fund-raising activities soon gave way to anti-tsarist propa-ganda, which took on an increasingly internationalist complexion. The newer Committee of Delegations was set up specifically to combat conscription of Russian subjects, and its focus for agitation was the East End of London. The secretary of the committee was Solomon Schwartz of the Bund.

Indeed, the Bund became affiliated to the Committee of Delegations which was Marxist-orientated. The group put out a series of well-printed pamphlets in support of the 'class struggle' of the Russian Jews against the 'West End' Anglo-Jewish establishment and against the Home Secretary, Herbert Samuel. Quite clearly, the Jewish element in the committee saw itself as part and parcel of the Russian revolutionary movement. There was a definite overlap, then, between the FJPC and the Russian revolutionary socialist exiles in London.

A police report of 1917 records that the Communist Club – sometimes referred to as the Herzen Club or the International Working Mens' Club at 107 Charlotte Street, off Tottenham Court Road in the West End – was used for a FJPC meeting on 28 July 1916. This venerable institution was as old as Marxist socialism itself; it was founded in 1840. The club attracted Russian émigrés from all over London, including from the colonies in Hampstead, Bloomsbury, Camden and Kentish Town, as well as from abroad. Before the war luminaries such as Kropotkin, Plekhanov and Lenin himself had met there. The police report stated: 'It is noteworthy that according to the list of members of the Communist Club from this date forward [28 July 1916] there was a large influx of Russian Jews.' Harold Edwards, the last secretary of the Communist Club, has confirmed that 'There were many Jewish Russian members.'[44]

The name of Z. Rafkin of the Industrial Workers of the World (IWW) also appears on the 1916 FJPC membership list. The existence of a London branch of the IWW, which was a pale reflection of the movement in the United States, is a reminder of the cross-fertilisation of the socialist and anarchist movements on both sides of the Atlantic. Jewish socialists and anarchists, like Morris Winchevsky in the 1880s and S. Yanovsky in the 1890s, had frequently stopped over in London on their way from eastern Europe to America, and briefly inspired radical activism in the East End. During the First World War, the English 'Wobblies' met at Great Tongue Yard, 76 Whitechapel Road, where, as in New York, they were kept under constant police surveillance.

The FJPC enjoyed a certain measure of support from interested English political organisations. Although the trade union movement as a whole did not come out against alien conscription, just as it remained silent on the aliens question in general, individual branches did express sympathy; for example, the Bethnal Green and London trades councils. In July 1916 the latter called a special meeting to discuss the aliens question at which it was resolved to back the FJPC.[45] Sylvia Pankhurst, organiser of the Marxist Workers' Socialist Federation (WSF) graced the FJPC's public rallies. Her memoir *The Home Front*, published in 1916, testifies to Sylvia's close involvement with East End life. She shared the platform with those two Liberal dissident parliamentarians, Lord Sheffield and Joseph King. They energetically took up the aliens' cause at Westminster, the latter earning himself the ironic nickname of 'King of the Jews' in the process.

Bezalel also enlisted the help of the National Council for Civil Liberties (NCCL) in a number of legal battles fought by the FJPC through the courts to uphold individual exemptions from military service. In February 1917, the NCCL and the Civil Liberties Group in Parliament backed the committee's defence of four Russian Jews in a test case brought at Bow Street. They had been arrested in November 1916 (while travelling on a neutral – American – ship) and charged with making false statements to the Russian consulate in order to obtain passports to proceed to Russia. The FJPC raised £600 to cover legal costs. The case went to the High Court and was dropped. They also contested cases where Russians were threatened with deportation. Bezalel argued that deportation to a specific destination was illegal, and this defence was upheld – with implications for the government's Convention legislation. Indeed, a Home Office minute remarks how 'highly organised' the East End Jews were when it came to legal action against conscription. Arguably it was in this field that the FJPC scored its main successes.[46] The influential Liberal newspaper the *Manchester Guardian* also supported the FJPC's legal battles, and invoked the precedent set by the French Assembly which had voted against the conscription of aliens.

The FJPC was, it may be concluded, primarily a political organisation, in terms both of its leadership and goals. Its stand against the twin evils (as it saw it) of conscription into the British Army or deportation back to Russia may be seen as a form of protest against the anti-alienism – if not outright antisemitism – then prevalent in the British media. The membership of the FJPC clearly derived strength from the growing anti-war sentiment on the left, among Jewish socialists, anarchists and trade unionists and, in some instances even from beyond the Jewish community, although it would be wrong to identify the FJPC exclusively with these elements. The outbreak of the Russian Revolution had a big impact on the committee. Henceforth, any decision to return to Russia would, willy-nilly, be regarded as a political expression of sympathy with the revolutionary regime.

Grass roots support? – exemption and evasion

We now come to the question as to how representative was the FJPC of Jewish feeling in the East End. How important was the stand taken against conscription or deportation to the 'average' East End Jew? How many Jews opted for these alternatives and what were the motives governing their choices? Before proceeding, however, it must be pointed out that the vast majority, in all probability, opted for *neither*. On the Jewish street, bread and butter was more important than political ideology. How to make ends meet in the daily struggle against poverty was the immediate problem, not pacifism or some Communist utopia. In this context, neither of the alternatives presented was exactly appealing, both involving physical upheaval and economic disruption. Hence, the preferred way out of the dilemma was either to apply for exemption from military service through the legal channels, or simply to resort to outright evasion of the call-up. The latter was a tried and tested stratagem dating from tsarist times.

The British authorities clearly viewed the FJPC as a bunch of agitators attempting to stir things up in the East End. The police did not regard Bezalel himself as a serious threat. He was a 'hanger-on' of the other more numerous and better-funded Russian émigré organisations. In April 1917, the Special Branch reported to the Home Secretary that the FJPC had:

> Failed to induce any other body ... to support them. Much of this failure is due to the fact that Bezalel is regarded with a certain amount of suspicion. It is common gossip among many Jews in the East End that before entering the anti-conscription movement, Bezalel was a corporal in the French army, engaged in the recruiting of Jews for the French army. They now suspect him to be in the pay of some Government and that his efforts among the Jewish population in East London now are for the purpose of bringing them into bad odour with the British authorities and general public.[47]

If the suspicions that Bezalel was an *agent provocateur* were real (and we have only Basil Thomson's word for it), then there seem to be no grounds for believing them to be true. He had, obviously, not been recruited by the Special Branch to make trouble. And it is hard to know who else might have had an interest. It is futile to speculate about secret conspiracies with so little evidence to go on.

In any case, the overwhelming impression is that the FJPC had accurately captured the mood of Russian Jews in the East End during the First World War. While casting doubts on Bezalel's credentials, the police had to admit that East End Jews in general were not keen on the idea of military service, whether in England or Russia. Memories of the cruelties inflicted by the tsarist army were too deeply ingrained and made them distrustful. The police doubted that many 'Russian' Jews would opt to go back. The Protection Committee's demand that they, at least, be given the choice was treated as a bluff. The ringleaders knew full well that there was not the transport available. Most of the so-called 'Russian' Jewish eligibles had been in England since childhood. They spoke no Russian and even their Yiddish was limited. In many cases, their closest relatives and business interests were in Britain. In short, their connection with the Old Country was minimal.[48]

In fact, some 10,000 Russian Jews applied for exemption from the call-up in Britain, out of a reputed total of 30,000. As the *News of the World*, a paper not known for its pro-alien sympathies, sarcastically put it: 'Domestic hardship in a hundred weird forms, work of all grades of national importance, and a hundred and one chronic diseases are quoted as reasons for keeping out of the Army.'[49] This diagnosis of the efforts which some Russian Jews made in order to evade military service in the British Army is amply born out by oral testimonies. The methods employed to evade service or to gain exemption were manifold and inventive. For example, Louis Wallis (born 1900 in Cracow and brought up in Stepney Green) remembers how many Jewish boys went to great lengths to get themselves listed as 'Grade 3' (unfit for army service). One of his personal friends ate an enormous quantity of apples so as to make himself sick and fail the medical examination.[50] Jack Miller (born 1912) writes: 'As a young lad I recall hearing accounts, sometimes maliciously related, as to how some men to avoid service, took toxic ingredients, or did things to impair their health.'[51] According to Israel Renson (born 1906 in the East End and trained as a pharmacist), at least two East End doctors were not unsympathetic to the plight of the Russian eligibles. Both Dr Sammy Sacks, who was himself Jewish, and Dr Bishop, who was not, were generous in bestowing exemption certificates after the obligatory medical. Indeed, Bishop got into trouble on this count and was struck off the register for a time. No doubt this was a result of the proximity of his practice to Leman Street police station!

Mr Renson also related how his older brother, who was born in Russia, fled to Dublin in order to avoid the call-up.[52] The Convention did not apply to Ireland. A similar story is told by Sam Elsbury, the leader of a breakaway garment workers' trade union in the late 1920s. Something of an agitator even during the war, the Russian-born Leeds tailor was arrested in 1917, fined and handed over to the military authorities for evading the draft; but he managed to escape and fled to Ireland. There, Elsbury 'purchased army discharge papers from an ex-soldier for ten shillings and assumed the ex-soldier's name of John Dillon'. And, late in 1917, ' "John Dillon", the Irish tailor with a Yorkshire accent, joined the Yiddish-speaking subdivisional branch of the tailor's union [the UGW] in London'. So began one deserter's rise to prominence in London labour politics.[53]

Even before the October Revolution, there were suspicions that the Russian consulate was freely issuing exemption certificates. Mick Mindel, the retired president of the United Ladies Tailors' Union, recalls how his father, Morris, made a successful application to the embassy in August 1917. Morris was born in 1885 in Vilna and emigrated to England in 1906. He was a bookbinder by trade, and worked for the anarchist printer Narodiczky. In eastern Europe he had been a member of the Bund; in the East End, an active member of the Workers' Circle. From 1915, meetings of the Circle took place regularly in the Mindels' flat in Rothschild Buildings. Morris's exemption certificate is still in the family. In March 1918, the Russian consulate admitted that it had issued some 2500 exemptions.[54]

The highly respected rabbi of the Machzike Hadass synagogue from 1916–19, Rav Avraham Yitskhok Kook, afterwards Chief Rabbi of Palestine, apparently did his bit to help the Russian Jews. The British Military Selection Board and the War Office traced a sudden increase in the number of qualified rabbis in the East End to Rav Kook's more than usually liberal bestowing of *semicha* (ordination) on his *yeshiva* students. He, like Salkind, was well aware that ministers of religion were exempt from military service. When questioned on the point by the authorities, Kook justified his stand by referring to the spiritual poverty of the Anglo-Jewish community! No action was taken against him.[55] Another subterfuge resorted to by 'alien eligibles' was to claim Polish or Lithuanian rather than Russian citizenship.

In July 1917, the General Registrar's Office reported a sudden rise in the number of marriages. The reason, it seemed, was 'to swell the agitation about the separation of wives and families and to claim separation allowances here'.[56] Certainly, it was the reluctance of many wives to uproot their families which prevented larger numbers of men from opting to return to Russia.

The Conventionists

Nevertheless, some men did make the journey back to Russia. But it was from the ranks of the ideologically committed that the majority of the so-called Conventionists came. For Jewish radicals, the decision to return was a positive one which was not taken merely out of a desire to avoid conscription. The Russian Revolution of February 1917 exerted an irresistible attraction upon these circles. It was the moment they had been waiting for; socialists and anarchists felt the need to go home and participate in the New Era. The ensuing exodus decimated the radical Jewish parties in the East End, and effectively spelt the end of Bundism and anarchism in England.

In his memoir *The London Years* (1956), Rudolph Rocker recalled that, while still interned in Alexandra Palace in 1917, he received a visit from the ex-editor of the *Arbayter Fraynt*, Alexander Shapiro. In 1916, Shapiro himself had been arrested and given six months for anti-war agitation.[57] Now he was returning with his wife to Russia. Indeed, Rocker

> [H]ad special visits about that time almost every day from friends and comrades who wanted to say goodbye to me before they left for Russia. They came jubilant and hopeful ... How differently things had turned out. I could see all my comrades in the East End rushing off to Russia! The Revolution had opened their native land to them! They would not hesitate one moment to give their

services to the Revolution! They would kiss the Russian earth from which Tsarist despotism had exiled them.

In October 1917 Rocker and his companion Millie Witcop were also given permission to leave for Russia – but were overtaken by events. In March 1919, when they were finally released, they made for Germany instead.

With regard to the Bund, the *Workers' Circle Jubilee Publication (1909–29)* records the following:

> The Revolution of 1917–18 led to the ruination [*fornunder-fulung*] of the J[ewish] S[ocial] D[emocratic] O[rganisation] in England, whose most active comrades went straight back to Russia and devoted themselves to the service of the Revolution; many comrades were deported by the then government, which wanted to preserve the land from the 'Red Spectre' which the Russian Revolution had called forth.

Solomon Schwartz was deported in March 1921; the Bundist newspaper *Dos Arbayter Vort* went out of existence in July 1917. The remnants of the Bund in Britain, besides joining the BSP, became the founder members of Division 9 of the Workers' Circle, afterwards the Communist Party Branch.

Indeed, the Workers' Circle itself suffered likewise. The Jubilee pamphlet also states that the Convention was 'a very severe blow' to the organisation and that 'many of our best members returned to Russia and most of those who remained, were forced to join the British Army'. Some 300 members were lost overall (from 831 in 1915 to 511 in 1918). Emigration must account for a fair proportion of this total – which represented the radical cream of the Ghetto. Two London divisions collapsed completely, and as for Division 8, based in Glasgow:

> The severest blow came in 1917, when the majority of our members became affected by the Convention between Britain and Russia. They were given the option of joining the British Army or going out to Russia. Both countries received a good contingent of our members, with the result that our numbers dwindled to 28.

The Manchester Jewish Museum has a copy of a list of five members of the local division who also went back.[58]

Disruption was caused by the Convention to other working-class institutions in the East End. The *Journal of the Amalgamated Society of Tailors* came to this conclusion about the state of its East London District in September 1917: 'The war and the calling to the colours, and the return to Russia of thousands of tailors working in the district made further attempts at organisation so much wasted labour.'

All the same, the popular impression of 'thousands' of Jewish returnees to Russia in 1917 is an exaggeration.[59] No precise figures either of the numbers applying to return, or of the numbers who actually went, were made available at the time. But from the somewhat piecemeal information in the extant Home Office files some conclusions may be drawn. A minute scrawled by J.F. Henderson in August 1917 gives the information set out below:

Applications to return to Russia under the Military Service Convention

Place of Residence	No. of applications	Other information
London	5000	Mainly Jews, tailors and cabinet makers
Lanarkshire	900–1000	Mainly Lithuanians, coalminers and blast furnacemen
Glasgow	500	
Scattered	1000 (including 180 from Manchester)	
Total	c. 7500	

Perhaps two-thirds of the applications came from Jews, hailing principally from the East End of London, but also from the provincial communities in Manchester, Leeds, Birmingham and Glasgow. The large number of Lithuanian Catholics living in Scotland who indicated a desire to return to their native land was 'disconcerting' to the Home Office, as these men were engaged in vital war industries.

The actual travel arrangements were made under a veil of secrecy. Fear that public knowledge of the acute shipping shortage would only encourage even more applications made the Home Office and the Admiralty equally opposed to publicity. It was put about officially that 4000 Russians had sailed for home by mid-October. The destination was the Black Sea part of Odessa. However, it appears from the records that the actual figure was smaller. Here is a breakdown of the information provided in Henderson's memos of October 1917:

Date of sailing (1917)	Number of men warned of departure	Number of Men who actually sailed
15 August	51	45
31 August	111	94
10 September (two ships)	3000	1700
19 September	136	–
30 September	2600	–
Total	5898	1839

A further sailing took place sometime in mid-October, which was scheduled to embrace the men who embarked on the aborted voyages of 19 and 30 September (56 plus 1050) 'together with such part of the remainder of the total number of applicants as decide to go (something between 900 and 1300)'. Given the high drop-out rate overall, it is safe to assume that the civil servant's calculations were somewhat over-optimistic. It may be guessed that the final figure of returnees was around the 3000 mark. Clearly the inaccuracies in the arithmetic mean that these statistics can only be regarded as an estimate.[60]

Arguably, a more valuable insight may be gained by looking at the case histories of individual Conventionists who returned to Russia on these ships. Here are two interesting, and probably fairly typical examples. The first is that of Lazarus Glick, a tailor who emigrated from Lithuania in 1902. He settled in Buxton Street, Whitechapel. His son, Alf, tells how Glick returned in 1917 to Russia – where he still had a brother and other relatives on his wife's side – leaving his wife, parents, Alf and his five older brothers and sisters behind in England. Glick subsequently came back to London in the spring of 1923. He carried a Soviet passport validated by a minor official, one G. Yagoda, afterwards the head of the OGPU under Stalin.[61] Our other example is that of Abraham Baron (Bar-On). He was born in the *shtetl* of Povyat-Ostrow in the Lomzher Gubernia of Poland and emigrated to the United States in 1905 in order to avoid conscription into the Russian army. Despite a traditional *yeshiva* education, Baron got involved with the anarchist circle in New York, and kept up the connection on his arrival in the East End. A machinist-tailor, he was a member of the Anarchist Club in Jubilee Street and of the Workers' Circle. Baron went back to Russia on the 10 September sailing, leaving behind his wife Rachel and their three children Harry, Leah and Jack. He sent the family a series of postcards written in Yiddish from Odessa. Such correspondence was sporadic and frequently censored. Baron, apparently, saw active service with the Red Army. Most of the cards are dated 1919, but did not arrive in England until as late as 1923. Eventually the contact ceased. The youngest son, Jack, who was six at the time of his father's departure, tells how, in 1927, he obtained a copy of the New York Yiddish daily *Forwerts*, which carried a report about anarchist political prisoners in the USSR. Among the list of names is 'A. Baron'.[62]

Divided families

Albert Meltzer, in his *Anarchists in London 1935–55*, writes:

> The bulk of the Anarchists in the Jewish Labour movement were of Russian origin and in most cases the men returned to Russia at the time of the Revolution, expecting to send for the women later – who had stayed to look after the children meanwhile. When most of the militants had perished, the women remained – a feature of Anarchist meetings in the East End in the 1920s and 1930s was the number of elderly Russian-Jewish women. It was something of a setback to the Young Communist League, then growing in influence, to find occasionally in the '20s and '30s that its members faced not merely the hostile criticism of a grand-

father or father from a conservative or orthodox religious stand-point, but the 'ultra-left' criticism of a grandmother or great-aunt.[63]

It is clear from the above examples that the departure of a significant number of Jewish males for Russia in the late summer of 1917 created a problem of divided families. In February 1918 the Home Office put the number of women left behind as some 900 in London and a further 100 in the provinces, while dependent children totalled 1500 in the Metropolis and 200 in the rest of the country. The total number of individuals affected was therefore around 2700. By 1920, the number of women had been reduced to between 550 and 600, but there were still some 1000 children without fathers at home. Nine-tenths of these children were British-born.[64] The reduction was, as we shall see presently, the result of either the subsequent return of the breadwinner or of the repatriation of the entire family to Russia. Emanuel Litvinoff, in his memoir *Journey Through a Small Planet* (1972),[65] has written movingly about his experiences of growing up in just such a one-parent family in the East End. He had only the vaguest recollection of his father:

> His picture hung on the wall, pink of cheek and red of mouth, tinted masterpiece of the enlarger's art. He had a waxed mous-tache and eyes that hunted you all over the room, accusing you of being alive. No father was more totally absent: for a long time I wasn't even sure of his name. It was either Max or Mark, and, having brought three sons into the hungry world and planted a fourth, he'd gone back to Russia when I was still sheltering from everyone behind the vast skirt of my towering mother.

Litvinoff goes on to describe how humiliated he felt when questioned by his teacher about his father's occupation:

> She'd gone round the class asking everybody what work their father did. I sat there miserably, wishing she'd ask about our mothers instead. 'And you, Emanuel, what does your daddy work at?' I closed my eyes tight, partly to think about it, partly in the hope that it would make the teacher go away ... Cissie Stoloff, who shared my desk, pursed her lips primly and put up her hand. 'Pleath, teacher,' she lisped, 'he'th got on'y a mummy.'

Miss Baker took out a tiny embroidered handkerchief from the sleeve of her dress and blew her thin nose. 'Oh, dear!' she said. 'Was he a soldier, then? Did your daddy fall on the battlefield?' ... Miss Baker was waiting for an answer. I didn't know if my father was a soldier, or if a father in Russia was a proper father, or if he did indeed fall on the battlefield. It was vexing to be so ignorant. 'He fell down,' I said. 'But I think he got up.'

It is obvious from Litvinoff's account that his mother had a hard time making ends meet: 'She'd been left, pregnant and twenty-two, with nothing but the three of us, a sewing machine and her skill in dressmaking.'

Jack Baron has a copy of a letter, sent by his older brother Harry to his father in Odessa, telling him not to worry about the family. Harry, who was aged 13 at the time, planned to leave school as soon as he turned 14 and to get a job as a book-keeper. In the event, the dependants were not entirely left to their own devices. Mutual support, a characteristic of East End Jewish life, was brought into play. Although the FJPC had collapsed with the deportation of Bezalel in August 1917, sympathisers regrouped in the United Russian Committee (URC) for matters of military service. Under the chairmanship of Dr David Jochelman, who had come to England in September 1915 in his capacity as the London manager of the Volga Insurance Company, the committee continued the fight on another front. Jochelman all along favoured a compromise solution for the Russian eligibles, such as non-combative national service. He served as a member of the government-appointed tribunal to hear cases for exemption. Thus he disapproved of the extremism of Bezalel. Now he campaigned for charitable assistance for the families of the returnees. The British government, via the Local Government Board, did undertake to pay half the cost of maintenance of these families (12s 6d per week per adult, 2s 6d – upped to 3s – per child). But this subsidy was classified as an 'out-relief' grant, that is one paid in cases of destitution rather than as a separation allowance and thus was not automatic. The rest of the money had to be found either from the Russian government (in fact the Provisional Government did make a contribution) or from the local Boards of Guardians or Jewish communal sources.[66] The URC regarded the government subsidy as hopelessly inadequate. It urged that the government raise the level of the grant, and meanwhile was forced to make up the shortfall itself.

Nevertheless, a conference of the United Russian Committee, meeting at the Old King's Hall, Commercial Road on 12 December 1917, voted to accept the government's offer, though not without vocal complaints about 'degradation' voiced by an impressive array of local leaders – anarchists, Bundists and trade unionists: Morris Myer, Sam Dreen, Nathan Weiner, and even the secretary of the committee itself, Louis Katzel. As a compromise, it was resolved that the families affected should be left to decide for themselves whether or not they wished to receive the government subsidy. The upshot was the formation of a rebel breakaway organisation, 'The Ladies Committee for Protecting the interests of the dependent families of Russian citizens', chaired by a Mrs Soloveitchik. The new committee's professed aim was to continue to agitate for the reunification of the divided families in *Russia*. Significantly, the Ladies Committee was established after the Bolshevik Revolution. No doubt this fact was sufficient justification for the Special Branch to pay special attention to its activities. They need not have worried, for the Russian Ladies Committee evidently settled down to cooperate with the URC and through it with officialdom. However, a year later, on 1 November 1918, an alternative grouping, the Russian Women's Protection Committee, was set up in opposition to the URC to demand 'Justice for the Russian Women'. Mrs Levene and her assistant M. Bachrach succeeded in attracting 400 members, if the records are to be believed – a substantial membership considering that a weekly subscription of 2d was required for friendly society purposes. The committee acquired offices at 23 Scarboro Street, off Leman Street, printed membership cards and organised a public meeting at the Old Kings Hall on 31 December. It is unclear whether this meeting actually took place, given that the police were made aware of the situation. The women did make links with English socialists such as George Lansbury and Sylvia Pankhurst and the Bolshevik emissary Maxim Litvinov. In January 1919 they appealed to the Home Office to allow back into Britain 17 Conventionists stranded in Rotterdam. The appeal was turned down. Little else is known about this Ladies Committee, except that both Basil Thomson and the old Russian Embassy regarded it with the deepest suspicion. Concerning Mrs Levene, A. Gambs (at the Embassy) wrote: 'This lady seems to have a very dark past. I hear that white slave traffic was one of her previous occupations.'[67]

Elderly East End Jews when called upon to give their reminiscences about the First World War, frequently claim that 'thousands' of Russian Jews went back to Russia during the revolution. The documentary evidence fails to substantiate this claim. Close on 3000 did in fact return, if the figures can be relied upon. Arguably, this amounted to a significant number, if not quantitatively – given the overall size of the immigrant community in Britain – then at least qualitatively. After all, the Conventionists represented the active radical political elite of the community. Their departure created a social problem regarding their wives and children which had to be dealt with by the British authorities and Anglo-Jewry. But the fact remains that the vast majority of Russian eligibles chose to remain behind, and went to great and sometimes comical lengths to keep out of the army – any army.

There was thus a kernel of truth in the contemporary allegations of the anti-alienists that the Jews were 'shirking' their duty. For East Enders this hostility may have been unpleasant, but it was not sufficiently intolerable to force large numbers to uproot themselves once again and return to an uncertain future back in the Old Country. In any case, by the end of 1917, the euphoria which had greeted the February Revolution had dissipated, to be replaced by more sober reflection that the destiny of Russia was still very obscure.

'East End' versus 'West End'

> The general disappointment of the English public in Russia, the long processions from Whitechapel to the 'tube' night after night [whether] a raid is expected or not, the noise and storm created by the Protection Committee, the behaviour of the parties of Russians leaving England and the comments of newspapers of the type of the *Daily Mail, Evening News, Western Despatch* etc. have created such a situation that I do not exaggerate when I say that another big disappointment from Russia ... and very regrettable incidents will occur.
>
> Mr Lazarus to Dr Chaim Weizmann, 12 September 1917[68]

Native-born, English-speaking Anglo-Jewry, headed by its 'Cousin-hood' of commercial families – Rothschilds, Samuels, Montefiores and the like – looked askance at the goings-on 'down the East End'. For the self-evident reluctance of the newcomers to do their bit for the war effort caused embarrassment to the communal establishment and challenged their bid to maintain communal discipline. 'English' Jews and 'Russian' Jews could all too easily be 'tarred with the same brush'. Moreover, the Board of Deputies was well aware that the media and the public at large viewed the activities of the FJPC as politically motivated – which, as we have seen, they largely were. The desire of Russian Jews to go back to their native land may have been regarded as commendable in the light of the February Revolution; by October it was taken as a sure sign that they were all Bolsheviks. The Protection Committee and the Conventionists thus only served to heighten anti-alien and anti-Bolshevik prejudice, and the combined result could not fail but be increased antisemitism.

Anglo-Jewish leaders therefore, overcompensated by strongly advocating conscription for the 'friendly alien'. Edmund Sebag-Montefiore, the chairman of the Jewish War Services Committee, had made his position plain in October 1916:

> It is evident that voluntary enlistment and attestation of Russian subjects must be regarded as a failure ... [thus] ... other methods must be adopted ... It must be appreciated that Russians in their own country are accustomed to compulsory service, and the idea of voluntary service is foreign to them.

And not only did Montefiore claim that he was giving expression to the 'unanimous desire' of the Jewish community in this matter, but he also assured the Home Office that:

> The [Conscription] Bill will have the active support of the large majority of those members of the House of Commons who are of the Jewish faith.[69]

It goes without saying that the 'New Court' Jewish War Services Committee did not enjoy the confidence of the East End. Indeed it was regarded with undisguised hostility.

But it was Lucien Wolf, the 'Foreign Secretary' of Anglo-Jewry, who was most outspokenly in favour of 'conscripting the alien'. His mind was made up on this point long before the Russian Revolution: 'Compulsion', he wrote in June 1916, 'is really indispensable if the Jewish community are to be spared an explosion of antisemitism, and if their good name in this country is to be maintained.' Wolf had no compunction about advertising his views, in articles for the *Daily Chronicle* in 1916. Apparently, the outbreak of the revolution only served to convince Wolf of the justice of his case. He bombarded the Home Office with unsolicited advice, which did not fall on deaf ears. He argued that the conscription of aliens was permitted under international law. And he came up with an ingenious method of applying 'indirect' compulsion to the East End Jews:

> The Russian Jews declare they are attached to this country, but they urge that, if they are to serve in the army, they should only do so in the capacity of full citizens.
> In my opinion, the proper course to pursue is to take them at their word.

In short, the British government should make an offer of immediate naturalisation for all Russians and their families intending to take up permanent residence in Britain. If this 'gracious' offer was turned down, then it could be safely assumed that the 'Russians' still regarded themselves as Russians and, thus, were obliged to discharge the military duties they owed to Russia. The implication was – although Wolf did not put it in so many words – that Russian Jews who chose to remain aliens should be deported back to tsarist Russia. This solution would not only clear up a bureaucratic mess, but would silence public objections:

> The anti-alien agitators cannot have it both ways. If they want the Russian Jews to serve, they must make them Englishmen. If they do not want to make them Englishmen, then they must cease from reproaching them with not serving.

In the end, Wolf was making himself crystal-clear: '[T]he only way of applying compulsion was by deportation, and without compulsion, I was sure there would be no enlistment.'[70]

As for the Protection Committee, Wolf dismissed them as a group of 'firebrands', new arrivals in the East End who were 'running the resident population who have no leaders of their own'. Hence, in July 1917 Wolf welcomed the Convention. Ironically, his only misgiving now was that the choice of voluntary repatriation had been incorporated under the terms of the agreement. This was now regarded as little more than an escape route for those still wishing to evade service. In a letter to the Home Office, Wolf confessed: 'I have all along been a strong supporter of the Act – indeed, much stronger than its sponsors, for if I had had anything to do with it, I should not have given the option of returning to Russia.'[71]

Wolf's views were shared by the vast majority of the communal establishment. Even the *Jewish Chronicle* came out in favour of the Convention in July 1917. The shift in Leopold Greenberg's editorial policy was really quite dramatic. Throughout 1916 Greenberg had consistently favoured persuasion with regard to military service for 'friendly aliens'; he now came out for coercion. Granted, he still had reservations of a liberal nature about the Bill: the secretive character of the negotiations, and the effect it had of singling out Russian Jews for special treatment. He campaigned successfully for the inclusion of certain legal safeguards such as the right of naturalisation, exemption and appeal, the guarantee of military equality and, indeed, the right of voluntary return to Russia. In the end, however, the editor announced his satisfaction with the Act in its final form and urged the Russian Jews to abide by it and give 'the minimum of trouble' to the authorities. He lashed out at the divisive tactics of the FJPC and, like Wolf, asserted that their demand that the British government provide shipping for the return of the 'eligible aliens' to Russia was just a pretext for evading service. They knew full well that there was a shipping shortage. And even if there was not, they were hoping that the dislocation in Russia would be such that they would be able to circumlocute the attentions of the Russian military authorities. In any case, Greenberg argued, it was simply hypocrisy to declare that one was a conscientious objector in England, whilst at the same time volunteering for military duty in Russia. As for the dependants, it was unreasonable to expect the government to take on the responsibility of arranging for them to accompany their menfolk home, for every soldier must necessarily be parted from his family in wartime. Besides, any alien who had elected to serve in the Russian rather than in the British army had elected to serve under Russian conditions. So, in spite of his subsequent softening on the question of charitable assistance for the families – he condemned the 'no khaki, no soup' mentality of David Lindo Alexander and the Board of Guardians for abdicating their communal responsibility on this score – Greenberg's attitude to the predicament of the Russian Jewish aliens in 1917 can hardly be described as sympathetic. According to Israel Cohen, the editor was obliged to 'leave his office under protection for several days' during this period.[72]

The reaction of Anglo-Jewry to the question of alien conscription may be seen as the function of an almost involuntary self-defence mechanism. It was indicative of a desire to put a certain distance between the West End and East End branches of British Jewry, between natives and immigrants, English and Russian, and even between rich and poor, in a bid to deflect anti-alien hostility away from the former. It was as if impeccable communal respectability was an insurance policy against antisemitism. The Convention and the conscription question as a whole thus throw an invaluable light on both the internal politics of the Anglo-Jewish community during the First World War and its relationship to surrounding society.

Postscript: after the Bolshevik Revolution

The October Revolution forced the question of military service for Russian Jews back to square one. The Soviet government tore up the Convention. Their representative in London, Maxim Litvinov, protested against conscription of Russian subjects into the Allied forces, given that the Treaty of Brest–Litovsk marked the end of Russian participation in the war. Thus the status of the Russian in England was effectively transformed from that of 'friendly alien' into that of suspect, if not 'enemy', alien. The Metropolitan Police at once took steps to compile a register of Russians in London. But the government as a whole responded with a compromise. They rejected the extreme options of internment or deportation. Instead, unannounced, they simply stopped recruitment. It was finally agreed to put Russian Jews into Labour Battalions rather than into the army proper.[73] The result was a bureaucratic muddle in which it is likely that not a few Russian Jews fell through the net.

The advent of the Bolsheviks clearly strengthened the resolve of the opponents of military service in the East End and created legal complications for the government, especially in relation to the dependants. The government had no real alternative but to continue the subsidy. By December 1920, the grant had been enhanced to 15s 6d per week for each adult and 5s for each child. The matter was under constant review. The Ministry of Health bore the brunt of the responsibility, although not without considerable opposition from both the police and the Treasury. The latter bodies wanted to deport these 'undesirables' without further delay. East End opinion concurred. Local Boards of Guardians were hostile to any further waste of ratepayers' money, while the *East London Observer* suggested that internment in 'concentration camps' would be a far more sensible (and cheaper) alternative.[74] The ex-Russian ambassador George Buchanan was in complete agreement. As spokesman for the White Russian Central Russian Committee, he resented government subsidising 'Bolshevik influences' in Great Britain. He only had misgivings about the political consequences of the deportation of such elements *en masse* to White-controlled areas of south Russia. In fact, any such idea was vetoed by the Home Office. This was not only on account of the sheer impracticality of 'dump[ing] a miscellaneous crowd of Russians, mostly Jews, in the Ukraine', given the shipping shortage and the possibility that the East End Russian '[might] simply [sit] down and [say] he wouldn't go'.[75] There were more serious implications to be considered. As a memo produced by the Aliens and Nationality Committee of the Home Office pointed out:

> A scheme of wholesale deportation of Jewish women (many with British-born children) to Eastern Europe ... would raise questions of practical and political significance which need to be weighed very carefully against the financial considerations put forward by the Treasury ... [It] ... involves issues which should probably be considered by the Cabinet.

Although the last sentence was crossed out in this particular memo (dated January 1921), there is every indication that the matter was discussed at the highest levels as far back as January 1918. The decision not to intern or deport aliens is recorded in a War Cabinet circular labelled 'Secret' of 13 February, 1918. A major factor influencing government policy was, apparently, the fear of reprisals by the Bolsheviks against British nationals in Russia.[76]

After the Armistice and the October Revolution it became exceedingly difficult for Conventionists to regain entry into Britain. A ban on Russian refugees entering Britain was put into operation in December 1917 and the extension of the Aliens Act in 1919 did not make life any easier. It was decided in November 1919 that only those who could prove that they had seen service with the Allied forces in Europe or Russia in the intervention would be readmitted. In most instances, this was almost impossible to verify. Some, however, did return, like Lazarus Glick and the cartoonist Harry Blacker's father (in 1922).[77] For the families in England the uncertainty was often hard to bear. Emanuel Litvinoff writes:

> A lot of the kids in fact were in our position. Some fathers never returned from the war, others had been sent back to Russia and got mixed up in the Revolution ... But as I crept more and more boldly out from behind my mother's skirts, it seemed to me that fathers were becoming more numerous. Unknown men tramped heavily up the stairs, shrieks of excitement came from one or another of the apartments, someone had a party. Next you knew, a boy who'd been running free was led off like a prisoner to school and synagogue classes and smacked if he was rebellious.
> They always made trouble, these fathers. Women sounded shriller, children wailed, neighbours banged broomsticks on each other's walls and ceilings. It reached a point where the arrival of a stranger at the entrance of the building filled me with panic in case it was our turn for trouble. Even when the newcomer entered turbulently into someone else's life my uneasiness remained. Next it might be the man in the picture, with his sad, sour eyes and waxed moustache, and he would stoop from his great height near the ceiling to rain hard and violent kisses on my only mother.

In the event, the worst never materialised. Litvinoff's mother even resorted to a fortune teller in the vain hope of finding out whether her husband would ever return.

On the other hand, a substantial number of wives and families were voluntarily repatriated; 200 sailed for Russia in March 1918. As steps were taken towards the normalisation of diplomatic relations as a preliminary to the signing of the Anglo-Soviet Trade Agreement in 1921, arrangements were made through the Russian Delegation for the return of more expatriates: on 4 March 1921, 232 'Russians' left for home.[78] Inspection of the passenger list reveals that the vast majority were East End Jews. They included BSP member Joe Fineberg's wife and three families from Rothschild Buildings, all known personally to the Mindels. Finally, it must be pointed out that even for those Conventionists who made it back to England (sometimes illegally), their future was not necessarily secured. In March 1923, the Board of Deputies presented the Home Office with a dossier of cases in which deportation orders had been carried out on individuals – in spite of an earlier court ruling that this was illegal. All those named were former Conventionists.[79]

The Jewish Legion

In the Summer of 1917, plans were announced to form a separate Jewish unit within the British Army. The principal attraction of this scheme, on the domestic front, was that it offered a way out of the Russian conscription problem. The instigator of the Legion, Ze'ev Jabotinsky (1880–1940), and his chief supporter Chaim Weizmann, both argued that the existence of a specifically Jewish regiment with a distinctly Jewish atmosphere, facilities for religious observance and Yiddish-speaking instructors, would induce the 'friendly aliens' to join up. From the purely military point of view, such a legion would be highly motivated and an effective fighting force.

The regiment idea evoked a certain response in governing circles. But it provoked fierce controversy within the Jewish community itself, controversy which cut across traditional divides. Differences of opinion on the subject of the regiment cannot be neatly classified according to 'class allegiances'. It was not simply another battle between 'East End' and 'West End'. Nor, given that the regiment raised the wider question of Jewish nationalism, can the debate be reduced to Zionist/anti-Zionist rivalry. On the contrary, protagonists on both sides of the fence found themselves in the company of some strange bedfellows. On the issue of the Regiment, the generally accepted pattern of communal politics broke down.[80]

The announcement of the regiment was greeted with a hostile reception in the East End. During 1916 Jabotinsky had made largely fruitless efforts to drum up support in Whitechapel. Copies of *Di Tribune*, a strongly Zionist newspaper edited by Meir Grossman (1888–1964), later head of the Jewish Telegraphic Agency, were freely distributed. In June, Jabotinsky organised a month long propaganda campaign consisting of public meetings and a petition to the War Office. The response was disappointing; only 300 signatures were collected, despite the interest shown by Herbert Samuel in Jabotinsky's work.[81] The Ministry assiduously took up the proposal put forward by Gregory Benenson, the Russian Jewish émigré banker, to set up a special Russian Jewish Committee to launch a last ditch recruitment drive in the East End – before the threat of deportation was carried out. Weizmann and Sokolov agreed to serve on the Benenson Committee. Again, its operations met with resistance from the East End 'tailors'.

After the revolution and once the Convention became a fact, Jabotinsky's 'Committee for Jewish Freedom' intensified its activities with the full support of the Recruiting Department. It put out circulars designed to persuade Russian Jews of the hazards entailed in returning to Russia and of the wisdom of opting for conscription here – into the Jewish Legion. The propaganda had little effect. It took four months to recruit 900 men for the first battalion, the 38th Royal Fusiliers. The rousing send-off given the volunteers when they finally set off for Palestine in February 1918 did little to obscure this fact. The colourful report of the scene printed in *The Times*, which claimed that the regiment had 'conquered Whitechapel', was far from the whole truth.[82]

The FJPC took a dim view of Jabotinsky's activities. It regarded government support for the regiment merely as a cynical move to facilitate the conscription of Russian Jews. Dr Jochelman concurred. He also feared that, in practice, the regiment would amount to the creation of a 'military ghetto' which Russian Jews would be forced to enter. This would ensure their complete segregation from the rest of the British Army, including Anglo-Jewish servicemen.[83] There was also considerable resentment in the East End at the way the project had developed; it had been sprung on the community more or less as a *fait accompli*. Neither the 'West End' establishment, nor the Jewish War Services Committee, let alone those directly affected – the East End masses – had been consulted. That was undemocratic. These opinions were shared right across the political spectrum in Whitechapel. Not only Jewish trade unionists, Bundists and anarchists condemned the scheme, but even Labour Zionists. Both *Di Tsayt* and *Yiddisher Ekspress* published hard-hitting editorials on the subject: Morris Myer condemned Jabotinsky as an 'adventurer'.[84] Nevertheless, official *Poale Tsion's* fierce opposition to the Jewish Legion was based exclusively on Zionist considerations. They objected on ideological grounds to the collective enlistment of Jews on one side in the 'imperalist' war in which Jews, as Jews, had no real interest. This gave rise to fears that Zionist 'neutralism' might be compromised, with the dangers inherent in that possibility. In any case, the very notion of a 'Jewish Legion' smacked of 'militarism'. In all these arguments the dilemma facing the 'friendly aliens' in East London was incidental.[85] Clearly, the regiment raised larger complications for Zionist politics, which took precedence over consideration of immigrant sensibilities. Thus, when it came to the issue of the Jewish regiment, East End Jewry was a target not only for 'Chicherin's boys' — the radical 'lefties' who broke up political meetings organised by Jabotinsky — but also for 'active Zionist counter-propaganda'.[86] The opposition of *Poale Tsion* did as much to weaken support for the regiment in Whitechapel as did that of the Marxist socialists. In August 1917, Scotland Yard informed the Home Office that the regiment was 'extremely unpopular ... amongst all but a small proportion of the Alien Jews in this country'.[87]

But East End hostility was not necessarily counterbalanced by West End enthusiasm. On the contrary, the issue of the regiment found English Jewry badly divided. Even the English Zionist Federation was split in two. Weizmann and Jabotinsky had a fight on their hands. Dr Gaster, through the medium of his Jewish National Union, registered strong sympathy for feeling in the East End, while other Zionists like Rabbi Samuel Daiches and Harry Sacher reiterated the arguments of *Poale Tsion* in Great Russell Street. Not that their efforts were inspired by any sympathy for the 'friendly aliens'. Sacher, writing from Manchester to his friend Leon Simon, confessed: 'Frankly I have very little sympathy with the opponents [of the Legion] at present. They won't fight for England, they won't fight for Russia and they won't fight for Palestine. All they want is to preserve their skins.'[88]

Oddly enough, when the battle-lines came to be drawn, the Zionist 'left' as a whole found itself in something of an unholy alliance with the

Swaythling camp. Naturally, the opposition of the communal establishment to the idea of the Jewish regiment started from basic anti-
nationalist assumptions; but there was more to it than that. The strong
resistance of the East End destroyed any merit the scheme might have
had in the eyes of the 'West End' as a solution to the vexed conscription
question. Indeed, the whole project could turn out to be a disaster.
There was great anxiety in the 'West End' that the so-called 'Jewish
regiment' – in reality made up of Russian Jewish conscripts – would
not acquit itself honourably in the field, and that would reflect badly on
Anglo-Jewry as a whole. Why, it was asked, should these half-hearted
'alien' conscripts, recruited so late in the day, be associated in the
public mind with the 40,000-odd English Jews who had participated
fully in the war effort since 1914? After all, as one letter writer to the
Jewish Chronicle protested, the Russian Jews were 'Not representative
of the Jews and not even [of] the English Jews and they must not
appropriate the name which [it] had taken English Jews two hundred
years to build up'.[89]

Other commentators were worried that 'bad elements' like 'revolutionists and BSP' would infiltrate the ranks. Such attitudes explain
the lobbying which went on to have the name of the regiment altered,
to 'Anglo-Russian', 'friendly alien', 'foreign legion' or anything, in fact,
which did not mention the adjective 'Jewish'. Hence the deputation to
Lord Derby in August 1917, which included as many of the big guns of
the 'Cousinhood' as could be mustered. The rationale which lay behind
this move is a now familiar one. The Swaythling delegation was
motivated by a concept of communal defence which entailed a
deliberate distancing of 'West' from 'East End' interests. That the
efficacy of such tactics was disputed even within the establishment was
demonstrated by the counter-deputation to the War Office a week
later, which asserted that 'Anglo-Jewry had no monopoly on the name
JEW'.[90]

Did an equivalent of the American 'Red Scare' of 1918–20 occur in
England? Did the deportation of hundreds of undesirable aliens, including many Jews, from New York City, for political reasons, that is
for their supposed 'Bolshevism' find an echo on the opposite side of the
Atlantic? It has recently been claimed that some 40 Jews were
deported, ostensibly as illegal immigrants, in 1919–20, and a further

29 interned in Brixton gaol.[91] In his memoirs, Detective Inspector Herbert Fitch of the Special Branch recalled how two Jewish individuals, Myer Hyman and Max Segal, were 'recommended for deportation' during the height of the English version of the 'Red Scare' in February 1919. Segal had, it transpired, 'come over as official representative of a powerful revolutionary society in Moscow, and he had brought with him the sum of £4000 in gold and bonds' – presumably to spend on propaganda and the purchase of arms in preparation for the 'World Revolution'.[92]

Russian Jews in England were put under considerable pressure after the outbreak of the Russian Revolution, which increased with the onset of civil war and British intervention. They found themselves the target of anti-alien and anti-Bolshevik prejudice. In July 1917, the crunch came in the form of the Anglo-Russian Military Convention. The 'friendly aliens' were given a choice between conscription into the British Army or voluntary repatriation back to Russia. Nevertheless, while there is little doubt that the Home Office was guilty of indulging in a measure of 'administrative justice' *vis-à-vis* the Jewish aliens, they avoided the extremes of mass internment or deportation. The latter was only resorted to in cases where criminal offences had taken place or of illegal immigration – under the more stringent provisions of the 1919 Aliens Act. Certainly, the atmosphere was hardly hospitable to the alien, but there is little evidence of mass deportations carried out against the will of the individuals concerned, on purely political grounds. The government remained sensitive to the charge that the almost sacrosanct right of asylum was being gradually whittled away.[93] The East End Jews achieved a considerable amount of success in resisting the Convention legislation. The Foreign Jews Protection Committee mobilised support in an overtly political fashion. Its membership represented the whole range of working-class organisations in Whitechapel, while its leadership consisted of some of the best brains of the radical intelligentsia. Much of this elite, being the most ideologically committed to the revolution, made the conscious decision to return to Russia, and in so doing impoverished the socialist and anarchist movement in England. It remains true, however, that the vast majority of Russian Jews in the East End were not politically motivated. Informal resistance manifested itself in widespread exemption and evasion of service in the British Army.

The effectiveness of this resistance made life uncomfortable for the established Jewish community which was stirring to prove its loyalty in wartime to the host society. Indeed, the twin issues of alien conscription and the Jewish Legion illustrate to what extent events in Russia could influence the course of Jewish communal politics in England. The Russian Revolution quickened the general debate on the conscription question and encouraged the Anglo-Jewish establishment in its campaign to persuade the immigrants to join up. This, in turn, ensured that Jabotinsky's scheme was looked at again in a fresh light, largely as a way out of the dilemma.

Not altogether unpredictably, the 'East End' – as the object of both plans – objected. The split in the 'West End' over the regiment throws a further interesting light on the attitudes adopted by the established Jewish community in Britain to the Russian Jews *in their midst*, as opposed to those still living in Russia.

The largely successful resistance put up by the Russian Jews to the Convention was in sharp contrast to the fate of the Lithuanian Catholics in Lanarkshire, the only other immigrant group of any significance (numbering about 8000 throughout the UK) to be affected by the legislation. Within a very short time some 85 per cent of Lithuanian eligibles were called up and the majority (about 1100) elected to return to Russia. In most cases where exemption was applied for, it was refused. Early in 1920 some 600 dependants were repatriated from Scotland to Lithuania, a move which more or less destroyed the viability of the émigré community. Superficially the Lithuanians had two advantages over the Jews which make their harsh treatment at the hands of the British government appear all the more surprising. Not only were they employed in essential war industries, coal mining, iron and steel, but they also enjoyed support from the local people, in particular the Lanarkshire County Miners Union. Yet the Lithuanians were unable to fight the Convention. It has been argued elsewhere[94] that, in this instance, it was the Catholic Lithuanians and not the Jews who served as the scapegoat. Like the Jews, the Lithuanians had a reputation for political militancy, but given that they formed a very much smaller community they could act as a convenient focus for anti-alien hostility. In the last analysis both the British government and the Jewish community knew that similar treatment of the Russian Jews could incite a storm of protest against infringement of the right of asylum and accusations of antisemitism which could be acutely embarrassing.

The Convention episode reveals much about Jewish responses to the Russian Revolution. Perhaps more importantly, however, the case of the Russian Jews, when set against that of the Lithuanian Catholics, tests the limits of governmental minority policies in Britain during the First World War.

JEWISH BOLSHEVIKS?

In England, as in Russia and elsewhere, there was an element of truth in the charge of 'Jewish Bolshevism'. The disproportionate number of individuals of Jewish origin in the top echelons of the Soviet government was evidence enough. In England, too, a significant number of Jews were active in left-wing politics at the time of the Russian Revolution. Research into Jewish activity on the left is beset with all sorts of problems, not least the complete absence of any statistical data. Trying to be precise as to the total number of Jewish participants in left-wing parties, their exact proportion and distribution, would be a very hazardous undertaking indeed. The dearth of hard facts is not at all surprising. The issue of Jewish involvement in radical politics in general, and in Bolshevism in particular, was, and still is, a sensitive one. Jewish and non-Jewish socialists alike shared an ideological aversion to making 'invidious' distinctions among themselves; this attitude was reinforced by an association of this practice with the tsarist regime. Jewish Communists especially, in England as in Russia, sought, subconsciously or otherwise, to subsume 'particularist' cultural, religious or national affiliations in the International Workers' Movement. It is often almost impossible for the researcher to distinguish between Jewish and non-Jewish Party members in the 1920s – even more so because 'Jewish identity' as such did not play any part in defining the political affiliations of Communists in this period, as it did later in the 1930s (positively, as far as the Party was concerned) and in the 1950s (negatively).

The issue of Jewish activity on the left was rendered doubly sensitive on account of the 'Jews and Bolshevism' agitation in sections of the Conservative press. The conspicuous presence of a number of Jews among the Bolshevik leaders in Russia was exploited in order to drum up support for the British intervention in the Civil War. Moreover, British military aid was going to prop up the reactionary White Guard generals – those same generals who were themselves using allegations of 'Jewish' Bolshevism as a pretext for massive pogroms in the Jewish Pale of Settlement in 1919 and 1920. Antisemitism was seen, even in Britain in certain quarters, as an instrument of foreign policy. It also had its uses in the domestic context. On the political right, the Russian Revolution was identified with the rise of Labour at home. And just as Conservatives regarded Bolshevism in Russia as a 'foreign import', so they regarded socialism at home in the same light. They blamed unrest on the 'alien'. Immigrants and subversion were linked; anti-Bolshevism, anti-alienism and antisemitism became intertwined in the public mind.

In the unstable political climate after the First World War, 'Bolshevism' became a term of abuse for every manifestation of leftist political tendencies. The popular adjective 'Bolshie' was coined in this period. If the label 'Bolshevik' is employed in this looser sense, rather than as a strict doctrinal definition, then the number of Jews involved in 'Bolshie' activity in Britain undoubtedly increases. Outside the bounds of the Communist Party of Great Britain (CPGB) itself, which was formed in 1920, individual Jews were prominent in an assortment of Marxist, anarchist and anti-war factions during this period.[95]

The best-known 'Jewish' Bolshevik in England was, of course, Maxim Litvinov (1876–1951). His prominence gave credence to the Jewish-Bolshevik connection. Litvinov was born Meir Genokh Moiseevitch Wallach, the son of an orthodox Jewish banker from Bialystok. He claimed to have joined the Marxist Russian Social Democratic Party at its inception in 1898 and thereupon to have embarked on a life-long revolutionary career. In 1902 he escaped from prison in Kiev and fled abroad. A period of political wandering in Europe, including a brief return to Russia during the 1905 upheaval, ended in 1908 when the writer Maxim Gorky found Litvinov a position with an English publishing company in London. Adopting the pseudonym Maxim Harrison, Litvinov settled in Parliament Hill. In 1916, he married Ivy Low, daughter of a Bloomsbury literary family and the granddaughter of Austrian Jews who had converted to Anglicanism. (One of her uncles was the journalist Sidney Low and her aunt Edith was married in turn to the Jewish Labour London County

Council member, Leslie Haden-Guest, and to the Fabian and Zionist, Dr David Eder.) Litvinov joined the Kentish Town branch of the British Socialist Party, the forerunner of the Communist Party. During the First World War he was associated with the BSP anti-war faction. Finally, in January 1918, Litvinov was granted semi-official status as Bolshevik representative in England. Enjoying diplomatic immunity, the Soviet 'ambassador' engaged in journalistic propaganda and organised a Bolshevik 'courier' service to and from Russia with the latest political news, pamphlets and funds. Very often these couriers were returning Jewish émigrés. In September 1918, Litvinov was deported to Russia in retaliation for the arrest of his opposite number, Bruce Lockhart, in Moscow. Litvinov went on to have a glittering career in the Bolshevik leadership, rising to the rank of Soviet Foreign Minister – until he was dropped by Stalin during his negotiations with Hitler in 1939.

A close associate of Litvinov's was Theodore (Fyoder Aronovitch) Rothstein (1871–1953).[96] After Litvinov's departure, Rothstein became the chief unofficial Soviet representative in Britain. He was born in Kovno, Lithuania and educated at Poltava in the Ukraine, the son of a non-practising Jewish chemist. In 1891 he emigrated to England via Germany, spent two years in Leeds and finally settled in Highgate. Like Litvinov, Rothstein remained a Russian citizen. He worked as a translator and journalist, writing not only for left-wing papers such as the Social Democratic Federation's (SDF) *Justice* and *Social Democrat*, and later the BSP's *The Call*, but also for the Liberal *Tribune*, *Daily News* and *Manchester Guardian* and the Russian émigré *Free Russia*. Rothstein also published articles in many foreign newspapers including *Neue Zeit* the journal of the Second International. He was London correspondent of the anti-colonialist *Egyptian Standard* between 1907 and 1912. Although he wrote in 'legal' Russian Marxist journals and in Trotsky's *Nashe Slovo*, in 1912 Rothstein became London correspondent for the Bolshevik *Pravda* and after 1915 for *Kommunist*. He collaborated on three short-lived Yiddish socialist papers which appeared in the East End in the early 1900s, at least two of which were Bundist in coloration. One of Rothstein's colleagues in this little-known period of his life was none other than Morris Myer.

Rothstein's varied journalistic activity reflected his overlapping political interests: in Russian émigré circles, in international socialism (he was a delegate at international socialist conferences before the First World War) and in the British socialist movement. In 1895 Rothstein had joined the Hackney Kingsland branch of the SDF, and served on the National Executive between 1901 and 1906. He soon clashed with H.M. Hyndman, over the latter's imperialism and antisemitism exhibited during the Boer War, and was to play a key role in the formation of the anti-war faction of the SDF's successor, the BSP, in 1916, which resulted in the break-up of the Party. After the Russian Revolution, Rothstein was a prime mover in bringing the BSP under the purview of the Russian Communist Party, ultimately leading to the formation of the CPGB and its affiliation to the Third International. Rothstein was responsible for providing 'Moscow Gold' for the far left in Britain as well as for the 'Hands Off Russia' campaign.[97] Although, according to one writer, 'Rothstein does not seem to have declared for Bolshevism until after the October Revolution', and thus, in the words of another, 'It is legitimate to question how deep the conversion actually was', there is no doubt that he was regarded as the mouthpiece of the Russian government in Britain. Whether Rothstein's role in the creation of the Party 'deals the view that the CPGB was a purely British phenomenon a heavy blow' is a strongly contested point.[98] In August 1920, ten days after the formation of the CPGB, Rothstein returned to Moscow to report on his activities. He was barred from re-entering Britain.

Other members of the Rothstein family carried on the revolutionary tradition in England. His brother-in-law, Boris Kahan (1877–1951), who was born in Kiev, became secretary of the East London branch of the SDF at the turn of the century. He was already prominent in this capacity at the time of Lenin's first visit to the East End in 1903. Associated with the anti-war wing of the BSP, Kahan was a member of the socialist delegation which welcomed the Soviet delegation to the Stockholm Conference on their stopover in London in July 1917. The latter delegation consisted of four prominent Bundists. Kahan was also present at the public meeting, held in honour of the Soviet guests, at the Brotherhood Church in Islington. The meeting was broken up after a pitched battle, by officially sponsored rowdies. Boris' sister Zelda, (1881?–1967), born in Lithuania and brought to England at the age of ten, became a member of the BSP executive on behalf of the Central Hackney branch in 1912. In 1915 she married William P. Coates, the

BSP's national organiser and later secretary of the 'Hands off Russia' committee. Together they joined the CPGB at its foundation and henceforth became leading publicists in the cause of Anglo-Soviet friendship. Finally, Theodore's eldest son Andrew Rothstein, born in London in 1898 and educated at Oxford followed in his father's footsteps. He joined the BSP in 1917. In his book *The Soldiers' Strikes of 1919* (London, 1980), Rothstein Junior recalls how, as a 20-year-old corporal based on Salisbury Plain just after the First World War, he played a modest role in the military opposition to recruitment for the North Russian Expeditionary Force. In 1921 he was appointed press officer for the Russian Trade Delegation and in 1923 to the executive of the CPGB, thus beginning a lifelong career in the service of Soviet Communism.[99]

Another Jewish 'BSPer' associated with the anti-war wing was Joe Fineberg (1886–1957). He was born in Zhoklin, Russian Poland, and brought to England at the age of 18 months. An East End tailor, Fineberg became the secretary of the Stepney and Whitechapel branch of the SDF in 1911; from 1914–18 he served on the BSP executive, where he was allied with the Fairchild faction. He played a key role at the anti-war Leeds Convention in June 1917 and from January 1918 was Litvinov's private secretary. In June 1918 he was deported back to Russia.[100]

The BSP had branches in Stepney and Bethnal Green and, no doubt, a Jewish grassroots following. *The Call* was on sale at East End bookstalls. A number of Jewish names appear on the list of delegates to BSP conferences in the period. For example, J. Valentine of Bethnal Green attended the April 1920 conference; he was also present at the Unity Convention held later the same year, and in 1922 stood as unsuccessful Communist Party candidate in the LCC elections. Nor must it be forgotten in this context that the Jewish Social Democratic Party, the Bund, had affiliated to the BSP soon after the Russian Revolution. J. Wolfe of the Glasgow Bund proposed an anti-Zionist resolution at the April 1918 BSP conference, which was held in Leeds. In the course of his speech he declared that 'it was well understood that the Jewish question had been solved by the Russian Revolution'. Joe Fineberg agreed, adding that 'The home of the modern Jew was in eastern Europe.' The resolution was carried by 92 to nil.[101]

The lesser known Marxist Socialist Party of Great Britain (SPGB), which had split from the SDF in 1904, also had connections with the East End and other centres of Jewish immigration. A prominent activist was Adolf Kohn, the London agent of a socialist publisher in Chicago. His friend Moses Baritz (1883–1938),[102] was born in Manchester and was a founder member of the SPGB branch there. The self-taught youngest child of poor immigrants who had come from Odessa in the late 1860s, Baritz graduated from the sweatshops of Red Bank to become a BBC broadcaster and music critic for the *Manchester Guardian*. But his hobby was political agitation. He apparently specialised in wrecking meetings of rival socialist groups and was a well-known local character in the debating clubs of Manchester. During the First World War both Baritz and Kohn adopted the SPGB anti-war line and consequently were forced to flee to the United States in order to avoid conscription. Baritz was arrested and interned in New York soon after the American entry into the war. Meanwhile, in 1917, Kohn sent a collection of inflammatory articles to London for publication in the SPGB's *Socialist Standard*. This led directly to a police raid on the SPGB's headquarters. Kohn's sister, Hilda, was questioned to no avail. Kohn evaded capture. Hilda, it turned out, was the SPGB's party secretary and carried a list of members in her handbag. In the 1920s Kohn and Baritz were responsible for the foundation of the Workers' Socialist Party of the United States in New York. Both men, it seems, later returned to England. One other SPGB member of Jewish origin was Alf Jacobs, a militant trade unionist who was on the executive of the (largely Jewish) Cigar Makers Mutual Association. He spoke every Sunday for more than 30 years in Victoria Park, Hackney.

Other fringe left-wing anti-war groupings with branches in East London also had a Jewish following: for example, the Stepney Herald League and Sylvia Pankhurst's Workers' Suffrage/or Workers' Socialist Federation (WSF). The latter contained a strong anarcho-syndicalist element, a characteristic it shared with the British Section of the American Industrial Workers of the World (IWW) set up in 1913. Indeed, the membership of these two organisations overlapped. The 'Wobblies' enjoyed a considerable expansion during the war. Their headquarters were situated in the heart of Jewish Whitechapel, and the 'Wobblies' were very active in a number of East End industries. In 1919, they played an important part in the 'Hands Off Russia' campaign. Several Jewish anarchists (as opposed to Yiddish-speaking anarchists, with whom we have already dealt) were active in the IWW. Albert Elsbury, the older brother of the breakaway garment workers' trade unionist, Sam Elsbury, was one-time editor of the IWW newspaper *Industrial Worker*. In 1921, Elsbury gained wider recognition as the chief strike organiser of the Shoreditch Unemployed Committee. Two radical Jewish feminists were also associated with both the WSF and the 'Wobblies'. Rose Witcop was the sister-in-law of one anarchist, the German Rudolf Rocker, and the common-law wife of another, Guy Aldred. She took over as the editor of the anarchist paper *The Spur* after the latter's internment in April 1916. Witcop's other interest was in the development of family planning. She met the pioneers in this field, Marie Stopes and the American, Margaret Sanger, and set up her own clinic in Highgate. Esther Archer (1897–1969) (née Argenband) was born to a German/Polish/Jewish immigrant family in Whitechapel. After leaving school at 13, she went to work in the Rothman's cigarette factory. By 1912 she was organising it for the IWW. 'During the war, she was a well-known open-air speaker, noted for her flaming red hair.' She eventually married her lover Charlie Lahr, who, like Rocker, was a German anarchist interned in Alexandra Palace from 1915 to 1919. For many years, Lahr ran an anarchist bookshop in Red Lion Square, Holborn, which was a meeting place for the radical literary intelligentsia. In 1920, the British IWW went into voluntary dissolution and its members joined the Communist Party *en bloc*. However, few stayed for long. Esther and Charlie, disillusioned by the Kronstadt Revolt and the introduction of NEP, unilaterally shut down the Central London branch in 1921.[103]

The Independent Labour Party (ILP) in Parliament adopted an anti-war stance in 1914. Of all the anti-war groupings, this 'most respectable' of parties had the least direct connection with East End Jewry. However, a few Jews were active in the ILP. One was Daniel Frankel, of the Whitechapel and Mile End branch, who was on the executive committee of the newly formed Stepney Trades Council in 1919. He represented Whitechapel at the 1920 ILP conference. Frankel went on to become mayor of Stepney and MP for Mile End in the 1930s. He came to be regarded as a 'right-winger' and was ousted by the Communist Phil Piratin in 1945.[104] Another Jewish ILP member was Joseph Leftwich, the Yiddish literary scholar, secretary of British *Poale Tsion* (1920-21) and a close friend of Rudolf Rocker. Like Zangwill he was a member of the Union of Democratic Control.[105] But among the ranks of the ILP, the title of 'Jewish Bolshevik' was reserved for Emanuel Shinwell (1884–1986). This was principally by virtue of his involvement in the 'Red Clydeside' unrest of 1919. Shinwell was not, in fact, born in Glasgow, but in Spitalfields, the eldest of 13 children of a Jewish tailor from Poland. His mother was descended from Dutch Jews. For economic reasons, the family moved to the Gorbals, the immigrant working-class district of Glasgow, and Shinwell was sent out to work at the age of 11. On his own admission, 'a Socialist before I was twenty',[106] Shinwell joined the ILP in 1903, was a delegate to the Glasgow Trades Council from 1906, and an organiser for the Seafarers' Union from 1911. Coopted onto the Glasgow Strike Committee in January 1919, he was arrested and imprisoned for five months after the George Square Riot on 'Black Friday' (31 January 1919). Despite his insistence in his memoirs that neither the Glasgow unrest, nor his own part in it, was revolutionary in intent, Shinwell's reputation for being something of a firebrand at the time was, apparently, not undeserved. Willie Gallacher, of the Clyde Workers' Committee, who later joined the CPGB, recalled Shinwell's conduct at an earlier demonstration, held in Glasgow in June 1917:

> The demonstration went off with gusto. MacDonald got a tremendous reception … and … contented [himself] with expressions of joy at the overthrow of the Czar and the emergence of 'Free Russia'. … But the best, and strongest, speech came from my pal Manny Shinwell. He too was pleased at the overthrow of the Czar, but he wanted to see the same thing happen here. He tore into the robber parasites in this country and left them stark naked before the eyes of a thoroughly receptive audience.
>
> 'They're squirming now' he exclaimed, 'but before we're finished we'll make their teeth rattle!'[107]

In the end, the 'revolutionary' went to Westminster instead. Shinwell, who had been nominated ILP candidate for the mining constituency of West Lothian (Linlithgow) in June 1918, was finally elected in 1922 – the first Jewish Labour MP. Thus began a career spanning 60 years in national Labour politics.

About left-wing anti-war groups in the period from 1914–18 Ken Weller has written the following: 'The fear of informers was *not* simple paranoia. The authorities did have networks of spies, and there was massive interception of letters and (for the first time) systematic telephone tapping.' Spies and *agent provocateurs* had some success in infiltrating the left, and a number of Jews were involved in this clandestine activity. Most of the information we have about the FJPC was provided by Yiddish-speaking employees of Basil Thomson at the Special Branch. An intriguing note, marked 'Confidential', from Thomson is amongst the papers of Ralph Blumenfeld:

> Among four Russian Jews who returned to Russia under the Military Convention and have just come back from Odessa, is one HARRY REISS, who has developed what appears to be a genuine abhorrence of Bolshevism. He is a costermonger, and lives with his wife and family at 94 Hessell Street, Commercial Road E. I suggest that he might be very useful for propaganda work in the East End, if you can get hold of him.[108]

This makes one wonder how many other returning Conventionists were approached with a view to 'propaganda work' by the Special Branch in 1919. A better-known Jew in the pay of the police was Alex Gordon, whose real name was F. Vivian. His activities at the Communist Club and the IWW hall in Whitechapel led directly to raids on these premises. But Gordon is perhaps best known for his part in the Wheeldon case of March 1917. He was the *agent provocateur* used to convict Mrs Alice Wheeldon, a socialist of Derby, and her family, in an alleged assassination plot against Lloyd George and Arthur Henderson. The story was headline news. Mrs Wheeldon was sentenced to ten years, while the chief witness, Gordon, was spirited away to South Africa. The trial was reputedly the outcome of a 'frame-up' by the Secret Service.[109]

In the realm of international espionage figure the names of Jacob Nosivitsky and Sidney Reilly. From 1919 to 1920, Nosivitsky, under various aliases, was the Soviet courier between Britain and the USA. However, in June 1919 he was arrested on his arrival in Liverpool and recruited by Basil Thomson. Nosivitsky's activities as a double agent enabled the British police to intercept mail between Moscow and Soviet representatives in the United States. In October 1920 he was responsible for the arrest of a Comintern agent, Erkhi Veltheim.[110] Sidney Reilly, otherwise Sigismund Gregorovitch Rosenblum, was the glamorous 'Ace of Spies' written about by the Bruce Lockharts, father and son, and the stuff of television drama. According to R.H. Bruce Lockhart, the official British representative in Russia in 1918, Reilly was 'a Jew with, I imagine, no British blood in his veins'.[111] He was born in Odessa, the illegitimate son of his Jewish mother's liaison with her doctor, whilst she was married to a Russian colonel. The son was brought up as a Catholic. Reilly himself is reputed to have been something of a Casanova; he was married at least three times and assumed the middle name of his first father-in-law, an Irishman named Callahan. In May 1918 he turned up in Moscow as an accredited British agent. (Lockhart: 'How he became a British subject, I do not know to this day. Prior to the War he had spent most of his time in St. Petersburg, where he had carved considerable sums of money as a commission agent in various forms of business.') Reilly was somehow implicated in the so-called 'Lockhart Plot' to overthrow the Bolshevik government. Since the exposure of this 'plot' was followed up by the unleashing of the 'Red Terror' against the opponents of the Bolsheviks, Reilly may well have been acting as a double agent in this instance. Be that as it may, Reilly was briefly back in England at the end of 1918 and, enjoying the full support of Churchill, joined the White Armies in south Russia in 1919. He was closely associated with Savinkov and is held to have been behind both the Sissons forgery and the Zinoviev letter which brought down the first Labour government in 1924. In 1926, on a subsequent mission to Russia, Reilly mysteriously disappeared. He was probably shot by the Bolsheviks.

Precisely what do these *ad hoc* examples of Jewish radicals add up to? Do they prove the reality of 'Jewish Bolshevism' in England, as some on the political right claimed? Hardly. The fact remains that, as in Russia, those Jews who were active in the general socialist and anarchist movement were unrepresentative of the Jewish community as a whole. Bolshevism, in the strict sense of the word, held little appeal for the mass of Jews, in England, in Russia or elsewhere. Marxist atheism and anti-nationalism cut across the aspirations of an overwhelmingly traditional community – and one, moreover, increasingly susceptible to Zionism. The Bolshevik social experiment also posed a threat to Jewish economic well-being, in that it had no patience with the petty-bourgeoisie. By 1919, much support for the Reds among Jews in

Britain, like their counterparts in Russia, was of the 'lesser evil' variety. After all, the only viable alternative was the blatantly antisemitic White Russian right.

Antipathy to Bolshevism was not only to be found among members of the established Anglo-Jewish community (something not entirely unexpected, if one is arguing from a class perspective), but equally among recent immigrants from Russia. This is perhaps surprising, given the latter's reputedly radical character and rich political life. Indeed, it was the militant hostility of the Russian Jewish immigrants to conscription into the British Army, under the terms of the Anglo-Russian Military Convention of July 1917, which more than any other factor reinforced the image of the East End as a stronghold of pro-Bolshevik and anti-war sentiment. The publicity courted by the FJPC was enough to convince outsiders that the aliens were deficient in patriotism. Besides, the Protection Committee, which enjoyed the support of many of the leading radical activists in the ghetto, also had links with the larger, left-wing, anti-war Russian émigré fraternity, not least with Georgi Chicherin. The activities of the FJPC in particular caused embarrassment to the Anglo-Jewish establishment and challenged their bid to maintain communal discipline.

Was the East End of London really a hotbed of leftist subversion as some conservatives would have it? In conclusion, the answer must be no. A perusal of the Jewish press suggests that the charge of 'Jewish Bolshevism' was wildly exaggerated. If this holds true for established English-speaking Jewry, then how much more so for the Yiddish-speaking immigrants of Whitechapel. East End Jewry backed the Labour Party line in relation to both the war and the revolution. The Yiddish press, led by Morris Myer's *Di Tsayt*, supported the prosecution of the war against 'German militarism' and a 'just' and democratic peace; the press was only pro-Bolshevik in the sense that it was opposed to military intervention in Russia to topple the Bolshevik regime and in favour of extending diplomatic recognition to the Soviet government. There is every reason to suppose that the attitude of the press reflected general feeling in the East End.

The information about Jewish voting patterns and Jewish involvement in wider Labour and trade union politics after the First World War bears out the contention that the radicalism of the East End fell far short of Communism. The Representation of the People Act (1918) extended the right to vote not only to women (who had to be both over 30 and local government electors) but also to men who had been resident in a constituency for six months. In other words, large numbers of Jews were now entitled to vote without undergoing the costly process of naturalisation. Thus, a working-class Jewish vote was created. Its impact was demonstrated at the 1918 general election. The anti-conscription Liberal James Kiley was convincingly returned for Whitechapel, whilst the Labour candidate was the runner-up, with strong Jewish support. In the 1922 election, Whitechapel went Labour.[112]

The same trend is also evident at the local level. In November 1919 Stepney Borough Council acquired a Labour mayor for the first time, the future Prime Minister of the first majority Labour government of 1945, Clement Attlee. Having never before held a single seat, the Labour Party now controlled two-thirds of the council and boasted six aldermen. Amongst these was a Jewish chemist, Oscar Tobin, president of the heavily Jewish Mile End Labour Party. He became the first Jewish mayor of Stepney in 1922. Other identifiable Jews on the council included Alfred Kershaw, secretary of the Mile End Labour Party, Solomon Levene, Abraham Valentine, an ex-Liberal and president of the Whitechapel and Spitalfields Costermongers Union, John R. Raphael and Isaac Sharp. Sharp stood unsuccessfully for the LCC elections of March 1919 (it was still early days for East End Jewish, if not for Labour, representation on the LCC). Sharp was also a regular at Trades Union Congress (TUC) conferences, indicative of the fact that Jewish trade unionists, encouraged by the war and the Russian Revolution, were cooperating to a far greater extent with their English counterparts. I. Lush of the United Ladies Tailors and Moses Sclare of the Leeds Amalgamated Jewish Tailors, Machiners and Pressers both spoke in support of a resolution welcoming the revolution passed at the September 1917 TUC conference. And at the 1919 conference, Sclare spoke out in favour of British recognition of the Soviet government.[113]

The Stepney Labour Party and Trades Council, founded in June 1918, had a substantial Jewish membership. All of the leading Jewish unions were affiliated to it, as were the BSP and the ILP, both represented by Jewish delegates. Oscar Tobin was secretary and John Raphael, Jacob Fine (general secretary of the United Ladies Tailors) and Daniel Frankel (of the ILP) served on the executive committee. The

Stepney Trades Council report for 1919 records that the organisation played a part in the 'Hands Off Russia' campaign, as well as in promoting the pro-alien cause. Not only was the council 'successful in preventing the deportation of a prominent trade union official in Stepney', but by means of concerted lobbying persuaded the Parliamentary Labour Party to put forward amendments to the 'worst features' of the Aliens Restriction Bill.[114]

The supposed Bolshevism of Russian Jews in England, like that of their counterparts in the 'Old Country', was thus largely a myth. The mass of East End Jewry aligned itself with the growing British Labour Party, and 'In 1918, Jews began, for the first time, to enter the foreground of East London Labour politics.'[115] It was their misfortune that, in the aftermath of the First World War and the Russian Revolution, some Conservatives failed to make the distinction between one type of socialist and another. The label 'Bolshie' became a blanket term of abuse for anyone with left-of-centre political preferences.

Conclusion

> Antisemitism is rampant even in the ranks of the Communist
> Party, of the Red Bureaucracy, and of the Red Army. When the
> Day of Judgement comes some of the worst enemies of the Jews
> will be found amongst their Russian Bolshevist accomplices.
> They will turn King's evidence; they will try to divert the anger of
> the mob from their own crimes and turn it against the Jews.
>
> Professor Charles Sarolea, 'Impressions of
> Soviet Russia XV: Bolshevism and the
> Jews', *The Scotsman*, 28 November 1923[1]

By the time Lenin died in 1924, British Jewry had made up its mind
about the Soviet Union. The subsequent internal transformation of the
community, the gradual absorption of immigrants, increasing economic prosperity and assimilation, did not materially alter fundamental attitudes towards Communist Russia. Even the increased Jewish
involvement in the British Communist Party in the 1930s may be
accounted for no less by preoccupation with the threat from German-
inspired Fascism, than by any real identification with Russian Communism.

All of the key issues with regard to Russia were well rehearsed in the
period 1917–21. Intense debate took place within the Anglo-Jewish
community on the political course of the Russian Revolution, British
intervention, the nature of Bolshevism and the Jewish role in the
Bolshevik Regime, on the fate of the Jews in Russia and the implications of the revolution for the future of the Zionist movement. Initial
euphoria at the overthrow of the oppressive tsarist Empire dissipated,
to be replaced by rueful reflection that the coming of the Communist
Revolution was not the beginning of the Messianic Era. Blatant antisemitism might be a thing of the past, but Bolshevik ideology brought
with it a new, more sophisticated intolerance of things Jewish. The
EVSEKTSIA (for a while at least) actively promoted a secular, socialist

242

Yiddish culture, at the expense of the Hebrew language, Zionism and Judaism itself.

We have found that Jewish responses to the Russian Revolution cannot be considered in isolation from the political climate in Britain. A significant increase in the incidence and extent of domestic antisemitism – reaching to the very top of British society – accompanied the war of intervention against the Bolsheviks. The belief that the October Revolution was a 'Jewish plot' gained currency even in sections of the 'respectable' press. Anti-Bolshevism became entangled with antisemitism in the public mind. It also got mixed up with anti-alienism. Immigrants were treated as suspect; the opposition of Russian Jewish 'friendly aliens' in the East End to conscription into the British Army hardened anti-alien sentiment during the war years. And, immediately after the war, rumours of impending revolution took hold of Britain. On the political right, the Russian Revolution was identified with the rise of Labour and trade union militancy at home. Just as Conservatives came to regard Bolshevism in Russia as a 'foreign import', so they ascribed socialism (of whatever hue) in Britain to 'alien influence', not least to immigrant Russian Jews.

This phenomenon was not confined to England. France, Germany and other countries in continental Europe suffered from the same malaise. Its most dramatic manifestation was the American 'Red Scare' of 1919–20: the Palmer Raids swept New York City clean of 'undesirable' aliens, including not a few Russian Jews.

Should the explosion of antisemitism in post-First World War Britain be regarded as an uncharacteristic lapse of passing consequence, or did it have more serious implications? Controversy rages amongst historians and social scientists about the problem of 'continuity' in the development of antisemitism in modern times. Leaving aside the whole debate as to whether twentieth-century antisemitism, especially in its most lethal Nazi form, was substantially different in quality from that which had gone before, what is certain is that the charge of 'Jewish Bolshevism' (which replaced the somewhat ironic one of Jewish pro-Germanism) gave more mileage to antisemitism in the years after the First World War. Combined with the growth of racial antisemitism, it provided nutrition for Fascist ideology in the 1930s. Thus the public outburst of anti-Jewish hostility in Britain from 1917 to 1921, if short-lived, left its legacy for the future.

There *was* an element of truth in the accusation of 'Jewish Bolshevism'. Trotsky had his imitators in Britain. Jews of British birth, although more often than not of Russian origin, were involved in the nascent Communist Party of Great Britain – not to mention in other, more obscure left-wing groupings. The fact remains, however, that as in Russia, these Jews were entirely unrepresentative of the Jewish community as a whole, with which their contact was usually minimal. Perhaps the most significant radical activity within the Jewish context was taking place in the East End of London during the war years. It centred on the Foreign Jews Protection Committee with its strong Yiddish anarchist input and its connections with mainstream Russian émigré circles. There was, without doubt, much passive sympathy for the Protection Committee's stand among immigrant Jews in London and Leeds.

Nevertheless, our reading of the Jewish press reveals that the influence of 'Jewish Bolshevism', particularly in the East End, was vastly overestimated. The Yiddish press sympathised with Labour Party policy on both the war and the Revolution. The war against German militarism was justified; intervention to topple Bolshevism was not. That the 'East End' no less than the 'West End' opposed intervention, emphatically did *not* imply that they supported Bolshevism.

That there was an element of truth in the charge of 'Jewish Bolshevism' also made life uncomfortable for the established Anglo-Jewish community, especially as antisemites regarded Jewry as indivisible. The First World War and the Russian Revolution challenged the major assumption of the 'Jewish liberal compromise' – the notion that British and Jewish interests coincided. In 1914, the Anglo-Russian Alliance cut diametrically across Jewish anxieties about tsarist persecution. In 1919, government remained largely deaf to Anglo-Jewish appeals on behalf of their co-religionists who were being massacred in their thousands by Britain's White Russian allies. A strain was put upon British/Jewish relations in this respect and the scope of Jewish diplomacy was actively curtailed. Lucien Wolf's efforts at the Paris peace conference and at the League of Nations bore precious little fruit.

The community had to be content to substitute philanthropy for diplomacy. Relief work compensated for the lack of progress on the political front, at least until relief work itself became mixed up with politics. At the same time, however, the war and the revolution accelerated the shift from emancipatory politics to 'the politics of cultural pluralism'. If 'West End' Jews were obliged to modify their responses to the Russian Revolution in the light of hostile public opinion, they were also goaded into a policy of communal self-defence.

More and more, the community moved from a cautious defence of its public image on to the counter-offensive against the antisemites. Meanwhile, the most enterprising wing of the leadership, spearheaded by the Zionist element, abandoned 'quiet diplomacy' in favour of 'public protest'. Here they were following the lead set by the 'East End'. But if this was a liberating development, in keeping with the true meaning of the word 'emancipation', the change of tactic did not herald any greater success in the political sphere. Arguably, it only succeeded in focusing even more unwelcome attention upon the Jewish community – and caused fresh dissension within it.

It is ironic that at the very same time that British Jewry was being forced to cope with an upsurge of antisemitism, fuelled by wartime xenophobia and anti-Bolshevism, Zionism was making great headway with the British government and public opinion. We have also seen how the genesis of the Balfour Declaration owed much to exaggerated Foreign Office fears about the Jewish part in Bolshevism. On this reading, the Declaration was designed primarily as a piece of wartime propaganda to wean Russian and American Jewry away from the competing attractions of socialism, pacifism and pro-Germanism, by the lure of Jewish nationalism. Chaim Weizmann and the Russian Zionists in London played up to such misplaced perceptions in the interest of promoting their cause. As far as the British government was concerned, the policy of 'Zionism versus Bolshevism' proved a failure. Yet Zionist success in the short-term notwithstanding, this policy was fraught with danger even for the Zionists themselves. Not only were they responsible for encouraging the myth of 'Jewish power', the charge was also levelled against them that 'Zionist Bolsheviks' were invading Palestine.

In 1945, the 'Jewish Communist' movement in the East End of London reached its apogee with the election of Phil Piratin as MP for the Mile End Division of Stepney. He won 47.6 per cent of the vote in a ward which was almost 50 per cent Jewish. In the autumn of the same year, ten Communists, seven of whom were Jews, were elected to Stepney

Borough Council. In the spring of 1946, two more Communists were elected to the LCC. Piratin claims in his memoirs that out of the 500 members of Stepney Communist Party in 1939, 'a half or more were Jewish'. The historian Geoffrey Alderman submits that perhaps as much as a third of the overall Communist Party membership in Britain (totalling 50,000) at that time was Jewish.[2]

Henry Srebrnik[3] argues that the electoral successes of the 1940s were the fruit of a decade in which the CPGB had mobilised the Jews of East London along ethnic lines. The Communist Party, often working through Popular Front organisations, established itself as the most active spokesman for issues of Jewish concern. It was at the forefront of the fight against poverty in the late 1930s, organising rent strikes against 'slum-lords'; it campaigned for proper Air Raid Precautions and for the provision of better housing at the war's end. On all these bread-and-butter issues the Communists proved themselves more effective than the Labour Party on the local council, which had acquired a reputation for corruption and was dominated by the Irish. But above all, the Communists were four-square against Fascism in both its domestic and international manifestations. The Battle of Cable Street (October 1936) became the symbol of a far wider Communist-inspired counter-offensive against the Mosleyites, whom it identified with home-grown antisemitism in general. Propaganda and street activism appealed to working-class Jews dissatisfied with the lukewarm approach of the established political parties (including Labour) and the 'low-profile' adopted by the Board of Deputies. Abroad, the CP condemned Franco and the Polish Ultras and sang the praises of Soviet Russia as the best insurance against Nazi Germany (an image little dented by the Ribbentrop–Molotov Pact of 1939–41). With the onset of Operation Barbarossa, the Party called for the opening of a second front in the west to divert German troops away from the Russian front. The Red Army could then advance across eastern Europe and, incidentally, liberate the Jews in its wake. Thus the defence of the Soviet Union and of European Jewry went hand in hand.

The CPGB was able to present an image of Soviet Russia which recommended itself to East End Jewry. Stalinist Russia's ideological and political opposition to Nazism was unrivalled in Europe. Moreover, at home, the Soviet Union was the only state on earth which had outlawed antisemitism in its constitution and was endeavouring to elevate the condition of the Jewish proletariat. The regime was actively promoting Yiddish culture through the World Jewish Cultural Union (1937) and the creation of the Birobidzhan Jewish Autonomous Region in the Soviet Far East. Pro-Soviet feeling in the East End peaked with the formation of the Soviet Jewish Anti-Fascist Committee and the visit to London of its two leading lights, Mikhoels and Feffer, late in 1943.

Srebrnik claims that the Communists were able to 'draw upon a long-standing legacy of pro-Soviet feeling' among the Jews of East London, in support of the wartime Anglo-Russian alliance, a legacy dating back to the Russian Revolution. Yet the continuity of this sympathy (outside the confines of the radical left) is far from certain, as our own researches have shown. However, he *is* right in his conclusion that the confluence of Communist and Jewish interest in the 1935–45 period was precisely that: a confluence of interests, and not a mutual ideological conversion. In conditions of impending and actual warfare, practical action – the struggle against Fascism – counted for more than political theory. The Communists went out (and were very successful in) enlisting Jewish support in unabashed 'ethnic' fashion. Jewish Communists 'thought, talked and behaved more like left-wing Jewish nationalists than Marxist internationalists'.[4] Committed Jewish Communists were undoubtedly sincere in their belief that, through a synthesis of Communist and Jewish ideas they were making 'a positive contribution to Jewish life'.[5] But in so doing they somehow 'managed to ignore much of Marxist–Leninist doctrine, including its analysis of the Jews and their ultimate place in society – an analysis highly unfavourable to any long-range Jewish ethnic ambitions'.[6] And in the afterglow of the triumph of 1945, Piratin and his supporters failed to acknowledge the compelling truth which patently did not fit their ideological construct, that it was ethnicity rather than class consciousness which had made it all possible.

In the late 1940s, the constellation of circumstances which had given rise to the Jewish-Communist alliance began to dissipate. Fascism had been defeated – and in the process six million Jews had met their deaths. The Cold War descended; initial Soviet support for the nascent State of Israel turned into hostility, and was accompanied by revelations of the extent of Stalin's own persecution of his Jews. Zionism was now in the ascendant. In Britain, the second generation was leaving the ghetto, their flight having been hastened by the Blitz. Upward social mobility and integration meant that Jewish identification with working-class causes lessened. By the end of the 1950s the Jewish Communist movement had collapsed. It had, in truth, all along contained the seeds of its own destruction.

Notes

INTRODUCTION

1. A start has been made on assessing the impact of the Russian immigration in general on British political life. See John Slatter (ed.) *From the Other Shore: Russian Political Emigrants in Britain 1880–1917* (London, 1984).
2. The literature on Russian Jewry, and indeed on the revolution, is vast. A few basic indispensable works are cited in the footnotes to the text.
3. According to the old Russian Julian calendar. After the revolution the Bolsheviks adopted the western Gregorian calendar, which is 12 days ahead. Hence the February Revolution actually took place in March, and the Great October Revolution in November.
4. The best and most detailed study of the intervention from the British point of view is Richard Ullman's three volume *Anglo-Soviet Relations 1917–1921* (Princeton 1968–72). Michael Kettle's *Russia and the Allies 1917–1920* has now reached Vol. II (London and New York 1981, 1988). See also Martin Gilbert, *Winston S. Churchill*, Vol. IV, *1917–22* (London, 1975).

1 'BOCHE, BOLSHIE AND THE JEWISH BOGEY'

1. The two major works dealing with antisemitism in Britain in the inter-war period are: Colin Holmes, *Anti-Semitism in British Society 1876–1939* (London, 1979) and Gisela C. Lebzelter, Political Anti-Semitism in England, 1918–1939, (Oxford, 1978). See also Leon Poliakov's *History of Anti-Semitism*, Vol. IV, *Suicidal Europe* (Paris, 1977, and London, 1985 English edn); 'Crucial event' Lebzelter, op. cit., p.16.
2. A.J.P. Taylor, *English History, 1914–1945* (Pelican edn, 1970), p. 150.
3. On the pogroms, see Elias Heifetz, *The Slaughter of the Jews in the Ukraine in 1919* (New York, 1921); Elias Tcherikower, *Antisemitizm un pogromen in Ukraine, 1917–1918* (Berlin 1923); *De Ukrainer Pogromen in yor 1919* (YIVO Institute, New York, 1965).
4. Sir Eyre Crowe, Assistant Under-Secretary of State FO, 1 Oct. 1919, quoted in Richard Ullman, *Anglo-Soviet Relations 1917–1921*, Vol. II, *Britain and the Russian Civil War, Nov. 1918–Feb. 1920* (Princeton, 1968), p.219, n. 40.
5. FO to Wolf, 19 April 1920, JFC C 11/12/121.
6. Gerald Spicer (FO) to Wolf, 17 Dec. 1919, JFC Minutes, 1919.
7. Ibid., 17 Nov. 1919.
8. Robert Cecil to Joshua Podruzhnik, 9 Aug. 1919, JFC C 11/12/121. Letter reprinted in Yiddish translation in *Di Tsayt*, 12 Sept. 1919.
9. Churchill to Holman, 18 Sept. 1919. Churchill Papers 16/18, quoted in Martin Gilbert, *Winston S. Churchill*, Vol. IV, *1917–22* (London, 1975), p. 330, and *Companion Vol. IV.II*, p. 860.

10. Churchill to Gough, 6 June 1919, WO 32/5692, quoted in Gilbert, op. cit., Vol. IV, p. 293, and *Companion Vol. IV.I*, p. 677.
11. Churchill to Lloyd George, 10 Oct. 1919. Churchill Papers, 16/12, quoted in Gilbert, op. cit., Vol. IV, p. 342, and *Companion Vol. IV.II*, pp. 912–13.
12. Churchill to Sir Richard Haking, *Outline of Instructions*, 21 Oct. 1919. Churchill Papers 16/18, quoted in Gilbert, op. cit., Vol. IV, p. 351, and *Companion Vol. IV.II*, p. 934. Warning to Yudenitch in the event of the capture of Petrograd.
13. Churchill to Gough, 6 June 1919 (as n. 10 above); also in Ullman, op. cit., pp. 218–19, n. 40.
14. Lloyd George to Churchill, 7 Oct. 1919, Churchill papers 16/25, quoted in Gilbert, op. cit., Vol. IV, p. 342., and *Companion Vol. IV.II*, pp. 899–900.
15. Churchill to Denikin, 9 Oct. 1919, Churchill papers 16/18, quoted in Gilbert, op. cit., Vol. IV, pp. 342–3, and *Companion Vol. IV.II*, p. 907; also press statement, 14 Oct. 1919, p. 918.
16. Churchill to Holman, 18 Sept. 1919 (as n. 9 above).
17. Winston S. Churchill, *Aftermath: A Sequel to World Crisis* (London, 1941), p. 274. See also Michael Cohen, *Churchill and the Jews* (London, 1985); Oskar Rabinowicz, *Winston Churchill on Jewish Problems* (London, 1956), pp. 89, 92–3.
18. Winston S. Churchill, 'Zionism versus Bolshevism: A Struggle for the Soul of the Jewish People', *Illustrated Sunday Herald*, 8 Feb. 1920.
19. Rabinowicz, op. cit., pp. 92–3.
20. Quoted in William Coates and Zelda Kahan, *Armed Intervention in Russia, 1918–22* (London, 1935), p. 290.
21. Ullman, op. cit., pp. 141–4.
22. JFC C 11/3/1. There is an original copy of the Arkhangel proclamation in the personal archive of a British soldier, J.H. Bracher, at the Imperial War Museum (File P 346).
23. Lucien Wolf, *Diary of the Peace Conference 1919* (UCL), 5 Sept. 1919. On Polish Jewry, see Norman Davies, 'The Poles in Great Britain 1914–1919', *Slavonic and East European Review*, Vol. 50 (1972), pp. 62–89; 'Great Britain and the Polish Jews, 1918–20', *Journal of Contemporary History*, Vol. 8, No. 2 (April 1973), pp. 119–42.
24. *Report by Sir Stuart Samuel on his Mission to Poland*, Command Paper No. 674 (1920), p. 29.
25. On the Diehards: Roger T. Schinness, *The Tories and the Soviets: The British Conservative Reaction to Russia 1917–27*, unpub. PhD State University of New York at Binghamton, 1972; also Maurice Cowling, *The Impact of Labour (1920–24)* (London 1971); Richard Thurlow, *Fascism in Britain: A History 1918–1985* (Oxford, 1987); G. Webber, *The Ideology of the British Right 1918–1939* (London, 1987), and his chapter on 'Intolerance and Discretion: Conservatives and British Fascism 1918–1926' in T. Kushner and K. Lunn (eds), *Traditions of Intolerance* (Manchester, 1989), pp. 155–72.
26. Reprinted in *JC*, 15 Aug. 1919. The following week's issue carried a letter to the editor from Mr Raper, denying any antisemitic intent.
27. Stephen Graham, *Russia in Division* (London, 1925), p. 6; his memoir *Part of the Wonderful Scene: An Autobiography* (London, 1964) throws no light on his antisemitism.
28. *The Times*, 11 April and 28 March 1917.
29. Letter from John Buchan to Geoffrey Robinson, 1 May 1917, quoted in Holmes, op. cit., p. 275, n. 12. Enclosed with this note was an intelligence memo on Wilton's

activities in Russia.
30. Robert Wilton, *Russia's Agony* (London, 1918), pp. 56–61.
31. Ibid., pp. 174–5.
32. Command Paper No. 8, *Russia No. 1: A Collection of Reports on Bolshevism in Russia*, (1919).
33. Robert Wilton, *The Last Days of the Romanovs* (London 1920), p. 148.
34. Anthony Summers and Tom Mangold, *The File on the Tsar* (London, 1976), pp. 102–4. Summers and Mangold also claim that Wilton was probably spying for the British and the Americans.
35. Phillip Knightley, *The First Casualty* (London, 1975), p. 162.
36. Summers and Mangold, op. cit., p. 104.
37. *The Times*, 14, 20–22, 25–9 Nov. and 1–4, 6, 20 Dec. 1919. Lucien Wolf did not take the press baron's antisemitic leanings seriously: 'I do not think that Northcliffe really takes any interest in antisemitism but I imagine he tolerates it as good yellow journalism. Wickham Steed, his *Times* editor, is quite a dangerous antisemite – absolutely monomaniacal.' Letter to Cyrus Adler, 15 July 1920. JFC, C11/3/4.
38. See *The Times*, 28 June 1919.
39. Henry Wickham Steed, *Through Thirty Years, 1892–1922*, Vol. II (London, 1924), pp. 8–9.
40. Ibid., pp. 390–3.
41. Ibid.
42. *The Times*, 10 Nov. 1919.
43. Steed, op. cit., pp. 30, 270.
44. Ibid., pp. 302.
45. Norman Cohn, *Warrant for Genocide* (London, 1970), p. 126.
46. Robert Cust to H.A. Gwynne, 11 Feb. 1920, Gwynne Papers, Bodleian Library, Oxford, quoted in Holmes, op. cit., pp. 147–8. For new research on the genesis of the English edition of *The Protocols* see Colin Holmes, *Anti-Semitism*, op. cit., and 'New Light on *The Protocols of Zion*', in *Patterns of Prejudice*, Vol. 6 (1977), pp. 13–21.
47. Poliakov, op. cit., p. 210 (English edn, 1985).
48. Quoted from A. Netshvolodov, *Emperor Nicholas II and the Jews* (Paris, 1924), in Poliakov, op. cit., pp. 197–8. Apparently this pamphlet was reprinted in English by The Britons Publishing Society, but I have not been able to locate a copy. See Victor E. Marsden, *Rasputin and Russia: The Tragedy of a Throne* (London, 1920) and *Jews in Russia: With Half Jews and Damped Jews. With a List of the names of the 447 Jews in the Soviet Government of Russia* (The Britons, n.d., [1921]). The list of Jewish Bolsheviks Marsden compiled was far more comprehensive than the one published in H.A. Gwynne's *The Cause of World Unrest* reproduced here, running to 16 pages. Marsden even claimed that Lenin was 'a full-blooded Jew'. Acknowledgements to Dr Keith Wilson of Leeds University.
49. H.A. Gwynne (ed.), *The Cause of World Unrest* (London, 1920), p. 9. Information about Ian Colvin cited in Holmes, *Anti-Semitism*, from *DNB*, *The Concise Dictionary 1901–1950* (Oxford, 1961), p. 94.
50. Gwynne, op. cit., pp. 131–2.
51. Ibid. Spellings are as in the original.
52. Nesta Webster, *The Origins and Progress of the World Revolution* (London, 1921, reprinted by Boswell in 1932). See John Michell, *Eccentric Lives and Peculiar Notions* (London, 1984), pp. 62–72; Richard M. Gilman, *Behind World Revolution: The Strange Career of Nesta H. Webster*, Vol. I (Ann Arbor, 1982).

BOLSHEVIKS AND BRITISH JEWS

BOLSHEVIKS AND BRITISH JEWS

53. Webster, op. cit., (1932 edn), p. 11.
54. *MP*, 26–27 April 1922, pp. 10–11, 15–16 June 1922.
55. Ibid., 26–27 April 1922. The *Morning Post* reprinted Nesta Webster and Kurt Kerlen's exchange in *Boche and Bolshevik* (New York 1923).
56. Webster, op. cit., p. 11.
57. *Spectator*, 15 May, 9, 16 Oct. 1920; Count de Soissons, 'The Jews as Revolutionary Leaven', *Quarterly Review*, Jan.–March 1920, p. 172ff.; Austin Harrison, 'Which God? or the World of the Jews', *English Review* Vol. 29 (July–Dec. 1919), pp. 553–64.
58. See also George Pitt-Rivers, *The World Significance of the Russian Revolution*, with an introduction by Oscar Levy (Oxford, n.d., [1920]). The DPhil dissertation upon which the present work is based contains a detailed analysis of Belloc and other literature indicated here.
59. For example: Sir Paul Dukes, *Red Dusk and the Morrow* (London, 1922); William T. Goode, *Bolshevism at Work* (London, 1920); John Ernest Hodgson, *With Denikin's Armies* (London, 1932); George Lansbury, *What I saw in Russia* (London, 1920); Capt. Francis McCullagh, *A Prisoner of the Reds* (London, 1921); John Pollock, *The Bolshevik Adventure* (London, 1919); Charles Sarolea, *Impressions of Soviet Russia* (London, 1924); Mrs Philip Snowden, *Through Bolshevik Russia* (London, 1920); H.G. Wells, *Russia in the Shadows* (London, 1920).
60. In 1924, The Duke of Northumberland purchased the *Morning Post*; in 1950 The Britons bought up Boswell.
61. See Holmes, *Anti-Semitism*, op. cit., and Lebzelter, op. cit., on The Britons. See also Lebzelter's 'Henry Hamilton Beamish and the Britons: Champions of anti-Semitism', in K. Lunn and R. Thurlow (eds), *British Fascism: Essays on The Radical Right in Inter War Britain* (London, 1980). The Wiener Library has a file on Beamish (now on microfilm in London); the British Library and the YIVO Institute for Jewish Research (Mowshowitch Papers) have some pamphlet material. Both Holmes and Lebzelter gained access to The Britons' own archives, at Chawleigh. C.C. Aronsfield, 'The Britons', *Wiener Library Bulletin*, Vol. 20, No. 3, (Summer 1966), pp. 31–5; and Barry Kosmin, 'Colonial Careers for Marginal Fascists: A Portrait of Hamilton Beamish', ibid., Vol. 27, No. 30/1 (1973/74), pp. 16–23.
62. The minister in question was Bark.
63. Cohn, op. cit., p.12.
64. The present quotation is taken from a letter by 'Anglus' to *The Globe*, 5 April 1919, and reprinted in Harold Sherwood Spencer, *Democracy or Shylockracy?* (London 1922), Wiener Library Collection.
65. Charles Whibley, 'Musings with Method', column in *Blackwood's Magazine* quoted in Spencer, op. cit. (undated). The 'Blood Libel' refers to the medieval Christian accusation that Jews used the blood of Christians for ritual purposes, especially in the preparation of *matzos* (unleavened bread) for the Passover feast.
66. Disease imagery, closely associated with biological race theories, constantly appeared in The Britons' pamphlets. Joseph Banister, one of their chief contributors, wrote in his *Our Judeo-Irish Labour Party* (London, 1923), 'There are in Russia, typhus, cholera, scarlet fever, bugs, beetles, lice, leeches – and seven million of Trotsky's tribesmen' (p. 56).
67. Holmes, *Anti-Semitism,* op. cit., p. 221.
68. See Hilary Blume, *A Study of Anti-Semitic Groups in Britain 1918–1940*, unpub. MPhil, University of Sussex, 1971.
69. Copy in the Wiener Library.

252

70. This silence was explained by antisemites by the fact that the editors of both papers, Lord Burnham and Ralph Blumenfeld, were of Jewish descent. This, coupled with the fact that the Reuters Press Agency had been founded by a Jew, gave credence to the antisemitic theory that Jews dominated Fleet Street in order to control the flow of information in their own interest. In reality Burnham and Blumenfeld's silence may be due more to insecurity than to the 'cover up' of a Jewish plot. However, after Beaverbrook fell out with Lloyd George in 1922, the *Express* took up a strongly anti-Zionist line. See David Cesarani, 'Anti-Zionist Politics and Political Anti-semitism in Britain, 1920–24', *Patterns of Prejudice*, Vol. 23, No. 1 (1989), pp. 28–45. It can only be assumed that Beaverbrook overruled his editor.

71. The *MG*'s Russian correspondents in 1917, David Soskice and Michael Farbman, were assimilated Russian Jewish émigrés with left-of-centre views. The editor, C.P. Scott, a friend of Weizmann and the EZF, played a key role in behind-the-scenes negotiations leading up to the Balfour Declaration on Palestine. On Soskice, see John Slatter, 'The Soskice Papers: A Guide', *Sbornik*, No. 8 (Summer 1982), pp. 49–68, the archive being in the House of Lords Record Library; Barry Hollingsworth, 'David Soskice in Russia in 1917', *European Studies Review*, Vol. 6 (1976), pp. 73–97. On Farbman, see obituary *MG*, 29 May 1933, *JC*, 2 June 1933, and his published works on Russia, listed in the bibliography below. Generally, see David Ayerst, *The Guardian: Biography of a Newspaper* (London, 1971).

72. This was especially true in the Marxist BSP, the forerunner of the CPGB, when in 1914 the pro-war faction used antisemitism to combat the anti-war faction one of whose leaders, Joe Fineberg, was a Jew.

73. See below, Ch. 5, pp. 229–30.

74. See Lloyd P. Gartner's pioneering study *The Jewish Immigrant in England 1870–1914* (New York, 1960); Bernard Gainer, *The Alien Invasion: The Origins of the Aliens Act of 1905* (London, 1972); J.A. Garrard, *The English and Immigration: A Comparative Study of the Jewish Influx, 1880–1914*, (London, 1971); and on the First World War, see C.C. Aronsfeld, 'Jewish Enemy Aliens in England during World War I', *Jewish Social Studies*, Vol. 18, No. 4 (1956), pp. 273–83; J.C. Bird, *The Control of Enemy Alien Civilians in Great Britain* (New York, 1986); Panikos Panayi, 'The Hidden Hand: British Myths about German Control of Britain during the First World War', *Immigrants and Minorities*, Vol. 7, No. 3 (Nov. 1988), pp. 253–72; 'Anti-German Riots in London during the First World War', *German History*, Vol. 7, No. 2 (Aug. 1989), pp. 184–203. On the Germans see also several essays in the major new collection Werner E. Mosse *et al.* (eds), *Second Chance: Two Centuries of German-speaking Jews in the United Kingdom* (Tubingen, 1991).

75. David Saunders, 'Aliens in Britain and the Empire during the First World War', *Immigrants and Minorities*, Vol. 4, No. 1 (March 1985), pp. 5–27, quotes pp. 9, 10. See also Bernard Porter, 'The British Government and Political Refugees c. 1880–1914', in John Slatter (ed.) *From the Other Shore: Russian Political Emigrants in Britain, 1880–1917* (London, 1983), pp. 23–45, and David Cesarani, 'Anti–Alienism in England after the First World War', *Immigrants and Minorities*, Vol. 6, No. 1 (March 1987), pp. 5–29 and his 'An Embattled minority: the Jews in Britain during the First World War', *Immigrants and Minorities*, Vol. 8, Nos. 1 & 2 (March, 1989), pp. 61–8.

76. Davies, 'The Poles in Great Britain', op. cit., p. 66.

77. Fewer than 400 had enlisted by 10 Oct. 1916, HO 45/10818/318095/62. Herbert Samuel gave way to the less sympathetic Sir George Cave in the Cabinet reshuffle

under Lloyd George in Dec. 1916. The exemption extended to the British born sons of non-naturalised Russian Jews.

78. Julia Bush, *Behind the Lines: East London Labour, 1914–19* (London, 1984) Ch. 6, 'The Jews and the War'.
79. *ELO*, 7 July 1917.
80. On Thomson see Porter, op. cit., pp. 33–8; Ivan Maisky, *Journey into the Past* (London, 1962) claims that the Convention was a conspiracy hatched in St Petersburg 'to hamper the anti-Tsarist agitation both in London and Paris,' p. 75.
81. Bush, op. cit.
82. See the list in the *Jewish Year Book* for the relevant years and also Geoffrey Alderman, *The Jewish Community in British Politics* (Oxford, 1983).
83. King is quoted as declaring 'People call me King of the Jews and I am proud of the title', in Banister, *Our Judeo-Irish Labour Party*, op. cit. According to Colin Holmes, 'Internment, Fascism and the Public Records', *Society for the Study of Labour History Bulletin*, Vol. 52, part 1 (1987), pp. 17–23, the Home Office file on King is closed (pp. 19–20), and the MP left no private papers. On Venetia Stanley's relationship with Montagu see Eugene Black, 'Edwin Montagu', *TJHSE*, Vol. 30 (1987–88), pp. 199–218.
84. See Bush, op. cit.
85. For government statistics see *Report of the Aliens Enlistment Committee*, 26 July 1916, PRO HO 45/10818/318095/57. On Anglo-Jewish recruits see Morris Adler, *The British Jewry Book of Honour* (London, 1919).
86. *JC*, 5 Oct. 1917.
87. See William J. Fishman, *East End Jewish Radicals, 1880–1914* (London, 1975).
88. *JW*, 16 May 1917.
89. See Thomson to HO, 4 April 1917, PRO HO 45 10820/318095/243. On the Leeds riots see Holmes, *Anti-Ssemitism*, pp. 130–8, and Abraham Gilam, 'The Leeds Anti-Jewish Riots 1917', *Jewish Quarterly*, Vol. 29, No. 1 (106) (Spring 1981), pp. 34–7; Garrard, op. cit., p. 57.
90. Hilaire Belloc, *The Jews* (London, 1922), p. 135.
91. *JC*, 15 June 1917; Garrard, op. cit., p. 59.

2 FROM BONDAGE UNTO FREEDOM?

1. Steven Gilbert Bayme, *Jewish Leadership and anti-Semitism in Britain 1898–1918*, unpub. PhD, Columbia University, 1977.
2. See Ch. 1, Section 4 on 'The dislike of the unlike', and Ch. 5.
3. See Chaim Bermant *The Cousinhood* (New York, 1971).
4. See anon. (Cecil Roth), *The Jewish Chronicle, 1841–1941: A Century of Newspaper History* (London, 1949).
5. Given the track record of tsarist antisemitism, and the apparently more civilised image of German *Kultur* before 1914, it must have seemed to many Anglo-Jews that Britain was entering the war 'on the wrong side'. See Mark Levene, 'Anglo-Jewish Foreign Policy in Crisis – Lucien Wolf, the Conjoint Committee and the War 1914–18', *TJHSE*, Vol. 30 (1987–88), pp. 179–97, esp. pp. 185–6.
6. Julia Bush, *Behind the Lines: East London Labour, 1914–19*, Ch. 6.

7. Reprinted in *JW*, 18 April 1917.
8. *JW*, 28 March 1917.
9. Ibid.
10. *JC*, editorial 21 June 1918.
11. Leopold de Rothschild to Lucien Wolf, 25 March 1917, RAL RFamAD/1/4. Original of Tereschenko telegram in RAL xi/89/12.
12. De Rothschild to Wolf, 18 March 1917, RAL RFamAD/1/4.
13. See Mark Levene, *Jewish Diplomacy at war and peace: A Study of Lucien Wolf*, unpub. DPhil, University of Oxford, 1982. I am grateful to Dr Levene for his advice. The major primary unpublished sources on Wolf are: Anglo-Jewish Association reports, minutes and correspondence at the BoD's Archives in London; Wolf's unpublished *Diary of the Peace Conference 1919*, a mimeographed copy of which is at University College London; the David Mowshowitch Collection at the YIVO Institute of New York; four Lucien Wolf Bound Correspondence Files at the headquarters of the Jewish Colonisation Association, and Wolf Papers 1905–17 at Rothschild Archive both in London.
14. Chimen Abramsky, 'Lucien Wolf's Efforts for the Jewish Communities in Central and Eastern Europe', *TJHSE*, Vol. 29 (1982–86), pp. 281–95; quote p. 284.
15. Conjoint Committee Report, No. X, 6 Feb.–17 May 1917.
16. The best biography of the writer remains the memoir *Israel Zangwill*, written by his friend Joseph Leftwich (London, 1957). Joseph H. Udelson's, *Dreamer of the Ghetto: The Life and Works of Israel Zangwill* (Alabama, 1990) appeared whilst this book was in press.
17. *MG*, 2 April 1917, p. 8.
18. Copy in the Zangwill archive (A 120/33) at CZA, Jerusalem. Subsequently reprinted in the Labour *Daily Herald*.
19. Leonard Schapiro.
20. De Rothschild to Wolf, 18 March 1917, RAL RFamAD/1/4 RA, see also 25 March; de Rothschild 'so excited by the Revolution', see Wolf to Montefiore, 16 March 1917, JFC C11/2/11. On similar caution expressed by the AJA, see Wolf to de Rothschild, 26 March 1917, MOW File 38; by David Lindo Alexander to de Rothschild, 5 April 1917, RAL/xi/1/13; by B'nai Brith, see 12 April 1917, File 326 (incoming), Gaster Papers, Mocatta Library, UCL.
21. This section based on the BoD Minutes, Bk 17, 22 April 1917. A full report appeared in the *JC* on 27 April.
22. *JC*, 6 April 1917.
23. *JW*, 11, 25 April 1917. The 'Communal Revolution' finally came in May of that year, ostensibly over Zionism.
24. Gaster to Rev. E. Sjoblom, Liverpool, 16 April 1917, Letter Book 1916–17, pp. 511–12; Gaster to Mr Weinstein, 14 May 1917, ibid., pp. 591–2; all in the Gaster Papers.
25. Dr Dillon in the *Fortnightly Review* as cited in *JW*, 2 May 1917.
26. *JW*, 25 July 1917.
27. *JW*, 26 Sep. 1917.
28. See George Katkov, *Russia 1917: The February Revolution* (London, 1967), where this thesis is treated at length.
29. Wolf to Claude Montefiore, 11 May 1917, MOW File 32, 2989.
30. Conjoint Committee Report, No. X, 6 Feb.–17 May 1917.
31. Wolf to Montefiore, 16 March 1917, JFC C 11/2/11, and similarly Wolf to Leopold de Rothschild, 16 March 1917, RAL/xi/1/13.

32. Conjoint Committee Report, No. X, 6 Feb.–17 May 1917.
33. *JW*, 28 March 1917.
34. Ibid., 17 July 1918.
35. *JC*, 3 May 1918.
36. *JC* report from Petrograd, 25 Jan. 1918.
37. Quoted in Hyman Lumer (ed.), *Lenin on the Jewish Question* (New York, 1974). Compare Lenin's position with that of Marx: Karl Marx, *On the Jewish Question* (1844). There is a good translation in David McLellan (ed.), *Karl Marx: Selected Writings* (Oxford, 1977).
38. See Henry J. Tobias, *The Jewish Bund in Russia from its Origins to 1905* (Stanford, 1972), and Leonard Schapiro, 'Jews in the Russian Revolutionary Movement', *Slavonic and East European Review*, Vol. 40, No. 94 (Dec. 1961), pp. 148–167. Schapiro cites the figure of 23,000 as the total membership of the Bund in 1905, as compared with a mere 8400 in the rest of the Russian Social Democratic movement (p. 160).
39. 1903 quoted in Lumer, op. cit.
40. Speech at the April Conference, 29 April 1917.
41. Lenin, *Critical Remarks on the National Question*, 1913.
42. Quoted in Zvi Gitelman, *Jewish Nationality and Soviet Politics: the Jewish Sections of the CPSU 1917–1930* (Princeton, 1972), which is the best study of this topic (p. 273).
43. The Black Hundred(s) (*Chornaya Sotnya*), otherwise known as the Union of the Russian People (*Soyuz Russkogo Naroda*), was an ultra-right national and antisemitic grouping formed during the reaction which followed the 1905 revolution.
44. *JC*, 1 Nov. 1918.
45. *JC*, 4 April 1919: Rev. Joseph's contributions, 25 April and 9 May 1919; Greenberg's reply, 16 May 1919. Zangwill in speech at the Albert Hall, *JC*, 12 March 1920.
46. Robert Wistrich, *Revolutionary Jews from Marx to Trotsky* (London, 1976), p. 199. See also his *Trotsky: Fate of a Revolutionary* (New York, 1982).
47. Joseph Nevada, *Trotsky and the Jews* (Philadelphia, 1971), pp. 116, 160.
48. *JW*, 9 Jan. 1918.
49. Ibid., 27 Feb. 1918.
50. Ibid., 2 Jan. 1918. Béla Kun and Rosa Luxemburg got the same treatment.
51. Quoted in Nevada, op. cit., p. 167.
52. *JC*, 12 July 1918.
53. Quoted in Zangwill, *The Voice of Jerusalem* (London, 1920), pp. 222–3 (1921 Macmillan edn), and Leftwich, op. cit., pp. 100–1. F. Anstey (Thomas Anstey Guthrie), *Vice Versa: Or A Lesson to Father* (London, 1882).
54. *JC*, 5 July 1918.
55. Wolf to Curzon, 2 Dec. 1918 (draft), JFC Minutes. Wolf's Russian correspondents Blank and Mowshowitch both opposed intervention as likely to strengthen the Bolsheviks.
56. *JW*, 30 July 1919.
57. Chief Rabbi Dr J.H. Hertz, *A Decade of Woe and Hope* (London, 1923). The comparison with the Armenian massacres is a quotation from the Samuel Report on Poland; see above, Ch. 1. Hertz admitted that at the time 'It was considered unpatriotic to draw attention to the horrors', address to the Third Annual Conference of the Federation of Ukrainian Jews, *The Call of the Ukraine: Report of the Third Annual Relief Conference* (London, 1923), p.4.

58. *JW*, 8 May 1918.
59. *JW*, 17 July 1918.
60. Martin Gilbert, *Winston Churchill*, Vol. IV, *1917–22* (London, 1975), p. 341.
61. *JW*, 18 June, and also 12 Nov. 1919.
62. On antisemitism in the White Armies see Ilya Trotzky, 'Jewish Pogroms in the Ukraine and in Byelorussia' (1918–20), in Jacob Frumkin *et al.*, *Russian Jewry, 1917–1967* (New York, 1969), pp. 72–87; and Peter Kenez, *Civil War in South Russia 1919–20: The Defeat of the Whites* (Philadelphia, 1977).
63. *JW*, 30 July 1919.
64. Entry for 12 Aug. 1919.
65. Quoted in *JW*, 12 Nov. 1919, and reprinted in Lucien Wolf, *The Jewish Bogey* (London 1921).
66. *JW*, ibid.
67. *JW*, 11 and 18 Aug. 1920.

3 'OUR OWN'

1. Contained in paper prepared for JFC meeting, 17 Sep. 1918, JFC C 11/4/1.
2. See official histories: Leon Shapiro, *The History of ORT: A Jewish Movement for Social Change* (New York, 1980); Theodore Norman, *An Outstretched Arm: A History of the Jewish Colonisation Association* (London, 1985). ORT and JCA, with headquarters in Berlin and Paris respectively, both had offices in London. ORT (est. 1880) in exile was very much a Russian emigré concern in the early years after the revolution. In London, the first ORT chairman was A. Halpern, the son of an ORT chairman in Russia. David Mowshowitch, S. Beloff, M. Shalet and J. Visotsky, all Russians, were on the committee, which met at Mowshowitch's home in St John's Wood and later in West Hampstead, a favourite area for well-to-do Russian emigrés. Elkan Adler was the only 'native' Anglo-Jew on the committee. On the Federation of Ukrainian Jews (FUJ), see the collection of FUJ Bulletins for 1921 in the Elkan Adler papers at the Jewish Theological Seminary, New York; also published reports at the YIVO Institute for Jewish Research, New York (see bibliography).
3. *JW*, 13 March 1918.
4. Swaythling to Sir Adam Samuel Block, Finance Section, Ministry of Blockade, 13 May 1918, JFC C 11/3/1. Block himself was, in fact, Jewish and an anti-Zionist.
5. Cf. Wolf's tactics in 1915 and see Ch. 4 below, *re* Zionists' similar methods in their dealings with the British government.
6. This paragraph is based on Zvi Gitelman, *Jewish Nationality and Soviet Politics: the Jewish Sections of the CPSU 1917–1930* (Princeton, 1972), and on Shapiro, *The History of ORT*, op. cit., esp. Ch. VIII. IDGEZKOM was replaced by KOMZET, which agreed with Joint to set up a new organisation, Agro-Joint, in 1924. ORT and the JCA made separate agreements with the Soviets.
7. Lucien Wolf, *Russo-Jewish Refugees in Eastern Europe: Report of Conferences on Russian Refugees, Held in Geneva under League of Nations Auspices, 22–24 August, 16–19 September 1921* (London, 1921), published by the Board of Deputies of British Jews.
8. In the *JC* of 30 March 1917, it had been predicted that the Russian Revolution would curtail the fresh injection of new blood into Anglo-Jewry for the next 50 years.

9. Sir John Hope-Simpson, *The Refugee Problem: Report of a Survey* (Royal Institute of International Affairs, London, 1939), Ch. V on the Russian Emigration; Eugene M. Kulischer, *Europe on the Move: War and Population Changes 1917–1947* (New York, 1948), pp. 53–7. He quotes figures ranging from 1500 to 10,000 Russians coming to Britain. Richard D. Barnett, 'The Sephardim of England', in R.D. Barnett and W.M. Schwab (eds), *The Sephardi Heritage*, Vol. II (Grendon, Northants, 1989), p.21 refers in passing to Jewish refugees from Soviet Bokhara (Turkestan) arriving in Britain after the war, but gives no figures. See below, p.222.

On well-to-do Russian Jewish emigrés in Britain, e.g. the Benenson family, see Manya Harari, *Memoirs 1906–1969* (London, 1972), and Flora Solomon and Barnet Litvinoff, *From Baku to Baker Street* (London, 1984). However, England was more important as a transmigration point for Russian refugees after the revolution.

10. There was also an economic depression in Palestine in the mid-1920s.
11. Lucien Wolf, *Diary of the Peace Conference 1919* (UCL), 6 Aug. and 5 Sep. 1919.
12. An Aliens Committee was set up at the Board of Deputies in February 1919 primarily to deal with this issue. The Home Office would only readmit those men who could prove that they had actually fought on the Allied side in Russia and who had first-degree relatives already in England. See below, Ch. 5.
13. Especially in their dealings with the Soviet government, which was reluctant to admit 'sectarian' relief agencies into Russia for fear of pogroms. League support also afforded the Jewish organisations some protection from the interference of the IDGEZKOM, the relief arm of the EVSEKTSIA.
14. JCA, Lucien Wolf Bound Files, Vol. I, 19 July 1921.
15. Wolf, *Russo-Jewish Refugees*, op. cit., Appendix, document No. 7, *Report of Mr Lucien Wolf on the International Emigration Commission*, 19 Aug. 1921. Copy also in JCA, Lucien Wolf Bound Files, Vol. I (1916–21).
16. Wolf to Cave (Chairman of International Emigration Commission, Geneva), 6 May 1921, JCA Bound Files, Vol. I; memo by Wolf, Stuart Samuel and Claude Montefiore, JCA Minute Books, 6 May 1921.
17. Lucien Wolf, *Memo: Interview with M. Frick*, 12 Dec. 1921, JCA Bound Files, Vol. I.
18. Wolf to Frick, 14 Oct. 1921, JCA Bound Files, Vol. I.
19. Wolf's reply to T.F. Johnson's (a British official at the League of Nations, Geneva) letter of 23 Feb. 1923: 2 March 1923, JCA Bound Files, Vol. III (Jan.–June 1923).
20. Wolf, *Report on the Refugee Question at Geneva*, London, 25 May 1923 (proof), JCA Bound Files, Vol. III.
21. Wolf to Johnson, 9 Oct. 1923, JCA Bound Files, Vol. IV.
22. Ibid., 8 Oct. 1923. In July 1921 Wolf requested that the International Emigration Commission recognise Soviet consuls abroad in order to facilitate the issuing of visas to refugees.
23. Wolf to JCA, Paris, 24 Oct. 1923, ibid.
24. See Mark Levene, *Jewish Diplomacy at War and Peace: A Study of Lucien Wolf*, unpub. DPhil, University of Oxford, 1982, Oscar Janowsky, *The Jews and Minority Rights 1898–1919* (New York, 1966); Eugene C. Black, *The Social Politics of Anglo-Jewry* (Oxford, 1988).
25. On Ukrainian–Jewish relations see Ch. 1, n. 3. See also John Hewko, *The Ukrainian–Jewish Political Relationship during the Period of the Central Rada – March 1917 to Jan. 1918*, unpub. MLitt, University of Oxford, 1981. Statistics

NOTES

based on Yakov Leshtinsky, *Di Sotsial-Economishe antviklung fun Ukrainishn Yidn*, p. 188 in *Yidn in Ukrainia*, Vol. I (New York, 1961).

26. *Report from Stockholm*, 14 Feb. 1918, JFC C 11/3/4/2. The original letter is in MOW File 80 10464–5 and is dated 11 Feb. 1918.
27. Stepanovsky in Lausanne to Wolf, 14 Dec. 1920, JFC C 11/12/121.
28. According to Wolf, *Diary*, 20 March 1919.
29. See interviews with Margolin and Vishnitzer, *JC*, 16 May and 12 Sept. 1919 respectively. In July 1920 Dr Jochelman warned Margolin off going to the Carlsbad Relief Conference, because of his unpopularity with the Zionists, CZA A 120/85/2; also material in Gaster Papers, Mocatta Library, UCL, File 364 no. 100.
30. Wolf's *Diary* 12 Sep. 1919.
31. This aspect of Zionist policy was grist to the Soviet propaganda mill – Zionists were accused of backing the Whites. See Ran Marom, 'The Bolsheviks and the Balfour Declaration, 1917–1920', *Wiener Library Bulletin* Vol. 29 NS No. 37/8 (1976), pp. 20–9; reprinted in R.S. Wistrich (ed.), *The Left Against Zion* (London, 1979), pp. 16–34.
32. 20 Jan. 1920, JFC C/11/3/1.
33. Leeper to Wolf, 9 July 1920, JFC C 11/12/121.
34. Wolf to Claude Montefiore, 2 Feb. 1920, MOW File 32 3018.
35. 25 Jan. 1921, JFC C 11/12/122/2.
36. Wolf, *Diary*, 13 Aug. 1919 and also 11 June 1919, interviews with Zarchi and Sydarenko (Ukrainian Delegation in Paris) and with Bakmetiev (Kolchak's 'ambassador' in Washington) respectively.
37. Zangwill, *The Voice of Jerusalem* (1921 Macmillan edn), p. 322.
38. *JC*, 31 May 1918.
39. *Memo on the Danger of Anti-Jewish Excesses from the Army of Denikin* by M. Naiditch, president of the Jewish Committee in Moscow, and member of the executive of the Zionist Organisation, dated 14 July 1919, JFC C 11/3/1 and CZA Z 4/1986.
40. Spicer to Wolf, 17 Nov. 1919, JFC minutes. The FO did, however, sanction Stuart Samuel's mission to Poland.
41. 10 Dec. 1919, JFC C 11/3/1.
42. Reported in Wolf, *Diary*, 6 June 1919. Kadets were members of the Constitutional Democratic Party.
43. For example, E.H. Carr, then at the FO, commented that he was 'very doubtful about [the] wisdom of the protest meetings [against pogroms] more especially as the Zionist telegraph agencies had spoilt their own good case by their exaggeration', Wolf, *Diary*, 28 May 1919. See Norman Davies, 'Great Britain and the Polish Jews', *Journal of Contemporary History*, Vol. 8, No. 2 (April 1973), pp. 119–42; argues that the Zionists were guilty of exaggerating 'pogroms in Poland', a slogan first given currency by Israel Cohen's articles in *The Times* in 1918, to the lasting detriment of Anglo-Polish relations and to the acute embarrassment of Lucien Wolf, who by 1920 was 'far more worried by the success of the Zionists in England than by the fate of the Jews in Poland'. Only nine issues of *La Tribune Juive* actually appeared in 1920.
44. Wolf, *Diary*, 6 June 1919, and also 24 Aug. 1919.
45. *JW*, 16 May 1917.
46. Dr Gaster to Joseph Super, 10 May 1917. Gaster Papers, Letter Book Nov. 1916–Dec. 1917 (outgoing), No. 581.
47. See *The Times*, 28 March, 11,12 April 1917. Also private correspondence with

Robinson in RAL RFamAD/1/4 and RAL/xi/1/13; see also Wolf to Montefiore, where he considered it pointless to take on *The Times*: 'A quarrel with *The Times* must be quite one-sided'. 12 April 1917, MOW File 32 2982.

48. Gunsburg to de Rothschild, telegram, n.d., April 1917, original in RAL/xi/1/13. The 'untrue' quote made by Vinaver, Conjoint Minutes, Vol. Sept. 1916–June 1917, entry for 25 April 1917.

49. Quoted in *JW*, 9 Jan. 1918. The authorship of this passage is uncertain. Perhaps it was Wilton himself – the style is certainly his. But he had returned to London from Petrograd in the autumn of 1917. See Robert Wilton, *Russia's Agony* (London, 1918), pp. 174–5; *The History of The Times Part I* (London, 1952, 150th anniversary edn), p. 248.

50. Gunsburg to de Rothschild, April 1917, op. cit. in n. 48 above.

51. De Rothschild to Gunsburg and Vinaver, Conjoint Minutes, Vol. Sept. 1916–June 1917, entry for 25 April 1917.

52. Wolf to de Rothschild, 4 April 1917, original in RAL/xi/1/13.

53. Wolf to Robinson, editor of *The Times*, 28 March 1917, JFC C 11/2/11. See also Wolf to M. Bigart of the French Alliance, 26 April 1917, MOW File 46, 4182–3.

54. The newly formed Propaganda Department of the FO under Sir William Tyrrell also asked for the Conjoint's cooperation. Wolf, Henriques and Adler rejected the idea as inappropriate. JFC Minutes, 6 March 1918.

55. H.J. Walpole (FO) to Greenberg, 28 Feb. 1918: Greenberg's statement 'To Our Brethren in Russia', Gaster Papers, File 337, Letter 21 (incoming). Copies were also sent to Joseph Cowen, Nahum Sokolov and Chaim Weizmann – the latter letter still extant in the Weizmann Archive.

56. Zangwill to Cecil, 10 March 1918, CZA A 120/68/2.

57. Israel Cohen, *Bolshevism and Jewry* (n.d. [early 1920s]), CZA A 213/15, and quotes following.

58. Quoted in Zangwill, *Voice of Jerusalem*, op. cit., pp. 221–2.

59. See Blank to Wolf, 12 April 1918, JFC C 11/3/1.

60. Quoted in *Voice of Jerusalem*, op. cit., p. 222. Zangwill offended some Russian emigré sensibilities with his claim that the Russians were 'analphabetic', CZA A 120/81/1.

61. As quoted in *JC*, 12 Dec. 1919, *JG*, 5 Dec. 1919 (apostle). For Zionist tendency towards exaggeration, see n. 43 above.

62. *JC*, 28 May 1920. *The Times* ran a series of articles on the murder between 19 Aug. and 6 Sept. 1920, the *Morning Post* on the *Protocols* in July 1920; See Ch. 1 above.

63. This section is based on JFC correspondence *re* the assassination of the tsar, C 11/3/4. See also *JC*, 20 Aug. 1920, for the published version. Blank encouraged Wolf to pursue the matter: JFC C 11/12/121, 9 May 1920 'Private'; Blank to Montefiore, 10 March 1920, CZA A 120/82/1.

64. Only the Blank interview with Starynkevitch had been quoted in the press before Aug. 1920 – in the original letter sent by Stuart Samuel and Claude Montefiore on behalf of the Board to *The Times* (25 March 1920).

On 10 Sept. 1920 Wolf wrote a letter of protest against *The Times*'s feature on the murder, which was published in a censored form on 25 Sept. Reference to 'the fierce antisemitic spirit' which inspired 'the articles' and their 'inflammatory' purpose 'to fix on "the Jews" the responsibility for the appalling crime of Ekaterinburg' were cut out – with the approval of the JFC. See *The Assassination of the Tsar: Correspondence with His Majesty's Government etc.*: BoD 1920.

NOTES

Copies in the BoD and Mocatta Library and JCA Archives (Minute Books). Correspondence between Wolf and *The Times*, MOW File 63 8435–40.

65. BoD meeting, 17 Oct. 1920, report in *JC*, 22 Oct. Ironically, the idea for the press agency came from Lord Northcliffe.
66. *JC*, 25 Feb. 1921.
67. *JC*, editorials of 27 Aug. and 1 Oct. 1920.
68. *The Times*, 28 June 1919.
69. *JC* report, 20 June 1919.
70. Chief Rabbi Dr J.H. Hertz, *Sermons, Addresses and Studies*, Vol. I *Sermons* (London, 1938), pp. 43–9. *Our Polish Brethren, Service of Prayers and Mourning for the Victims of the Pogroms in Poland, Queen's Hall*, 26 June 1919.
71. For this controversy and the correspondence it generated see the *JC* and *JW* for the relevant weeks in June/July 1919. Members of the BoD were so incensed that they refused to pass a resolution thanking Sir Philip on his retirement, for 30 years of loyal service to the community.

   For biographical information on Magnus see Chaim Bermant, *The Cousinhood* (New York, 1971), and Ruth Sebag-Montefiore, *A Family Patchwork: Five Generations of an Anglo-Jewish Family* (London, 1987).
72. *Unzer Veg*, Vol. I, Nos. 5–6, 25 July 1919.
73. This section is based on Wolf, *Diary*, 2, 11 and 12 Aug. 1919. See above, Ch. 1, p. 18.
74. CZA A 120/33. See also *JC*, 23 Jan., 14, 21 May 1920 for other examples of anti-interventionist sentiment.
75. Quoted in *JW*, 2 April 1919.
76. *JW*, 5 Feb. 1919.
77. 'Red flags' quote, *JW*, 2 April 1919. Before agreeing to speak at a second rally on 28 Feb. 1920, Zangwill took the precaution of requesting that the chairman make an official disclaimer about his (Zangwill's) non-Bolshevik politics in his welcoming remarks. Afterwards, somewhat disillusioned, Zangwill confided to Joe (Cowen?): 'I shall certainly not speak again with a gang which is not only Bolshevist, but Sinn Fein, Republican and revolutionary.' 3 March, 1920 CZA A 120/82/1, and see also 26 Feb. 1920, A 120/82/3.
78. Predictably, the *Morning Post* did make capital out of Greenberg's 'apparent Bolshevik sympathies'; see editorial reprinted in *JW*, 22 Oct. 1919. The ultra-right-wing Britons organisation was also fond of quoting Greenberg in its publications, most notably in *The Jews' Who's Who* (1920). Lucien Wolf was furious with Greenberg, but did not involve himself publicly in the row at the time. See Wolf to Greenberg, 27 July 1920, MOW File 26, 2370.
79. *JW*, 25 June 1919.
80. *MP*, 24 April 1919.
81. *MP*, 5 May 1919. Back on 21 March, the *JC* had already warned against 'walk-[ing] into the trap' set by the *MP* in its 20 March editorial. 'We refuse to purchase immunity from the *Morning Post*', Greenberg had then declared. He subsequently denied the charge that his papers were propagating Bolshevism in the East End, on the quite logical grounds that the average Jewish immigrant from eastern Europe did not have sufficient command of English to read them (assuming he could afford to buy a copy).
82. H.A. Gwynne (ed.), *The Cause of World Unrest* (London, 1920), pp. 13–14.
83. *JW*, 30 April 1919. The term is derived from the Hebrew root meaning to deliver up or hand over. The *MP* commented: 'Now if this article was not a Bolshevist

89. threat against these ten *mosserim* or informers, pilloried by name and photograph, we should like to know why it was printed' (quoted in *JW*, 13 Aug. 1919).

84. *JW*, 7 May 1919.

85. See the editorial in *Di Tsayt*, 2 May 1919, and *Ovend Nayes* editorials by Joshua Podruzhnik, 1 and 8 May 1919.

86. *JC*, 9 May 1919.

87. Quoted *JG*, 5 Dec. 1919.

88. BoD Minutes, Bk 17, 29 April 1919. A full report was also published in the *JC* on 2 May. The wording of this motion was suggested by Neville Laski and S.E. de Haas. Especially since only one of the signatories, Philip Magnus, was actually a member of the Board.

90. *MP*, 24 April 1919.

91. Quoted in *JC*, 31 Oct. 1919.

92. Quoted in *JC*, 1 Feb. 1918.

93. *JW*, 7 May 1919.

94. *JC*, 20 Feb. 1920.

95. *JW*, 30 July 1919. Cf. Lucien Wolf's comment: 'I did not think, however, it would be wise to assert … that 90 per cent of the Jews were bourgeois. The effect of this would only be that we should make enemies of all schools of socialism.' Wolf, *Diary*, 26 June 1919.

96. Ibid. Cf. the following statement:

> [W]e must in no circumstances attempt to pledge the Jewish community as a whole against socialism. Apart from the fact that socialism is bound to win in the new political struggle, the immediate result is that we should fall between two stools. We should never really conciliate antisemitic reaction while we should probably alienate, or arouse the suspicions of, the great bulk of the democracy. (JFC C 11/2/5, Wolf to Montefiore, 4 Nov. 1920.)

97. Stuart Cohen, *English Zionists and British Jews* (Princeton, 1983). David Cesarani in 'The Leadership of Anglo-Jewry Between the Wars', a paper delivered at the Oxford Centre for Postgraduate Hebrew Studies, 21 Nov. 1984, criticises Cohen for not paying enough attention to class factors when analysing the communal power struggle.

98. As Magnus himself put it, he regarded his paper as 'a stick with which to beat … Master Greenberg, who has run the community long enough and it seems to me that he tries to "boss it" with his *J[ewish] C[hronicle]* and *J[ewish] W[orld]*, as Northcliffe tries to "boss" the country with his *Times* and *Mail*' (quoted in Cohen, op. cit., p. 309). There was also an element of personal animosity between Greenberg and the Magnuses, father and son. The *JG* had the dubious distinction of being the only Anglo-Jewish journal to be praised by the *MP*; see Gwynne, op. cit., p. 24.

99. BoD Minutes, Bk 17, 29 April 1919. This motion, one of three amendments debated, was put forward by Lord Rothschild and S.H. Emanuel.

100. Except that 'the Ten' inserted one crucial word into their quotation from the *MP* editorial of 8 April 1919, without any explanation: '[T]he British Jewish community – most of whom … are by no means in sympathy with this [Nationalist] crusade … are being served very badly by their newspapers.'

101. *Illustrated Sunday Herald*, 8 Feb. 1920. Minute books of the League of British Jews, made available at the Rothschild Archive after this section was completed, throw no new light on the genesis of the 'Letter of the Ten'.

4 ZIONISM VERSUS BOLSHEVISM

1. In fact Krassin was not of Jewish origin, although his wife was. Weizmann, who became a naturalised British subject in 1910, was elected president of the EZF in Feb. 1917. He occupied a 'curious double status', seeking to represent both English and Russian Jewry, yet possessing doubtful credentials to speak for either. Sokolov, as a member of the pre-war Actions Committee, was arguably better placed and Weizmann enlisted his support. See David Vital, *Zionism: The Crucial Phase* (Oxford, 1987), pp. 226, 261. This is the third volume in a trilogy, the others being *The Origins of Zionism* (Oxford, 1975) and *Zionism: The Formative Years* (Oxford, 1982).

2. Draft by Harold Nicolson, 24 April 1917; dispatched to Petrograd, Paris and Cairo in the form of a telegram. PRO FO 371/3053/84173, cited in Isaiah Friedman, *The Question of Palestine 1914–18* (London, 1973), p.182.

3. William Ormsby-Gore, 'Appreciation of Eastern Report No. XVIII', 31 May 1917, PRO CAB 24/143; Ormsby-Gore to Graham, 30 May 1917, PRO FO 371/3012/95062, cited in Friedman, op. cit., pp. 192–3.

4. Henry Brown in Nikolayev to Bagge in Odessa, 23 April 1917; received at FO from Buchanan in Petrograd, 26 May, FO 371/2996/811; cited in Friedman, op. cit., pp. 191–2.

5. Leonard Stein, *The Balfour Declaration* (London, 1961), the classic work on the subject.

6. In the words of a *JC* editorial of 13 Feb. 1920.

7. Graham to Hardinge, 13 June 1917, PRO FO 371/3058/123458, cited in Friedman, op. cit., p. 246.

8. Buchanan to FO, 27 April 1917, telegram No. 590, PRO FO 371/3053/84713, cited in Friedman, op. cit., p. 182.

9. Milyukov, as foreign minister of the Provisional Government, sent the note which committed revolutionary Russia to continue the war against Germany (April 1917). It provoked angry demonstrations in the capital and brought about Milyukov's resignation and the fall of the government.

10. As Ormsby-Gore put it cynically: 'I think we ought to use pogroms in Palestine as propaganda ... any spicy tales of atrocity would be eagerly welcomed by the propaganda people here – and Aaron Aaronsohn [in Palestine] could send some lurid stories for the Jewish papers.' Gore to Mark Sykes, 8 May 1917, Sykes Papers No. 47, cited in Friedman, p. 187. It must also be remembered that the United States did *not* declare war on Turkey.

11. Conor Cruise O'Brien: see n. 23 below.

12. Graham to Gore, 9 June 1917, PRO FO 371/3012/95062; Friedman, op. cit., p. 193. Boris Goldberg was chosen in the absence of Sokolov, whose negotiations in Paris led to the publication of the Cambon note, the French equivalent of the Balfour Declaration.

13. I.e. on the controversy generated by the Conjoint Foreign Affairs Committee's anti-Zionist letter to *The Times*, 24 May 1917. The debate at the Board took place on 17 June.

14. Minute by Cecil, n.d., June 1917, PRO FO 371/3058/123458; cited in Friedman, op. cit., p. 247.

15. Webster, Military Intelligence report, quoted in Friedman, op. cit., p. 196.

16. Philip Kerr to Ronald Graham, 5 May 1917, PRO FO 371/3101/65760; Fried-

man, op. cit., p. 184. The best history of the regiment is Elias Gilner, *War and Hope – A History of the Jewish Legion* (New York, 1969). There are also memoirs by Colonel Patterson and Jabotinsky himself.

17. In the words of H.J. Creedy, secretary to General Kitchener, to H.G. Locock (FO), 17 Jan. 1916, private letter, PRO FO 371/2835/18095, Friedman, op. cit., p. 45.

18. Philip Kerr to Ronald Graham, 5 May 1917, PRO FO 371/3101/65760; Friedman, op. cit., p. 184.

19. To say nothing of the split within the Zionist movement itself.

20. Elizabeth Monroe, *Britain's Moment in the Middle East, 1914–17* (2nd edn, London, 1981), p. 43. Balfour to War Cabinet, PRO CAB 23/4, No. 261 (12), 31 and 4 Oct. respectively; Friedman, op. cit., pp. 278–9. It was felt necessary to approve the Declaration before the arrival of Tschlenov, the Russian Zionist leader, in London.

21. Graham to Balfour, 24 Oct. 1917, PRO FO 371/3054/84173; Friedman, op. cit., pp. 274–5.

22. David Lloyd George, *Memoirs of the Peace Conference*, Vol. II (New Haven, 1939), Ch. XXIII, 'The Turkish Treaty, Palestine', pp. 723–4; Henry Wickham Steed, 'A Non-Jewish View of Zionism', in Paul Goodman (ed.), *Chaim Weizmann: Tribute in Honour of his Seventieth Birthday* (London 1945). Steed noted:

> I have always attributed some importance to Ludendorff's statement that 'The Balfour Declaration was the cleverest thing done by the Allies in the way of propaganda,' and that he wished Germany had thought of it first. (op. cit., pp. 74–5)

23. Conor Cruise O'Brien, 'Israel in Embryo', *The New York Review of Books*, 15 March 1984, a review of Ronald Sanders, *The High Walls of Jerusalem: A History of the Balfour Declaration and the Birth of the British Mandate for Palestine* (New York, 1984) – the latest in-depth study of the subject. It follows both Stein, op. cit., and Friedman, op. cit. Thanks are due to Roger Goodman for drawing my attention to the O'Brien article. Other recent relevant works are: Vital, *Zionism: The Crucial Phase*, and Ruddock F. Mackay, *Balfour, Intellectual Statesman* (Oxford, 1985).

24. Frank Hardie and Irwin Herrmann, *Britain and Zion: The Fateful Entanglement* (London, 1980), Introduction. Monroe and Christopher Sykes both regard the Russian argument as being of merely 'transient' importance, not seriously entertained by the FO until Oct. 1917, just prior to the Cabinet meeting of the 31st of that month. See Monroe, op. cit., and *The Times*, 2 Nov. 1967. The evidence we have mustered proves otherwise. Most commentators agree that the influence of 'Gentile Zionism' was too ambiguous to have been a factor.

25. *JC*, 25 Jan. 1918. There was a delay of three weeks before news of the Declaration got through to Russia.

26. Sykes to Picot, PRO FO 371/3054/84173, telegram No. 1181, 12 Dec. 1917, Friedman, op. cit., p. 292. Sykes, the architect of the secret Sykes-Picot agreement of 1916 between Britain, France and Russia for the post-war internationalisation of Palestine, had become Secretary to the War Cabinet in December 1916 and supported Zionist aspirations in the Middle East.

27. Graham and Balfour minutes, 3 Nov. 1917, PRO FO 371/3083/143082, quoted in Friedman, op. cit., pp. 280–81, 292.

28. Hardinge minute, 3 Nov. 1917, PRO FO 371/3083/143082.

29. WO memo by Charles Webster, circulated at Versailles, Jan. 1918, and quoted in

NOTES

Friedman, op. cit., p. 293; see n. 52, p. 369 and Stein, op. cit., p. 570. 'Counting heads' quoted from O'Brien, op. cit.

30. H.J. Walpole (Dept. of Information) to Leopold Greenberg, 28 Feb. 1918. Copy enclosed in letter from Greenberg to Gaster, 5 March 1918, stamped 'Secret'. Gaster Papers, File 337 (incoming) No. 21.

31. Webster, memo: see n. 29 above.

32. Barter in Petrograd to FO, 26 Nov. 1917, FO 371/3054/84173, telegram No. 1389; Friedman, op. cit., p. 280.

33. Lloyd George, op. cit., p. 737.

34. Stein, op. cit., pp. 571.

35. Robert Cecil to the War Cabinet, 21 Dec. 1917, War Cabinet 304, PRO CAB 23/4 (10); quoted in Michael Kettle, *Russia and the Allies* (London, 1981), Vol. I., pp. 164–5.

36. Cecil to the War Cabinet, 19 Dec. 1917, Kettle, p. 162; CAB 28/3, 23 Dec. 1917, Kettle, p. 172.

37. Quoted in Lloyd George, op. cit., p. 743.

38. The Star of David actually has six points.

39. CZA Z4 16033, quoted in Bernard Wasserstein, *The British in Palestine* (London, 1978), p. 67.

40. Chaim Weizmann, *Memo on the Fifth Meeting of the Advisory Committee to the Palestine Office* (at Herbert Samuel's residence, Jerusalem), 10 May 1919, WA.

41. But Leopold Greenberg had already predicted that 'Bolshevik Zionism' was the logical outcome of Churchill's thesis: *JW* editorial, 11 Feb. 1920.

42. Sir Thomas Haycraft, *Palestine: Disturbances in May 1921: Report of the Commission of Inquiry with Correspondence relating thereto*, Command Paper 1540 (Oct. 1921). See M. Mossek, *Palestine Immigration Policy under Sir Herbert Samuel* (London, 1978).

43. Lloyd George, op. cit., pp. 767–8.

44. Churchill to Samuel 12 May 1921, PRO CO 733/3 237 42; Martin Gilbert, *Winston S. Churchill*, Vol. IV, *1917–22* (London, 1975), pp. 585–7. Privately, the Zionists were not averse to a slowing down of immigration, due to their own financial difficulties; see also Mossek, op. cit.

45. Lloyd George, op. cit., pp. 767–8.

46. Deedes to Major Young, 18 May 1921, PRO CO 733/17; Gilbert, op. cit., pp. 585–7.

47. Wasserstein, op. cit., p. 11.

48. Chaim Weizmann, *Trial and Error* (2nd edn, London, 1949), p. 273.

49. *The Times*, 8,15,17 Feb. 1922; *Daily Mail*, 23 Feb. 1922. See Michael Cohen, *Churchill and the Jews* (London, 1985), pp. 136–8. See also David Cesarani, 'Anti-Zionist Politics and Political Antisemitism in Britain, 1920–24', *Patterns of Prejudice*, Vol. 23, No. 1 (1989), pp. 28–45; and 'The Anti-Jewish Career of Sir William Joynson-Hicks, Cabinet Minister', *Journal of Contemporary History*, Vol. 24, No. 3 (July 1989), pp. 461–82, also published under the title, 'Joynson-Hicks and the Radical Right in England after the First World War' in T. Kushner and K. Lunn (eds), *Traditions of Intolerance* (Manchester, 1989), pp. 118–39.

50. Such arguments explain, for example, the apparent contradiction between Balfour's support of Zionism and for the Aliens Act in 1905. See also speech by Lord Sydenham of Combe: 'The Arabs would have kept the Holy Land clear from Bolshevism', House of Lords Debates, 21 June 1922.

51. Stein, op. cit., pp. 339–41. There are numerous biographies and memoirs of

Weizmann, the latest being Norman Rose, *Chaim Weizmann: A Biography* (London, 1986), and the second part of Jehuda Reinharz's *Chaim Weizmann: The Making of a Zionist Leader* (Oxford, 1985), covering the post-1914 period is still awaited; see also Ben Halpern, *A Clash of Heroes: Brandeis, Weizmann and American Zionism* (New York, 1987).
52. Speech to EZF conference, 20 May 1917, reprinted in Nahum Sokolov's *History of Zionism*, Vol. II (London, 1919).
53. Stein argues that Weizmann plumped for cooperation with the British largely because of practical considerations – that a British and not a French conquest of Palestine was imminent.
54. Mayir Vereté, 'The Balfour Declaration and its Makers', *Middle Eastern Studies*, Vol. 6 (1970), pp. 48–76.
55. *The Times*, 3 Sept. 1917.
56. Jabotinsky to FO, 8 May 1917, PRO FO 371/3101/65760, Friedman, op. cit., p. 181.
57. Jabotinsky especially linked pacifism in Russia with that of Russian Jews in Britain; see note to Col. French, CO, 2 Jan. 1918, Jabotinsky Institute, Tel Aviv 8/2/1/Aleph. On the reception accorded to Jabotinsky's plans in the East End, see below, Ch. 5.
58. Weizmann to C.P. Scott, 26 April 1917, in Chaim Weizmann, *Letters* (Jerusalem/Oxford/London, 1969–80), Vol. VII, No. 357.
59. Weizmann interview with Robert Cecil, 25 April 1917, Weizmann, *Letters*, Vol. VII, No. 356 and PRO FO 371/3053/84173, Friedman, op. cit., pp. 157–9 (Cecil's version).
60. *Palestine*, 19 May 1917.
61. Weizmann, *Letters*, Vol. VII, No. 359 and No. 364.
62. Weizmann, *Letters*, Vol. VII, No. 386, 14 May 1917. Sokolov, who was at the time busy in France with the negotiations leading up to the publication of the Cambon note, was, in fact, not quite as keen as Weizmann to press for an exclusively British Protectorate. See Sanders, op. cit., pp. 536–7.
    Weizmann did not have the unanimous backing of the EZF either. See, for example, Gaster's diary notes of 6 June 1917, Balfour Declaration File II, Gaster Papers.
63. Stein, op. cit., p. 441, and see also Vital, op. cit., p. 256.
64. Tschlenov to Sokolov, 24 Sept. 1917, Stein, op. cit., p. 440.
65. Weizmann, *Letters*, Vol. VII, No. 489, 1 Sept. 1917; The *Zionist Review* of Sept. 1917 carries the full text of Tschlenov's speech in English. *Carte blanche*, Friedman, op. cit., p. 196.
66. Sokolov to Tschlenov, 22 Aug. 1917 (CZA), quoted in Stein, op. cit., p. 440.
67. Vera Weizmann's Diary, 31 Oct. 1917, quoted in Stein, op. cit., p. 441.
68. Typed memo by Gaster of an interview with Tschlenov, Nov. 1917, Gaster Papers. Sacher, unlike Weizmann and Sokolov, was British-born.
69. Stein, op. cit., p. 348.
70. Weizmann (Tel Aviv) to Brandeis (Washington), Weizmann, *Letters*, Vol. VIII, No. 175, 25 April 1918.
71. Weizmann, speech to the Council of Ten at the peace conference, Paris, 27 Feb. 1919. Reprinted in *Foreign Relations of the United States: The Paris Peace Conference* (Washington, 1943), Vol. IV, p. 164; quoted in Stein, op. cit., p. 348.
72. *Report of the Twelfth Zionist Congress* (1921) (London, 1922), p. 67.
73. Weizmann, *Memo of an Interview with Balfour*, 15 Feb. 1919, WA 1919; also

copy in CZA Z4 16008. Lucien Wolf gives us a useful, if biased, insight into Weizmann's tactics in his *Diary* 'Weizmann is making great use of this Bolshevik Bogey', he wrote on 25 March 1919; *Diary of the Peace Conference, 1919* (UCL).

74. Weizmann, *Letters*, Vol. VIII, No. 14, 23–6 Nov. 1917. Weizmann sent a similar note to Aaronsohn in Washington, instructing him to put pressure on the Russians from his end (No. 18, 3 Dec. 1917).
75. Weizmann, *Letters*, Vol. VIII, Introduction, p. 4.
76. Report of the London Zionist Bureau, Feb. 1918. WA.
77. Weizmann, *Letters*, Vol. IX, No. 38, to Gilbert Clayton, GHQ Palestine, 27 Nov. 1918.
78. Weizmann, *Letters*, Vol. VIII, No. 37, 21 Dec. 1917.
79. Report of the London Zionist Bureau, Feb. 1918, WA. The 'natural channel' sentence is identical to that which appeared in Charles Webster's report to the WO in Jan. 1918. So who got the idea from whom?
80. Quoted in Christopher Sykes, *Two Studies in Virtue* (London, 1953), pp. 212–14.
81. Lucien Wolf, 'The Jewish National Movement', published in the *Edinburgh Review*, April 1917, and subsequently in pamphlet form, ZBPs.
82. Laurie Magnus, *Studies of the Jewish Question*, 1917, No. IV, Mocatta Pamphlets File A 89; see Ruth Sebag-Montefiore, *A Family Patchwork* (London, 1987), the author being the daughter of Laurie Magnus.
83. Philip Magnus, *Jewish Action and Jewish Ideals* (1891, repr. 1917), footnote p. 9; ZBPs.
84. Laurie Magnus, op. cit.
85. Lucien Wolf, *Notes on Palestine and the Jews* (1917), CZA A 77/3/1; *Edinburgh Review*, op. cit.
86. Copy of Levene sermon in Mocatta Library, UCL. Wolf, *Notes*, op. cit.
87. Wolf, *Edinburgh Review*, op. cit.
88. JFC C 11/3/1, 21 May 1917.
89. Wolf to de Rothschild, 22 March 1917, CZA A 77/3/2. This was ironic, given that it was Wolf who had first suggested the usefulness of propaganda sympathetic to Zionism in winning over Jewish opinion in the United States. This was in 1915, a year before Weizmann came on the scene. See Mark Levene, 'Anglo-Jewish Foreign Policy in Crisis – Lucien Wolf, the Conjoint Committee and the War 1914–18', *TJHSE*, Vol. 30 (1987–88), pp. 190–4, and Vital, op. cit., p. 236; Halpern, op. cit., 144–6.
90. Montefiore's version of the meeting is contained in Conjoint Report X, p. 464, 16 May 1917. AJ/204/3. Milner was a member of Lloyd George's War Cabinet from Dec. 1916.
91. ITO Constitution, copy in CZA A 36 (ITO).
92. Zangwill to Wise, 29 May 1917, CZA A 120 68/2.
93. *JW*, 8 Aug. 1917.
94. 1923 speech to the American Jewish Congress, quoted from Joseph Leftwich, *Israel Zangwill* (London, 1957), p. 217. See also Zangwill, *The Voice of Jerusalem*, (1921 Macmillan edn), p. 279. In 1926, just before his death, Zangwill displayed an interest in the Birobidzhan plan.
95. Stuart Cohen, *English Zionists and British Jews* (Princeton, 1983), p. 159.
96. Leon Simon, *The Case of the Anti-Zionists: A Reply* (London, 1917).
97. *JC*, 23 March 1917.
98. *Palestine*, 24 March 1917.
99. *JC*, 25 May 1917, interview with Dr Jochelman.

100. Rebecca D. Sieff, 'The Jewish National Question and the Russian Revolution', *ZR*, Aug. 1917. Mrs Sieff was the President of the Women's International Zionist Organisation (founded 1920—WIZO) and a leading member of its precursor, the British-based Federation of Women Zionists (1918).
101. Chaim Weizmann, 'What is Zionism?', in Leon Simon (ed.), *Zionism and the Jewish Future* (London, 1918). See also Weizmann's article 'The Russian Revolution and Zionism' *ZR* May 1917.
102. Webster, Military Intelligence Report, quoted in Friedman, op. cit., p. 178. Naturally, the contradictory information put out by the Zionists and anti-Zionists in London reflected the contradictory and biased reports being sent back to both sides from Russia.
103. Gaster Papers, File 337 (incoming) No. 21, March 1918.
104. Friedman, op. cit., p. 241.
105. Lord Rothschild to Weizmann, 19 April 1917, WA.
106. Harry Sacher, *Jewish Emancipation: The Contract Myth* (London, 1917).
107. Leon Simon, 'Palestine and Jewish Nationalism' (March 1918), in Simon (ed.), *Studies in Jewish Nationalism* (New York, 1920).
108. Zangwill, *Voice of Jerusalem*, op. cit., p. 225. The ZR (March 1920) commented: 'One is tempted to reply with the old Hebrew proverb, "Keep your sting and keep your honey".'
109. Wolf, *Edinburgh Review*, op. cit.

5 JEWISH BOLSHEVIKS?

1. *Di Tsayt*, 19 March 1917. On the Anglo-Yiddish press and journalists the following works of reference have been indispensable: Leonard Prager, 'A Bibliography of Yiddish periodicals in Great Britain, 1867—1967', *Studies in Bibliography and Booklore*, Spring, 1969 pp. 4—32 and the 8 volume *Leksikon fun der Nayer Yiddisher Literatur* (New York, 1956—81). I am also deeply indebted to the late Mr I.A. Lisky for much previously unrecorded information given in two interviews on 13 and 20 Oct. 1985. Lisky (real name Yehuda Itamar Fuchs) was one of the last surviving Yiddish journalists in England. He was born in East Galicia in 1899 and came to England in 1930. He knew all of the leading writers in the East End personally.
2. *Di Tsayt*, 24 April 1917.
3. *MG*, 2 April 1917. There was also a noticeable Jewish contingent at the Royal Albert Hall meeting which was addressed by Israel Zangwill. See Ch. 2 above, pp. 62—4.
4. *Ovend Nayes*, 29 March, 18 April 1917.
5. *Yiddisher Ekspress*, 4 April 1917, *Di Tsayt*, 26 March 1917.
6. *Di Tsayt*, 8 May 1917, *Yiddisher Ekspress*, 7 Aug. 1918.
7. *Di Tsayt*, 21 March 1917.
8. *Di Tsayt*, editorials 8 and 14 May, 6 Aug., 12, 14 Sept., 11 Nov. 1917.
9. *Di Tsayt*, 12 Nov. 1917.
10. *Di Tsayt*, 7 Dec. 1917, 4 Jan., 21, 24, 28 Feb., 11 March 1918; also *Yiddisher Ekspress*, 7, 13 Feb. 1918.
11. *Di Tsayt*, 3 Sept. 1918, 21 Feb. 1918 ('military methods').
12. *Di Tsayt*, 27, 31 May 1918, 10 Jan. 1918.

13. *Di Tsayt*, 4 July 1918, *Ovend Nayes*, 8 July 1918.
14. *Di Tsayt*, 24 July 1918, 29 Jan. 1918 (Litvinov), 22 July 1918 (tsar).
15. *Di Tsayt*, 24 Feb. 1918, 29 July 1918, 14 Aug. 1918.
16. 'How long, how long? How much more?' an oft-quoted – and untranslatable line from Chaim Nachman Bialik's poem *On the Slaughter*, written to commemorate the Kishinev pogrom in 1903.
17. *Di Tsayt*, 11 April 1919. Leon Kreditor at the *Ekspress* took a similar view.
18. *Yiddisher Ekspress*, 19 June 1918.
19. *Yiddisher Ekspress*, 17 July 1918.
20. *Di Tsayt*, 7 March, 6 May 1920; 12 Sept., 15 Dec. 1919. *Yiddisher Ekspress*, 2 July 1919, 2 April 1919.
21. *Di Tsayt*, 28 May 1920.
22. *Di Tsayt*, 19 May, 14 Oct. 1920.
23. *Yiddisher Ekspress*, 30 July 1919.
24. *Di Tsayt*, 26 Jan. 1920.
25. *Di Tsayt*, 11 June 1920, 9 June 1920, 1 Feb. 1920 ('democratic parliament').
26. *Di Tsayt*, 14 June, 16 Sept. 1920.
27. *Di Tsayt*, 8 Oct. 1920 ('sensible'), 16, 18 March 1921; *Yiddisher Ekspress*, 30 March 1921.
28. This section is largely based on information gleaned from the Home Office files at the Public Record Office, Kew; HO 45 Series, the most important files being 10810, 10818, 10819, 10820, 10821, 10822, 10823, 10839 (10810–10823 inc. PRO sorting code 318095; 10839/333052). See also the relevant sections in Colin Holmes, *Anti-Semitism in British Society 1876–1939* (London, 1979), and Julia Bush, *Behind the Lines: East London Labour, 1914–19* (London, 1984).
29. PRO HO 45/10820/261, minute signed J.F.H[enderson], 21 April 1917. Nor was the Russian government, neither tsarist or Kerensky, keen on taking back its erstwhile citizens who would in all likelihood engage in anti-war propaganda in the army. See the memoirs of the Russian chargé d'affaires Constantine Nabokoff, *Ordeal of a Diplomat* (London, 1921).
30. PRO HO 45/10820/309, 8 June 1917: see Gaster Papers at Mocatta Library, UCL, for a copy of Bezalel's telegram to the Stockholm Conference, File 327/2/92 (incoming), May 1917. For similar steps taken by the Lithuanian Socialist Federation (LSF) in Glasgow see Rogers, n. 94 below. Branches of the FJPC were established in North and West London and in the provinces: Glasgow, Edinburgh, Manchester, Leeds, Liverpool, Birmingham, Blackpool and Cardiff – in fact in all of the major British cities with a concentration of immigrant Jews. The Leeds branch, for example, was active between July and Oct. 1916. Phil Freeman of the Leeds Amalgamated Jewish Tailors was the chairman and Aaron Rollin of the No. 2 branch of the UGW was secretary. Rollin's minute book is preserved in his papers at Warwick University (MSS/240 Box marked 'Glasgow/Leeds Jewish Representative Council: Russian Jews'). See the *Workers' Circle Jubilee Publication (1909–29)*, for the fact that the Manchester Division became affiliated to the local branch of the FJPC.
31. See Basil Thomson, *Queer People* (London, 1922); *The Scene Changes* (London, 1937).
32. PRO HO 45/10821/327. It appears that files on Bezalel have been destroyed by the HO. See Colin Holmes, 'Problems of Research: Government Files and Secret Access', *Social History*, Vol. 6 (1981), pp. 333–50, p. 341; also his 'Internment, Fascism and the Public Records', *Society for the Study of Labour History Bulletin*,

Vol. 52, part 1 (1987), pp. 17–23. The file on Joseph King is closed under Section 5(1) of the 1958 Public Records Act, as amended in 1967, as are those on other radicals dealt with in section 3 of this Chapter, besides Chicherin, Litvinov and Rothstein. The file on Joe Fineberg has met a similar fate to that on Bezalel.

33. *Leksikon*, op. cit., and *JC*, 24 Aug., 21 Dec. 1917, 22, 29 Nov. 1918, for Salkind's army exemption and scandalous private life. In 1917 he claimed to be rabbi of the West Central synagogue, an independent congregation based in Berwick Street, Soho, but was disowned by its members and by the Chief Rabbi for his apparently unacceptable behaviour. Interview with I.A. Lisky in London, 20 Oct. 1985.

34. Rudolph Rocker, *The London Years* (London, 1956); English translation with an invaluable introduction by Joseph Leftwich. Rocker regarded Salkind's 'attempt' at reviving the *Arbayter Fraynt* after the war as 'without success'.

35. PRO HO 45/10818 n.d. 1916.

36. Interview with the late Sam Bornstein, London, 10 Nov. 1985. Bornstein made a tape of an interview with Capitanshchik's daughter, Rose Selner, of which I have read the transcript, dated 23 June 1984.

37. These were branches 115, the East London International Mantle Makers; and 116, the Gentlemen's Tailors E., based at 12a Colchester Street, off Commercial Road. See the *Journal of the Amalgamated Society of Tailors and Tailoresses*, kept at the headquarters of the NUGW in London. On the history of the UGW, which was created as a result of amalgamations in 1916, see Shirley W. Lerner, *Breakaway Unions and Small Trades Unions* (London, 1961). As for the United Ladies Tailors, it was the most successful Jewish garment union in the East End, with a membership of 3000 in 1918. (Minute books are preserved at Hackney Library). Acknowledgements to Mick Mindel, the president of the union in the 1930s. On the furnishing unions see *NAFTA Monthly Reports* at the TUC Library.

38. PRO HO 45/10818/54; *Notes of an Interview by the Secretary of State with Russian Jewish Trades Unionists*, at the Home Office, 14 Aug. 1916; HO 45/10818/57, letter from a conference of all the Jewish trade union committees in London, 20 Aug. 1916.

39. *The Workers' Circle Jubilee Publication 1909–29*. Other material is being catalogued by the Hackney Archives Department and consequently is not available to researchers; Mr Louis Appleton possesses materials pertaining to the 1930s and 1940s. Oral reminiscences of the Circle provided in interview by Netty Alexander, Jack Baron, Mick Mindel and the late Israel Renson.

40. *Dos Arbayter Vort* gave its editorial backing to the FJPC. PZ in Britain became affiliated to the Labour Party in 1920. See S. Levenberg, *The Jews and Palestine: A Study in Labour Zionism* (London, 1945); Joseph Gorny, *The British Labour Movement and Zionism* (London, 1983); Gideon Shimoni, 'Poale Zion: A Zionist Transplant in Britain (1905–45)', in *Studies in Contemporary Jewry, II* (Indiana, 1986), pp. 227–69.

41. Zangwill wrote to Colonel Patterson of the Jewish Legion complaining of the 'martyrising' of Bezalel by the War Office, 7 Aug. 1917 (Patterson File, Jabotinsky Institute, Tel-Aviv). Moses Gaster, the Sephardi *Haham*, also showed sympathy for the FJPC; see his letter of support to the Camperdown Hall meeting, *MG*, 26 March 1917 and copy in Gaster Papers, Letter Book Nov. 1916–Dec. 1917, p. 430. The secretary of his congregation at Bevis Marks, Paul Goodman, wrote to protest to the Chief Rabbi about his 'identification' with the FJPC, 5 April 1917, Gaster Papers, File 326/2, No. 25 (incoming). Bezalel's family begged Gaster for financial support after the latter was deported; they wished to join him in Berlin;

NOTES

letter from Bezalel's brother, 18 Feb. 1920, Gaster Papers, File 1920, No. 62 (incoming).

42. PRO HO 45/10819/110, Assistant Commissioner of Police, *Anti-Conscription Movement among East End Aliens*, 16 Sept. 1916 plus enclosures and HO minutes. The government claimed there were some 30,000 Russian political refugees in Britain in Feb. 1917; the Committee of Delegations countered that the number of 'strictly political exiles ... hardly exceeds 1,000 persons' (PRO HO 45/10818/14).

43. See Richard K. Debo, 'The Making of a Bolshevik: Georgi Chicherin in England 1914–18', *Slavic Review* Vol. 25 (1966), pp. 651–62; Ron Grant, 'G.V. Chicherin and the Russian Revolutionary Cause in Great Britain', in John Slatter (ed.) *From the Other Shore: Russian Political Emigrants in Britain, 1880–1917* (London, 1984), J. McHugh and B.J. Ripley, 'Russian Political Internees in First World War Britain: the Cases of George Chicherin and Peter Petroff', *Historical Journal*, Vol. 28, No. 3 (1985), pp. 727–38. On Mrs Bridges-Adams see the biography by John Saville in *Dictionary of Labour Biography*, Vol. VI (London, 1982), pp. 1–7. Her private papers are at St Antony's College, Oxford, but I have not been given sight of them. There seems to be some confusion in the available sources as to how far the Committee of Delegates was identifiable with the Emigrés Committee set up in cooperation with Constantine Nabokoff, the acting chargé d'affaires at the Russian Embassy in London: Nabokoff, op. cit., pp. 94–110; Barry Hollingsworth, 'The Committee for Correct Information about the New Russia, a Note and a Query', *Sbornik*, No. 1 (1975), pp. 17–19; An offshoot of the Committee of Delegations appeared in Glasgow as the Russian Political Refugees Defence Committee. See Grant, op. cit., pp. 128, 133. However, Grant also produces evidence to show that certain tensions existed between the internationalist-orientated Committee of Delegations and the FJPC. In a pamphlet entitled *To all Jewish Trades Unions and Workers' Organisations*, 15 March 1917, the former accused the latter of adopting a 'chauvinist "All Israel" policy' to the detriment of the wider proletarian movement (pp. 129–30).

44. Police report PRO HO 45/10821/368 n.d. July 1917. Harold Edwards, letter to the author, 28 Nov. 1985. Mr Edwards added: 'Most went back to Russia and regretted it.'

45. Bush, op. cit., Ch. 6.

46. *The Case of the Russian Jews*, a pamphlet printed by the FJPC dated 20 Feb. 1917, PRO HO 45/10820/219. The organisation enjoyed the moral support of E.R. Morel of the pacifist Union of Democratic Control and of ILP leaders George Lansbury, Herbert Morrison, Philip Snowden and Robert Williams of the Transport Workers' Union. 'Highly organised': PRO HO 45/10822/545.

47. PRO HO 45/10820/229, Special Branch report, 1 April 1917.

48. The government was fully aware that repatriation would not be a popular option, PRO HO 45/10820/300. Nevertheless it took the HO six months to institute a police inquiry into the practice of evasion in London, HO 45/10823/633.

49. 24 Sept. 1917. For the figures see *Report of the Aliens Enlistment Committee*, 26 July 1916, PRO HO 45/10818/57. The medical commission established on the initiative of the URC had exempted 250 Russians as unfit by mid-September 1917 and a further 300–400 'white ticket' holders were due to be examined; Jochelman to Wolf, 14 Sept. 1917, RAL xi/1/13. In Glasgow, 'No less than 293 Jewish appeals were held at the local Military Tribunal between autumn of 1917 and the end of the War'. In Sept. 1917 the Glasgow Jewish Representative Council secured

Jewish representation on the Tribunal. See Kenneth E. Collins, *Second City Jewry* (Glasgow, 1990), p. 192. The Leeds Council did likewise, see Ernest C. Sterne, *Leeds Jewry and the Great War: 1914–18: The Homefront*, JHSE (Leeds, 1982), p.212.

50. Interview with Louis Wallis, Beaumont Settlement, Stepney Green, East London, 6 Aug. 1985.
51. Letter to the author, 18 Nov. 1985; Dr Samuel Sacks, obituary, *JC*, 29 June 1990; and reminiscences of Israel Renson, 12 Jan. 1986.
52. Interview with Israel Renson, East London, 12 Jan. 1986. He was associated with the Socialist Party of Great Britain in the 1930s and 1940s. See 'Obituary: Israel Renson 1906–1986' by Jerry White, *History Workshop*, issue 25 (Spring 1988).
53. Lerner, op. cit., pp. 103–4. Elsbury was a member of the SDF.
54. Interview with Mick Mindel, London, 22 Aug. 1985. See also Jerry White, *Rothschild Buildings* (London, 1980), which contains reproductions of memorabilia connected with the Mindel family – not least Morris' exemption certificate. The 2500 figure is cited from a note by Gambs of the Russian Consulate to the Director General of Recruiting, 27 March 1918, in PRO HO 45/10822/585; and 10821/422 and see 437, and 10823/633. It appears that the consulate was under pressure from the Russian Emigrés' Committee in Aug. 1917.
55. On Rav Kook's role see Jacob Agus, *High Priest of Rebirth: The Life, Times and Thought of Avrohom Yitskhok Kook* (New York, 1972). See also Evelyn Wilcock, 'The Revd. John Harris: Issues in Anglo-Jewish Pacifism 1914–18', *TJHSE*, Vol. 30 (1987–88), pp. 163–77, for a rare example of a native-born Anglo-Jewish minister who became a conscientious objector. His stand cost him his job at the Prince's Road synagogue, Liverpool, in 1916. But he was not charged under the Defence of the Realm Act.
56. PRO HO 45/10821/372, General Registrar's Office to HO, 31 July 1917.
57. Rocker, *The London Years*, op. cit., pp. 325–7. Like Rocker, Shapiro was an anti-war anarchist. Nevertheless he remained on good terms with Kropotkin even after they had both returned to Russia in 1917. Shapiro joined the Bolsheviks in the hope of pushing the revolution towards anarchism. See George Woodcock and Ivan Avakumovic, *The Anarchist Prince: A Biographical Study of Peter Kropotkin* (London, 1950), pp. 385, 387, 390, 408, and Martin A. Miller, *Kropotkin* (Chicago, 1976), p. 238.
58. Acknowledgements to Bill Williams of Manchester Polytechnic and see Tony Kushner, 'The Manchester Jewish Museum', in *Society for the Study of Labour History Bulletin*, Vol. 51, No. 3 (1986)), pp. 18–19.
59. In a letter to the *JC*, 17 Feb. 1989, Asher Tropp of Milford Haven writes: 'Those who returned to Russia are difficult to count, but not "countless". My best estimate is between 2,000 and 2,500 from the whole of Britain. From the East End, less than 10 per cent of Russian Jews of military age returned to Russia.' On returnees from Leeds see Nigel Grizzard, *Leeds Jewry and the Great War 1914–18* JHSE (Leeds, 1981), p.11.
60. PRO HO 45/10821/434 and HO 45/10822/481.
61. Letters to the author from Mr Alf Glick of Bristol, 3 Oct., 19 Nov. 1985, in response to the former's notice in the *JC* of 27 Sep. 1985, seeking ex-Conventionists and their descendants.
62. Interview with Jack Baron, London, 1 Feb. 1986. Acknowledgements to the London Museum of Jewish Life.
63. Albert Meltzer, *The Anarchists in London* (Cienfuegos Press, Orkney Islands,

1976). Acknowledgements to Sheila Leslie.

64. For statistics see PRO HO 45/10822/563, 10839/52 and 169; Dr Jochelman's appeal addressed to Anglo-Jewish leaders, 15 Jan. 1919, copies in MOW File 87, 11188–9, and in the Chief Rabbi's correspondence at Woburn House, London (Box File marked 'Russia' 1919); Jews' Temporary Shelter 31st, 32nd, 33rd, 34th *Annual Reports* (1918–24) available at the Shelter's new premises in Willesden, North London.

65. Ch. II, 'Growing up with Mother'.

66. In Feb. 1920 the Board of Deputies finally took over responsibility for the families, the Jewish Board of Guardians having been most reluctant to cooperate. The URC, whose offices were at 10 Great Garden Street, also enjoyed the moral support of Morris Myer's *Di Tsayt* (see editorial of 10 Sep. 1917) and the financial support of the Workers' Circle and the Russian Delegates Committee. The Provisional Government via the Embassy in London donated £1500. See Jochelman to Wolf, 14 Sept. 1917 RAL/xi/1/13.

67. PRO HO 45/10822/525, 10823/661 and 679. It appears that the Jewish women had made some attempt to organise in Aug. 1917. Thomson reported that the Glasgow Lithuanian Women's Committee had received 'strong support' from 'the Jewish Protection Society for Women', PRO HO 45/10821/431. On Bachrach see entries in *Register* of Jews' Temporary Shelter 9, 12 Sept. 1914. The Glasgow Jewish Representative council raised funds for the families and in Edinburgh an aid organisation was set up in Aug. 1917. See Collins, op. cit., pp. 191–2, 219.

68. WA.

69. PRO HO 45 10819/157, 25 Oct. 1916.

70. *Memorandum* by Lucien Wolf, 20 June 1916; *Russian Jews and Military Service* ('Strictly Confidential'), by Lucien Wolf, 15 Aug. 1916, MOW File 203; *The Alien and the Army: Can we conscript foreigners?* by Lucien Wolf, n.d. 1916, MOW File 87. Another copy of *Memorandum* in RAL/xi/1/13. The threat of deportation was first used by Herbert Samuel in July 1916 and was made public in his speech in the House of Commons on 22 Aug. 1916. In fact the government offered free naturalisation, waiving the £5 fee after three months' service.

71. PRO HO 45/10821/371, Wolf to Oliphant (HO), 25 July 1917. 'Firebrands' cited from HO 45/10819/91, an HO minute quoting Wolf, Sept. 1916.

72. See *JC*, 27 July 1917; on dependants, 21 Sept. 1917 and editorials in subsequent weeks. Dr Jochelman complained: 'The Anglo-Jewish community, with a very few exceptions, has turned a deaf ear to all the appeals of the [United Russian] Committee.' Jochelman to Chief Rabbi Hertz, 22 Oct. 1918, Chief Rabbi's correspondence, 'Russia' File No. I.

Even Morris Myer, the editor of the East End's *Di Tsayt*, although by no means for the Convention, took care, officially, not to oppose the government's plans. He regarded the FJPC as a bunch of *tomel mukhers* (rabble rousers); see *Di Tsayt*, 25, 27 July 1917. After the war, Myer got himself elected to the Board, and was widely looked upon as having 'sold out' to the 'establishment' by those to his left in the East End.

73. Jack Miller's father was one of those enlisted in the Labour Corps (interview, Beaumont Settlement, 6 Aug. 1985). Those already serving with the colours (some 4–5000 officially, but closer to 3100 in actual fact) were not released in the winter of 1917–18. To all intents and purposes they had become British citizens. Recruitment into the Jewish Legion, however, was soon resumed. The War Office was afraid that Litvinov would release all the East End Jews from military service if

he was given half a chance. See PRO HO 45/10822/545, 551, 556, 562, 579, 605.

74. *ELO*, 28 July 1917. *Di Tsayt* defended the aliens who, after all, were not responsible for the change of regime in Russia (15 Feb., 31 May 1918).

From April 1920 to July 1922, the URC was replaced by the Russian Dependents Committee, on which sat representatives of the Jewish Board of Deputies, Board of Guardians, Workers' Emergency Relief Fund and the Lithuanian Colony of London. The Committee received a grant from the Ministry of Health and made use of the Shelter's premises in Leman Street. Responsibility for funding subsequently reverted to the local Board of Guardians. See Shelter's *Annual Reports* and Minute Book (1885–1935), and above n. 66, 72.

75. Buchanan to HO, 16 Dec. 1918, PRO HO 45/10823/656, 690; Pedder (HO) to Basil Thomson, 20 Jan. 1919, HO 45/10823/667.

76. Aliens and Nationality Committee Memo No. 132, 17 Jan. 1921, PRO HO 45/10839/333052/169; For War Cabinet Circular and related documents see HO 45/10822/545.

77. In Nov. 1919, British Consulates abroad were given confidential orders not to issue visas to Conventionists. See David Cesarani 'Anti-Alienism in England after the First World War', *Immigrants and Minorities*, Vol. 6, No. 1 (March 1987), p. 11. Interview with Harry Blacker, Oxford, 22 May 1985; see also his memoir *Just Like it Was* (London, 1974).

78. PRO HO 45/10839/184; 10822/579. An entry for 15 Jan. 1924 in the Shelter's Minute Book states that 'the work of repatriation [is] to cease on Aug. 31st next, and applications for repatriation to be received up to July 31st only.' The Shelter had taken over responsibility from the Russian Dependants' Committee in July 1922. The number of Russians seeking temporary shelter dropped dramatically after the revolution.

79. PRO HO 45/24765/432156/5,13,17. A minute of 8 May 1924 states that a minimum of 15 years' residence was required in the case of Russians and Poles seeking naturalisation – the official requirement was five years. 'This figure [of 15 years] cannot be stated in public ... It is merely a practical rule for the internal guidance of the Department, based on experience ... and may be altered by experience.' The Board's protestations had no effect. In Oct. 1920 they advised Conventionists seeking readmission to stay away and outstanding cases of divided families were dropped. See Cesarani, op. cit., p. 14.

80. Ronald Sanders in *The High Walls of Jerusalem: A History of the Balfour Declaration and the Birth of the British Mandate for Palestine* (New York, 1984), p. 568 terms the regiment a 'visceral issue'.

81. See Jabotinsky's *The Story of the Jewish Legion* (New York 1945) and Elias Gilner, *War and Hope – A History of the Jewish Legion* (New York, 1969). The nucleus of the regiment was made up of veterans of the Zion Mule Corps, some 120 men, who made their way to London. See also Cyril Silvertown, 'The "Righteous Colonel" and the Jewish Legion', *Jewish Quarterly*, Vol. 32, No. 2 (118) (1985), pp. 37–40. Mr Silvertown quotes from correspondence between Jabotinsky and Dr Hertz which I came across in the Chief Rabbi's Office, see n. 90 below. For one example of Jabotinsky's propaganda see *The Right Way: Foreign Jews and Military Service*, English translation, MOW File 203, n.d. July/Aug. 1917; and for the FJPC counter-attack a poster in Yiddish entitled *Jews, do not let yourselves be deceived!*, n.d., MOW File 87 11172.

On Grossman see David Vital, *Zionism, the Crucial Phase* (Oxford, 1987), pp. 142, 150–3, that author being Grossman's son. *Di Tribune* was begun in Copenhagen in Oct. 1915. In Sept. 1916 Jabotinsky attempted to publish the pro-Legion *Unzer Tribune* which was so poorly received in London that it collapsed within a month. See Oscar Janowsky, *The Jews and Minority Rights, 1898–1919*, (New York, 1966), p. 197.

82. Quoted in Gilner, op. cit., p. 113. The march took place on 23 Feb. 1918. See PRO HO 45/10821/422 for a 'protest against the Regiment on behalf of the Russian JPC elected at a representative conference of over 80 organisations'.

83. *MG*, letter from Jochelman, 25 Aug. 1917. Israel Zangwill, on the other hand, came out in support of the regiment, as did Joseph King.

84. *Di Tsayt*, 30 July, 10 Aug. 1917; *Yiddisher Ekspress*, 5 Sept. 1917.

85. See Ch. 4 above, pp. 143–4.

86. Quotation from Gilner, op. cit., pp. 96, 106.

87. Bigham (New Scotland Yard) to HO, 24 Aug. 1917, PRO HO 45 10821/446.

88. Sacher to Simon, 30 May 1917, CZA A 289 (Sacher). Joseph Cowen's public support for the Regiment and for Herbert Samuel's proposed sanctions against the Russian eligibles cost him the presidency of the EZF. Weizmann, who was more discreet in his backing for Jabotinsky's project, got the job instead. However, he was forced to rein-in the EZF executive when it threatened formally to denounce the Legion during the summer of 1917: see Ben Halpern, *A Clash of Heroes: Brandeis, Weizmann and American Zionism* (New York, 1987), pp. 164–5.

89. And in a debate at the Board of Deputies, see *JC*, 17 Aug. 1917. The speaker was A.E. Franklin.

90. *JC*, 31 Aug., 7 Sep. 1917. The counter-delegation was led by Elkan Adler and M.M.J. Landa. Jabotinsky wrote an impassioned plea for support to the Chief Rabbi, who was endeavouring to keep 'above party' in the whole dispute. Jabotinsky/Hertz correspondence in First World War File, folder labelled 'Jewish Recruiting Committee and Jewish Regiment', Chief Rabbi's Office. Hertz did not join the second delegation despite his Zionist sympathies.

91. Cesarani, op. cit., p. 13.

92. Herbert T. Fitch, *Traitors Within* (London, 1933), p. 71.

93. See Bernard Porter, 'The British Government and Political Refugees c. 1880–1914', in Slatter, op. cit., on government reluctance to tamper with the rights of *political* refugees in the earlier period.

94. On the Lithuanians see two articles by Murdoch Rogers in *Immigrants and Minorities*: 'The Anglo-Russian Military Convention and the Lithuanian Immigrant Community in Lanarkshire Scotland, 1914–20', Vol. 1, No. 1 (March 1982), pp. 60–88, and 'Political Developments in the Lithuanian Community in Scotland c. 1890–1923', in Slatter, op. cit., pp. 141–56. See also James D. White, 'Scottish Lithuanians and the Russian Revolution', *Journal of Baltic Studies*, Vol. 6, No. 1 (Spring 1975), pp. 1–8. According to White 'only a hundred or so' Lithuanian Conventionists were able to return to their families in England. Rogers puts it at 'fewer than 350'. Similar 'class' divisions were apparent in the Lithuanian as in the Jewish community; the Catholic priests, like the Anglo-Jewish establishment, urged the aliens to join up, whilst the socialists, led by the LSF, favoured repatriation.

95. Walter Kendall, *The Revolutionary Movement in Britain, 1900–1921* (London, 1965) is a useful source on Jews in the CPGB. I am grateful to Professor Kendall for his advice. On Litvinov see A.U. Pope, *Maxim Litvinov* (London, 1943); John Carswell, *The Exile: A Life of Ivy Litvinov* (London, 1983); Ivan Maisky, *Journal into the Past* (London, 1962), pp. 53–69.

96. On Rothstein see Maisky, op. cit., Ch. 8; biography by Keith Nield in *Dictionary of Labour Biography*, Vol. 7 (1984), pp. 200–9; David Burke, 'Theodore Rothstein: Russian Emigré and British Socialist', in Slatter, op. cit., pp. 81–99. In the course of his research on Rothstein for an MA (Thames Polytechnic, 1981), Burke was refused access to the Rothstein archive in Moscow. Also see Andrew Rothstein, *Lenin in Britain* (A Communist Party pamphlet, n.d. [1970]). Rothstein's connections with the Yiddish press based on Prager, op. cit., and a letter from his son Andrew to the author, 23 Nov. 1985. Rothstein Junior writes:

> My father was a revolutionary Social-Democrat, a member of the SDF and subsequently of the BSP. As such, he had no contact whatsoever, so far as I know, with what I assume you mean by the 'Anglo-Jewish Community' and 'East End Jewry'. Early in this century he edited two workers' Socialist papers published in Yiddish, but so far as I am aware these were strictly anti-bourgeois papers, and therefore hardly likely to fall under that category either. Moreover as an atheist he had no interest whatever in either the Jewish religion or in Zionism, of which he was a convinced opponent.

Andrew Rothstein is currently the president of the Marx Memorial Library, Clerkenwell, and of the British-Soviet Friendship Society. On the occasion of his eighty-fifth birthday in 1983, he was awarded the 'Order of the October Revolution' by the Soviet government. See report in *Daily Telegraph*, 26 Sept. 1983.

97. Directorate of Intelligence (Basil Thomson), *Report on Revolutionary Organisations in the UK*, Secret Report No. 88, 13 Jan. 1921; *A Survey of Revolutionary Movements in Great Britain in the Year 1920*, Jan. 1921, PRO CAB 24/118 and other reports on 1920 in CAB 24/97–111; and also CAB 21/197 (1921).

98. Kendall, op. cit., p. 245 and p. 388, n. 32; Raymond Challinor, *The Origins of British Bolshevism* (London, 1977), p. 226; Andrew Rothstein, *Labour Monthly*, Dec. 1969, pp. 563–8 review of Kendall; Burke, op. cit.

99. On Boris and Zelda Kahan see Kendall, op. cit., and Andrew Rothstein's books and article, op. cit., and letter re 'an uncle of mine' written to the author, 20 Dec. 1985. The Kahans' father Isaac was hardly a revolutionary; he ran a passenger shipping agency in Commercial Road working with the White Star and Cunard lines, see Nield, op. cit., p. 201. On the brawl at the Brotherhood Church, see Ken Weller, *Don't be a Soldier! The Radical Anti-War movement in North London 1914–1918* (London History Workshop 1985), pp. 87–90, and Thomson, *The Scene Changes*, op. cit., p. 383.

100. On Fineberg, see Kendall, op. cit., and B. Lazitch and M.M. Drachkovitch, *A Biographical Dictionary of the Comintern* (Stanford, 1973), pp. 100–1 for his subsequent career in Russia.

101. *BSP, Report of the Seventh Annual Conference*, Leeds, 31 March–1 April 1918.

102. Robert Barltrop, *The Monument: The Story of the Socialist Party of Great Britain* (London, 1975). Acknowledgements to Philip Benesch; also articles by Bill Williams in *Manchester Jewish Telegraph*, 7 May, 2 July 1976; Tommy Jackson, *Solo Trumpet* (London, 1953), pp. 83–6.

103. On the IWW see p. 203 above and Weller, op. cit. ('Red hair'), p. 67, n. 4. On Esther Archer and Charlie Lahr see David Goodway, 'Charles Lahr: Anarchist, Bookseller, Publisher', *The London Magazine*, June–July 1972; R.M. Fox, *Smokey Crusade*, (London, 1938); interview with their daughter Sheila Leslie, 10 Nov. 1985. Acknowledgements to the late Sam Bornstein. On Rose Witcop see also J. Quail, *The Slow Burning Fuse* (London, 1978), and Guy Aldred's autobiog-

raphy, *No Traitor's Gate* (Glasgow, 1955–63). Another woman Jewish radical was the English-born Rose Cohen who married the Comintern agent D. Petrovsky (alias A.J. Bennett). She returned with him to Russia and was shot during the purges. See Kendall, op. cit., and Carswell, op. cit., Appendix II.

104. *Stepney Trades Council and Central Labour Party, Annual Report 1919–1920*, copies at Tower Hamlets and Hackney Library: ILP *Report of the Annual Conference*, Glasgow, April 1920, list of delegates.

105. Bush, op. cit.

106. Emanuel Shinwell, *Conflict Without Malice* (London, 1955); *I've Lived Through It All* (London, 1973); *Lead with the Left! My First Ninety Six Years* (London, 1981); and (ed. John Dexat) *Shinwell Talking* (London, 1984). In reply to a letter I wrote to him in 1985, Lord Shinwell stated 'I ... consider that you should seek to obtain the information you require from somebody who knows more about the Jewish community than I do' (2 Aug. 1985). He died at the age of 101 on 8 May 1986; see obituary notices in the national press and *JC* the following week. His papers are being left to the Library of the London School of Economics. 'Socialist before I was twenty' quoted from *Conflict Without Malice*, p. 38.

107. William Gallacher, *The Last Memoirs of William Gallacher* (London, 1966), pp. 100–1. See also his earlier *Revolt on the Clyde* (London, 1936). Gallacher became Communist MP for West Fife in 1935.

108. Thomson to Blumenfeld, editor of the *Daily Express*, 21 March 1919, Blumenfeld Papers, House of Lords. 'Spies' Weller, op. cit., p. 64.

109. See Kendall, op. cit., and Basil Thomson, *The Story of Scotland Yard* (London, 1935), pp. 237–40; Harold Brust, *I Guarded Kings: the Memoir of a Political Police Officer* (London, n.d. [1935]), pp. 209–15.

110. See Kendall, op. cit., pp. 243, 246–9.

111. See R.H. Bruce Lockhart, *Memoirs of a British Agent* (London, 1932); ed. Kenneth Young, *The Diaries of R.H. Bruce Lockhart* (London, 1973); *Retreat from Glory*, (London, 1934). Richard Deacon, *A History of the British Secret Service* (London, 1969), quotes Lockhart on Reilly's origins. However, Michael Kettle, *Sidney Reilly: The True Story* (London, 1983), gives an entirely different version. Kettle claims that Reilly was the only son of Pauline and Gregory (Hirsh) Jakovlevitch Rosenblum – 'a rich Polish-Jewish landowner', with an estate in the Grodno region. The family were reputed to be related to Leon Bramson, the chairman of ORT. He even produces a photograph as proof of Reilly's ancestry. The truth must remain shrouded in mystery. See, finally, Robin Bruce-Lockhart, *Ace of Spies* (London, 1967). Deacon casts doubt on the generally accepted belief that Reilly was killed by the Bolsheviks – he was much too useful to them.

112. See Geoffrey Alderman, *The Jewish Community in British Politics* (Oxford, 1983), and his *London Jewry and London Politics 1889–1986* (London, 1989) on Jewish support for Labour at national, local and LCC level after the First World War.

113. *Stepney Trades Council and Central Labour Party Annual Report 1919–20*; TUC *Report of Proceedings of the 29th Annual TUC*, Blackpool, 3–8 Sept. 1917, pp. 309–10; *Report of Proceedings of the 31st Annual TUC*, Derby, 1919, pp. 345–352; Bush, op. cit. On Sclare see Rosalind O'Brien, *The Establishment of the Jewish Minority in Leeds*, unpub. PhD, Bristol University, 1975, p. 170, and acknowledgements to Anne Kershen of Warwick University. Acknowledgements also to Elaine Smith of Leicester University *re* Oscar Tobin and other Jewish Labourites mentioned in this section. Relevant articles by both Mrs Kershen and

Dr Smith are to be found in David Cesarani (ed.), *The Making of Modern Anglo-Jewry* (Oxford, 1990) which appeared whilst this book was in press.
114. *Stepney Trades Council Report 1919–20*, op. cit.; *Labour Party Annual Conference Report*, Southport, June 1919, Scarborough, June 1920.
115. Bush, op. cit., p. 190.

CONCLUSION

1. Published in book form, London 1924, p. 165.
2. Phil Piratin, *Our Flag Stays Red* (London, 2nd edn, 1978), p. 49; Geoffrey Alderman, *London Jewry and London Politics 1889–1986* (London, 1989), p. 95. One of the LCC members was Jack Gaster, son of the late *Haham*.
3. Henry F. Srebrnik, *The Jewish Communist Movement in Stepney: Ideological Mobilization and Political Victories in an East London Borough 1935–1945*, PhD, University of Birmingham, 1983 (forthcoming). See also Elaine R. Smith, 'Jewish Responses to Political Antisemitism and Fascism in the East End of London 1920–1939', in T. Kushner and K. Lunn (eds), *Traditions of Intolerance* (Manchester, 1989), pp. 53–71.
4. Srebrnik, op. cit., p. 160.
5. Ibid., p. 16.
6. Ibid., pp. 4–5.

Bibliography

UNPUBLISHED SOURCES

Board of Deputies of British Jews, London
Class A: BoD Agenda and Reports
  /3   Foreign Affairs Committee/Joint Foreign Committee Minutes 1918–21
  /17   BoD Minutes Volume 17 1915– 21
Class C: Foreign Affairs
  /C   11/2   General Joint Foreign Committee Correspondence
  /C   11/3   World War I, Peace Conference, League of Nations, Emigration and Refugees 1915–24
  /C   11/4   Papers prepared for JFC meetings 1918– 19
  /C   11/5   Lucien Wolf JFC Correspondence
  /C   11/12   JFC filed by country: 118, 119, 120, 121, 122 Russia

Bund Archives of the Jewish Labour Movement, New York

M 16/84   Dr Joseph Kruk file
M 18/125   Israel Zangwill
M 18/127   Aaron Zundelevitch
M 18/132   Vladimir Jabotinsky
Workers' Circle File

Central Zionist Archives, Jerusalem

A 18   Nahum Sokolov
A 36   ITO
A 77   Lucien Wolf
A 99   Morris Myer
A 120   Israel Zangwill
A 185   Leonard Stein
A 213   Israel Cohen
A 289   Harry Sacher
A 354   Chief Rabbi Dr J.H. Hertz
K 11/46   Papers relating to the Balfour Declaration
Z4/305/2   Leon Simon

Chief Rabbi' s Office, London
Box Files: War 1914–18, Russia (two files), Misc. correspondence 1916–23 (alphabetical by subject).

Paul Goodman Papers
By permission of Mr Cyril Goodman, Essex

House of Lords Record Library
Ralph Blumenfeld Papers
Herbert Samuel Papers
Stuart Samuel Papers
David Soskice Papers

Imperial War Museum, London
p. 346   J.H. Bracher file

Jabotinsky Institute, Tel Aviv
Colonel Patterson file
Jabotinsky letter book 1915–18

Jewish Colonisation Association, London
Minute Books 1917–21
Lucien Wolf Bound Files (four) 1916–23

Jewish Theological Seminary, New York
Elkan Adler Collection

Jews' Temporary Shelter, London
General Committee Minute Book (1885–1935)

Mocatta Library, University College London
Archives of the Anglo-Jewish Association
    AJ/204/3   Conjoint Foreign Affairs Committee of the BoD and AJA
            Special Branch Reports IX, X, XI, XII (1916–17)
    AJ/204/4   Conjoint Committee Confidential Minutes, March 1912–June
            1917 (One volume)
Moses Gaster papers

Public Record Office, London
Cabinet Papers
    CAB 21/197
    CAB 24/97–111, 118
Foreign Office
    371/3052
Home Office
    HO 45/10810
            10818
            10819
            10820
            10821

BIBLIOGRAPHY

    10822
    10823
    10831
    10839
    10963
HO 45/24765

Rose Lipman Library (Hackney Archives Department), London
United Ladies Tailors' Trades Union
    DS/24 1&2 Minute Books, June–Nov. 1922; Nov. 1922–Sept. 1923
    DS/24/53/1&2 Misc. Box and press cuttings

Rothschild Archive, London
RFamAD/1/4 Lucien Wolf papers 1905–1917
RAL/xi/1/13 Conjoint Foreign Committee
League of British Jews minute books: No. 1 Nov. 1917–July 1923; n.d. Nov.
1917–March 1919

St Antony' s College, Oxford, Middle East Centre
Balfour Declaration File
Herbert Samuel papers

University College London
Lucien Wolf, *Diary of the Peace Conference, 1919*

Warwick University, Modern Records Centre
Aaron Rollin Collection

Wiener Library, London
Hamilton Beamish File

Weizmann Institute, Rehovot
Weizmann Archive: Letters received by Chaim Weizmann (arranged chrono-
logically)

YIVO Institute for Jewish Research, New York
Lucien Wolf/David Mowshowitch Collection

Unpublished theses
Bayme, Steven Gilbert, 'Jewish Leadership and Antisemitism in Britain
    1898–1918', Columbia University PhD, 1977
Blume, Hilary, 'A Study of Antisemitic Groups in Great Britain 1918–1940',
    University of Sussex, MPhil, 1971
Fuller, Stephen Merle, 'The British Press and European Antisemitism', Univer-
    sity of New Mexico, PhD, 1974

Hewko, John, 'The Ukrainian-Jewish Political Relationship during the period of the Central Rada March 1917–January 1918', University of Oxford, MLitt, 1981

Levene, Mark, 'Jewish Diplomacy at War and Peace: A Study of Lucien Wolf 1914–19', University of Oxford, DPhil, 1981

O' Brien, Rosalind, 'The Establishment of the Jewish Minority in Leeds', University of Bristol, PhD, 1975

Schinness, Roger T., 'The Tories and the Soviets: The British Conservative Reaction to Russia 1917–27', State University of New York at Binghamton, PhD, 1972

Srebrnik, Henry F. 'The Jewish Communist Movement in Stepney: Ideological Mobilization and Political Victories in an East London Borough 1935–45', University of Birmingham, PhD, 1983–4

PUBLISHED SOURCES

Government Papers and Annual Reports

Board of Deputies of British Jews, *Annual Reports* 1917–20

British Socialist Party, Annual Conference Reports 1917–20

Command Papers

No. 8   *Russia No. I: A Collection of reports on Bolshevism in Russia* (April 1919)

No. 674   *Report by Sir Stuart Samuel on his mission to Poland* (1920)

No. 1540   *Sir Thomas Haycraft, Palestine, Disturbances in May 1921: Report of the Commission of Inquiry with correspondence relating thereto* (Oct. 1921)

Communist Unity Convention, London, 31 July–1 Aug. 1920, *Official Report* (Sept. 1920)

House of Commons/Lords Debates, *Hansard* 5th series, 1917–21

Independent Labour Party, Annual Conference Reports 1917–21

Jews' Temporary Shelter, Annual Reports 1916–24

    31st Annual Report 1916–1918 (London, 1919)

    32nd Annual Report (for three years ending 31 Oct. 1921) (London, 1921)

    33rd Annual Report (for the year ending 31 Oct. 1922) (London, 1923)

    34th Annual Report (for the two years ending 31 Oct. 1924) (London, 1925)

Labour Party Annual Conference Reports, 1917–21

Metropolitan Borough of Stepney, *Minutes of Proceedings of the Council*, Vol. XVII–XX (1916–1920)

Metropolitan Borough of Bethnal Green, *Minutes of Proceedings*, Vol. XVII (1916–1917)

NAFTA Monthly Reports, Aug. 1917–Dec. 1921

Stepney Trades Council and Central Labour Party, *Annual Report 1919–20*

TUC Annual Conference Reports 1917–21

BIBLIOGRAPHY

Report of the XII Zionist Congress, Carlsbad, 1–14 Sept. 1921: Addresses, Reports, Resolutions (London 1922)

Contemporary Newspapers and Periodicals

Der Arbayter Fraynt
Dos Arbayter Vort
The Call
The Communist
Daily Express
Daily Herald
Daily Mail
Daily Telegraph
East London Advertiser
East London Observer
English Review
Illustrated Sunday Herald
Jewish Chronicle
Jewish Guardian
Jewish Opinion
Jewish World
Journal of the Amalgamated Society of Tailors
Justice
Manchester Guardian
Morning Post
National Review
Nashe Slovo
New Age
Nineteenth Century and After
Observer
Ovend Nayes
Palestine
Quarterly Review
Round Table
Russian Outlook
Spectator
The Spur
The Times
La Tribune Juive
Di Tsayt
Unzer Veg
Der Yiddisher Ekspress
Zionist Review

Memoirs, diaries, letters, speeches

Aldred, Guy, *No Traitor's Gait* (Glasgow, 1955–63)

283

Amery, Leo, ed. Barnes, John and Nicholson, David, *The Leo Amery Diaries*, Vol. I (1896–1929) (London, 1980)

Blacker, Harry, *Just like it was* (London, 1969)

Brust, Harold, *I Guarded Kings: The Memoir of a Political Police Officer* (London, n.d. [1935])

Churchill, Sir Winston, *Aftermath: A sequel to World Crisis* (London, 1941)

—, ed. Gilbert, Martin, *Companion Volumes* to *Winston S. Churchill*, Vol. IV 1917–22 (London, 1975)

Fitch, Herbert T., *Traitors Within* (London, 1933)

Fox, R.M. *Smokey Crusade* (London, 1938)

Gallacher, William, *Revolt on the Clyde* (London, 1936)

—, *The Last Memoirs* (London, 1966)

Graham, Stephen, *Part of the Wonderful Scene: An Autobiography* (London, 1964)

Harari, Manya, *Memoirs, 1906–69* (London, 1972)

Hertz, Chief Rabbi Dr J.H., *Sermons, Addresses and Studies*, Vol. I, Sermons (London 1938)

Hodgson, John Ernest, *With Denikin' s Armies: Being a Description of the Cossack Counter-Revolution in South Russia 1918–20* (London, 1932)

Jabotinsky, Ze'ev, *The Story of the Jewish Legion* (New York, 1945)

Jackson, Tommy, *Solo Trumpet* (London, 1953)

Litvinoff, Emanuel, *Journey through a Small Planet* (London, 1972)

Lloyd George, David, *Memoirs of the Peace Conference*, Vol. II (New Haven, 1939)

Lockhart, R.H. Bruce, *Memoirs of a British Agent* (London, 1932)

—, *Retreat from Glory* (London, 1934)

Maisky, Ivan, *Journey into the Past* (London, 1962)

Meinertzhagen, Col. Richard, *Middle East Diary 1917–1956* (London, 1959)

Piratin, Phil, *Our Flag Stays Red* (London, 2nd edn, 1978)

Reilly, Sidney (ed. by his wife), *The Adventures of Sidney Reilly* (London, 1931)

Rocker, Rudolf, *The London Years* (London, 1956)

Sebag-Montefiore, Ruth, *A Family Patchwork: Five Generations of an Anglo-Jewish Family* (London, 1987)

Shinwell, Emanuel (Lord), *Conflict Without Malice* (London, 1955)

—, *I've Lived Through It All* (London, 1973)

—, *Lead with the Left! My First Ninety-Six Years* (London, 1981)

—, (ed.) Dexat, John, *Shinwell Talking* (London, 1984)

Solomon, Flora and Litvinoff, Barnett, *From Baku to Baker Street*, (London, 1984)

Thomson, Sir Basil, *Queer People* (London, 1922)

—, *The Story of Scotland Yard* (London, 1935)

—, *The Scene Changes* (New York, 1937)

Ukrainian Information Bureau Munich, *Materials Concerning Ukrainian-Jewish Relations during the Years of the Revolution (1917–1921)*

BIBLIOGRAPHY

(Munich, 1956)

Webster, Nesta, *Spacious Days* (London, 1950)

Weizmann, Chaim, *The Letters and Papers of Chaim Weizmann*, Series A, *Letters* (Jerusalem/Oxford/London, 1969–80): Vol. VII (Aug. 1914–Nov. 1917); Vol. VIII (Nov. 1917–Oct. 1918); Vol. IX (Oct. 1918–July 1920); Vol. X (July 1920–March 1921)

—, *Trial and Error* (London, 1949)

Contemporary publications: books and pamphlets (1917–30) including memoirs

Adler, Morris, *The British Jewry Book of Honour* (London, 1919)

American Jewish Congress, *The Massacre and Other Atrocities Committed Against the Jews in Southern Russia* (New York, 1920)

Banister, Joseph, *Our Judeo-Irish Labour Party* (London, 1923)

Belloc, Hilaire, *The Jews* (London, 1922)

Board of Deputies of British Jews, *The Assassination of the Tsar* (1920)

—, Lucien Wolf, *The Jewish Bogey and the Forged Protocols* (1920)

—, *The Peace Conference* (1920)

—, *League of Nations: Reports of the Secretary and Special Delegates of the JFC on Jewish Questions dealt with by the First Assembly of the League* (Feb. 1921)

—, Ditto, Third Session (1922); Fourth Session (1924)

—, Lucien Wolf, *Russo-Jewish Refugees in Eastern Europe: Report of the Conference on Russian Refugees held in Geneva under League of Nations Auspices* (1921)

—, Lucien Wolf, *Russo-Jewish Refugees in Eastern Europe: Report on the Fourth Meeting of the Advisory Committee of the High Commissioner for Refugees of the League of Nations* (1923)

—, Lucien Wolf, *Russo-Jewish Refugees in Eastern Europe: Report to JCA on a Meeting of the Advisory Committee of the High Commissioner for Russian Refugees – Geneva September 3rd 1924 and on Certain Emigration Questions Arising during the Fifth Session of the Assembly of the League of Nations* (1924)

—, JFC and AJA *Memo on Correspondence with the Soviet Government Respecting Persecution of Judaism in Russia* (1923)

Brailsford, Henry Noel, *Beyond the Blockade: The Russian Workers' Republic* (London, 1921)

The Britons, Collection of pamphlets at the British Library, Wiener Library, YIVO (Mowshowitch Papers)

Chesterton, G.K., *The New Jerusalem* (London, 1920)

Clarke, J.H., *White Labour versus Red* (The Britons, 1922)

Committee of Jewish Delegations, *The Pogroms in the Ukraine under the Ukrainian Governments 1917–20* (Paris, 1927)

Dukes, Sir Paul, *Red Dusk and The Morrow: Adventures and investigations in Red Russia* (London, 1922)

285

Farbman, Michael, *Russia and the Struggle for Peace* (London, 1918)
—, *Bolshevism in Retreat* (London, 1923)
Federation of Ukrainian Jews, *The Ukraine Terror and the Jewish Peril: Report of pogroms in the Ukraine by the Kiev Pogrom Relief Committee of the Russian Red Cross* (London, 1921)
—, *In and Around the Ukraine: Report of the Work of the London Federation of Ukrainian Jews, October 1921–March 1923* (London, 1923)
—, *Report of the Third Annual Relief Conference of the London FUJ, September 16th 1923* (London, 1923)
—, *Two Years Relief Work: Report of the Activities of the London FUJ, April 1923–March 1925* (London, 1925)
Foreign Jews Protection Committee, *The Case of the Russian Jews* (London, 1917)
Friends of the Ukraine, *The Jewish Pogroms in Ukraine: Authoritative Statements on the Question of Responsibility for Recent Outbreaks against the Jews in Ukraine* (Washington, DC, 1919)
Goode, William T., *Bolshevism at Work* (London, 1920)
Goodman, Paul, *Zionism and Liberal Judaism* (repr. from the *Zionist Review*, Nov. 1917)
Graham, Stephen, *Russia in Division* (London, 1925)
Gwynne, H.A. (ed.), *The Cause of World Unrest* (London, 1920)
A Handbook for Anti-Socialists (Boswell, 1924)
Heifetz, Elias, *The Slaughter of the Jews in the Ukraine in 1919* (New York, 1921)
Hertz, Chief Rabbi Dr J.H., *A Decade of Woe and Hope* (London, 1923)
The Jewish Peril: Protocols of the Learned Elders of Zion (London, 1920)
The Jews' Who's Who (anon = H.H. Beamish) (London, 1920)
Lansbury, George, *What I Saw in Russia* (London, 1920)
Levene, Rev. Ephraim, *The Mission of the Jew* (London, 1917)
McCullagh, Capt. Francis, *A Prisoner of the Reds: The Story of a British Officer Captured in Siberia* (London, 1921)
Magnus, Laurie, *Studies of the Jewish Question* (repr. and revised from *Aspects of the Jewish Question*, (1902) (London, 1917)
Magnus, Sir Philip, *Jewish Action and Jewish Ideals* (London, 1891, repr. 1917)
Marsden, Victor E., *Rasputin and Russia: The Tragedy of a Throne* (London, 1920)
—, *Jews in Russia* (The Britons, n.d. [1921])
Montefiore, Claude G., *Liberal Judaism and Jewish Nationalism* (London, 1917)
—, *Nation or Religious Community* (London, 1917)
—, *The Dangers of Zionism* (London, 1917)
—, *Race, Nation, Religion and the Jew* (London, 1918)
Nabokoff, Constantin, *Ordeal of a Diplomat* (London, 1921)
Pitt-Rivers, George, *The World Significance of the Russian Revolution*

BIBLIOGRAPHY

(Oxford, n.d. [1920])

Pollock, John, *The Bolshevik Adventure* (London, 1919)

Rosenberg, Alfred, *The Jewish Bolshevism* (Munich 1922 repr. in English by The Britons, 1923)

Sacher, Harry, *Jewish Emancipation: The Contract Myth* (London, 1917)

Sarolea, Charles, *Impressions of Soviet Russia* (London, 1924)

Simon, Leon, *The Case of the Anti-Zionists: A Reply* (London, 1917)

—, *Zionism and the Jewish Future* (London, 1918)

—, (ed.) *Studies in Jewish Nationalism* (New York, 1920)

Snowden, Mrs Philip, *Through Bolshevik Russia* (London, 1920)

Sokolov, Nahum, *History of Zionism*, Vol. II, (London, 1919)

Spencer, Harold Sherwood, *Democracy or Skylocracy?* (The Britons, 1922)

Steed, Henry Wickham, *Through Thirty Years*, Vol. II 1892–1922 (London, 1924)

Tcherikower, Elias, *Antisemitizm un Pogromen in Ukraine 1917–18* (Berlin, 1923)

—, *Di Ukrainer Pogromen in Yor 1919* (YIVO, New York, 1965)

Wassilevsky, I., *Jewish Refugees and Military Service: The Ethical Aspect of Compulsion under Threat of Deportation: Why the Russian Jew Hesitates to Join the Army* (Manchester, n.d. [1916])

Webster, Nesta, *The Origins and Progress of the World Revolution* (London, 1st edn, 1921)

—, *Secret Societies and Subversive Movements* (London, 1924)

—, and Kerlen, Kurt, *Boche and Bolshevik* (New York, 1923)

Wells, H.G., *Russia in the Shadows* (London, 1920)

Wilton, Robert, *Russia's Agony* (London, 1918)

—, *The Last Days of the Romanovs* (London, 1920)

Wolf, Lucien, *The Jewish National Movement* (repr. from the *Edinburgh Review*, April 1917)

Workers' Circle Jubilee Publication 1909–1929 (London, 1929)

Zangwill, Israel, *The Melting Pot* (1908)

—, *The Voice of Jerusalem* (1920)

—, *The Forcing House* (1922)

SECONDARY SOURCES

Works referred to directly in the text are cited in the footnotes.

INTERVIEWS

Netty Alexander, 12 Jan. 1986

Jack Baron, 20 Jan. (letter), 1 Feb. 1986

Harry Blacker, 22 May 1985

The late Sam Bornstein, 10 Aug., 23 Sept. (letters), 10 Nov. 1985

BOLSHEVIKS AND BRITISH JEWS

Harold Edwards, 28 Nov. 1985 (letter)
Alf Glick, 3 Oct., 19 Nov. 1985 (letters)
Cyril Goodman, 2–3 Jan. 1986
Sheila Leslie, 10 Nov. 1985
The late I.A. Lisky, 13, 20 Oct. 1985
Jack Miller, 6 Aug., 18 Nov. 1985 (letter)
Mick Mindel, 22 Aug. 1985
The late Israel Renson, 9 Dec. 1985 (letter), 12 Jan. 1986
Andrew Rothstein, 23 Nov., 20 Dec. 1985 (letters)
Peter Sand, 23 Dec. 1985
The late Lord Shinwell, 2 Aug. 1985 (letter)
Louis Wallis, 6 Aug. 1985
Kitty Weitz, 21 Jan. 1984, 8 Jan. 1986

Index

INDEX

Councils of Action, 85, 193
'Cousinhood', 55, 132, 217, 226
Crimea, 173
Cromie, Captain, 13
Curzon, Lord, 13, 80, 142

Daiches, Rabbi Samuel, 65, 103, 130, 225
Daily Chronicle, 218
Daily Express, 42
Daily Herald, 49, 195
Daily Mail, 47, 52, 154, 216
Daily News, 43, 231
Daily Telegraph, 42, 84
Danby, Reverend H., 150–1
'Day of Mourning' (for Polish Jewry), 27–8, 115–16, 193
Deedes, General Sir Wyndham, 152, 153
Defence of the Realm Act (DORA), 57, 67
Denikin, General, 6, 12, 13, 15, 16, 17, 21, 27, 81, 84, 99, 102, 103, 150
Derby, Lord, 226
Deterikhs, General, 26, 113
Dimanshtain, Semyon, 72
Directory (Ukrainian), 97, 98
Dmovsky, Roman, 19, 103
Domville, Admiral, 20
Dorpat (Yuryiev), 106–7
Douglas, Lord Alfred, 38
Dreen, Sam, 201, 215
Drummond, Sir Eric, *see* Perth, Earl of
Dubnov, Simon, 96, 170
Duma, 4, 65, 88

East London Observer, 47, 48, 221
Eder, David and Edith, 230–1
Edinburgh Review, 96, 170
Edwards, Harold, 203
Egyptian Standard, 231
Ekaterinburg, 26, 112
EKOPO (Jewish Help Committee), 89
Eliot, Sir Charles, 113
Elsbury, Albert, 235
Elsbury, Sam, 207, 235
Emmott Report (1919), 17–18, 26, 112
English Review, 23
English Zionist Federation (EZF), 56, 132, 138, 174, 177, 185, 225

Evans-Gordon, William, 47
Evening News, 47, 216
Evening Standard, 47, 109
EVKOM (Commissariat for Jewish Affairs), 72, 89
EVSEKTSIA (Jewish Sections of the Communist Party), 4, 6, 73, 89, 90, 242

Fairchild, E. C., 50, 233
Farainigte, 96, 97, 171
Federation of Synagogues, 122
Federation of Ukrainian Jews (FUJ), 87, 193
Feffer, Itzik, 247
Fine, Jacob, 240
Fineberg, Joe, 50, 223, 233
Finkelstein *see* Litvinov, Maxim
'First Universal' (Ukraine), 96
Fisher, Victor, 21, 47, 50
Fitch, Herbert, 227
Folkspartai, 96, 171
Foreign Jews' Protection Committee (FJPC), 50, 52, 197–206, 214, 216, 217, 219, 224, 227, 237, 239, 244
Fourteen Points (1918), 142
'Fourth Universal' (Ukraine), 97, 99
France, French, 5, 25, 30, 36, 45, 46, 87, 91, 102, 140, 143, 156, 159, 199, 204, 243
Frankel, Daniel, 235, 240
Friedman, Isaiah, 146
'Free Russia', 231
Friedman, N.M., 65
Fund for the Relief of Jewish Victims of the War in Eastern Europe, 87
Furstenberg *see* Ganetsky

Gallacher, William, 236
Galveston Project, 173
Gambs, A., 215–16
Ganetsky, 36
Garrard, John A., 53
Gaster, *Haham* Moses, 66–7, 106, 117, 130, 161–2, 225
General Registrar's Office, 208
George Square Riot (1919), 236
Gilbert, S., 65
Glasgow, 199, 209, 210, 233; Trades Council, 236; Strike Committee, 236